D1233090

Early English Dramatists

"LOST" TUDOR
PLAYS WITH
SOME OTHERS

𝔈𝔞𝔯𝔩𝔶 𝔈𝔫𝔤𝔩𝔦𝔰𝔥 𝔇𝔯𝔞𝔪𝔞𝔱𝔦𝔰𝔱𝔰

Recently Recovered

"LOST" TUDOR PLAYS

WITH SOME OTHERS

COMPRISING

Mankind—Nature—Wit and Science
Respublica—Wealth and Health
Impatient Poverty—John the Evangelist
Note-Book and Word-List

EDITED BY

JOHN S. FARMER

This edition, published in 1966,
is a facsimile of the edition published by the
EARLY ENGLISH DRAMA SOCIETY, LONDON
in 1907

BARNES & NOBLE, Inc.
NEW YORK
PUBLISHERS AND BOOKSELLERS SINCE 1873

PREFACE

UNQUESTIONABLY the chief interest of this volume will centre in the three recently recovered "lost" Tudor Plays: *Wealth and Health*, *Impatient Poverty*, and *John the Evangelist*. It was, in truth, a unique and notable "find"—one that gladdened the world's scholarship. In June 1906 it was announced that no fewer than seventeen of the rarest pre-Shakespearean interludes, including three "lost" plays and four apparently unknown or unrecorded editions, had been unearthed in an Irish country house. Yet the owner of this quarto volume of old plays, the hammer value of which ultimately proved to be over £2600, thought so little, or knew so little, of its value that it was sent over to the London auctioneers without a cover!

It is a matter of surmise, perhaps idle enough, how these old plays got so far afield from the usual centres of early dramatic interest and effort. Still it shows that we need not despair of further "recoveries"; in the most unlikely quarters and when least expected other lost plays of the Tudor period may turn up; and, it must be confessed, if only a tithe of known plays not now traceable are restored, the gain to scholarship will be invaluable.

Public interest in this recent recovery was

at once aroused ; and the contest for possession, when brought to the hammer, was of the keenest. Mr. Bernard Quaritch secured every one. It is, however, a matter of profound satisfaction to know that the rarest and best items of the collection, the "lost" plays and unrecorded editions, were bought for the nation.

As a matter of record I may state that the British Museum authorities secured—the prices given are the hammer prices—*King Darius* (unknown edition, £132) ; *John the Evangelist* (lost play, £102) ; *The Nice Wanton* (unknown edition, £169) ; *Play of the Weather* (unknown edition, £90) ; *Wealth and Health* (lost play, £95) ; *Lusty Juventus* (unknown edition, £140) ; and *Impatient Poverty* (lost play, £150).

America took *The Trial of Treasure* (£160) and *Apius and Virginia* (£101). I have not, however, as yet, been able to locate them more definitely.

Mr. T. J. Wise purchased *Cambyses* (£169) and *Gammer Gurton's Needle* (£180).

Octavia (£82) was purchased for Mr. J. H. Wrenn.

Others were announced for sale by Mr. Quaritch in his catalogue (No. 254) dated Dec. 1906. The titles of these plays and the auction price were: *Jacob and Esau* (£148) ; *The Tide Tarrieth for no Man* (£176) ; *The Disobedient Child* (£233) ; *Youth* ; and *The New Custom* (£155).

It is my good fortune in the present volume to be the first to make the three "lost" plays available for scholars. The greatest care has been taken to furnish a faithful rendering of the original texts; these have been set from rotary-bromide photographs of the unique copies now in national custody. Moreover, to meet the requirements of "textual experts" and the "higher criticism" these three plays form the first series of my *Tudor Fascimile Texts*, and will shortly be available in collotype. The four "unknown" editions already noted are also being reproduced by the same process and will form Series II. of the same collection.

Space—this volume is already much overgrown—forbids further comment. Nor would it be proper here and now. The recovery is too recent to have afforded an adequate opportunity for more than the most cursory examination; indeed, my strong feeling has been that I should best serve the wishes of the subscribers to the Early English Drama Society's publications by losing no time in placing these texts before them.

The other early interludes which complete the present collection are likewise rare and more or less difficult of access.

JOHN S. FARMER.

18 Bury Street, W.C.

CONTENTS

[MANKIND

c. 1475

A MORALITY PORTRAYING THE
LIFE OF NE'ER-DO-WEELS IN
LATE PLANTAGENET AND
EARLY TUDOR TIMES]

[The Names of the Players:

MERCY   NEW GUISE
MANKIND   NOUGHT
MISCHIEF   NOW-A-DAYS
          TITIVILLUS]

MANKIND

[Enter MERCY.*]*

Mercy. The very Founder and Beginner of
   our first creation,   [magnified ;
Among us sinful wretches He oweth to be
That, for our disobedience, He had none
   indignation
To send His own Son to be torn and crucified.
Our obsequious service to Him should be
   applied :   [of nought,
Where He was Lord of all, and made all thing
For the sinful sinner, to have him revived,
And, for his redemption, set His own Son at
   nought.   [dear bought ;
That may be said and verified : Mankind was
By the piteous death of Jesu he had his
   remedy ;   [had wrought—
He was purged of his default—that wretchedly
By His glorious passion, that blessed lavatory.
O sovereigns ! I beseech you your conditions
   to rectify ;   [remotion
And, with humility and reverence, to have a
To this blessed Prince, that our nature doth
   glorify ;
That ye may be participable of His retribution.
I have be[en] the very mean for your restitution:
Mercy is my name, that mourneth for your
   offence.

3

Divert not yourself in time of temptation,
That ye may be acceptable to God at your
    going hence ;   [eminence,
The great mercy of God, that is of most pre-
By meditation of our Lady, that is ever abund-
    ant   [negligence :
To the sinful creature that will repent his
I pray God, at your most need, that Mercy be
    your defendant.
In good works I advise you, sovereigns ! to
    be perseverant ;
To purify your souls that they be not corrupt ;
For your ghostly enemy will make his avaunt,
Your good conditions if he may interrupt.
O ! ye sovereigns that sit, and ye brothern that
    stand right up,
Pryke not your felicities in things transitory !
Behold not the earth, but lift your eye up !
See how the head the members daily do
    magnify.
Who is the head ? forsooth ! I shall you certify :
I mean our Saviour that was likened to a lamb ;
And His saints be the members, that daily He
    doth satisfy   [womb.
With the precious river that runneth from His
There is none such food by water, nor by land ;
So precious, so glorious, so needful to our
    intent ;   [bond
For it hath dissolved Mankind from the bitter
Of the mortal enemy, that venomous serpent :
From the which, God preserve you all at the
    last judgment !
For, sikerly, there shall be a strerat examination:
The corn shall be saved ; the chaff shall be
    brent—
I beseech you heartily have this premeditation.

[Enter Mischief.]

Mischief. I beseech you heartily leave your
calculation!

Leave your chaff! leave your corn! leave
your dalliation!

Your wit is little; your head is mickle; ye are
full of predication!

But, sir! I pray [you] this question to clarify:

Driff, draff! mish, mash!

Some was corn, and some was chaff;

My dame said my name was Raff.

Unshut your lock and take an halfpenny!

Mer. Why come ye hither, brother? ye were
not desired.   [hired.

Mis. For a winter corn thresher, sir! I have

And ye said: the corn should be saved and the
chaff should be fired;   [verse:

And he proveth nay, as it showeth by this

Corn serveth breadibus, chaff horsibus, straw
firibusque.   [standing,

This is as much to say, to your lewd under-

As: the corn shall serve to bread at the next
baking; chaff horsibus, et reliqu[i]d,

The chaff to horse shall be good produce;

When a man is for-cold the straw may be
brent;

And so forth, etc.

Mer. Avoid, good brother! ye been culpable

To interrupt thus my talking delectable.

Mis. Sir! I have nother horse nor saddle;

Therefore, I may not ride.

Mer. Hie you forth on foot, brother! in
God's name!

Mis. I say, sir! I am come hither to make
you game;

Yet, bade ye me not go out in the devil's name,
And I will abide.

[*A leaf of the manuscript has probably been lost
    at this point. It commences again by the
    entry of* New Guise, Nought, *and* Now-
    a-days *with a band of minstrels.*]

New Guise. And ho, minstrels! play the
    common trace ;
Lay on with thy bales till his belly brest !
    Nought. I put case : I break my neck—
        how than ?
    New G. I give no force, by saint Anne !
    Now-a-days. Leap about lively! thou art a
        white man ;
Let us be merry while we be here !
    Nought. Shall I break my neck to show
        you sport ?
    Now. Therefore, ever beware of thy report !
    Nought. I beshrew you all ! here is a
        shrewd sort ;
Have there at them, with a merry cheer !
                [*Here they dance.* Mercy *saith,*
    Mer. Do way ! do way this revel, sirs !
        do way !
    Now. Do way, good Adam ! do way !
This is no part of thy play.
    Nought. Yes, marry ! I pray you ; for I
        love not this revelling ;
Come forth, good father ! I you pray ;
By a little ye may assay.
Anon, off with your clothes ! if ye will pray.
Go to ! I have had a pretty scottling.
    Mer. Nay, brother ! I will not dance ;
    New G. If ye will, sir ! my brother will
        make you to prance.

Now. With all my heart, sir! if I may
    you avance ;
Ye may assay by a little trace.
    Nought. Yea, sir! will ye do well?
Trace not with them, by my counsel!
For I have traced somewhat to fell ;
I tell [you] it is a narrow space.
But, sir! I trow, of us three I heard you
    speak.
    New G. Christ's curse have ye, therefore!
    for I was in sleep.
    Now. A[nd] I had the cup in my hand, ready
    to go to meat—
Therefore, sir! curtly, greet you well!
    Mer. Few words! few, and well set! [jet.
    New G. Sir! it is the new guise and the new
Many words and shortly set—
This is the new guise every deal.
    Mer. Lady, help! how wretches delight in
    their simple ways!   [a-days !
    Now. Say no[ugh]t again the new guise now-
Thou shall find us sh[r]ews at all assays :
Beware! ye may soon lick a buffet.
    Mer. He was well occupied that brought
    you hither !
    Nought. I heard you call New Guise, Now-
    a-days, Nought: all these three together.
If ye say that I lie, I shall make you to slither :
Lo, take you here a trepitt !
    Mer. Say me your names ! I know you not.
    New G. [*Now. and Nought. in turn*]. New
    Guise, I ! Now-a-days, [I] ! I, Nought !
    Mer. By Jesu Christ! that me dear bought ;
Ye betray many men.
    New G. Betray? nay, nay, sir ! nay, nay !
We make them both fresh and gay.

But, of your name, sir, I you pray !
That we may you ken.   [tion.
    Mer. Mercy is my name and my denomina-
I conceive ye have but a little force in my
      communication.   [Latin.
    New G. Ay, ay ! your body is full of English
    Now. I pray you heartily, worshipful clerk !
I have eaten a dishful of curds,
And I have shitten your mouth full of turds.
Now, open your satchel with Latin words,
And say me this, in clerical manner :
Also, I have a wife ; her name is Rachael ;
Betwixt her and me was a great battle ;
And fain, of you, I would hear tell
Who was the most master.
    Nought. Thy wife, Rachel, I dare lay
      twenty lice !
    Now. Who spake to thee ? fool ! thou art
      not wise ;
Go and do that longeth to thine office :
Osculare fundamentum !   [limit ;
    Nought. Lo, master ! here is a pardon by
It is granted of Pope Pockett :
If ye will put your nose in his wife's socket,
Ye shall have forty days of pardon.
    Mer. This idle language ye shall repent ;
Out of this place I would ye went.   [assent ;
    New G. Go we hence, all three, with one
My father is irk of our eloquence ;
Therefore, I will no longer tarry.
God bring you, master, and blessed Mary !
To the number of the demonical frayry—
    Now. Come wind : come rain !
Though I come never again ;
The devil put out both your eyne !
Fellows ! go we hence tight !

Nought. Go we hence, a devil way!
Here is the door ; here is the way!
Farewell, gentle Geoffrey !
I pray God give you good night !   *Exiunt sil.*
   Mer.   Thanked bè God ! we have a fair
      deliverance
Of these three unthrifty guests :
They know full little what is their ordinance.
I preve by reason they be worse than beasts :
A beast doth after his natural institution ;
Ye may conceive, by their disport and be-
      haviour,
Their joy and delight is in derision
Of their own Christ, to His dishonour.
This condition of living, it is prejudicial ;
Beware thereof ! it is worse than any felony or
      treason.
How may it be excused before the justice of
      all
When, for every idle word, we must yield a
      reason ?
They have great ease ; therefore, they will take
      no thought ;
But how then, when the angel of heaven shall
      blow the trump,
And say to the transgressors that wickedly have
      wrought :
"Come forth unto your Judge, and yield your
      account !"
Then shall I, Mercy, begin sore to weep ;
Nother comfort nor counsel, there shall none
      be had ;
But, such as they have sown, such shall they
      reap ;
They be wanton now ; but, then, shall they be
      sad.

The good new guise, now-a-days, I will not
    disallow ;
I discommend the vicious guise—I pray have
    me excused—
I need not to speak of it ; your reason will tell
    it you :
Take that is to be taken, and leave that is to
    be refused !

[*Enter* MANKIND.]

    Mankind.   Of the earth and of the clay we
    have our propagation ;
By the providence of God thus we be derived :
To whose mercy I recommend this whole con-
    gregation.
I hope unto His bliss ye be all predestinate :
Every man, for his degree, I trust shall be
    participate ;
If we will mortify our carnal condition,
And our voluntary desires that ever be perver-
    tionate—
To renounce these and yield us under God's
    provision.
My name is Mankind ; I have my composition
Of a body and of a soul, of condition contrary.
Betwixt the twain is a great division : [victory.
He that should be s[u]bject, now he hath the
This is to me a lamentable story :
To see my flesh, of my soul to have governance ;
Where the good wife is master, the goodman
    may be sorry.
Alas ! what was thy fortune and thy chance
To be associate with my flesh, that stinking
    dunghill ?
Lady, help ! Sovereigns ! it doth my soul much
    ill

To see the flesh prosperous, and the soul trodden
under foot.
I shall go to yonder man ; and assay him I
will ;
I trust of ghostly solace he will be my boot.
           [MANKIND *approaches* MERCY.
All hail, seemly father ! ye be welcome to this
house ;
Of the very wisdom ye have participation.
My body with my soul is ever querulous ;
I pray you, for Saint Charity ! of your support-
ation.   [fort ;
I beseech you, heartily, of your ghostly com-
I am unsteadfast in living ; my name is Man-
kind ;
My ghostly enemy, the devil, will have a great
disporte
In sinful guiding, if he may see me end.
    Mer.   Christ send you good comfort ! ye be
welcome, my friend !
Stand up on your feet ! I pray you, arise !
My name is Mercy ; ye be to me full hend :
To eschew vice I will you advise.
    Man.   O, Mercy ! of all grace and virtue ye
are the well :
I have heard tell, of right-worshipful clerks,
Ye be approximate to God and near of His
counsel ;
He hath institute you above all His works—
Oh ! your lovely works to my soul are sweeter
than honey.
    Mer.   The temptation of the flesh ye must
resist, like a man ;
For, there is ever a battle betwixt the soul and
the body :
Vita hominis est milicia super terram.

Oppress your ghostly enemy, and be Christ's
    own knight ;
Be never a coward again your adversary ;
If ye will be crowned, ye must needs fight !
Intend well ; and God will be you[r] adjutory !
Remember, my friend ! the time of continuance ;
So, help me God ! it is but a chery-time.
Spend it well ! serve God with heart's affiance !
Distemper not your brain with good ale, nor
    with wine !
Measure is treasure ; I forbid you not the use ;
Measure yourself ! ever beware of excess !
The superfluous guise, I will that ye refuse :
When nature is sufficed, anon that ye cease.
If a man have an horse, and keep him not too
    high,
He may then rule him at his own desire ;
If he be fed over well he will disobey ;
And, in hap, cast his master in the mire.

    New G. Ye say true, sir ! ye are no faitour ;
I have fed my wife so well till she is my master.
I have a great wound on my head ; lo ! and
    thereon layeth a plaster ;
And another—there ! I piss my peson.
And my wife were your horse, she would you
    all to-samne.   [man !
Ye feed your horse in measure : ye are a wise
I trow and ye were the king's palfry-man,
A good horse should be gesumme.

    Man. Where speaks this fellow ? will he
    not come near ?   [for you.

    Mer. All too soon, my brother ! I fear me
He was here right now—by Him that bought
    me dear !—   [sorrow.
With other of his fellows ; they can much
They will be here right soon, if I out depart.

Think on my doctrine! that shall be your
    defence ;
Learn while I am here ! set my words in heart !
Within a short space I must needs hence.

[NOW-A-DAYS *and* NOUGHT *return.*]

   Now. The sooner the liever ; and that be
    even anon !   [from home ;
I trow your name is Do-little—ye be so long
If ye would go hence we shall come, everyone,
Mo than a good sort !
Ye have liever, I dare well say !
To them ye will go forth your way—
Men have little dainty of your play
Because ye make no sport.
   Nought. Your pottage shall be for-cold, sir !
    when will ye go dine?   [time ;
I have seen a man lost twenty nobles in as little
Yet it was not I, by saint Quintin !
For I was never worth a potful a' worts sithen
    I was born.   [merry ;
My name is Nought ; I love well to make
I have be sithen with the common tapster of
    Bury.   [weary :
I played so long the fool that I am even very
Yet shall I be there again, to-morrow. [*Exeunt.*
   Mer. I have much care for you, my own friend !
Your enemies will be here anon ; they make
    their avaunt.   [kind—
Think well in your heart—your name is Man-
Be not unkind to God, I pray you ! be His
    servant !   [variant !
Be steadfast in condition ! see ye be not
Lose not, through folly, that is bought so dear.
God will prove you soon ; and, if that ye be
    constant,

Of His bliss perpetual ye shall be partner.
Ye may not have your intent at your first
    desire ;
See the great patience of Job in tribulation :
Like as the smith trieth iron in the fire,
So was he tried by God's visitation.
He was of your nature, and of your fragility :
Follow the steps of him, my own sweet son !
And say, as he said, in your trouble and
    adversity :
Dominus dedit, Dominus abstulit, sicut sibi
    placuit ; sit nomen Domini benedictum !
Moreover, in special, I give you in charge :
Beware of New Guise, Now-a-days and
    Nought !
Nice in their array, in language they be large ;
To pervert your conditions all their means shall
    be sought.   [pany !
Good son ! intermise yourself not in their com-
They heard not a mass thi[s] twelvemonth, I
    dare well say ;
Give them none audience ! they will tell you
    many a lie ;
Do truly your labour, and keep your holyday !
Beware of Titivillus—for he leseth no way—
That goeth invisible and will not be seen ;
He will rond in your ear, and cast a net before
    your eyne ;
He is worst of all : God let him never thene !
If ye displease God, ask mercy anon ;   [bridle.
Else Mischief will be ready to brace you in his
Kiss me now, my dear darling ! God shie[l]d
    you from your fone !
Do truly your labour, and be never idle !
The blessing of God be with you, and with all
    these worshipful men !

Man. Amen! for saint Charity, Amen!
Now, blessed be Jesu! my soul is well satiate
With the mellifluous doctrine of this worshipful
man.
The rebellion of my flesh, now it is superate,
Thanking be [to] God, of the cunning that I can.
Here will I sit, and tittle in this paper
The incomparable estate of my promotion.
Worshipful Sovereigns! I have written here
The glorious remembrance of my noble con-
dition,
To have remo[r]se and memory of myself: thus
written it is
To defend me from all superstitious charms:
*Memento, homo, quod cinis es, et in cinerem
reverteris.*
Lo! I bear on my breast the badge of mine
arms.

> [NEW GUISE *enters, but remains in the
> background.*]

New G. The weather is cold; God send us
good fires!   [*verteris.*
Cum sancto sanctus eris, et cum perverso, per-
Ecce quam bonum et quam jocundum, quod the
devil to the friars,
Habitare fratres in unum.
Man. I hear a fellow speak; with him I will
not mell.
This earth with my spade I shall assay to delve;
To eschew idleness I do that mine own self;
I pray God send it His fusion!

> [*Enter* NOW-A-DAYS *and* NOUGHT.]

Now. Make room, sirs, for we have be long!
We will come give you a Christmas song.

Nought. Now, I pray all the yemandry, that is here,

To sing with us with a merry cheer :

[Nought *sings.*

It is written with a coal, it is written with a coal—

New G. and Now. It is written with a coal, it is written, etc.

Nought. He that shitteth with his hole, he that shitteth with his hole—

New G. [and] Now. He that shitteth with his hole, etc.

Nought. But he wipe his arse clean, but he, etc.—

New G. [and] Now. But he wipe his arse clean, but he, etc.

Nought. On his breech it shall be seen, on his breech, etc.—

New G. [and] Now. On his breech it shall be seen, on his breech, etc.

Cantant omnes. Hoylyke, holyke, holyke ! holyke, holyke, holyke !

New G. Hey, Mankind ! God speed you with your spade !

I shall tell you of a marriage :

I would your mouth and his arse, that is made,

Were married junctly together !

Man. Hie you hence, fellows ! with breeding ;

Leave your derision and your japing !

I must needs labour ; it is my living.

Now. What, sir ! we came but late hither—

Shall all this corn grow here

That ye shall have the next year?

If it be so, corn had need be dear ;

Else ye shall have a poor life.

Nought. Alas, good father! this labour
     fretteth you to the bone ;
But, for your crop I take great moan ;
Ye shall never spend it alone—
I shall assay to get you a wife.   [tion ?
How many acres suppose ye here, by estima-
     New G. Hey ! how ye turn the earth up and
     down !
I have be, in my days, in many good town,
Yet saw I never such another tilling !
     Man. Why stand ye idle ? it is pity that
     ye were born !
     Now. We shall bargain with you ; and
     nother mock nor scorn—
Take a good cart in harvest, and load it with
     your corn,
And what shall we give you for the leaving ?
     Nought. He is a good, stark labourer ; he
     would fain do well—
He hath met with the good man, Mercy, in a
     shroud cell :
For all this, he may have many a hungry meal.
Yet, well ye see, he is politic :
Here shall be good corn ; he may not miss it ;
If he will have rain, he may overpiss it ;
And if he will have compos[t] he may overbliss it
A little, with his arse like.
     Man. Go, and do your labour ! God let
     you never thee !
Or, with my spade, I shall you ding, by the
     holy Trinity !   [me ?
Have ye none other man to mock, but ever
Ye would have me of your set ?
Hie you forth, lively ! for hence I will you
     driffe !

          [MANKIND *belabours them with his spade.*
MAN.   2

New G.   Alas, my jewels ! I shall be shent
  of my wife !   [thrive ;
  Now.   Alas ! and I am like never for to
I have such a buffet !   [days, and Nought !
  Man.   Hence, I say, New Guise, Now-a-
It was said beforn : all the means shall be
  sought   [nought—
To pervert my conditions and bring me to
Hence, thieves ! ye have made many a leasing !
  Nought.   Marred I was for cold, but now
  am I warm !
Ye are evil advised, sir ! for ye have done harm.
By Cock's body sacred ! I have such a pain
  in my arm
I may not change a man a farthing !   [knee :
  Man.   Now, I thank God, kneeling on my
Blessed be His name ! He is of high degree.
By the aid of His grace, that He hath sent me,
Three of mine enemies I have put to flight ;
                          [*Shows his spade.*
Yet this instrument, sovereigns ! is not made
  to defend—
David saith : *Nec in hasta, nec in gladio, saluat
  Dominus.*
  Nought.   No, marry ! I beshrew you ! it is
  in spadibus !
Therefore, Christ's curse come on your
  headibus,
To send you less might !   [*They go out.*
  Man.   I promit you, these fellows will no
  more come here ;
For some of them, certainly, were somewhat
  too near !
My father, Mercy, advised me to be of a good
  cheer,
And again my enemies manly for to fight.

I shall convict them, I hope, every one—
Yet I say amiss ; I do it not alone—   [fone
With the help of the grace of God I resist my
And their malicious heart.   [sovereigns !
With my spade I will depart, my worship[f]ul
And live ever with labour, to correct my
    insolence.   [patience ;
I shall go fet corn for my land ; I pray you of
Right soon I shall revert.   [*Exit.*

[*Enter* MISCHIEF.]

Mis.   Alas, alas ! that ever I was wrought !
Alas ! the while I [am] worse than nought !
Sithen I was here, by Him that me bought !
I am utterly undone !   [game,
I, Mischief, was here, at the beginning of the
And argued with Mercy ; God give him shame !
He hath taught Mankind, while I have be vane,
To fight manly again his fone ;
For, with his spade—that was his weapon—
New Guise, Now-a-days, Nought hath [he] all
    to-beaten :
I have great pity to see them weeping.
Will ye list ? I hear them cry !

[NEW GUISE, NOW-A-DAYS, *and* NOUGHT *enter.*]

Alas, alas ! come hither ! I shall be your
    borrow.   [sorrow !
Alack, alack ! *veni, veni !* Come hither, with
Peace, fair babies ! ye shall have a napple
Why greet you so, why?   [to-morrow :
    New G.   Alas, master ! alas my privity !
                [*Commences to untruss.*
    Mis.   A ! where ? alack ! fair babe, ba me !
Abide ! too soon I shall it see !   [master !
    Now.   Here, here ! see my head, good

Mis.   Lady, help! silly darling! *veni, veni!*
I shall help thee of thy pain;
I shall smite off thy head, and set it on again.
   Nought.   By our Lady, sir! a fair plaster!
Will ye off with his head? it is a shrewd
     charm!
As for me I have none harm;
I were loth to forbear mine arm.
Ye play: *in nomine Patris*, chop!   [may!
   New G.   Ye shall not chop my jewels, and I
   Now.   Yea, Christ's cross! will ye smite
     my head away?   [assay—
There! we're on anon; out! ye shall not
I might well be called a fop!
   Mis.   I can chop it off, and make it again.
   New G.   I had a shrewd recumbentibus,
     but I feel no pain.
   Now.   And my head is all safe and whole
     again.
Now, touching the matter of Mankind,
Let us have an interlection sithen ye be come
     hither;
It were good to have an end.   [aught?
   Mis.   Ho, ho! a minstrel! know ye any
   Nought.   I can pipe on a Walsingham
     whistle, I, Nought, Nought.
   Mis.   Blow apace! thou shall bring him in
     with a flowte.
          [TITIVILLUS *roars from outside.*
   Titivillus.   I come with my legs under me!
   Mis.   Ho! New Guise, Now-a-days, hark!
     or I go: [didero."
When our heads were together I spake of "Si
   New G.   So! go thy way! we shall gather
     money unto;
Else there shall no man him see.

Now, ghostly to our purpose, worshipful
    sovereigns !   [negligence,
We intend to gather money, if it please your
For a man with a head that [is] of great omni-
    potence—
    Now.   Keep your tail ! in goodness, I pray
    you, good brother !—   [reverence !
He is a worshipful man, sirs, saving your
He loveth no groats, nor pence, nor two pence ;
Give us red royals if ye will see his abominable
    presence !
    New G.   Not so ! ye that mow not pay the
    tone, pay the tother—   [assay !
At the good man of this house first we will
God bless you, master ! ye say us ill, yet ye
    will not say nay.
Let us go by and by, and do them pay !
Ye pay all alike ? well mu[s]t ye fare !
    Nought.   I say, New Guise, Now-a-days !
Estis vos pecuniatus ?   [patus !
I have cried a fair while, I beshrew your
    Now.   *Ita vere magister* ; come forth now,
    your gatus !   [beware !
He is a goodly man, sirs ! make space and

[*Enter* TITIVILLUS *dressed devilwise, net in hand.*]

    Titi.   *Ego sum dominantium dominus,* and
    my name is Titivillus !   [*Caveatis !*
Ye that have good horse, to you I say,
Here is an able fellowship to trise him out at
    your gates.   [*Loquitur ad* NEW GUISE.
Ego probo sic : sir New Guise, lend me a
    penny !
    New G.   I have a great purse, sir ! but I
    have no money :   [penny ;
By the mass ! I fail two farthings of an half-

Yet had I ten pounds this night that was.

               [*Loquitur ad* NOW-A-DAYS.

    Titi.   What is in thy purse? thou art a
      stout fellow!   [clean gentleman

    Now.   The devil have [thee]! while I am a

I pray God I be never worse stored than I am!

It shall be otherwise, I hope, or this night
      pass.

               [*Loquitur ad* NOUGHT.

    Titi.   Hark now, I say! thou hast many a
      penny?

    Nought.   *No*[*n*] *nobis, Domine, non nobis;* by
      saint Denis!   [penny;

The devil may dance in my purse for any

It is as clean as a bird's arse.

    Titi.   Now I say, yet again, *Caveatis!*

Here is an able fellowship to trise them out of
      your gates.   [Nought,

Now, I say, New Guise, Now-a-days, and

Go and search the country, anon, that be
      sought!   [aught—

Some here, some there—what if ye may catch

If ye fail of horse, take what ye may else!

    New G.   Then speak to Mankind for the
      recumbentibus of my jewels!

    Now.   Remember my broken head in the
      worship of the five vowels!   [arm—

    Nought.   Yea, good sir! and the sitica in my

    Titi.   I know full well what Mankind did to
      you;   [through;

Mischief hat[h] informed [me] of all the matter

I shall venge your quarrel, I make God a vow!

Forth! and espy where ye may do harm!

Take W[illiam] Fide if ye will have any mo—

I say, New Guise! whither art thou advised to
      go?

New G.   First, I shall begin at m[aster]
  Huntington of Sanston ; [Hanston,
From thence I shall go to William Thurlay of
And so, forth to Pichard of Trumpington :
I will keep me to these three.
 Now.   I shall go to William Baker of
  Walton ;
To Richard Bollman of Gayton ;
I shall spare Master Wood of Fulbourn :
He is a *noli-me-tangere* !
 Nought.   I shall go to William Patrick of
  Massingham ;
I shall spare Master Allington of Bottisham,
And Hammond of Swaftham,
For dread of *In manus tuas queck.* [gether !
Fellows, come forth ! and go we hence to-
 New G.   Sith we shall go, let us see well
  where and whither ;
If we may be take, we come no more hither ;
Let us con well our neck-verse that we have
  not a check. [way, all !
 Titi.   Go your way—a devil way—go your
I bless you with my left hand : foul you befall !
Come again, I warn, as soon as I you call,
A[nd] bring your advantage into this place !
   [*They go out and leave* TITIVILLUS.]
To speak with Mankind I will tarry here this
  tide,
And assay his good purpose for to set aside ;
The good man, Mercy, shall no longer be his
  guide :
I shall make him to dance another trace !
Ever I go invisible—it is my jet—
And before his eye, thus, I will hang my net
To blench his sight ; I hope to have his foot
  met.

To irk him of his labour I shall make a frame :
This board shall be hid under the earth,
    privily ;
His spade shall enter, I hope, unreadily.
By then he hath assayed he shall be very
    angry,
And lose his patience, pain of shame !
I shall menge his corn with drawk and with
    darnel ;
It shall not be like to sow nor to sell—
Yonder he cometh : I pray of counsell ;
He shall ween grace were wane.

[*Enter* MANKIND.]

   Man. Now, God, of His mercy, send us of
    His sonde !
I have brought seed here to sow with my lond ;
While I over-delve it, here it shall stond.
In nomine Patris, et Filii, et Spiritus sancti !
    now I will begin.
This land is so hard, it maketh unlusty and
    irk ;
I shall sow my corn at winter, and let **God**
    work.
Alas ! my corn is lost ; here is a foul **work** !
I see well, by tilling, little shall I win ;
Here I give up my spade, for now and for
    ever.
    [*Here* TITIVILLUS *goes out with the spade.*
To occupy my body, I will not put me **in**
    dever ;
I will hear my evensong here or I dissever.
This place I assign as for my kirk ;
Here, in my kirk, I kneel on my knees :
    Pater noster, qui es in celis—

[*Enter* TITIVILLUS.]

Titi.   I have no lead on my
    heels ;
I am here again to make this fellow irk.
Whist ! peace ! I shall go to his ear and tittle
    therein—

[*Goes to* MANKIND.
A short prayer thirleth heaven—of thy prayer
    blin !
Thou art holier than ever was any of thy kin :
Arise, and avent thee ! nature compels !
    Man.   I will into thi[s] yard, sovereigns !
    and come again soon ;
For dread of the colic, and eke of the stone,
I will go do that needs must be done ;
My beads shall be here for whosomever will
    come.   [MANKIND *goes out.*
    Titi.   Mankind was busy in his prayer, yet
    I did him arise ;
He is conveyed, by Christ ! from his divine
    service.
Whither is he ? trow ye ?   I-wis, I am wonder-
    wise :
I have sent him forth to shit lesings.
If ye have any silver, in hap pure brass,
Take a little pow[d]er of Paris and cast over
    his face ;
And even in the owl-flight let him pass—
Titivillus can learn you many pretty things !
I trow Mankind will come again soon,
Or else, I fear me, evensong will be done :
His beades shall be triced aside, and that anon.
Ye shall [see] a good sport if ye will abide—
Mankind cometh again ; well fare he !
I shall answer him *ad omnia quare.*

There shall he set abroach a clerical maller ;
I hope of his purpose to set him aside.

[*Re-enter* MANKIND.]

Man.   Evensong hath be in the saying, I
      trow, a fair while ;
I am irk of it ; it is too long by one mile.
Do way ! I will no more, so oft, on the church
Be as it may, I shall do another.   [stile ;
Of labour and prayer, I am near irk of both ;
I will no more of it though Mercy be wroth.
My head is very heavy ; I tell you, forsooth !
I shall sleep, full my belly and he were my
      brother.

[MANKIND *sleeps and snores.*]

Titi.   And ever ye did, me keep now your
      silence !   [pence !
Not a word ! I charge you, pain of forty
A praty game shall be showed you or ye go hence.
Ye may hear him snore ; he is sad a-sleep.
Whist ! peace ! the devil is dead ! I shall go
      rond in his ear :   [mare ;
Alas, Mankind, alas ! Mercy [has] stolen a
He is run away from his master, there wot no
      man where ;
Moreover, he stale both a horse and a neat.
But yet, I heard say, he brake his neck as he
      rode in France ;
But I think he rideth over the gallows, to
      learn for to dance,
Because of his theft : that is his governance.
Trust no more on him ; he is a marred man !
Mickle sorrow with thy spade beforn thou
      hast wrought ;
Arise, and ask mercy of New Guise, Now-a-
      days, and Nought !

They come! Advise thee for the best; let
    their good will be sought;   [leman!
And thy own wife brethel, and take thee a
Farewell, everyone! for I have done my
    game;
For I have brought Mankind to mischief and
    to shame.   [TITIVILLUS *goes out.*
    Man. Whoop! ho! Mercy hath broken
    his neckercher, a vows!   [gallows.
Or he hangeth by the neck high up on the
Adieu, fair master! I will haste me to the
    ale-house,   [Nought;
And speak with New Guise, Now-a-days, and
A[nd] get me a leman with a smattering face.

[Enter NEW GUISE.]

    New G. Make space! for Cock's body
    sacred, make space!   [grace!
Aha! well! on! run! God give him evil
We were near saint Patrick's way, by Him
    that me bought!   [begun;
I was twitched by the neck; the game was
A grace was; the halter brast asunder—*Ecce
signum!*—   [run!
The half is about my neck: we had a near
"Beware!" quod the good wife when she
    smote off her husband's head—"beware!"
Mischief is a convict, for he could his neck-
    verse—   [casse.
My body gave a swing when I hung upon the
Alas! who will hang such a likely man, and a
    fierce,   [care!
For stealing of an horse? I pray God give him
Do way this halter! what [the] devil doth
    Mankind here? with sorrow!—
Alas, how my neck is sore, I make avow!

M[an].   Ye be welcome, New Guise ! Sir !
   what cheer with you?   [mourn.
New G.   Well, sir ! I have no cause to
M[an].   What was there about your neck?
   so God you amend !   [bend ;
New G.   In faith ! saint Audrey's holy
I have a little dishele, as it please God to send,
With a running ringworm.

[*Enter* NOW-A-DAYS.]

   Now.   Stand, aroom ! I pray thee, brother
   mine !
I have laboured all this night ; when shall we
   go dine?   [and wine ;
A church, here beside, shall pay for ale, bread,
Lo ! here is stuff will serve.
   New G.   Now, by the holy Mary ! thou art
   better merchant than I !

[*Enter* NOUGHT.]

Nought   Avaunt, knaves ! let me go by !
I can not geet, and I should starve.

[*Enter* MISCHIEF.]

   Mis.   Here cometh a man of arms ; why
   stand ye so still?   [fill.
Of murder and manslaughter I have my belly
   Now.   What, Mischief ! have ye been in
   prison? and it be your will,
Meseemeth ye have sco[u]red a pair of fetters.
   Mis.   I was chained by the arms ; lo ! I
   have them here.   [jailor ;
The chains I brast asunder and killed the
Yea, and his fair wife halsed in a corner :
A ! how sweetly I kissed that sweet mouth of
   hers !

When I had do, I was mine own bottler ;
I brought away with me both dish and doubler.
Here is enou' for me : be of good cheer !
Yet, well fare the new che[vi]sance !

    Man.   I ask mercy of New Guise, Now-a-
    days, and Nought ;
Once, with my spade, I remember that I fought ;
I will make you amends if I hurt you aught,
Or did any grievance.

    New G.   What a devil liketh thee to be
    of this disposition ?

    Man.   I dreamt Mercy was hang[ed] : this
    was my vision ;   [and remotion.
And that, to you three, I should have recourse
Now, I pray you, heartily, of your good will ;
I cry you mercy of all that I did amiss !

    Now.   [*Aside.*] I say, New Guise, Nought !
    Titivillus made all this ;
As siker as God is in heaven, so it is !

    Nought.   Stand up on your feet ! why stand
    ye so still ?   [exhort,

    New G.   Master Mischief ! we will you
Mankind's name, in your book, for to report.

    Mis.   I will not so ! I will set a court—
Ah ! do it [*in*] *forma juris d'hasard !*

        [Now-a-days *make*[*th*] *proclamation.*

    Now.   Oyez ! oyez ! oyez !
All manner of men, and common women,
To the Court of Mischief either come or send ;
Mankind shall return, he is one of our men !

    Mis.   Nought ! come forth ! thou shall be
    steward.   [may be sold ;

    New G.   Master Mischief ! his side-gown
He may have a jacket thereof, and money told.

    Man.   I will do for the best, so I have no
    cold.

Hold ! I pray you, and take it with you,
> *Nought (scri[bit]).*   And let me have it again
> in any wise.
> *New G.*   I promise you a fresh jacket after
> the new guise.   [office ;
Man.   Go ! and do that longeth to your
A[nd] spare that ye may !

> > > [NEW GUISE *goeth out.*
> *Nought.*   Hold, Master Mischief, and read
> this !
Mis.   Here is *blottibus in blottis,*
Blottorum blottibus istis :
I beshrew your ears ! a fair hand !
> *Now.*   Yea ! it is a good running fist ;
Such an hand may not be missed !   [*Goes out.*]
> *Nought.*   I should have done better, had I
> wist.
Mis.   Take heed, sirs, it stand you on hand !
Curia tenta generalis,
In a place—there good ale is !—
Anno regni regitalis.
Edwardi millatene,
On yestern-day in Febru'ry—the year passeth
fully—
As Nought hath written—here is our Tulli,
Anno regni regis nulli.
> *Now.*   What ho, New Guise ! thou makest
> much [tarrying] ;
That jacket shall not be worth a farthing.

> [*Re-enter* NEW GUISE.]

> *New. G.*   Out of my way, sirs ! for dread of
> fighting !
Lo ! here is a feat tail, light to leap about !
> *Nought.*   It is not shapen worth a morsel of
> bread ;

There is too much cloth ; it weighs as any lead.
I shall go and mend it ; else I will lose my
    head—
Make space, sirs ! let me go out !

                      [NOUGHT *goes out.*

    Mis. Mankind, come hither ! God send you
    the gout !
Ye shall go to all the good fellows in the
    country about ;
Unto the good-wife when the good-man is
    out—
" I will," say ye !
    Man. I will, sir !
    New G. There arn'[t] but six deadly sins ;
    lechery is none ;
As it may be verified by us brethels everyone.
Ye shall go rob, steal, and kill, as fast as ye
    may gone—
" I will," say ye !
    Man. I will, sir !   [betime,
    Now. On Sundays, on the morrow, early
Ye shall with us to the ale-house early, to go
    dine ;   [prime—
A[nd] forbear mass and matins, hours and
" I will," say ye !
    M[an]. I will, sir !   [pacem,
    Mis. Ye must have by your side a long da-
As true men ride by the way, for to unbrace
    them ;   [facc them—
Take their money, cut their throats ; thus over
" I will," say ye !
    Man. I will, sir !

               [*Re-enter* NOUGHT.]

    Nought. Here is a jolly jacket—how say
    ye ?

New G. It is a good jake of fence for a
man's body—
Hi, dog ! hi ! whoop, ho ! go your way lightly !
Ye are well made for to ren !
Mis. Tidings ! tidings ! I have espied one !
Hence with your stuff ! fast we were gone !
I beshrew the last shall come to his home !
Amen !   [*Dicant omnes.*

[*Enter* MERCY.]

Mer. What ho, Mankind ! flee that fellow-
ship, I you pray !
Man. I shall speak with [thee] another time ;
to-morn or the next day.   [*To the others.*
We shall go forth together to keep my father's
year-day :
A tapster ! a tapster ! stow, statt, stow !
Mis. A mischief go with [thee] ! here I have
a foul fall.   [all !
Hence ! away from me ! or I shall beshit you
New G. What ho, ostler ! ostler, lend us a
foot-ball !
Whoop ! ho ! anow, anow, anow !
                                   [*They go out.*
Mer. My mind is dispersed ; my body
tir-trimmeleth as the aspen leaf ;
The tears should trickle down by my cheeks,
were not your reverence !   [death !
It were to me solace, the cruel visitation of
Without rude behaviour I can[not] express
this inconvenience :
Weeping, sighing, and sobbing, were my
sufficiance ;   [odible ;
All natural nutriment, to me, as carene, is
My inward affliction yieldeth me tedious unto
your presence ;

I cannot bear it evenly that Mankind is so flexible.
Man unkind, wherever thou be! for all this
    world was not apprehensible
To discharge thine original offence, thraldom
    and captivity,   [and passible:
Till God's own well-beloved Son was obedient
Every drop of His blood was shed to purge
    thine iniquity.   [bility!
I discommend and disallow this often muta-
To every creature thou art dispectuous and
    odible—
Why art thou so uncurtess, so inconsiderate?
    alas, woe is me!
As the vane that turneth with the wind, so
    thou art convertible!
In trust is treason: thy promise is not credible;
Thy perversious ingratitude I cannot rehearse;
To go over, to all the holy court of heaven thou
    art dispectable,   [verse:
As a noble versifier maketh mention in his
" *Lex et natura, Christus et omnia jura*

Damnant ingratum; lugetur eum fore natum."
O, good Lady, and Mother of Mercy! have pity
    and compassion
Of the wretchedness of Mankind, that is so
    wanton and so frail!
Let mercy exceed justice, dear Mother! admit
    this supplication!   [prevail!
Equity to be laid over part[l]y, and mercy to
Too sensual living is reprovable, that is now-a-
    days,   [specified.
As by the comprehence of this matter it may be
New Guise, Now-a-days, Nought, with their
    allectuous ways
They have perverted Mankind, my sweet son,
    I have well espied.

    MAN.   3

A ! with these cursed caitiffs, and I may, he
    shall not long endure ;

I, Mercy, his father ghostly, will proceed forth
    and do my property.

Lady, help ! this manner of living is a detest-
    able pleasure ;

Vanitas vanitatum : all is but a vanity!

Mercy shall never be convict of his uncurtess
    condition ;

With weeping tears, by night and by day, I
    will go and never cease.

Shall I not find him ?   Yes, I hope ; now, God
    be my protection !   [*Ubi es ?*

My predelict son ! where be ye? Mankind !
      [MISCHIEF *re-enters with his companions.*

   Mis.   My prepotent father ! when ye sup,
    sup out your mess !

Ye are all to-gloried in your terms ; ye make
    many a lesse.

Will ye hear ? he cryeth over Mankind, *Ubi es ?*

   New G.   Hic, hic, hic ! hic, hic, hic ! hic, hic !

   .   .   .   .   .   .

That is to say: here ! here ! here ! nigh dead
    in the crick.

If ye will have him, go and seek, seek, seek !

Seek not over long, for losing of your mind !

   Now.   If ye will have Mankind—ho, *domine,*
   domine domine !—

Ye must speak to the shrive for a *cepe coppus* ;

Else ye must be fain to return with *non est*

How say ye, sir ? my bolt is shot !   [*inventus.*

   Nought.   I am doing of my needings ; beware
    how ye shoot !

Fie, fie, fie ! I have foul arrayed my foot !

Be wise for shooting with your tackles, for,
    God wot !

My foot is foully over-shit.

    Mis. A parlement! a parlement! come
    forth, Nought, behind!   [him find.
A counsel, belive! I am afeared Mercy will
How say ye? and what say ye? how shall we
    do with Mankind?

    New G. Tush, a fly's wing! will ye do well?
He weeneth Mercy were hung for stealing of
    a mare.   [everywhere;
Mischief! go say to him that Mercy seeketh
He will hang himself, I undertake, for fear.

    Mis. I assent thereto; it is wittily said, and
    well.   [done!

    Now. I whip it in thy coat! anon it were
Now, saint Gabriel's mother save the clothes
    of thy shoon!   [undone,
All the books in the world, if they had be
Could not a counselled us bet.

    Hic exit MISCHIEF [*apparently meeting* MAN-
KIND *as he is going out, and salutes him*].

    Mis. Ho, Mankind! Come and speak with
    Mercy; he is here, fast-by!

    Man. A rope! a rope! a rope! I am not
    worthy.   [ready;

    Mis. Anon, anon, anon! I have it here
With a tree also that I have get.
Hold the tree, Now-a-days! Nought! take
    heed and be wise!

    New G. Lo, Mankind! do as I do! this is
    thy new guise;   [advice.
Give the rope just to thy neck: this is mine

    Mis. Help thyself, Nought! lo, Mercy is
    here!   [tarry.
He scareth us with a bales; we may no longer

    New G. Queck, queck, queck! alas, my
    throat! I beshrew you, marry!

A, Mercy! Christ's copped curse go with you,
    and saint Davy!   [near!
Alas, my weasand! ye were somewhat too
          [*All but* MERCY *and* MANKIND *go out.*
    Mer.   Arise, my precious redempt son! ye
    be to me full dear.
He is so timorous; meseemeth his vital spirit
    doth expi[re].
    Man.   Alas! I have be so bestially disposed;
    I dare not appear;   [desire.
To see your solicitous face, I am not worthy to
    Mer.   Your criminous complaint woundeth
    my heart as a lance.
Dispose yourself meekly to ask mercy, and I
    will assent.
Yield me neither gold nor treasure, but your
    humble obeisance,   [am content.
The voluntary subjection of your heart, and I
    Man.   What! ask mercy yet once again?
    alas! it were a wild petition.
Ever to offend, and ever to ask mercy—that is
    a puerility.
It is so abominable to rehearse my worst
    transgression;   [bility.
I am not worthy to have mercy, by no possi-
    Mer.   O, Mankind! my sing'ler solace! this
    is a lamentable excuse!
The dolorous fears of my heart, how they
    begin to amount!   [to redeem!
O, blessed Jesu! help thou this sinful sinner
Nam hæc est mutatio, dexteræ Excelsi; vertit
    Impios, et non sunt.
Arise! and ask mercy, Mankind! and be
    associate to me.
Thy death shall be my heaviness; alas! 'tis
    pity it should be thus.

Thy obstinacy will exclude [thee] from the
    glorious perpetuity.
Yet, for my love, ope thy lips and say, *Miserere*
    mei, Deus!
    Man. The egal justice of God will not per-
      mit such a sinful wretch
To be revived and restored again : it were
    impossible.
    Mer. The justice of God will, as I will, as
      Himself doth precise :   [reducible.
Nolo mortem peccatoris, inquit, and if he will [be]
    Man. Then, mercy, good Mercy ! what is
      a man without mercy ?   [where.
Little is our part of paradise were mercy ne
Good Mercy ! excuse the inevitable objection
    of my ghostly enemy ;
The proverb saith : the truth tryeth thyself.
    Alas ! I have much care !
    Mer. God will not make you privy unto
      His last judgment :
Justice and equity shall be fortified, I will not
    deny ;   [argument
Truth may not so cruelly proceed in his straight
But that mercy shall rule the matter, without
    controversy.
Arise now, and go with me in this deambulatory.
Incline your capacity ; my doctrine is convenient.
Sin not in hope of mercy ; that is a crime
    notory ;   [expedient.
To trust overmuch in a prince, it is not
In hope, when ye sin, ye think to have mercy—
    beware of that adventure !
The good Lord said to the lecherous woman of
    Canaan—   [Scripture—
The holy gospel is the authority, as we read in
" *Vade ! et jam amplius noli peccare !* "

Christ preserved this sinful woman taken in
    advoutry ;   [more !"
He said to her these words : "Go, and sin no
So to you ; Go, and sin no more ! Beware of
    vain confidence of mercy !
Offend not a prince on trust of his favour ! as
    I said before.   [ghostly enemy,
If ye feel yourself trapped in the snare of your
Ask mercy anon : beware of the continuance !
While a wound is fresh it is proved curable by
    surgery ;   [grievance.
That, if it proceed over long, it is cause of great
    Man. To ask mercy and to have—this is a
    liberal possession :
Shall this expeditious petition ever be allowed,
    as ye have in sight ?
    Mer. In this present life mercy is plenty, till
    death maketh his division ;
But when ye be go, *usque ad minimum quad-
rantem*—ye sha[ll] reckon this right.
Ask mercy and have, while the body with the
    sou[l] hath his annexion ;
If ye tarry till your decease, ye may hap of
    your desire to miss ;
Be repentant here ; trust not the hour of death ;
    think on this lesson :   [*salutis !*
Ecce nunc tempus acceptabile ! ecce nunc dies
All the virtue in the wor[l]d, if ye might
    comprehend,
Your merits were not premiable to the bliss above ;
Not to the lowli'st joy of heaven, of your
    proper effort to ascend ;
With Mercy ye may : I tell ye no fable—
    Scripture doth prove.
    Man. O, Mercy ! my suavious solace and
    singular recreatory !

My predelict special ! ye are worthy to have
    my love ;
For, without desert and means supplicatory,
Ye be compatient to my inexcusable reproof.
A ! it swimmeth my heart to think how un-
    wisely I have wrought !
Titivilly, that goeth invisible, hung his net
    before my eye ;   [sought,
And, by his fantastical visions, sedulously
By New Guise, Now-a-days, Nought, caused
    me to obey.
    Mer. Mankind ! ye were oblivious of my
    doctrine manitory ;
I said before : Titivilly would assay you a bront.
Beware from henceforth of his fables delusory !
The proverb saith : *Jacula prefata minus ledunt.*
Ye have three adversaries—he is master of
    them all—
That is to say, the devil, the world, the flesh,
    and the fell ;
The New Guise, Now-a-days, and Nought, the
    world we may them call ;   [hell ;
And, prope[r]ly, Titivilly signifies the fiend of
The flesh, that is the unclean concupiscence of
    your body.
These be your three ghostly enemies in whom
    ye have put your confidence ;
They brought you to Mischief to conclude your
    temporal glory :   [audience.
As it hath be showed before this worship[f]ul
Remember how ready I was to help you ; from
    such I was not dangerous ;
Wherefore, good son ! abstain from sin ever-
    more after this !
Ye may both save and spoil your soul, that is
    so precious :

Libere velle, libere velle! God may not deny, I
    wis.
Beware of Titivilly with his net, and of all his
    envious will ;
Of your sinful delectation that grieveth your
    ghostly substance :   [will.
Your body is your enemy : let him not have his
Take your leave when ye will ; God send you
    good perseverance !
    [*Man*]. Sith I shall depart, bless me, father !
    hence then I go—
God send us all plenty of His great mercy !
Mer. Dominus custodi[a]t te ab omni malo!
In nomine Patris, et Filii, et Spiritus Sancti.
    Amen !   *Hic exit* MANKIND.

(EPILOGUE.)

Worship[f]ul sovereigns! I have do my property;
Mankind is delivered by my several patrociny.
God preserve him from all wicked captivity ;
And send him grace, his sensual conditions to
    mortify !   [humanity,
Now for His love, that for us received His
Search your conditions with due examination !
Think and remember : the world is but a vanity,
As it is proved daily by d[i]verse transmutation,
Mankind is wretched ; he hath sufficient proof ;
Therefore, God [keep] you all *per suam*
    misericordiam,
That ye may be pleyseris with the angels above,
And have to your portion *vitam eternam.*

                          Amen !

FINIS.

O liber, si quis cui constas forte queretur,
Hyngham, quem monacho dices, super omnia
consta[s].

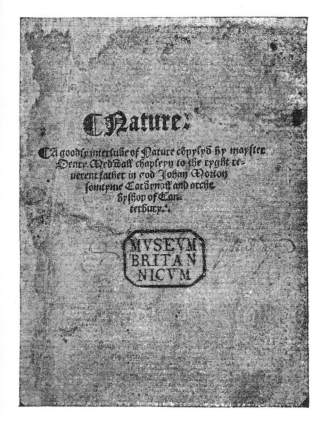

¶Nature.

¶A goodly interlude of Nature cōpylyd by mayster
Henry Medwall chapleyn to the ryght re-
uerent father in god Johan Morton
somtyme Cardynall and arche-
byshop of Can-
terbury.

MVSEVM
BRITAN
NICVM

NATURE

A GOODLY INTERLUDE OF NATURE, COMPILED BY

MASTER HENRY MEDWALL

CHAPLAIN TO THE RIGHT REVEREND FATHER IN GOD

JOHN MORTON

SOMETIME CARDINAL AND ARCHBISHOP
OF CANTERBURY

The Names of the Players:

NATURE	WRATH	CHASTITY
MAN	ENVY	GOOD
REASON	SLOTH	OCCUPATION
SENSUALITY	GLUTTONY	SHAME-
INNOCENCY	HUMILITY	FACEDNESS
WORLDLY	CHARITY	MUNDUS
AFFECTION	ABSTINENCE	PATIENCE
BODILY LUST	LIBERALITY	PRIDE
	GARCON	

Cum Privilegio

NATURE

First cometh in MUNDUS, *and sitteth down,
and saith nothing; and with him* WORLDLY
AFFECTION, *bearing a gown and cap and a
girdle for* MAN.
Then cometh in NATURE, MAN, REASON, *and*
INNOCENCY; *and* NATURE *sitteth down and
saith.*

Nature.   Th' almighty God that made each
   creature,
As well in heaven as other place earthly,
By His wise ordinance hath purveyed me,
   Nature,
To be as minister, under Him immediately,
For th' encheson that I should, perpetually,
His creatures in such degree maintain
As it hath pleased His grace for them to
   ordain.
   To me it longeth, by natural engendure,
Thing to continue that hath spirit of life;
Which, nor were my help, should never
   endure,
But suddenly perish and wax all caitiff.
Atwixt th' elements, that whilom were at strife,
I have suaged the old repugnance
And knit them together, in manner of alliance.
   Eke, I have ordained the goddess Diane,
Lady of the sea and every fresh fountain,

43

Which commonly decreaseth when she ginneth
    wane,
And waxeth abundant when she creaseth again.
Of ebb and flood she is cause certain ;
And reigneth, as princess, in every isle and
    town
That with the sea is compassed environ.
    I am causer of such impression
As appeareth wondrous to man's sight :
As of flames that, from the starry region,
Seemeth to fall in times of the night ;
Some shoot sidelong, and some down right :
Which causeth the ignorant to stand in dread
That stars do fall, yet falleth there none indeed.
    What needeth it to speak of things here
    below ?
As fowls, beasts, and fishes in their kind ;
Of trees, herbs, and stones, how they grow.
In which, men sundry and many virtuous find
One thing, be ye sure, and think it in your
    mind :
No manner creature may take on him the cure
Of these works, but only I, Nature.
    And, plainly, there is in earth no manner
    thing
That is not partner of my influence ;
I do provide, for every beast living,
Of natural food always sufficience ;
And give them, also, a manner of prudence
Whereby they may naturally ensue
Thing that is delectable, and th' other eschew.
    Who taught the cock his watch hours to
    observe,
And sing of courage with shrill throat on high ?
Who taught the pelican her tender heart to
    carve

For she nold suffer her birds to die?
Who taught the nightingale to record, busily,
Her strange entunes in silence of the night?
Certes! I, Nature, and none other wight.
  But if that I should clepe to memory
Each strange effect, and every great marvel
That I have caused, I ensure you faithfully
That rather time than process should me fail.
It were your pain, and to me but travail
All such matters as now to bring in place;
Wherefore, I let pass them till other time and
    space.
  But, if ye covet now to know th' effect
Of things natural, by true conclusion,
Counsel with Aristotle, my philosopher elect;
Which hath left in books of his tradition
How every thing, by heavenly constellation,
Is brought to effect; and, in what manner
    wise,
As far as man's wit may naturally comprise.
  Wherefore, sith God, of His great largesse
Hath thus enriched me with dower of His
    grace,
And made me, as who saith, a worldly goddess,
Of duty I can no less do in this case
But with heart's joy and entire solace
Myself address to do His high pleasures,
And to this same move all other creatures.
  Enforce you, therefore, His creatures each one
To honour your Maker with humble obeisance—
Namely, thou man! I speak to thee alone
Before all other, as chief of His creance.
Think how He hath made thee this semblance;
Pluck up thine heart, and hold thine head
    upright;
And evermore have heaven in thy sight.

Ovid in his book, cleped *The Transformation*,
Among all other his fables and poesies
Maketh special mention of thy creation ;
Showing how God wondrously gan devise
When He thee made, and gave to thee th'
emprise
Of all this world, and feoffed thee with all
As chief possessioner of things mortal.
In token whereof He gave thee upright
visage ;   [eye
And gave thee in commandment to lift thine
Up toward heaven, only for that usage
Thou shouldest know Him for thy Lord Al-
mighty,
All other beasts as things unworthy ;
To behold th' earth with grovelling counten-
And be subdued to thine obeisance.   [ance ;
But, as touching the cause specially
Wherefore I have ordained thee this night to
appear,
It is to put thee in knowledge and memory
To what intent thou art ordained to be here.
I let thee wit thou art a passenger
That hast to do a great and long voyage,
And through the world must be thy passage.
Address thyself now towards this journey ;
For, as now thou shalt no longer here abide,
Lo ! here Reason to govern thee in thy way,
And Sensuality upon thine other side.
But Reason I depute to be thy chief guide,
With Innocency that is thy tender nourice ;
Evermore to wean thee from th' appetite of vice.
Man.   O Lord of Lords, my Lord God
immortal !
To Thee be honour and joy ever to endure ;
Whose heavenly empire shall never be final,

But world without end remain stable and sure ;
Whom heaven and hell and earthly creature,
With one assent, and all with one accord,
Honoureth, praiseth, and knowledgeth for
    their Lord.
  To Thee mine head I humbly incline,
Thanking Thy grace that first hast ordained me
To be as a silly creature of Thine ;
And, after that, of Thy great bounty
Thou hast me set in sovereign degree,
And given me the profits of every earthly thing,
As well of fruits as of beasts living ;
And that, that is also most precious,
Thou hast me inspired with heavenly wisdom,
Whereby I may do works marvellous.
In every place, wheresoever I come,
Of each perfection Thy grace hath lent me some;
So that I know that creature nowhere
Of whose virtue I am not partner.
  I have, as hath each other element
Among other in this world, a common being ;
With herbs and trees continual nourishment
That is sufficient to natural living ;   [ing
With sensual beasts I have a manner of know-
Whereby I should in good things delight,
And flee the contrary of mine appetite.
  And, over all this, Thou hast given me virtue
Surmounting all other in high perfection :
That is, understanding, whereby I may aview
And well discern what is to be done ;
Yet, for all that, have I free election
[To] do what I will, be it evil or well ;
And am put in the hand of mine own counsel.
  And, in this point, I am half angelic ;
Unto Thy heavenly spirits almost egal ;
Albeit in some part I be to them unlike.

For, they be ordained to endure perpetual ;
And I, wretched body ! shall have my funeral
When it pleaseth Thy grace so to provide :
Man is not ordained alway here to abide.
    Wherefore, unto Thy sovereign and high
        estate,
Most heavenly prince ! I make mine orison
Sith it hath pleased Thy noble grace algate
That I, unworthy of so great renown,
In this world shall have possession :
Thou give me grace myself to enure
As may me profit, and be to Thy pleasure.
    Nature.   God hath heard thy prayer, Man-
        kind, no doubt,
In all thy requests and right full petition.
Now, forth thy journey ! and look well about
That thou be not deceived by false prodition.
Let Reason thee govern in every condition ;
For, if thou do not to his rule incline,
It will be to thy great mischief and ruin.
    I wot well Sensuality is to thee natural,
And granted to thee in thy first creation.
But, notwithstanding, it ought to be over all
Subdued to Reason, and under his tuition.
Thou hast now liberty, and needest no main-
        mission ;
And, if thou aband thee to passions sensual,
Farewell thy liberty ! thou shalt wax thrall.
    Sensuality.   What, lady Nature ! have **I**
        none intress
As well as Reason or Innocency ?
Think ye this, lady ! a good process
That they are advanced and I let go by ?
Ye know right well that I ought naturally,
Before all other, to have of him the cure :
I am the chief perfection of his nature.

Alas ! what could the silly body do?
Or, how should it live nor were the help of me?
Certes ! it could not well creep nor go ;
At the leastwise it should neither feel here nor
    see,
But be as other insensate bodies be ;
In much worse case than worms of the ground
In which unneth any token of life is found.

Meseemeth it should abhor him for to hear
That I destrained should be in any wise,
Standing that I was create to be his fere ;
Of all his guiding to take the enterprise :
And now ye put me out of his service,
And have assigned Reason to be his guide—
With Innocency, his nourice, thus am I set
    aside.

Ye clepe him lord of all beasts living ;
And nothing worthy, as far as I can see.
For, if there be in him no manner of feeling,
Nor no lively quickness, what lord is he?
A lord made of clouts, or carved out of tree ;
And fareth as an image graved out of stone
That nothing else can do but stand alone.

If ye intend him to continue long
In honour, or worldly felicity,
He must needs follow his appetite among ;
And conform himself to the more part.
I tell you men will have no dinty
To do service or homage to a block :
All the world will think it but a mock.

Suffer me, therefore, to have with him a
    room,
And to be with him as chief counsell[or] ;
And if he do so, I think to doom
He shall reign in the world as chief governor.
But, if Reason tickle him in the ear,

NATURE 4

Or bear him on hand the cow is wood,
He shall never be able to do earthly good.
   Nat.   My friend ! as I said to you before,
A room shall ye have : no man saith nay ;
But Reason must be preferred evermore.
For he can best lead him to the way
Of virtue and grace, whereby he may
Longest continue to God's high pleasure ;
To the which end God hath ordained this His
    creature.
   Content thyself now with Reason, my friend !
And meddle thee no further than thou hast
    to do.
Thou has brought many a man to a wretched
    end
And so thou wouldst spoil His creature also.
But whatsoever he say take no heed thereto
Without that Reason will allow the same ;
For whoso doth the contrary deserveth much
    blame.   [case
   God and I, Nature, have set thee in better
Than any creature under the firmament.
Abuse not, Man ! abuse not thy grace
Of God Almighty that from above is sent !
Thou shalt be the first that shall repent
If ever thou flee Reason and sue folly,
When once thou feelest the smart of misery.
   But, be of comfort ! hardely God shall send
Both ghostly aid and worldly help also ;
And I shall never fail, unto thy life's end,
To minister unto thee as me oweth to do.
Lo ! yonder the world which thou must needs
    to :   [say—
Now, shape thee thither ; there is no more to
Thy Lord and mine guide thee in thy way !
                    Then NATURE *goeth out.*

Sen.   Well, lady Nature! leave ye me in this
     case?
Shall I have of you none other comfort?
By Christ! yet will I not hide my face;
For, as soon as we shall to the world resort,
I put no doubt he will me support.
He hath been my good master many a day;
And he will not see me thus cast away.
     Rea.   Siker thyself, man! I advise thee
     hardely.
Be not so passionate, nor yet so furious;
Thou tormentest thyself and wottest not why.
No well-advised body will demean him thus;
Be sure thy mind is all erroneous;
Thou takest a self will and wrong opinion
Which shall be thine and others confusion.
     Sen.   Yea, Reason! sir, ye speak like a
     noble man;
But yet are ye taken with a point oversight.
What, would ye make me stand as a lurdan,
And not speak one word for mine own right?
I see it well that if your lordship might,
By means possible, once bring it about
Yourself should be a ruler, and I but a cast-
     out.
     Rea.   A ruler? certes! and so I ought to be;
And a lord also, though ye say it in scorn.
     Sens.   A lord! whose lord?
     Rea.   Thy lord.
     Sens.   Nay, so mote I thee!
Thou liest! it may no longer be forborne;
Thou camest but to-night and mayst hap go
     to-morn.
For, if thou be as haughty as thou beginnest,
Thou shalt avoid much sooner than thou
     weenest.

Rea. As for mine avoidance, how soon
    soever it be,
It shall not skill as for this intent ;
But he that first fleeth or forsaketh me
He shall have greatest occasion to repent.
It shall be to his great trouble and torment
That he hath left Reason, and sued his own
    folly,
That thereby is fallen to wretched penury.

    But now, as touching the honour and degree
That I am ordained to, I will thou understand
That Almighty God, of His grace and bounty,
Of thee and such hath given me the overhand ;
And will that I use thee as a servant,
To advise thee and reform thee when thou
    ginst to err ;   [far.
And to clepe thee homeward if thou rail too

    And, where thou sayst thou art so necessary
That man without thee can have no living,
As in that point we shall not much vary :
I wot thou art necessary to his being.
But, be thou sure that is not the very thing
That maketh him to appear so wondrous ;
And to be, in his nature, so noble and precious.

    It is a thing that doth right far exceed
All other perfections and virtues natural.
For sensuality, in very deed,
Is but a mean which causeth him to fall
Into much folly, and maketh him bestial ;
So that there is no difference, in that at the
    least,
Betwixt man and an unreasonable beast.

    But this other cometh of great tenderance
And spiritual love that God oweth to mankind,
Whom He hath created to His own semblance ;
And endued with a wondrous mind

Whereby he may well discern and find
Sufficient difference betwixt good and bad :
Which is to be left, and which is to be had.
　　Lo ! this is it that doth him dignify ;
And causeth him to be reputed so excellent.
And of all this the chief doer am I,　　　[sent,
Which from Heaven into earth by God am
Only for that cause and final intent　　　[guide
That I should this, His creature, demean and
For the season that he doth in this world
　　　abide.　　　　　　　　　　　　[gether,
　　Now, compare thy virtues and mine to-
And say which is the worthier of them two.
　　Sens.　Which is the worthier ? forsooth !
　　I trow neither ;
We be good fellows.
　　Rea.　　　　　　Nay, my friend, not so !
Thou ought to obey me wheresoever I go.
　　Sens.　Nay ! that shall I never do ; for,
　　to-day
I shall thy fellow be, look thou never so high.
　　And, therefore, hardly be somewhat fellow-
　　　like ;　　　　　　　　　　　　　[way.
Leave thy haut conceits, and take a meetly
For shame of the world, man ! let us not stick
At a matter of right nought, and traverse here
　　　all day.　　　　　　　　　　　　[say :
Have me in few words, man ! and hark what I
Meddle thou in no point that belongeth to me,
And I shall promise thee never to meddle with
　　　thee.
　　And, standing the nonage of this gentleman,
On my peril take no care therefore.
I shall demean it as well as I can
Till he be passed forty years and more ;
And Reason then, if ye will undershore

His crooked old age, when lusty youth is
        spent,
Then take upon you : I hold me content.
    For, trust ye me ! the very truth is this :
This man is put in his own liberty ;
And, certainly, the free choice is his
Whether he will be governed by thee or by me.
Let us, therefore, put it to his own jeopardy,
And therein stand to his arbitrament
To which of us twain he had liefer assent.
    Rea. Nay, sir, not so ! I know his frailty ;
The body is disposed for to fall
Rather to the worse than the better part ;
But it be holpen by power supernal.   [all,
    Sens. Yet, Reason ! when thou hast said
If thou see him not take his own way,   [day.
Call me cut when thou meetest me another
    Rea. For certain yet, according to mine office,
I must advertise and counsel him, at the least,
To haunt virtue and 'schew all vice ;
And therein assist him to the uttermost ;
And if he will algates be a beast,
And take none heed to my lore and doctrine,
The peril and hurt shall be his, not mine.
    Inno. Sirs ! I shall answer for this man, as
        yet
That he is maiden for all such folly
As should disdain nature, or dishonour it.
Brought up with me, full well and tenderly,
Wherefore I dare the surelier testify
For Innocency, that he is yet virgin,
Both for deed and eke consent of sin.
    And longer will not I be of his acquaintance
Than he is virtuous, and of good living ;
For, fleshly lust and worldly pleasance
Is, with Innocency, nothing according.

But, if his behaviour and daily demeaning
Be of such draught as reason will allow,
I shall him favour and love, as I do now.
    Sens.   Well spoken and wisely! now have
      ye all done?
Or, have ye ought else to this man to say?
    Rea.   O, sir, yea!   [disputation!
    Sens.   Peace, no more of this
Here be many fantasies to drive forth the day;
That one chattereth like a pie; that other like
    a jay;   [can,
And yet, when they both have done what they
Maugre their teeth, I shall rule the man.
    Man.   O, blessed Lord! what manner strife
      is this
Atwixt my reason and sensuality,   [amiss.
That one meaneth well, and that other all
In one is sikerness, and in tother great frailty;
And both they be so annexed to me
That needest I must with one of them abide.
Lord, as Thou thinkest best for me, do provide!
  For, I am wondrously entriked in this case,
And almost brought into perplexity;
Notwithstanding, thanked be Thy grace,
As I did never assent, nor agree   [Thee;
To things that should be contrarious unto
Of sinful deed and thought all innocent,
Subdued to Reason as his obedient.
    Rea.   Christ grant you therein good con-
      tinuance!
To be ever of the same mind and intent.
But now, will ye call to your remembrance
For what cause ye be hither sent?
I hold it well done, and right expedient
That ye were brought unto the world's
    presence.

   Man.   Be it so! in God's name I pray you
      go we hence!
   Rea.   And will ye that I shall for you declare
Unto the world the cause of your coming,
What is your intent, and what person ye are?
   Man.   Yea! I would be glad that everything
Be done even after your devising.   [tied?
   Sens.   Shall I then stand as I were tongue-
   Man.   Yea, hardely! till Reason have said.
   Rea.   Sir World! it is the mind and also
      pleasure
Of lady Nature, as she bade us to you tell,
That ye accept and receive this her creature
With you, for a season here to dwell;
Desiring you heartily to entreat him well,
With all the favour that ye can devise;
Wherein ye shall do her great pleasure and
      service.   [heartily.
   The World.   Sirs! ye be welcome to us
Your message is to us right acceptable.
Be ye assured there is nothing earthly
To us so joyful, nor yet so delectable,
As to be acquainted with persons honourable;
Namely, such as ye seem to be,
Men of high honour and of great dignity.
   And, as touching the message that ye have
      brought,
Have thereof the full mind and intent;
Assuring you that our busy thought
Shall be to do dame Nature's commandment.
And, thereunto, we will be diligent
To do her pleasures in that we may;
And so we would ye should to her say.
   And where ye show unto me that this man
Is ordained to reign here, in this empery
I assent well; for, or nature began

To shape the world she thought finally
To ordain man therein to occupy ;
He to take upon him as mighty governor,
Having all things subdued to his power.
    Wherefore, I receive greatly his coming.
Mankind, sir, heartily welcome ye be !
Ye are the person, without feigning,
That I have evermore desired to see :
Come ! let me kiss you.   O, benedicite !
Ye be all naked ! alas, man ! why thus ?
I make you sure it is right perilous.
    Man.   I thank you ; but I need none other
      vesture ;
Nature hath clothed me as yet sufficiently.
Guiltless of sin, and as a maiden pure,
I wear on me the garment of innocency.
    Inno.   Yea, hardely wear that garment
      continually :
It shall thy body sufficiently safeguard
From stormy weather, my life to jeopard.
    The World.   Be peace, fair woman ! ye are
      not very wise ;
Care ye not if this body take cold ?
Ye must consider this is not paradise,
Nor yet so temperate by a thousandfold.
Whoso liveth here, be he young or old,
He must suffer both fervent cold and heat ;
And be out of temperance oft time in his diet.
    Also, he must needs do as the world doth
That intendeth any while here to reign ;
And follow the guise that now-a-day goeth,
As far as his estate may it maintain.
And who doth the contrary—I will be plain—
He is abject and despised utterly ;
And standeth ever banished from all good
    company.

Sith   God,   therefore,   had   ordained   this
To dwell here in this earthly region,   [body
Of convenience he must himself apply
To worldly things ; and be of such condition
As all men be ; and leave each fond opinion
That is not approvable of wiser men than he ;
To take such way it is but vanity.

Take this garment ! man, do as I you bid !
Be not ashamed hardly to do it on.
So, lo ! now this girdle have gird it in the mid ;
And this for your head go set it upon :
By the charge of me ! you be a goodly one
As ever I saw sith that I was born ;
Worth a thousand that ye were beforne.

Give me your hand ! be not in fear !
Sit down as ye are born to occupy this place !
I give you here authority and power
Over all thing that conceived is, in the space
Of all the earth that round is in compass,
To be as lord of every region ;
And, thereof, I give you peaceable possession.

Man.   Blessed be Thou, my Lord, most boun-
That of Thy great abundant charity   [teous !
Me, Thy wretched creature, hast honoured thus
With natural gifts and worldly dignity.
Now, I beseech Thee, for Thy great pity,
Sith Thou hast set me in so noble way,
Suffer me not hereafter wretchedly to decay.

For, certes ! it is mine heart's desire
So to demean me in this life present
As may be most unto Thy pleasure,
And unto nature not disconvenient.
This is my will and my chief intent ;
This will I observe, Thy grace to borrow,
Though   I,   therefore,   suffer   much   worldly
        sorrow.

Rea. Forsooth! these words be greatly to
  allow
If they from meek and lowly heart proceed.
Now, Mankind, sith thou hast made this vow,
Shape thee, thereafter, thy life to lead ;
And let thy word be cousin to thy deed :
That is to say, do thou none otherwise
Than thou here openly to God dost promise.
  Inno. Yea, sir! and ever look that ye
    abstain,
Not only from deed, but also from the assent ;
See that ye commit neither of them twain
If ye will observe the high commandment.
For, surely ye may not be cleped innocent,
Nor guiltless of sin, as far as I can find,
If once ye assent to folly in your mind.
  Mun. This is an hard word, sister, that ye
    have spoken ;
An hard word, surely, and an heavy sentence!
But think ye God's commandment broken
For a light trifle and matter of insolence?
Alas! have ye such a spiced conscience
That will be entriked with every merry
    thought?
Leave it, woman! leave it! For it is nought.
              Loquitur ad ho[minem].
  And man! as for you, ye shall not take that
    way ;
That manner of observance is too hard and
    strait.
Ye must attempt the world ; and, therein assay
Whether ye can live after that endrait.
These two folk harp both on refrait ;
And ever enbusieth them to rebuke you of sin
That never was spotted, nor found guilty
    therein.

Take no heed of them! their words be but
    wind;   [silence.
And, as for this time, I command them to
And let us see now how prately ye can find,
By sage policy and worldly prudence,
To maintain the state, in honour and reverence,
That ye shall be in while ye in the world dwell.
Speak of this matter and ponder it well!

    First, meseemeth necessary to provide
What manner folks your servants shall be;
For, surely, ye are nothing accompanied
According to a man of your degree:
Ye have here with you two persons or three
That pleaseth you happily, in the best wise;
Yet it appeareth not so to every man's guise.

    What man is this?

    Man.   Reason, sir! my chief counsellor;
And this Innocency, my nourice hitherto;
And Sensuality that other, by whom I have
To do as all sensate beasts do.   [power
But Reason and Innocency, chiefly these two,
Have the whole rule and governy of me;
To whom eke is subdued my Sensuality.

    Sens.   For certain, sir! Reason hath done
    me wrong;
More than ever he shall be able to recompense.
God knoweth, sir! I thought the season very
    long
Till we were brought unto your presence.
But now, I pray you to annul the sentence
That Nature gave unto me by Reason's advice,
To my great hurt and utter prejudice.

    And sir! I ask none amends earthly,
But that Reason may have a checkmate;
A little knack, a little pretty congy,
His haut courage some thing to abate.

For, hitherto, he hath kept great estate ;
And had of me the over hand and stronger :
But be not displeased ! I will suffer it no
    longer.
    Mun.   Thou hast had great wrong, and that
    is pity ;
For, if thou be the person that I take thee for,
Thou should'st be as honourable as he.

    .   .   .   .   .   .

    Sens.   Lord ! ye say well ; but would God
    ye would see
Some manner help and remedy for this evil ;
And let me not alway live thus like a drivel.
    Mun.   Sir ! ye know well that if so it were
A man should suddenly come to a strange
    place,
Wherein he is but alien and stranger,
He must needs be compelled, in that case,
To put himself in the favour and grace
Of some singular person, that can show him the
    way
Of all the behaviour and guise in that country.
    So it is now that ye be hither sent ;
This country, as yet, to you unknown.
In mine opinion it is expedient
To take some other counsel than your own,
Of well inured men, such as have grown
In worldly experience, and have thereof the
    drift,
And can best for you in time of need shift.
    Homo.   Certes ! ye move right well and pru-
    dently ;
And I am well content that it so be ;
But, as yet, have I not the policy
To know which men have most ability.
    Mun.   Dare ye commit the matter unto me ?

Homo.   Yea, sir ! right well; I am fully content
That all thing be done by your assignment.
   Mun.   Then thus I will, that above all thing,
From henceforward, ye be like and conformable
Unto other persons in all your demeaning ;
Namely, to such as be companable,
Be they never so vicious or abominable ;
For every man clepeth him wise
That doth after the common guise.
   And, as for men that should do you service,
I know divers persons that be right honourable
That can you serve, alway point device.
In all the world be there none so able,
So wise, so politic, nor yet so profitable.
Lo ! here is one of them that I speak for ;
And he himself can tell you where ye shall have more.
   Worldly Affection is this man's name ;
He is well brained, and wondrous of invention ;
A forecasting man and, payne of shame !
Ye shall not find in any Christian region
A wiser fellow in things to be done ;
Specially of matters that be concerning
Worldly pleasure, that is for you according.
   Suffer him, therefore, never to depart ;
But, if it be for matters of great substance,
And for sensuality, I pray you with all my heart
To accept him to your favour and tendrance.
He hath been long of mine acquaintance ;
And, on my faith ! my heart cannot but grudge
To think that ye should use him as a drudge.
   Do as he adviseth you, hardely now and then ;
And despise not utterly his counsel
Think that ye be here a worldly man ;

And must do as men that in the world dwell.
Ye are not bound to live like an angel ;
Nor to be as God, alway immutable :
Man's nature of himself is full miserable.
    I have told you now my counsel and advice ;
And ye have promised to be ruled thereby.
Now, let each man execute his office ;
And see how wisely ye can them occupy
To increase the world, and it thereto ye must
      apply.   [thus :
Now, address you thereto ; and demean you
I shall be to you ever good and prosperous.
    Man.   Sir ! I thank you of this courtesy,
Undeserved as yet ; but, be ye sure,
I shall myself endeavour busily
To do that may be to your pleasure.
And, for the season that I shall here endure,
I shall them cherish ; and to my power maintain
That unto you in anywise do pertain.
    The Wor[ld].   Then, to begin withal, I will
      advise you
To put this man from your company.
I tell you every man will despise you
As long as ye be ruled by Innocency :
To follow such counsel it is but folly ;
For, he can neither good, neither evil ;
And, therefore, he is taken but for a drivel.
    Man.   By my faith ! even as ye say :
It liketh me not right well
With Innocency long to dwell ;
Therefore, according to your counsel,
I will not, after this day,
With his company myself affere ;
As mute as it were a grey friar.
I suppose there is no man here,
Whatsoever he be,

That could in his mind be content
Always to be called an innocent.
Wherefore, it is mine intent
To do as ye advise me.
 The World. Yea, hardly, do even so!
 Inno. Forsooth, and I hold me well content
To depart at your commandment,
Ye shall find me obedient
Whatsoever ye bid me do.

      Here INNOCENCY *goeth out.*
 Sens. So, the company is well amend;
Let him go the devil of hell!
He is but a boy, I warn you well;
And, should ye follow his counsel,
Almighty God defend!
If ever ye lust to play the man
It is time that ye now began.
Marry! to play the boy, now and then,
For your disport and solace,
It forceth not though ye do
When ye may have leisure thereto;
And among I will help you also
In due time and place.
 The World. Yea, that ye will indeed!
But now, sir! will ye anything
Command me before my departing?
 Man. Nothing at all, to my witting;
But our Lord have you in His keeping,
And send you well to speed!

  [*He goeth out.* MANKIND *calls to* WORLDLY
    AFFECTION.]
Worldly Affection, come hither! ye are politic;
And much better inured in this world than I.
I pray you dispose for me, as ye think most
  like,
That I may live here well and honourably.

    [*Wor. Affec.*] Yea, sir! I shall. Doubt ye
    not, hardely!
If it like you to put me in so great trust,
And I trow ye shall find me true and just.
    Man. I wot well I shall. Surely you be
    bound
To the world that hath given you so great
    commendation?
    [*Wor. Affec.*] Yea, sir! some men had liever
    than a thousand pound
They might be commended of the same fashion.
But, sir! let pass all this commendation;
And answer to me, I pray you, fruitfully,
In that I shall move you substantially.
    Sir! at few words I you exhort,
Sith that ye be come to your own,
Cast yourself to bear such a port
That, as ye be, ye may be known;
Eke it is necessary, for that behove,   [ance
That there be made some manner of purvey-
Whereby ye may bear out your countenance.
    Will it like you, therefore, that I survey
And see th' extent of all your land,
And thereupon in all thee hast purvey,
Both for you and yours, all manner of viand,
With other utensils ready at your hand;
So that ye be purveyed all times, early and
    late,
Of each thing that belongeth to your estate?
    Man. Your counsel is good; do as ye think
    best;
I commit all such thing to your discretion.
    [*Wor. Aff.*] I shall do my true business, at
    the least
To bring all things to good conclusion.
                [*He maketh to go out.*

Man.   Abide, Worldly Affection ! ye made
        no mention
Who should await and give attendance ;
I must have mo servants whatsoever chance.
    Wor. Aff.   What ? ye have Sensuality ! ask
        never other counsel
Of such matter ; he can you best advise.   [dwell
He knoweth where all such manner persons
As be most apt to do you worldly service.

                              Then he goeth out.
    Sens.   Yea, on my peril, sir !   I shall take
        the enterprise
Of all such matters ; and, look ! where I find
Any man of pleasure, on him set your mind.
Lo ! will ye see—lo ! here cometh one ;
Even the last man that was in my thought.
    Man.   What is he ?
    Sens.   Ye shall see anon.
A well-drawn man is he ; and a well-taught,
That will not give his head for nought ;
And, thereto goodly, as ye shall see in a day
As well-apparelled at each point of his array.

                              [Mankind *goes aside.*
    [*Pride.*]   Who dwelleth here ? will no man
        speak ?
Is there no fool nor hoddypeak ?
Now, by the bell ! it were alms to break
Some of these knaves' brows.
A gentleman comes in at the doors,
That all his days hath worn gilt spurs,
And none of these knaves nor cutted whores
Bids him welcome to house !
    Wot ye not how great a lord I am ?
Of how noble progeny I came ?
My father a knight ; my mother called madame ;
Mine ancestors great estates.

And now the livelood is to me fall
By both their deaths natural :
I am spoken of more than they all,
Hence to Paris gates.
    How say ye, sirs, by mine array ?
Doth it please you, yea or nay ?
In the best wise, I dare well say !
By that ye know me awhile
And one thing I put you out of doubt ;
I have wherewith to bear it out
As well as any man hereabout
Within these hundred mile.   [*indecipherable.*]
    Behold [*the rest of the line, almost cut away, is*
A staring colour of scarlet red :
I promise you a fine thread
And a soft wool.
It cost me a noble at one pitch—
The scald capper sware sithich
That it cost him even as mich—
But there Pride had a pull.
    I love it well to have side hair
Half a wote beneath mine ear ;
For, evermore, I stand in fear
That mine neck should take cold.
I knit it up all the night ;
And the daytime comb it down right ;
And then it crispeth and shineth as bright
As any purled gold.
    My doublet is on-laced before—
A stomacher of satin and no more ;
Rain it, snow it never so sore,
Methinketh I am too hot.
Then have I such a short gown,
With wide sleeves that hang a-down—
They would make some lad in this town
A doublet and a coat.

Some men would think that this were pride ;
But it is not so—ho, ho, abide !
I have a dagger by my side
Yet thereof spake not I.
I bought this dagger at the mart,
A sharp point and a tart ;
He that had it in his heart
Were as good to die.
  Then have I a sword or twain ;
To bear them myself it were a pain ;
They are so heavy that I am fain
To purvey such a lad,
Though I say it, a pretty boy—
It is half my life's joy.
He maketh me laugh with many a toy,
The urchin is so mad.
  I begat the whoreson in bast ;
It was done all in haste :
Ye may see there was no waste,
He occupied no great place.
Sometime he serveth me at board ;
Sometime he beareth my two-hand sword—
Come forth, thou little lick-turd !
Look in thy father's face !
  But, now to do that I come for,
And of these things to speak no more—
Hark, sirs ! me longeth sore
To hear some novelty.
I hear say there is a great state
Come into this country late ;
And is disposed algate
An householder to be.
  Father's soul, sirs ! ye shall understand
That, if he keep household in this land,
I will thrust in on hand,
Whosoever say nay.

Whatsoever the man intend,
To appair the world or to amend,
I will be with him at that one end ;
Hap what hap may !
　I met Worldly Affection erewhile,
From this town scant a mile ;
And he hath showed me a pretty wile,
If I may put it in ure.
He tells me that Sensuality
Begins a great ruler to be ;
And, if it be so, care not for me—
The matter is cock sure !
　Ay, good lord, what man is that ?
Father's soul ! this is some great wat.
　Garcon.　This is he that ye seek.
　Pride.　　　　　　See this, brat !—
This boy is passing taunt—
Come behind, and follow me ;
Set out the better leg, I warn thee !
　Garcon.　Yes, in the best wise trust ye me !
Allez, seigneur ! allez vous avant !
　Pride.　Salutem to you, sir !
　Man.　　　　　　And to you also !
Whence are ye ?
　Pride.　　　　I shall tell you or I go ;
But, first would I speak a word, and no mo,
With this servant of yours.　　　　　[me ?
　Sens.　With me, sir ? Would ye speak with
　Pride.　Yea, fore God ! are ye not Sensuality ?
　Sens.　Yes, surely !　　　　　　　[be.
　Pride.　Yea, such a gentleman ye seem to
　Sens.　Your poor servant at all hours !
　　　　　　Then PRIDE *speaketh to* SENSUALITY
　　　　　　　in his ear that all may hear.
　Pride.　Sir ! I understand that this gentle-
　　man is born to great fortunes, and intendeth

to inhabit herein the country. And I am
a gentleman that alway hath be brought
up with great estates, and affeed with them;
and, if I might be in like favour with this
gentleman, I would be glad thereof, and
do you a pleasure.

Sens.   Where is your dwelling?

Pride.   I dwell hereby.

Sens.   What is your name?

Pride.   Pride!

Sens.   Pride?

Pride.   Yea, sikerly!
But I am cleped Worship, commonly,
In places where I dwell.

Sens.   Worship, now, in faith, ye say true;
Ye be *radix viciorum*—root of all virtue.

Pride.   Yea, yea, man! ye would say so if
ye me knew.

Sens.   Turd! I know you well.
Sir! ye are welcome, as I may say;
I shall bring you in service if I may;
And if one man stand not in the way.

Pride.   One man? what the devil is he?

Sens.   By God! one that loveth not thee,
Nor me neither.

Pride.   I pray thee tell me
What manner of man he is,
And I shall give him a lift, as I guess.

Sens.   Wilt thou so, doubtless?

Pride.   Yea, and that within a short process—
In faith! I will not miss.

Sens.   Surely I cannot spy the ways how!

Pride.   Let me alone; I shall do well enow.
Acquaint me with that man, and care not thou!
The matter shall speed.

Sens.   Hark, cousin! first speed this matter,

And if yonder man make thee not good cheer
As any man that ever came here
Let me, therefore, be dead!   [in
   Pride.   Sir! I shall tell thee how when I am
To thy master's service; I will first begin
To set his heart on a merry pin,
And bid him make good cheer.
I will bid him think how he is create
To be a worthy potestate,
And eke that he is predestinate
To be a prince's peer.
And other things more than this:
I shall bring that heart of his
To be more haut than it is
By a deuce ace.
Specially, I will commend his wit
That no man can amend it;
And that he is able thereby to sit
As a judge in common pleas;
And when I praise him this wise
I think his heart will begin to rise
And after that utterly despise
Any opray counsel to hear;
He shall trust all to his own brain;
And then would Reason never so fain,
Though he come and such opry twain:
He shall be never thee near.
   Sens.   Surely this conceit is well found!
I shall bring thee in service for twenty pound.
   Pride.   Gramercy, brother! I think me much
      bound
To thee for thy courtesy.
But, sir! abide here one thing—
I will not be known that it is my seeking.
   Sens.   No more would I, for forty shilling:
Let me alone hardely! [MANKIND *comes forward.*

  Sens. Sir! if it please you, here is come a
   stranger
That never was acquainted with you ere;
Somewhat shamefaced, and half in fear
To put himself in prese;
A goodly person, be ye sure,
Both of countenance and of feature
If he were drawn in portraiture;
And a good man, doubtless!
Yea, and a wise man at all—
Will it please you that I him call
To speak with you?
  Man.   Bid him come!
  Sens.   I shall.
Sir! will ye come near? [*To* MANKIND.]
Sir! bid him welcome for the manner sake;
Another day I am sure he will crake
And say, such a gentleman did him make
Very great cheer.
Desire him for to dwell with you;
I tell you he is a man for your prow,
And knoweth the world well; I know
No man better than he.
  Man. Sir! ye be welcome to this place.
  Pride. I thank you, sir! but I do you
   trespass
To come thus homely.
  Sens.   Yea, a parlous case!
God wot ye are welcome hither.
On my faith, by my will
Ye shall dwell with us still.
Go near to him and talk your fill:
I leave you together.

          [*He goeth forth.*
  Man. Now, sir! what have ye to say to
   me?

    Pride.   No great thing, sir! but I come to
    see
And to know what manner man ye be
That all men praiseth so much.
    Man.   Praise! whom praise they?
    Pride.   Marry, you!
    Man.   Me?
    Pride.   Yea, sir! I make mine avow
They give you a praising good I know;
I heard never none such.
And, surely, ye be right worthy!
I see well now they do not lie;
And, therefore, I did me hither hie
To acquaint me with you—
But ye may say that I am bold.
    Man.   Nay, ye are worth thy weight of gold!
Methinketh me to you much behold;
I pray you what is your name?
    Pride.   My name is Worship.
    Man.   Worship? now, surely,
The world told me it was my destiny
To come to Worship or I die.
    Pride.   Truly, I am the same.
    Man.   Now, Worship, I pray you me tell
Your wisdom and also counsel;
Ye can advertise me passing well
In things that I have to do.
    Pride.   In good faith! anything that I
May do to your pleasure it is ready;
I am your own, and pray you, heartily,
That ye accept me so.
But where ye ask counsel of me
Meseemeth ye save not your honesty!
    Man.   Mine honesty? Wherefore, let see;
I pray you show me why!
    Pride.   Marry, sir! for it is right fitting

That a man of your behaving
Should have alway sufficient cunning
Of worldly wit and policy
To guide himself everywhere ;
And not to be led by the ear,
And beg wit, here and there,
Of every Jack-a-pie.
Ye are well complexioned, be ye sure ;
And Nature hath done on you her cure
As much as upon any creature
That ever I saw with mine eye.
And, by likelihood, sir ! I wis
Ye have wit according to all this ;
Or else Nature hath wrought amiss :
And that is not likely.   [king !
 Man. Now, certain, thanked be heaven's
I have a right quick understanding.
If ye show me anything
I can soon perceive it ;
But I was forbid by Reason
On mine own fantasy to run,
Or to take any presumption
Of mine own wit.
 Pride. Said Reason so ? Marry, fie on
  him, knave !
It were better the hangman were in his grave
Than ever the lewd fool should have
The governance of you.
 Man. Certain, Nature advised me
To follow Reason what time that she
Put me first in authority
That I stand in now.
 Pride. Alas, alas, man ! ye be mad—
I see well ye be but a very lad.
On my faith ! I was very glad
Of your first acquaintance ;

And now, I forthink it utterly
That ever I knew you : fie, fie, fie !
I heard never, certainly,
Of such another chance.
   Will ye draw to that fellowship?
I would ye had three stripes with a whip,
Even upon the bare hip,
If I should you not grieve.
He that would lordship enjoy,
And play ever still the old boy,
Meseemeth he doth but make a toy
And ye will me believe.   [not.
   Man.   Worship! for God's sake grieve ye
   Pride.   I wis ye are but an idiot—
I pray you, sir, make not me a sot ;
I am no trifler !
I have been in honour heretoforne,
Ye allow the counsel of a carl born,
Before mine I have it in scorn—
It is a thing I cannot bear.
   Man.   Whom mean ye, Reason?
   Pride.   Yea, that same daw !
   Man.   What, is he a wise man?
   Pride.   He is a straw
Because he keeps you under awe ;
Ye be therein blind.
   Man.   And so doth he, without faining ;
For, hitherto, I`might do nothing
But after his will and bidding :
And that groged my mind.
   Pride.   Groge, quotha ! it is no marvel,
      hardely ;
It shall grieve me, certainly,
As long as I am in your company
To see you demeaned in that wise.
Ye be now in good way ;

But, in faith! I like not your array ;
It is not the fashion that goeth now-a-day,
For now there is a new guise.
It is now two days agone
Sith that men began this fashion,
And every knave had it anon ;
Therefore, at this season,
There is no man that setteth thereby
If he love his own honesty.
    Man.   So seemeth, certainly,
That every man is fresher than I,
And I wis that is no reason.
               Here cometh in WORLDLY AFFECTION
                   and SENSUALITY.
    Sens.   Reason, quotha ! no, no!
But, sir ! wot ye what ye shall do?
Hardely let us two go
To some tavern here beside.
Come on ! I can bring you there ;
And let them alone with all this gear.
Care ye nothing for the matter ;
But, let them here abide ;
And ye will suffer, and let them alone,
Ye shall see them devise you a new fashion
That all the world shall wonder thereon.
    Man.   By God! that will I do goodly ;
But, I pray you, sirs ! do your diligence
For this array, and spare none expense ;
And, for a while, I will go hence
And come again shortly.
               Here MAN *and* SENSUALITY *go out.*
    Wor. Aff.   Brother Pride ! now the weight
Of all this matter resteth in thee.
    Pride.   Tush ! thou shalt see me devise it
       even straight ;
It is but japes, that gear, with me.

I have none other study a-days, parde !
But how I may new fashions find ;
And, thereon, I set all my labour and mind.
 Sir ! Our master shall have a gown
That all the gallants, in this town,
Shall on the fashion wonder :
It shall not be sewed but with a lace
Betwixt every seam, a space
Of two handful asunder.
 Then a doublet of the new make ;
Close before, and open on the back,
No sleeve upon his arm ;
Under that a shirt as soft as silk,
And as white as any milk
To keep the carcase warm.
 Then shall his hosen be striped
With corselets of fine velvet, sliped
Down to the hard knee ;
And, from the knee downward,
His hosen shall be freshly gard
With colours two or three.
 And when he is in such array—
" There goeth a rutter," men will say ;
" A rutter, huffa gallant ! "
Ye shall see these fools on him gaze,
And muse as it were on a maze
New brought into the land.   [Virgin !
 Wor. Aff. Ha, ha, ha ! now, by the Mary
This will set him on a merry pin,
Even as it should be.
But ever I am in great fear
That Reason will whister him in the ear,
And turn his mind clean from this gear :
This thing feareth me !
 Pride. Reason ! nay, nay, hardely !
He is forsaken utterly

Sith I came to his company ;
He would not once appear.
Nevertheless, for a surety,
Worldly Affection, I advise thee
As shortly as ever it may be
For speed of the matter,
To bring him shortly in acquaintance
With all the company of mine affiance ;
And let them give continual attendance,
Every man busily,
After the property of his office ;
Then shall ye see him utterly despise
Reason's counsel, on warrantise,
And forsake him, utterly.
   Sens. Nay, nay, sirs ! care ye nothing
That matter is sped well and fine.
   Pride. Is it so ?
   Sens.   Yea, by heaven king !
Even as we sat together at the wine.
   Wor. Aff. Thou shalt have God's blessing
     and mine—
But is it true ?
   Sens.   Yea, sir ! by this day !
Our master and Reason have made a great fray.
   Pride. How so ?
   Sens.   By my faith ! we sat together
At the tavern, next hereby ;
And, anon, who should come together
But flee[r]ing Kate and Margery,
She that beguiled you, parde ! so prately
And bare away your shirt the last morning
Stead of her smock, while ye lay sleeping.
   Pride. I wot whom ye mean, well I know ;
But that is nothing to this purpose—
Tell on thy tale, for God avow !
   Sens. I shall, anon, had I wiped my nose :

Sir ! when I spied them, anon I rose ;
And called them unto me by name ;
And, without more tarrying, anon they came ;
  And sat down with us, and made nothing
    strange,
As they be full courteous—ye know it well.
And, anon, our master's colour began to
  change—
Whereof it came I cannot tell ;
His cheer was appalled, every deal,
And scant that he could speak to me one word ;
But start him even up and rose from the board.
  He said he would go lie down on a bed ;
And prayed me, for the manners' sake,
That Margery might come hold his head
Which, as he told me, began to ache.
And so she hath him undertake
To make him whole, in an hour or twain,
Whensoever he hath any such sudden pain.
  What it meaneth, I wot never ;
But he liketh her physic so well
That I trow the devil of hell
Can not them two dissever !   [more ?
  Lo ! this have I done ; and what trow ye
Yet can I tell you better tiding.
  Wor. Aff. What is that ?   [before,
  Sens. Marry ! Reason, that ye two spake of
Came even to us as we sat so drinking ;
And gave our master a heat, worth a hanging,
Because that Margery sat on his knee,
While that other whore sat talking with me.
  My master saw that he could have no rest,
Nor never be rid of this controlling,
He played the man and thought it best—
And with an angry look to my seeming—
Drew out his sword without more tarrying

And smote Reason so on the head
That I have great marvel but he be now dead.
    Wor. Aff.   Marry! then fill all the cups at
      once
If this be true.
    Sens.   Yes, by these ten bones!
I lie never a word.
    Pride.   Trowest thou it is no feigned strife
Betwixt them two?
    Sens.   No, on my life!
For, when they fought, I ran between
And cried, "Keep peace and leave debate!"
But ye would have laughed had ye seen
How I departed them; and, for all that,
Sometime I clapped Reason on the pate,
And cried "Keep the peace," as fast as I could
Till I was hoarse, I cried so loud.   [now
    Wor. Aff. But, can our master play the man
And fare with this gear?
    Sens.   Yea, make God avow!
And, beware ye of one thing:
Meddle ye no more with Margery;
For, by Cock's precious body!
If our master may it espy,
Or have an understanding
That ye use her company,
I tell you he will be angry;
He is so full of jealousy
As ever I knew man.
    Wor. Aff. Jealousy? peace, man, be still!
He can thereof no manner of skill.
    Sens.   No! but say what ye will
I am sure he can.
   He is now as familiar
With bodily lust as ever ye were;
Yea! and thereto as great a swearer.

When time requires
Knew I never, of his age,
A man of better courage
To do all manner of outrage
After our desires.
  Sith Reason and he were thus at variance
He hath be full of such dalliance ;
And hath called to his favour and acquaintance
Your kinsmen by and by—
Envy, Wrath, Gluttony, and Covetise,
Sloth and Lechery become to his service ;
And utterly he hateth their contrariwise,
And that he professeth openly.
  Wor. Aff.   And be these folks of his retinue?
  Sens.   Yea, every one, I tell you true.
But, marry ! their names be changed new
For to blear his eye.
I tell you he is a serefull man,
For Reason stirreth him, now and than ;
And, therefore, do we what we can
It is little enow, hardely !
  Sirra ! there is first Pride, as ye wot well,
The sweet darling of the devil of hell :
How his name is changed ye can tell.
  Wor. Aff.   Yea, marry ! on the best wise—
Worship I ween is now his name.
  Sens.   Yea, by the rood ! even the same.
And Covetise, to eschew all blame,
Doth his name disguise,
And calleth himself Worldly Policy.
Wrath, because he is somewhat hasty,
Is called Manhood.   Then is there Envy,
And he is called Disdain.
Gluttony, for Good Fellowship is taken ;
And Sloth his old name hath forsaken,
And as fair a name hath he shapen

NATURE   6

As ever man could ordain—   [blood,
He is called Ease; right comfortable to the
Specially for them that lust to do no good.
And, among all other, I would ye understood
That Lechery is called Lust.
Lo! these be fair names, parde!
Both good and honest as seemeth me;
As for their conditions, what they be,
Ye know well!
   Wor. Aff. Very just!
I know their conditions on the best wise
If they keep still their old guise.
   Sens. Yes! that they do, on warrantise.
   Wor. Aff. But yet, I have great marvel
That Covetise should dwell in his company.
   Sens. By my troth, lo! and so have I.
But one thing I ensure you faithfully,
And that I have espied well;
That, hitherto, our master setteth no store
By his counsel, nor his lore.
Marry! when his head waxeth hoar
Then shall be good season
To follow Covetise and his way;
Yea, time enow another day—
Even so I heard our master say.
   Wor. Aff. By my faith! he said but reason—
But all the remanent be well retained?
   Sens. Yea, be ye sure it is matter unfeigned;
And wot ye who is greatly disdained
With our master now?
   Pride. Who?
   Sens. By God! even Shamefacedness.
When he shall do any such excess
No shame can fear him, doubtless,
I may say to you.
   Pride. No! then the craft were nought.

But now, sirs ! well bethought,
Sith the matter is hereto brought,
It is time for me
To go and make some provision
Of garments after the new invention,
As he commanded me to be done :
Thereto must I see.
For it is committed to my negligence ;
And, if he come hither while I am hence,
I pray thee excuse mine absence.
 Sens. Yea, and mine also !
 Pride. Why, wilt thou go with me ?
 Sens. Will I, quod a ? yea, parde !
It is according for Sensuality
With Pride for to go.
     [SENS. *and* PRIDE *go out.*]
 Wor. Aff. Now the matter is almost in good
  case,
After the world's mind and pleasure ;
There is no more but now must I compass,
With all my wit and busy endeavour,
How it may be stablished and continued sure.
For, a little fantasy of man's own will
May quail this matter, and utterly it spill.
And if he vary again
Of scruple imagination,
Or else by the suggestion
Of the foresaid Reason,
One thing I am certain—
He will no longer me support ;
And that were a shrewd crank dort.
Therefore, it is best that I resort
To my master's presence,
And see of what demeanour he is.
I am greatly to blame, I wis,
For that I saw him not or this

Sith he departed hence.

> [*He goeth out and* REASON *cometh in.*
>> *Rea.*   O good Lord ! to whom shall I
>>   complain

And show the sorrows of my mind?
And nothing for mine own cause, certain ;
But only for the decay of mankind ;
Which now, of late, is waxen so blind
That he hath despised and forsaken me,
And followeth every motion of his Sensuality.

   What availed at the beginning
That Nature committed me to his service?
And charged me that, before all thing,
Of all his guiding I should take th' enterprise
When he lusteth not to follow mine advice,
But followeth th' appetites of his sensual
   affection,
As a brute beast that lacketh reason?

   And yet, notwithstanding
That he doth me disdain,
I will resort to him again ;
And do my labour and busy pain
To assay if I can him refrain
From such beastly living.
But, first will I stand hereby,
In secret manner, to espy
Some token of grace in him, whereby
I may discern and find
That he hath any shamefacedness
After his great surfeit and excess ;
And, if it be so, doubtless,
It shall content my mind.

> [REASON *goeth aside.*]
>> MAN *cometh in* [*followed by* WOR. AFFEC.
>> *Man.*   I say, sirs ! where is Worship, can ye
>>   tell?

In this place I left him last.
   Wor. Aff. Sir, I warrant you he is occupied
    well
In ordaining your garments, full fast;
He departed from me in great haste
For that intent; and so he desired
That I would tell you when need required.
   He showed me his mind or he went;
How he had devised your garment;
And, if it be made after that intent,
As he told me,
When ye wear on that vestour
Every man shall do your honour,
As becometh a man of your haviour;
And so it should be.
   Man. Yea, but what will Reason say
When he seeth me in that array?
   Wor. Aff. Reason? Marry! let him go play
To the devil of hell:
Ye promised me, at the beginning,
That ye would no more be under his guiding.
   Man. No! but yet it were according
To have therein his counsel;
Man, without Reason, is but blind;
And, if I should speak after my mind,
I can well a difference find
Betwixt man and a beast
When he hath Reason in presence,
And duly obeyeth his law and sentence.
   Wor. Aff. Why have ye such a spiced
    conscience
Now, within your breast,
That changeth your mind so suddenly?
I am sorry and ashamed, truly,
On your behalf!
   Man.   No force, hardely!

Thou leadest me all wrong ;
And, therefore, will I no more follow thee.
    Wor. Aff.   Not Worldly Affection?
    Man.   No, parde !
Nor yet thy brother Sensuality :
I have followed you too long.
    Wor. Aff.   Is that your mind?
    Man.   Yea, doubtless !
And now will I seek Shamefacedness,
By whom I trust I shall redress
All my misdeed.   [Shame bow,
    Wor. Aff. And, sith thou wilt needs to
I pray God send thee shame enow.
And yet I trust, make God avow !
Once thou shalt have need
To call me again to thy service.
    Man.   Nay, nay, on warrantise !
Now, sirs ! who can me advise
What is best to do?

      [*Enter* SHAMEFACEDNESS.]

    Shame. Sir ! if ye lust to have mine ac-
        quaintance
I am ready to give you attendance ;
Happily my service shall you advance :
I am called Shamefacedness.
    Man. By your troth ! are ye the same?
    Shame. Yea, forsooth ! that is my name.
Almsdeeds I can atame ;
And help for to repress
When ye have done offence or sin ;
If ye will mercy and grace win
With Shamefacedness ye must begin :
This way must ye take.
    Man. Ye be the man, without feigning,
That I wished for or ye came here ;

And glad am I now of your coming,
Praying you with heart entire
When I have need thus to come near.
   Shame. So will I do ; ye may trust it, verily !
Whensoever ye call ye shall find me ready.

            He goeth out [and REASON *cometh*
               forward.]

   Rea. Sir ! is it your mind to do as ye say ?
   Man. Yea, that is it, as God me speed !
Heard ye all this matter—yea or nay ?
   Rea. Yes, that I did, in very deed !   [need
   Man. O ghostly Reason ! I have greater
Of your help than ever I had before :   [more.
Help me now and I shall never forsake you
Sith I forsook your company
I have committed much folly ;
I am ashamed, certainly,
When I think thereon.
But now have I refused utterly
All such manner of company ;
And thus have I done, verily !
Of mine own motion.   [ye me call ;
   Rea. Then my help shall be ready as oft as
It is my duty so for to do.
And of your offences will I make no rehearsal ;
But whatsoever ye have done, hitherto,
To me ward let it pass and go :
Against God your offence is great ;
Of the which matter I will not long treat.
   But this comfort of me ye shall have :
If ye be contrite, as ye pretend,
God is merciable if ye lust to crave ;
Call for grace and soon He will it send.
And be not in purpose hereafter to offend ;
Accustom yourself in the ways of virtue,
And—be not in doubt—grace will ensue.

    Man.   Sir ! it is my mind and intent
Hereafter to be your true obedient ;
And never more to assent
To such folly again.
    Rea.   And, upon that condition,
I take thee unto my tuition
With all heart's affection,
Never to part atwain.
And, for this season,
Here we make an end
Lest we should offend
This audience ; as, God defend !
It were not to be done.
Ye shall understand, nevertheless,
That there is much more of this process ;
Wherein we shall do our business,
And our true endeavour
To show it unto you, after our guise :
When my lord shall so devise
I shall be at his pleasure.
            Thus endeth the first part.]

THE SECOND PART.

REASON *and* MAN *come in.*

Rea. I assemble the life of mortal creature
To the assiege again a strong town or castle:
In which there is much busy endeavour;
Much worldly policy; with diligent travail,
On every side, which part shall prevail
By sleight of engines, or by strong power,
That other to subdue and bring into danger.

  In such case and manner of condition
Is wretched man, here in this life earthly,
While he abideth within the garrison
Of the frail carcase and caronous body;
Whom to impugn laboureth incessantly
The world, the flesh, the enemy—these three—
Him to subdue and bring into captivity.

  And, for to show you what wise they us
    impugn,
First doth the world give us an allective
To covet riches and worldly renown,
With other vanities that be used in this life.
Next, that our flesh, which ever is in strife,
Again our spirit doth provoke and excite
Us to accomplish our sensual appetite.

  The last of all is our great enemy;
Which ever hath us in continual hatred
Of old encankered malice and envy
That he oweth to us, and all the kindred

Of all the ancestors of whom we do succeed ;
Nor yet ceaseth his malice, unto this day,
Us to endanger in all that he can or may.

    And certes ! these, our said enemies,
Be of their nature so mighty and so strong
That hard it will be for us, in any wise,
Again them war or battle to underfong ;
Also our garrisons and fortress to maintain long
Again their engines ; without spiritual grace
We can not perform in no manner case.

    Wherefore, it is to us right behovable
Busily to pray to God, that is immortal,
Beseeching Him, as He is merciable,
To have compassion and pity on us all ;
And not to suffer us any wise to fall
Into such folly and utter mischance
As should them grieve and do displeasance.

    Also, it behoveth on our part
To flee all such manner of occasion
As may us put in fear and jeopardy
Of their displeasure, in any condition.
Newfangleness, and other nice invention,
We must forsake in all manner wise ;
And acquaint us with their contraries :
Quia contraria contrariis curantur. etc.
I tell this tale, sir ! to you,
Trusting that it be not done in waste :
Ye remember, as I suppose, well enow,
How it is not fully three days past
Sith ye me promised, and bound it fast,
From that day forth to be obedient
Unto my counsel and advisement ?

    Man.   Yea, sir ! so I did, in very deed ;
And yet it is my mind and intent
To follow the same—have ye no dread !

    Rea.   If ye do not, yourself shall repent ;

Now, fare ye well ! for I must be absent
As for a season ; and, for your comfort,
Whensoever ye call me I shall to you resort.
> *Then he goeth out and* SENSUALITY
> *cometh in.*

Sens.   God forbid that ever he come again !
Jesu ! how may ye this life endure ?
Meseemeth it should be to you a great pain,
Sith ye be of good complexion and nature,
To forbear the worldly sport and pleasure ;
As ye have done now a great season,
And all by the foolish counsel of Reason.

Where is your lusty heart become
That served you so well this other day ?
Now, so help me God and halidom !
I have great marvel how ye may
Live in such misery ; and, this dare I say,
Without ye take some other ways,
By my troth ! it will shorten your days.

And, though I say it, that were pity ;
For, by Christ ! and ye were gone
Many a good fellow would make great mone.
> *Then he weepeth.*

Man.   Why weep ye so ?
Sens.   Let me alone !
It will none otherwise be.
And ye saw the sorrowful countenance
Of my company, your old acquaintance,
That they make
For your sake—
I daresay ye would mone them in your mind
They be so loving and so kind
That I am sure
If ye endure
In this peevish opinion,
It will be their confession

There is none other remedy
But, for sorrow, they shall die.
 Man. Nay, God forbid they should so do!
 Sens. In faith! without ye help thereto
There is none other way.
 Man. I will help it in all that I may
And I wist by what mean.
 Sens. Marry! call them to your company!
 Man. 'By Saint John! I am content.
For, I may say here to thee,
Since I forsook my liberty
And did to Reason assent
I had never merry day;
But lived under awe and dread alway,
Nothing to mine intent.
Another while I will me disport
And to mine old company resort.
 Sens. O then shall ye them comfort,
And your self also.
Wot ye who will be very glad?
 Man. Who?
 Sens.   Margery!
 Man.   Why, was she sad?
 Sens. Yea, by the mass! she was stark mad,
Even for very woe
When she heard tell of this chance;
And, because she would live in penance
Her sorrow for to quench,
She hath entered into a religious place,
At the Green Friars hereby.
 Man.   Yea, has'e?
Alack, good little wench!
Is it an house of strait religion?
 Sens. Yea, as any that ever was bygone
Sith the world stood.
 Man. Be they close nuns as other be?

Sens.   Close, quod a? nay, nay, parde!
That guise were not good—
Ye must beware of that gere!
Nay, all is open that they do there;
As open as a goose eye!
   Man.   And cometh any man into their cells?
   Sens.   Yea, yea, God forbid else!
It is free for everybody;
And, beside all this, they be
Ex omni gente cognite.
No nation they forsake;
Without it be beggars, going by the way,
That have never a penny to pay
For that that they do take.
   And yet can I beggars thither lead
Where they shall, for lumps of bread,
Satisfy their desire:
Such drabs some there be
That require none other fee,
Not yet any other hire.
   Man.   Be they not wedded, as other folk be?
   Sens.   Wedded, quod a? no, so mot I thee!
They will not tarry therefore;
They can wed themselves alone.
"Come kiss me, John;" "Gramercy, Joan!"
Thus wed they evermore.
And it is the more to commend;
For, if the woman hap to offend,
As it is their guise,
A man may let her alone with sorrow
And wed another whore on the morrow;
Even of the same wise.
   Man.   Forsooth! this is a noble religion;
It stirreth me to great devotion
For to see that place—
Canst thou bring me thither, well enow?

Sens.   Yea, and it were midnight, I make
   God avow!
As dark as ever it was.
   Man.   But, where is Bodily Lust now?
                    Then cometh in BODILY LUST, *with*
                              him WORLDLY AFFECTION :
                         SENSUALITY *standeth aside.*
   Bod. Lust.   Marry, sir! I have seeken and
   sought you
This three or four hours.
   Man.   I make God avow!
Ye give shrewd attendance ;
All this two days I could not thee espy.
   Bod. Lust.   Sir! ye know well that ye and I
Be never much asunder
Albeit I be from you among.   [too long,
   Man.   And now meseemeth thou hast tarried
Which is to me great wonder.
   Bod. Lust.   Wonder? yea, parde! for an
   hour or twain ;
Forth for a passing while and come again—
Here is a sore matter :
When was I so long absent as now?
And yet I was for to seek you
At the other side of the water ;
The place that ye wot of, parde!
Understand ye what I mean?
   Man.   Yea, yea!
   Bod. Lust.   Tell me in mine ear!
   Man.   *Quid est Latinum propter le stewys?*
   Bod. Lust.   What! Latin? now this of the
I heard never this ere :   [news ;
I trow ye begin to wax shamefaced!
   Man.   Nay, nay, hardely! that gear is past,
Many days agone.
I am as wanton as ever I was.

    Bod. Lust. It were alms to hang you else—
      by the mass !—
By the hard neck bone.
But will ye now go with me to a place
And I shall show you the smorterst place
That ever ye saw with eyes ?
    Man. What thing is it ? young or old ?
    Bod. Lust. Whatever it be, it is able to be
    sold :
It shall like you on the best wise.
    Man. For my love let us some night be
At a banket or a rare supper ;   [there,
And get us some wanton meat
So we may have some dainty thing—
Yet would I spend twenty shilling
Wheresoever I it get.
    Bod. Lust. Nay, nay ! will ye spend a couple
    of crowns ?
And there shall no gentleman in these ten towns
Be better served than ye ;
Nor be received more honestly,
As to an house of bawdry,
For a banket or a junkery,
For a dish two or three.
    Man. Yes ! that will I spend with all mine
    heart.
    Bod. Lust. By your leave, I will depart
To make ready this gear.
    Man. What ! now, in all this haste ?
    Bod. Lust. Yea, fore God, sir ! I am aghast
That other knaves will come thither
Before us and take up all.
    Man. See thereto, I pray thee !
    Bod. Lust.   So I shall ;
Else, fie on all together !

                    [Then goeth he out.

Wor. Aff.   Now will Margery make great
mone
Because ye come not.
Man.   Yea, let her alone !
I am not her bondman, parde !
She hath disappointed me or now.
Wor. Aff.   Yet, on my faith, sir ! and I were
as you
At the least I would excuse me.
Send her word that ye in no wise
May this night keep her promise ;
And, if ye do not so,
She will so mourn that, as I think,
Of all this night she will sleep no wink,
She shall be so full of woe.
Man.   Yea, on my peril ! take no care ;
This answer will I defer and spare
Till I be certain
What answer Bodily Lust shall bring
Of this other pretty new thing
When he cometh again.
Wor. Aff.   Will it please you that I go to
Margery
In your stead ?
Man.   Marry ! that were merry ;
Wouldst thou serve me so ?
Wor. Aff.   Why, sir, by my troth ! I mean
but well.
Man.   Yea, what thou meanest I can not tell,
But that shall thou not do   [worse ;
Wor. Aff.   In good faith, sir ! ye may do
For, while I have anything in my purse,
Or any penny to spend,
I will make her even such cheer
As I would mine own wife if she were here ;
Else, God defend !

Man. Yea, I thank thee for thy good will ;
But as for that cheer, keep it still
Till I call thereon !   [spake it ;
    Wor. Aff. By God, sir ! for good love I
And now that I see ye will not take it
I shall let it alone.   [*Re-enter* BODILY LUST.]
    Man. How now? hast thou been yonder
      away ?
    Bod. Lust. Yea, sir !
    Man.   Et que novellys ?
    Bod. Lust.   Je nescey.
I could not speak with her
No[r] with none of her folks.
    Man.   Not with one ?
    Bod. Lust. No ! they be asleep everyone :
All that ever dwell there.
    Man. How knowest thou whether they be
      asleep or no ?
    Bod. Lust. Marry ! she herself told me so
When I rapped at the door.
    Man. It seemeth she was not asleep then.
    Bod. Lust. No ! she was abed with a strange
      man.
    Man. A mischief on her, whore !
I would this fire were in her tail, I make God
      avow !   [enow ;
    Bod. Lust. That needeth not ; she is hot
It were more alms to get
Some cold water her fire to quench :
I tell you, it is as warm a wench
As any in all this street—
I supposed I had angered her ill.
    Man. How so ?
    Bod. Lust.   For I rang her a knil
That waked her from her sleep ;
I gave her a peal for her friends' souls—

A man might have heard the noise from Poules
To the farthest end of Cheap.
She saw that I would not cease but knock
And rap still at the gate ;
She opened a window and put forth her head—
Hence, Forty Pence ! quo' she, Jack Noble is
    a-bed !
This night ye come too late.
Ah ! standeth the wind so cold, quod I ?
K. q. tytle ! we have a bry—
This gear goeth all wide.
And so I came thence a great pace
Till I came hither ; lo ! this is the case—
Have I not well hied ?
    Man.   Well, man ! there is no more to do ;
That we cannot have we must forego ;
There is none other remedy.
Lo, Worldly Affection ! now mayst thou see
Thy counsel was nought that thou gavest me.
    Wor. Aff.   No more it was truly !
    Man.   Yea, I told thee as much before,
It is good to be sure evermore ;
Therefore, now let us go
And resort again to our old hostess :
That is the best way now, as I guess.
    Wor. Aff.   Yea, hardely do so !
            Then they three go out [, SENSUALITY
              remaining,] *and* PRIDE *cometh in.*
    Pride.   Sirs ! remember ye that this other
    day
Man promised me, even in his stead,   [say
That I should with him dwell ; and now, I hear
The wild worm is come into his head ;
So that by Reason only he is led :
It may well be so ; but, I am sure
That Reason shall not alway with him endure.

Methinketh that Sensuality doth not his part
According to the duty of his office;
For, nobody can better turn a man's heart,
Nor yet a readier mean devise
To put away such foolish fantasy,
Than Sensuality if he lust to assay,
For he is chief ruler when Reason is away.

Sens. [*coming forward*]. Yea, a ruler will I
be though Reason say Nay. [day!

Pride. Ah, Sensuality! welcome, by this
What, tidings good?

Sens. Yea, by my fay!
As good as can be told.
I have brought this man to his old guise.

Pride. Hast thou so?

Sens. Yea, on warrantise!

Pride. Now, forsooth! I give thee prick
and praise;
Thou art worth thy weight of gold.
Of this tidings I am glad and fain;
But shall I be welcome to him again
And all our company?

Sens. Yea, hardely!
As welcome as ever ye were before. [therefore;

Pride. God's blessing have thine heart,
Thus am I in thy debt, more and more.

Sens. Japes! why say ye so?

Pride. For—I speak it after my mind—
Thou art to me alway so kind.
But, where shall I our master find?
To him will I go.

Sens. He is busy—hark! in your ear—
With little Margery—ye wot where?
And, as soon as I had brought him there
I came my way apace.
And, because he should not be alone,

I left with him Worldly Affection,
And other errand had I none.
Now to this place,
But even to show you what is done ;
And from hence I must anon,
For to seek another companion
To give attendance.
 Pride. Who is that?
 Sens.   Marry ! Gluttony.
Our master calleth for him busily—
Sawest thou him not?
 Pride.   No, certainly !
To my remembrance.   [tarrying—
 Sens. I must go seek him without any
But, Pride ! I warn you of one thing
While I think thereon :
When my master and ye shall meet,
In any wise see that ye him greet
In the old fashion ;
And make as though ye know nothing
Of his divers and variable dealing ;
Keep that in your breast.
Ye cannot do him more displeasure
Than thereof to make reporture ;
Therefore, let it rest !
To speak thereof it is high treason.
        Then he goeth out.
 Pride. I am glad ye warn me thus in season ;
I shall be the better ware.
By this warning I shall be wise
And do as ye me advertise :
Take thereof no care. [*Enter* SLOTH.]
 Sloth. Will ye be wise, quod a? marry !
  that is a thing—
By God ! ye had need to have better warning
Or ye bring that about.

Pride. What, brother Sloth ! from whence
  comest thou ? [avow !
Sloth. Straight from my bed, I make God
Mine eyes be almost out
For lack of sleep—but this, sir ! to you :
Methought ye called me Sloth, right now ;
Peace, no more of that !
I have a new name as well as ye.
  Pride. What is that ? Ease ?
  Sloth. Yea, parde !
But it forceth not
While our master is not present.
Between us twain I am content
Call me what ye will—
But where is our master ?
  Pride. Wottest thou ne'er ?
  Sloth. No !
  Pride. No more do I.
  Sloth. There, there, there !
Thou shalt dwell with me still ;
Thou art as good a waiter as I.
  Pride. I shrew the better of us both, hardly !
But, surely we do not well ;
We shall not continue with yonder man
But we await better, now and than.
Therefore, by my counsel,
Let us twain go together
To seek our master.
  Sloth. But wottest thou whither
We shall now go
To find our master ?
  Pride. I shall assay.
Thou shalt see me guess the way ;
And, happily, find him too.
Now must I to the stewes, as fast as I may,
To fetch this gentleman ; but, sirs ! I say,

Can any man here tell me the way?
For I came never there.
Ye know the way, parde! of old;
I pray thee tell me which way shall I hold—
Will ye see this whoreson cuckold?
I trow he cannot hear—
Now it were alms to clap thee on the crown!
              [*Then cometh in* MAN *and* WORLDLY
                AFFECTION.

    Man.   Why, be there any cuckolds in town?
    Pride.   Yea, I durst hold thereon my gown
That there be a score;
But, fore God! I cry you mercy;
For, by my faith! I wist you not so nigh.
Had I wist it I ensure you, faithfully,
That word I would have forbore.
    Man.   No force, hardely! it toucheth not me—
But worship! tell me, where have ye be?
Methinketh long sith I you see:
    Pride.   Sir! it is no marvel.
Bade ye not me, the last day,
To go purvey for your array,
And ye remember well.
    Man.   Yea, fore God! have ye done the same?
    Pride.   Yea, by the rood! else were I to blame.
All thing is ready, in pain of shame,
Else I quit me ill.
The tailor told me yester night
That all your garments were ready dight—
Will ye go thither and have a sight?
    Man.   Yea, marry! with a good will.
    Sloth.   Will ye that I go with you also?
    Man.   I wot never whether ye may attend
    thereto;
For ye do nothing
But even after your own sweet will.

Sloth. Why should I ever wait nay that I nill?
For, to be a king,
I may not endure continual business.
I was never used thereto ; doubtless
I should not live a year
If I followed you, I am sure ;
Ye stir and labour out of measure :
I saw never your peer :
Ye ween there can nothing be do
But if ye put your hand thereto ;
And I wis that is no need.
Ye have servants, that be true and just,
If it would like you to put them in trust,
And quit well their meed.
What should I attend you for to please,
When I see well ye set by none ease,
Which belongeth to me?   [to say?
    Man. Why, Ease ! what meaneth thee thus
I do but eat, drink, sleep, and play,
And none other labour, parde !
    Sloth. Yea, ye may say what ye will
But I can never see you idle,
And quiet as ye should be.
Your body laboureth as doth an hackney
That beareth the burden every day,
That pity it is to see ;
And your mind, on that other side,
Is never idle, nor unoccupied.
I wis it grieveth me
To see you demeaned that wise :
I trow ye be set all on covetise !
    Man. Covetise? nay, let be !
It is a thing of greater cure
That sticketh in my mind, be thou sure !
    Sloth. So methought, by the rood !
I wist as much there was something,

By your lowering cheer and your sighing,
That was not all thing good—
But, what is the matter? I pray you, heartily!
   Man.   I wis thou canst not devise the remedy
With all the wit thou hast.
But this is the case, to tell it shortly:
A thing was told me as I came hereby
How Reason purveyeth fast,
And maketh very great labour and ordinance
To dash us all out of countenance;
And, for that purpose,
He hath gathered a great company.
   Sloth.   What to do?
   Man.   I wot ne'er I.
But, as I suppose,
It is to bring me in captivity;
And to take from me my liberty—
So he hath oft said.
   Pride.   Fear ye that matter?
   Man.   Nay, never a deal!
But I care for it, wit ye well,
Yet am I not afraid.
For I will withstand it proudly;
And, sirs! I trust ye will stand thereby
When it shall be need.
   Pride.   Yea, by the way that God went!
Or he have of you his intent
First shall I bleed
The best blood that is in this carcase.
   Man.   Well, Ease! go thy way hence, apace,
And make therein good speed.
Call my company all together,
And bid them every man come hither
That is with me affeed.
   Sloth.   Marry, sir! that shall be do.
                        [Then he goeth out.

Man. Worship ! in the meantime let us go
To see my new apparel. [sake,
  Pride. Will ye so? Now, for your lady's
Go do it on you ; and I undertake
It shall become you well.
  Man. Worldly Affection ! abide thou here
For I will go do on this new gear
As Worship doth me counsel.
                    [*Then* MAN *and* PRIDE *goeth out.*
  Wor. Aff. Marry, I shall ! with all mine
      heart !
This good fire and I will not depart ;
For very cold mine hands do smart :
It maketh me woe-begone.
Get me a stool ! here ! may ye not see ?
Or else a chair will it not be—
Thou pild knave ! I speak to thee ;
How long shall I stand ? [*Enter* GLUTTONY.]
  Glut. Let him stand, with a foul evil !
[*The lower margin is shaved off*] the devil
Will ye see—lo ! every drivel,
Nowadays I warrant,
Must command as he were a king :
Let him stand on his feet with breeding.
  Wor. Aff. What, Gluttony ! I can tell thee
      one thing :
In faith you will be shent !
  Glut. Why?
  Wor. Aff. My master hath sent Sensuality
To seek thee all about the country—
Spakest thou not with him?
  Glut. Yes, parde !
I know all his intent ;
And, thereupon, I am come here
For to await ; but wottest thou where
Our master is now ?

Wor. Aff.   Nay, I wot ne'er ;
I am not very certain
But Pride and he together be gone.
He said he would come again, anon,
Within an hour or twain.
Tarry thou here, and go not away !
I will go break my fast and I may,
For I ate never a morsel this day.
                              Then he goeth out.
   Glut.   Marry ! that is a thing :
Go when thou wilt, I will abide.
My stomach he shall not rule or guide
That is now fasting—
Nay, of all thing earthly I hate to fast ;
Four times a day I make repast ;
Or thrice as I suppose.
And, when I am well fed
Then get I me to a soft bed
My body to repose ;
There take I a nap or twain.
Up I go straight and to it again ;
Though nature be not ready,
Yet have I some meat of delight,
For to provoke th' appetite
And make the stomach greedy.
After all this needs I must
Sometime follow the wanton lust
   [*This line is shaved off at the foot of the page.*]
For hot drinks and delicate refection
Causeth fleshly insurrection :
Ye know it as well as I.   [MAN *entereth.*]
   Man.   Troth ! as ye say, I know it well.
   Glut.   What gentleman is this, can ye tell ?
   Bod. Lust.   Wottest thou never ?
   Glut.   No, by the bell !
I saw him never before.

Bod. Lust.   Is it our master?

Glut.   Nay, by the rood!
It is not he; wouldst thou make me wood?

Man.   Yes, I am the same.

Glut.   I cry you mercy! I see it well now;
Before, I knew you not, I make God avow!
In earnest nor in game.

Man.   Why? Because I have changed mine
    array?

Glut.   For that cause, trow ye? nay, nay!
That is not the thing
That can deceive me, be ye sure.
But, I pray you, who hath had you in cure
Since my last departing?

Man.   By my faith! a little season
I followed the counsel and diet of Reason.

Glut.   There went the hare away!
His diet, quod a! it may be, verily:
For ye be haltered marvellously—
Altered, I would say.
Alas! the while had ye no meat
As long as ye were under his diet?

Man.   Meat? yes, I had some,
Without it were on fasting days;
Then he withdrew my supper always
And gave me never a crumb.

Glut.   No force, hardely; why would ye then
Favour him as ye did like a madman?
Ye look now as it were a ghost.
Had ye dwelt with him till this day
Ye had been pined even away,
As ye be now almost:
Your flesh is gone every deal—
A vengeance on the morsel
That is left thereon!

Bod. Lust.   Now, talk of the remedy.

Glut. Marry! now must he eat and drink
Other remedy is there none.   [fast;
    Bod. Lust. Yea, but where is the meat?
    now let us see!
    Glut. Ye are passing hasty, benedicite!
First must ye go
Whereas provision thereof is made;
Let us go thither and it shall be had.
    Man. But what is the mistress of the inn?
A wedded woman or a virgin?
    Glut. Neither of both, I wis!
    Bod. Lust. No! but for a maiden she goeth.
    Glut. Yea, fore God! that she doth;
But yet she is none, by Jis!
    Bod. Lust. No, no! what then?
    Glut. I wis I not; but, as men clatter,
They say she is innupta mater,
Hardely an holy woman.
    Man. Well, thither we will! go we hence!
    Bod. Lust. Sir! ye will give me licence
To sport me for a season?
    Man. Yes, for a while ye well enow;
But go not out of the way, I charge you;
For hither will come, anon,
All my company, as I suppose:
Keep them together! for I purpose
To come again anon,
And show them my mind what I will do.
                 Then he goeth out.
    Bod. Lust. Marry! I shall do what I can
And yet, it is hard for me   [thereto;
To keep them together any while.
But I shall tell you what:
I had liever keep as many fleas,
Or wild hares in an open lese,   [ENVY.]
As undertake that. [*Entereth* WRATH *and*

Wrath. Where be these knaves that make
this array? [way—
Bod. Lust. Marry! they be gone that other
Tell me whom ye mean.
Wrath. I trow, thou scornest!
Bod. Lust. Nay, certainly!
Howsobeit, if I should not lie
At the first blush, I ensure you, faithfully,
I had forgot you clean;
Because ye be thus defensibly arrayed.
What meaneth that? are ye afraid?
Who hath you grieved? [head;
Wrath. Nay, I fear no man that beareth a
Yet had I liever that I were dead
Than that should be proved.
Bod. Lust. By my faith! ye are wont to be
as bold
As it were a lion of Cotswold;
But now, to my question:
What meaneth all this defensible array?
Wrath. Marry! Sloth warned us two this
same day,
Even sith it was noon, [fray;
That our master and Reason should make a
And, therefore, he had us, without delay,
To await on our captain.
Bod. Lust. Ah! now I know the matter
right well;
But what shall come thereof I cannot tell:
It passeth my brain.
Our master willed that we twain
Should tarry here till he come again.
Envy. What wilt thou do then?
Bod. Lust. Who, I? nay, care not for me!
I will not come where strokes be;
I am not so mad a man.

And I wis it is not for any fear ;
But it is a thing that I can well forbear,
And will as long as I can.
Of lust and pleasure is all my mind ;
It longeth to me of property and kind ;
And if I should to the war,
And lie in mine harness, as other men do,
With hunger and thirst a day or two,
It should me utterly mar.

    Envy. It were a great loss if thou were
        married !
Now, fie on the stark whoreson coward !
By Cock's precious blood !
It were no sin to slay such a knave.
Hast not thou wages as other men have ?
And few of us so good ;
Yet wilt thou fail us at this need !
Now, whosoever shall quit my meed,
I will no further go
Till I have slain him [with] mine own hand,
Though I should forswear the land
Even when I have do.

            Then goeth out BODILY LUST.
Hold him in, sirs ! I you require—
Alas ! would ye not, at my desire,
Do so much for me ?
I wis it would have done me more good
To have seen the knave's heart-blood
Than twenty shillings of fee. [MAN *returneth.*]

    Man. What ho, sirs ! what meaneth this gear ?
Will ye slay each other here ?
No more of this work !   [abiden

    Envy. By the heart of God ! and he had
A little while he should never have spoken
With priest nor with clerk.

    Man. Who was that ?

Envy.   Your own minion,
Bodily Lust.
Man.   Why, what hath he done?
Envy.   Even like a lurden
He saith that ye have given him licence
To abide at home, and keep residence
While we bear the burden,
And serve you now at your need!
Man.   He prayed me so, in very deed,
Within these two days.
He said he would serve me with a good will;
But of the wars he could no skill,
Nor knew thereof the ways:
Howbeit I gave him thereof none answer.
Envy.   No! but I am sure he will not come
And now may ye see   [there;
That no man is so much to blame
As yourself.
Man.   I?
Envy.   Yea, by Saint Jame!
No man but even ye.
For, I am well assured of one thing,
Ye gave him better clothing
Than ye did me;
And better wages and fees also;
And though I said but little thereto,
But suffered evermore,
Yet I disdained it ever in my mind;
And though[t] that ye were to me unkind
To set so great store
By such a knave as he was—
I would I had him here, by the mass!
And no man but we twain.
Man.   By my troth! this is ever thy guise:
Look! by whom I set any prize
Him thou wilt most disdain.

Wrath. By Christ ! he can do none otherwise.
But now, sir ! is there any service
That ye will command me ?

Man. Yea, marry is there ! but my company
Dresseth them forward, passing slowly ;
I trow it will not be.
Manhood ! thou art good I know for one.

    Wrath. Yea, by Christ ! and they came
        everyone
I will not greatly fear.

    Envy. By my troth ! because he saith so
I shall tell you what I saw him do.
I was present there—
Sir ! it happened in Westminster Hall,
Even before the judges all—
His hands were bound fast ;
And, never upon him, that ever God made,
Dagger, sword, nor knife he had.
And yet, at the last,
He drave twelve men into a corner ;
And an hour after durst they not appear.
How say ye hereto ?
And his hands had been at liberty
He would have put them in great jeopardy—
It is to suppose so.

    Man. Marry ! there he quit him well—
But where be mine other folk, can ye tell ?

        Then cometh in GLUTTONY *with a cheese*
           and a bottle.

    Wrath. Marry ! here cometh one—
Good Fellowship meseemeth it should be.

    Glut. Sirs, God speed ye !

    Man. What tidings with thee ?

    Glut. I shall tell you anon   *[page.]*
[*A line has been shaved away at the foot of the*
Marry, sir ! I am come here

For to attend upon you ;
We shall a warfare it is told me.
   Man.   Yea, where is thy harness?
   Glut.   Marry ! here may ye see—
Here is harness enow.   [but this ?
   Wrath.   Why, hast thou none other harness
   Glut.   What the devil harness should I
    miss,
Without it be a bottle?
Another bottle I will go purvey
Lest that drink be scarce in the way ;
Or happily none to sell.
   Wrath.   Thou must have other harness
    than this, man !   [then !
   Glut.   Other harness? nay, I shrew me
I can no skill thereon—
Why, trowest thou that I will fight?
   Envy.   Yea, so I trow !
   Glut.   Nay, by God Almight !
Thereof will I none ;
I was never wont to that gear.
But I may serve to be a victualler—
And thereof shall ye have store—
So that I may stand out of danger
Of gun shot ; but I will come no near ;
I warn you that before !   [devil !
   Envy.   Now, such a knave I betake to the
This is even such another drivel
As was here whilere :
They be two knaves anointed.
I fear me, sir ! ye shall be disappointed ;
I like not this gear.   [avow !
   Glut.   O ! I had forgotten, I make God
Sir ! my fellow, Ease, commandeth me to you.
   Man.   Commandeth thee to me?
   Glut.   You to me !

  NATURE   8

Man.   Me to thee!   [have said.
Glut.   Commandeth you to him, I would
Man.   Why cometh he not hither?
Glut.   By God! for he is afraid;
And lieth sick in his bed.   [gear
He took such a conceit when he heard of this
That for thought and very fear
[*A line is shaved away at the foot of the page.*]
    Wrath.   And he were hanged it were no
        reck:
I pray God, the devil break his neck!
And all such as he is.
    Man.   Well, let us suffer for awhile;
I will go walk hence half a mile;
And for all this,
Happily, all this gear shall not need
Howbeit that I doubt and dread
The worst, as wise men do.
Manhood! come thyself with me.
    Glut.   And I too, sir?
    Man.   Yea, parde!
Wouldst thou be prayed thereto?
        Then goeth out MAN, GLUTTONY *and* WRATH.
    Envy.   Now, he that would have war or
        strife
I pray God send him a shrewd wife;
And then shall he have enow.
But, I shall tell you, sirs! as for me,
I am none of them; so mot I thee!
I may say to you
I will no such reckonings abide.
God's body! here cometh Pride
As crank as a peacock!
As soon as he and I meet,
Without he stand right upon his feet,
He shall bear me a proud mock. [PRIDE *entereth.*]

Pride. What tidings, sirs? can any man
tell?

Envy. Yea, marry! that can I do as well
As any that was in field;
Ye have tarried so long about your gay gear
That the field is done or ye come there.

Pride. Done? marry, God shield!

Envy. It is done without fail;
But which of them hath won the battle
I cannot tell you certain.   [thereby!

Pride. Thou were not there it seemeth

Envy. Not I there, quod a? yes, hardely!
And that to my great pain;
But, as soon as the battles joined together,
I came my way straight hither
For to tell tidings.

Pride. What the devil tidings canst thou
tell?   [the battle,

Envy. Marry! I can show you nothing of
But of many other tidings.
Ye are out of conceit, I tell you, for ever;
Because ye did not you[r] endeavour
At this great voyage;
Insomuch that ye are like to lese,
Both your office and all your fees,
And put clean out of wages.

Pride. That is not true, as I suppose.

Envy. Sir! and it be not, take my nose
And my head also!
Your office was given or I came thence.

Pride. Marry! that was a very short
sentence;
And I not called thereto.
Now, Envy, what counsel wilt thou give me?

Envy. By my troth, Pride! thou mayst
believe me,

If I were in thy case
I would withdraw me for a season ;
Though it be neither felony, nor treason,
Nor yet wilful trespass.
Yet the same is worst of all ;
For every knave will thee call
A coward to thy face.
    Pride.   I am unhappy, I see it well,
For th' expense of mine apparel
Towards this voyage,
What in horses and other array,
Hath compelled me for to lay
All my land to mortgage.
And now, when I have all do,
To lose mine office and fees also
For my true intent,
I may say that all my cost
And all my time is evil lost
In service that I have spent.
Well, whatsoever betide me,
For a season I will hide me,
After thy counsel.
And, sith it will no better be,
Farewell ! I take my leave of thee.
    Envy.   Now, gentle Pride, farewell ! [*Exit.*]
Alas ! that I had no good fellow here
To bear me company, and laugh at this gear :
This game was well found.

                       [Sensuality *entereth.*]
    Sens.   Yes, and ye lust to play the knave
Some manner of company ye might have,
Here within this ground.
    Envy.   Some I can think, young or old ;
And else it were a small household
As any might be found.   [well ;
    Sens.   It is not small ; the company showeth

But, methought thou were about to tell
Of some merry jest,
Or some merry game at my coming.
    Envy.   Yea, hardely ! it is a game for a king,
When he lusteth best,
To laugh for his disport and solace.
Sir ! I shall tell thee this is the case :
Right now, as I stood
In this place, and never a man with me,
In came Pride garnished as it had be
One of the royal blood.
It grieved me to see him so well besene ;
But, I have abated his courage clean,
For a little season.
By the rood ! I have given him a checkmate ;
For I bare him a hand that he came too late,
And that the field was done,
And how his office was given away
Because he failed our master that day :
I made him to believe so.
And when I had told him all this tale,
Anon, he began to wax all pale,
Full of care and woe.
And now he hideth himself for shame ;
I gave him mine advice to the same ;
And so he is gone.   [do !
    Sens.   Now, on my faith ! this was madly
But, in faith ! what moveth thee thereto ?
    Envy.   Marry ! cause had I none ;
But only that it is my guise
When I see another man arise,
Or fare better than I,
Then must I chafe and fret for ire,
And imagine, with all my desire,
To destroy him utterly.
But now, in earnest, Sensuality !

Tell me when this fray shall be ;
I pray ye heartily !
    Sens.   What, against Reason?
    Envy.   Yea, the same !
    Sens.   Tush ! they be agreed, in pain of
    shame !
And good company they keep.
    Envy.   Agreed, quod a ? in the mere name ;
Marry, sir ! that were a game
To make some of us weep.
    Sens.   Weep or laugh, man ! so it is ;
And who, trow ye, is the cause of this ?
    Envy.   Who ?
    Sens.   Age, the devil him quell !
    Envy.   Why, is Age now come in place ?
    Sens.   Yea, and that may ye spy by his face
And ye mark it well.
His stomach fainteth every day ;
His back crooketh ; his head waxeth gray ;
His nose droppeth among ;
His lust is gone and all his liking ;
I see it well, by everything,
He may not live long ;
And all maketh Age, as I said before.
He is the doer, and what trow ye more
This Age hath done ?
    Envy.   What ?
    Sens.   By my faith ! he hath brought in
    Reason
In such wise that, at no season,
Nothing can be wrought
But Reason must be called thereto :
I fear me he will us all undo
Within few days.
As soon as Gluttony had espied
All this gear, he would not abide ;

But went even his ways.
Our master prayed him to tarry a season—
Nay, nay, quoth he! now have I done ;
I may no longer tarry :
For Age and I may not together dwell.
And straightway he departed, fair and well.
Bodily Lust stood by,
And saw that Gluttony would needs be gone.
Have with thee, Gluttony, quod he! anon,
For I must go with thee.
So that two be gone together ;
Came there none of them both hither?
    Envy.   Never a one, that I see !
    Sens.   Well, they be gone some other way
To get a new master as soon as they may ;
They cannot be unpurveyed.
And, as soon as they two were gone,
Our master sent for Covetise anon,
And heartily him prayed
To await on him well for a year or two ;
And he hath promised him so to do,
As for a year or twain ;
But Reason may not thereof know.
    Envy.   Reason, quod a ? no, so I trow !
He will that disdain ;
But where hath Covetise been many a day ?
    Sens.   He dwelt with a priest, as I heard
       say ;
For he loveth well
Men of the church, and they him also ;
And lawyers eke, when they may tend thereto,
Will follow his counsel.
    Envy.   So men say there, as I dwell.
But, Sensuality ! canst thou tell,
Now in this case,
What were best for us to do ?

Sens.   Marry! I hold it best that we go
Hereby, to some place,
And semble together all our company;
To hear their minds, by and by,
And every man's opinion
What shall be best for to do.
    Envy.   By my troth, and be it so!
I hold it well done.
                    [*Then they go forth and* REASON *and*
                        MAN *come in.*
    Rea.   Sir! I have ofttimes you advised
To live virtuously, and showed you the way;
And that notwithstanding ye have me despised,
And followed Sensuality many a day.
Will ye so continue? yea, or nay?
If ever ye purpose yourself to amend,
It is time; for your life draweth fast to th' end.
    Man.   I cannot continue though I would;
For Age hath wained me clean therefro.
And yet, Reason! when ye me told
Of this gear, many day ago,
I thought little I should have come hereto,
But had of your words great scorn and disdain.
Would God that my life were to begin again!
    Rea.   Speak not thereof! that may not be.
A thing done cannot be called again;
But the thing that most feareth me,
On your behalf, I tell you plain,
Is that ye would in nowise abstain
From sinful lusts, as I willed you to do
Till now that age compelleth you thereto.
    Man.   That is full true, without feigning;
As long as mine appetite did endure
I followed my lusts in everything;
Which now, by the course and law of nature,
And not of my policy or good endeavour,

Is taken from me for evermore :
And so can I deserve no meed therefore.
   But notwithstanding this mine abusion,
I trust that by the help of your good advice
I may be made the child of salvation.
   Rea. Yes, and ye will, sir ! on warrantise ;
So that ye utterly forsake and despise
All your old servants, in will and deed,
And do by my counsel.
   Man.   Yes, have ye no dread !
   Rea. Then, my soul for yours I lay to wed ;
Ye shall do well—have ye no mistrust !
And first, to begin with, I you forbid
All manner of despair ; and secondly, ye must
Put to your mind and good will
To be recured of your great excess ;
For, without your help, it cannot be, doubtless !
   As in this example : if so be the patient
Of himself be willing to have any remedy,
It is a great furtherance to that intent
So that to the precepts of physic he apply ;
And whoso doth the contrary, no marvel, truly,
Though he miscarry. What ! should I bring
Any mo examples for so plain a thing ?
   Man. It shall be no need, as in this case ;
I know right well what ye mean thereby ;
And that will I follow, by God's grace !
   Rea. Then, as I told you, it shall be no
     maistry
Yourself to comfort, and to have good remedy
Against the great surfeits that thou hast done,
By which thou hast deserved endless dam-
    nation.   [dread ;
   But do as I shall tell thee, and have no
And, for to give thee medicines most according
Ayenst thy sores, do by my rede.

Look ! what disease is hot and brenning
Take ever such a medicine as is cold in work-
    ing ;
So that the contrary, in all manner of wise,
Must heal his contrary, as physic doth devise.
    Right so whoso lusteth from sin to arise,
Where he hath in pride done any offence,
He can be helpen thereof none otherwise
But only by meekness : that is the recompense.
Again wrath and envy, take charity and
    patience ;
Take alms deed again the sin of covetise.
    And, to repress gluttony, acquaint ye with
    abstinence ;   [continence.
Again foul lust of body, take chastity and
Much sin groweth by sloth and by idleness,
And that must be eschewed by men of good
    business.
Lo ! these be preparatives, most sovereign,
Against thy sores, which be mortal
Unless that these medicines to them be lain.
When thou hast received these preparatives all
I will come again, if thou me call,
And order thee further after my mind.
    Man.   Yea, but where shall I these prepara-
    tives find ?   [breast.
    Rea.   Thou shalt them find within thine own
Of thee it must come ; it must be thy deed ;
For voluntary sacrifice pleaseth God best.
Thou canst not thereof have help or meed
But if this gear of thine own heart proceed.
    Man.   Well, I shall endeavour me to the
    uttermost ;
And till I have found them I shall never rest.
But how shall I know them ? that wot I ne'er ;
I pray you show me that before your departing.

Rea. It needeth not thereof to inquire :
Thou shalt know them at the first meeting.
Of two contraries there is but one learning ;
That is to say, when thou knowest well that
The other contrary is known anon.   [one
  Then he goeth out and MEEKNESS *cometh in.*
  Meekness. Whoso wotteth histories of scrip-
      ture well
Shall find that for pride and presumption
Lucifer, which sometime was a glorious angel—
For that his offence had such correction
That both he, and eke many a legion
Of his order—was cast down to hell
By rightful Justice, perpetually there to dwell.
  Remember also Adam, the first of our line,
What pain he suffered for pride and disobedi-
Causeth he not a great decay and ruin, [ence !
In all the progeny, for the same offence ?
In suchwise that he, and all that were born
      since,
Be utterly disherited and put from paradise ;
And so we be made thrall unto sin and vice.
  And lost should we be all, of very justice,
Ne had be that God of His merciful good-
      ness
Did us, soon after, with His own blood main-
      prize
And us redeemed from pains endless ;
So that we do not disobey or transgress
His high commandments, but demean us well
After His laws while we here dwell.
  And forasmuch as man's nature
Is frail, and lightly to sin will assent,
Either of purpose or on witting peradventure,
There the said good Lord hath him sent,
Again every sin, a remedy convenient.

For He ne would have one soul to be lore
Whom He hath dear bought, as I said before.
The root of all sin is pride, ye know well ;
Which is mine adversary in all that he may ;
Where I am in place he may not dwell.
His malicious power I can right well allay ;
And teach every creature the remedy and way
How to subdue pride ; which no man can do
Without that I, Meekness, must help thereto.

Man. Then your help and counsel is necessary
    to me :
Whereof, I pray you, with all heart's affection !

Meek. All ready at hand—whosoever it be
That lusteth to have me for his consolation.

Man. I myself have sinned in pride and
    elation :
Show me your counsel what way shall I take
A due satisfaction for that sin to make.

Meek. Thou must, before all thing, set little
By thine own self ; and take no heed   [prize
Whether the people do thee praise or despise.
Be thou meek in heart, in word, and in deed ;
Think not that thou wouldst any man over
    lead ;
Be soft and lowly in speech to every wight ;
And use none array that staring is to sight !
Lo ! in these three things only standeth pride
If thou commit the least of them three.

Man. From this day forth I will set them
    aside
And follow the counsel that ye give me.

Meek. Do so, and I will clearly discharge
    thee :
As for the sin of pride, my soul for thine,
Thou shalt be all whole if thou take this
    medicine.   *Then he goeth out.*

Man. Yes, I shall take it; think not the
   contrary!
Now am I well eased, yet have I not done all.
                              [*Enter* CHARITY.]
   Charity. There is no living physician, no
      poticary
That can devise so sovereign cordial
Again the sore of envy, which is mortal.
No man living, I you ensure,
Without my help may undertake that cure.
For, I am called Charity, the salve for that
   sickness,   [larly,
Whom th' Apostle Paul commandeth singu-
In divers his epistles: I can well repress
The rancour of Envy and give therein good
   remedy.   [necessary:
   Man. Then is your counsel to me full
If ye be Charity ye are bound, doubtless,
To have some compassion of your neighbours'
   distress.   [this day?
   Char. Why, hast thou been envious before
   Man. Yes, as God knoweth well! and that
      I rue sore.   [mark what I say:
   Char. Well, this must be the remedy—
There is no sin that displeaseth God more
Than doth this sin of Envy; and, therefore,
If so be thou wilt thine own soul safeguard,
Be thou never envious from this day forward.
   Also, that sin is to man unnatural;
More than any other, in mine opinion.
For all other sins—mark therein well—
A man committeth with some delectation;
But Envy is ever full of pain and passion,
And tormenteth himself with sorrowful sadness
When he seeth his neighbour's prosperity or
   gladness.

He is never glad, nor taketh any solace
But at his neighbour's harm, loss, or heaviness.
He speaketh sometime fair before a man's face,
And yet within his heart he is full of
    doubleness ;
For, behind his back, he will never cease
With slanderous words, to appair his good
    name ;   ⌈same.
And many a-falsely doth he report for the
    Ye know, sir ! whether it be thus or no ;
But now another while to speak of remedy.
If ye will be holpen, sir ! thus must ye do :
First, before all things, love God entirely ;
Next, that thy neighbour love as thine own
    body ;
That is to say, thou must thee to him behave
And do him such courtesy as thou wouldst of
    him have.
    Observe these two things : and do no more
In recompense of thy great trespass,
Touching the sin of envy, rehearsed before.
    Man. To observe them well, God send me
    His grace !
And I thank you for your comfort and counsel
    in this case :
I shall myself endeavour according thereto.
    Char. God send thee His grace well so to do !
    Then he goeth out [*and* PATIENCE *cometh in*].
    Patience. The remedy of wrath and out-
    rageous ire
Must needs come of me, and none otherwise.
For I am called Patience, which quencheth
    the fire
And flames of wrath : it is also my guise,
By soft words and sufferance, to overcome
    mine enemies.

Man. Now, welcome Patience, for whom
    I have sought !
Help me with your counsel for His love that
    all wrought.   [stand
    Pat. This is my counsel : if thou wilt with-
Thy ghostly enemy, and this temptation,
Thou must have me, Patience, ever ready at
    hand ;
Specially in suffering of worldly tribulation.
Remember how Christ died, in time of His
    passion !
There mayst thou learn how to be patient
In any adversity that to thee shall be sent.
    And yet there may be no comparison
Betwixt the least part of His pain   [done :
And the greatest wrong that to thee can be
Wherefore, thou, wretch ! shouldst not disdain ;
But gladly thou shouldst thyself refrain
From ireful passions, as I said before,   [fore.
Sith thou shalt have a reward in heaven there-
    Man. It is my full mind and intent,
Hereafter, to do as ye me advertise.   [sent,
    Pat. Now, He that all goodness to us hath
Send you His grace to demean you that wise !
                    Then he goeth out.
    Man. I shall do my good will, on warrantise !
Now, who can me best direct,
My slothful idleness for to correct ?
            [GOOD OCCUPATION *cometh in.*]
    Good Occupation. The sin of sloth I can well
    repress ;
And I shall teach thee to do the same.
    Man. How should I do it ?
    Good Occ. By mean of me, Good Business,
And so am I called, for that is my name.
Idleness is never without sin or blame ;

By mean thereof much sin cometh in:
For it is the very mother and mistress of sin.
  In eschewing thereof thou must ever use
Some good occupation, in body or mind;
And if thou do this my counsel refuse,
So that the devil in idleness thee find,
Then according to his property and kind
He laboureth fast, by mean of temptation,
To bring thy soul unto endless damnation.
  Therefore do some good occupation alway,
As well with the body as with mind inward.
And if thou do not this counsel obey,
Thou shalt thine own soul greatly enjeopard.
On that other side thou mayst be no coward,
Nor fearful of penance, or other good deed,
Sith thou shalt be sure to have heaven to thy
    meed.   [therefore;
  Man.   This counsel is good; I thank you,
My mind is well eased therein, be ye sure!
  Good Occ. Is there anything else that I can
    do more?   [done your cure.
  Man. None to my knowledge, for ye have
  Good Occ. See that ye wisely now put in ure.
    Then he goeth out [and LIBERALITY *cometh in].*
  Man. Yes, hardely think not the contrary!
Sith it is to me so behoveful and necessary.
  Liberality. I am Liberality, the virtue
    cardinal;
By whom is confounded the sin of avarice.
Whosoever lusteth on me to call
I am ready therein to give mine advice. [wise,
  Man. Sir! I pray you, in my most hearty
[Help] to reform and order my mind. [abusing
  Lib. First, thou must be sorry for the
Of temporal goods, before this day;
Next, that I will advise thee, before all thing.

If thou hast wrongfully taken away
Any man's good, go without delay
And thereof to thy power make due restitution ;
For erst shalt thou have of thy sin no remission.
    Man.   Why, trow ye that I shall not be
      excused
By alms deed of that offence ?   [abused :
    Lib. No, no, hardely ! thou art greatly
Think not thereby to make recompense ;
For, by that alms, thou doest great offence
And displeasure to God.
    Man.   Why say ye so ?
Christ Himself bade that we should alms do.
    Lib. Yea, fore God ! but that should be do
Of well-gotten goods ; else it is nought.
    Man. Well, I assent gladly thereto ;
As in that one point I am fully taught :
Wit is nothing worth till it be dear bought !
But what other amends shall I make,
The foul sin of avarice to suage and a-slake ?
    Lib. Thou must have compassion, and also
      be liberal
Unto thy neighbour at his necessity.   [all,
    Man. I trow ye would have me to give away
And leave myself nought !
    Lib.   I mean not so, pardy !
For that is waste and sinful prodigality.
Take the midway, betwixt them two,
And flee the extremities howsoever thou do.
  Thou must thy worldly goods so employ,
In charitable deeds with due compassion,
That thou mayest buy everlasting joy
For the good intent of that distribution.
Thou mayest also give them to thy damnation ;
As when thou doest it to win thereby
Praising of the people, or some other vain glory.
    NATURE   9

For, trust it well ! thou must give a reckoning
Of all the goods that come to thine use.
The high Judge that knoweth all thing,
To whom thou shalt thyself accuse,
Without any appeal or feigned excuse
. . . . . . in this case
From whom thou canst not hide thy face.
    There shalt thou openly show and confess
How that goods came to thy possession ;
What mind and pleasure thou had'st in riches ;
And why thou had'st therein such affection ;
What alms-deed or other good distribution ;
Or how thou hast these goods wasted or
    abused—
There it shall be known : it cannot be refused.
    Then, as I said to thee before,
Thou shalt receive after thy deserving :
Joy or else pain to endure evermore.
    Man.   Truly this is a fearful thing !
    Lib.   Therefore, remember well my saying ;
Mark well my counsel, and follow the same.
    Man.   If I did not I were greatly to blame !
        Then LIBERALITY *goeth out and* ABSTINENCE
            and CHASTITY *come in.*
    Abst.   The remedy of Gluttony I can well
        teach :
I am ordained only for that intent.
    Man.   And I have great need of such a leech ;
Your counsel to me is right expedient.
    Abst.   Sir ! if ye lust to be my patient,
And take such remedy as I shall devise
I shall make you whole of that sin, on
        warrantise !
    Man.   What is your name ?
    Abst.   My name is Abstinence ;
And this other that cometh with me

Is called Chastity, or else Continence:
It is his guise, and his property,
To follow me wheresoever I be;
Likewise as lechery, that deadly sore,
Followeth the beastly sin of gluttony evermore,
   Quia delicia sunt instrumenta voluptatis.
But now to do that I came for.
Again the sin of gluttony the remedy is this:
Use scarcer diet than thou did'st before;
Beware of superfluity and surfeit evermore;
Take no more than sufficeth nature;
Nor of delicate meat set thou no store.
Now have I said all that longeth to my cure.
   Chas.   And I must needs confirm his saying:
For, as he rehearsed now right well,
Glutting of hot meats and delicate feeding
Causeth sinful lusts in a man to swell;
And, over that, this is my counsel:
Eschew idleness before all thing
If thou wilt be chaste and clean of living.
   Flee also the company and the occasion
Of that sin, which is damnable;
As soon as thou feelest any temptation
Put it clean away, by means convenable.
Of all other sins it is most abominable;
And soonest will thy soul endanger and blame—
There be so many great sins annexed to the
   same.
   If thou list not, for fear of damnation,
This sin to forbear; then, on that other side,
Do it for love of thine own salvation.
Think what rewards in heaven doth thee abide
Which, if thou live chaste, cannot be denied.
My wit sufficeth not to tell and express
What joy thou shalt have for thy chaste
   cleanness.

Man.   I thank you both for your advice.
And now would I speak with Repentance fain.
   Abst.   I can bring you to him on the best
      wise.
Man.   Then will I await upon you twain ;
And after that I will come hither again,
Trusting that God will send me the grace
To comfort my soul with ghostly solace.
          Then they go out and REASON *cometh in.*
   Rea.   I hear say, to my great joy and glad-
      ness,
That according to my counsel and advice,
This mortal creature doth well his business
To correct and forsake all his old vice.
And that he is in good way, and likely to arise
From the vale of sin, which is full of dark-
      ness,
Toward the contemplation of light that is
      endless.
   Lo, sirs ! are not we all much behold
To our Maker for this great patience.
Which, notwithstanding our sins manifold
Wherein we daily do Him offence,
Yet of His merciful and great magnificence
He doth not punish as soon as we offend,
But suffereth in hope that we will amend.
   He suffereth a sinner sometime to endure
A long life in honour and great prosperity :
It is a thing that daily is put in ure.
And many a great danger escapeth he
Where good men perish : this may ye see ;
And all because that He would him win
And have him to turn and forsake his sin.
                    [MANKIND *returns.*]
   Oh, here cometh he that I look for.
Sir ! have ye done as I willed you to do ?

Man. Yea, that have I done ; and what
    trow ye more ?
I have been with Repentance also,
Which from my heart shall never go ;
For he brought me unto Confession ;
And anon I was acquainted with heart's con-
    trition.   [faction ;
    They advised and charged me to do satis-
And so have I done, to my best power.
Rea. Then art thou fully the child of salva-
    tion !
Have good perseverance, and be not in fear ;
Thy ghostly enemy can put thee in no danger ;
And greater reward thou shalt therefore win
Than he that never in his life did sin.
    And to the intent that thou mayest well
Persevere and continue in this sure way,
Or we depart hence, by my counsel,
Let us by one accord together sing and pray
With as humble devotion as we can or may ;
That we may have grace from sin thus to rise
As often as we fall ; and let us pray this wise.
       [Then they sing some goodly ballet.

*[Here follow " The Names of the Players " as given
on page 42.]*

[THE PLAY OF WIT AND SCIENCE

MADE BY MASTER JOHN REDFORD

The Names of the Players:

WIT	IDLENESS
SCIENCE	INGNORANCY [1]
REASON	SHAME
EXPERIENCE	COMFORT
CONFIDENCE	QUICKNESS
HONEST RECREATION	STRENGTH
STUDY	FAME
DILIGENCE	RICHES
INSTRUCTION	FAVOUR
TEDIOUSNESS	WORSHIP

[1] INGNORANCY, but see pp. 152-157]

[*Reduced facsimile of the penultimate page of manuscript copy of "Wit and Science" now in the British Museum.*]

THE PLAY OF WIT AND SCIENCE.

[By John Redford.]

Reason. Then, in remembrance of Reason,
   hold ye
A glass of Reason, wherein behold ye
Yourself to yourself. Namely, when ye
Come near my daughter, Science, then see
That all things be clean and trick about ye;
Lest of some sluggishness she might doubt ye;
This glass of Reason shall show ye all;
While ye have that, ye have me, and shall.
Get ye forth, now! Instruction, farewell!
   Instruction. Sir, God keep ye!
              Here all go out save REASON.
   Rea. And ye all from peril!
If any man now marvel that I
Would bestow my daughter thus basely,
Of truth I, Reason, am of this mind:
Where parties together be inclined,
By gifts of graces, to love each other,
There let them join the one with the tother.
This Wit such gifts of graces hath in him
That maketh my daughter to wish to win him:
Young, painful, tractable and capax—
These be Wit's gifts which Science doth axe.

And, as for her, as soon as Wit sees her,
For all the world he would not then lese her.
Wherefore, since they both be so meet matches
To love each other, straw for the patches
Of worldly muck !   Science hath enough
For them both to live.   If Wit be through
Stricken in love, as he since hath showed,
I doubt not my daughter well bestowed :
Th' end of his journey will prove all.
If Wit hold out, no more proof can fall ;
And, that the better hold out he may,
To refresh me soon, Wit, now, by the way,
Some solace for him I will provide.
An honest woman dwelleth here, beside,
Whose name is called Honest Recreation ;
As men report, for Wit's consolation
She hath no peer ; if Wit were half dead,
She could revive him—thus is it said.
Wherefore, if money or love can hire her,
To hie after Wit I will desire her.

                                    [REASON *goeth out.*

CONFIDENCE *cometh in with a picture of* WIT.

   [*Confidence.*] Ah, sir ! what time of day is't,
      who can tell ?
The day is not far past, I wot well ;
For I have gone fast, and yet I see
I am far from whereas I would be.
Well ! I have day enough yet, I spy ;
Wherefore, or I pass hence, now must I
See this same token here, a plain case,
What Wit hath sent to my lady's grace.
                                    [*Examines his packet.*
Now, will ye see a goodly picture
Of Wit himself? his own image sure !

Face, body, arms, legs, both limb and joint,
As like him as can be, in every point ;
It lacketh but life.   Well I can him thank ;
This token indeed shall make some crank ;
For, what with this picture so well favoured,
And what with those sweet words so well
    savoured—
Distilling from the mouth of Confidence—
Shall not this appease the heart of Science ?
Yes ! I thank God I am of that nature,
Able to compass this matter sure ;
As ye shall see now, who list to mark it,
How neatly and featly I shall work it.
                    [CONFIDENCE *goeth out.*

    WIT *cometh in without* INSTRUCTION, *with*
            STUDY, *etc.*

  [*Wit.*]   Now, sirs ! come on ! which is the
    way now ?
This way or that way ?   Study ! how say you ?
                    [STUDY *reflecteth.*
Speak, Diligence ! while he hath bethought him.
  Diligence.   That way, belike ; most usage
    hath wrought him.   [now stay
  Study.   Yea, hold your peace ! Best we here
For Instruction ; I like not that way.
    Wit.   Instruction, Study ? I ween we have
    lost him.   INSTRUCTION *cometh in.*
  [*Inst.*]   Indeed, full gently about ye have
    tossed him !
What mean you, Wit, still to delight
Running before thus, still out of sight ;
And, thereby, out of your way now quite.
What do ye here except he would fight ?
Come back again, Wit ! for, I must choose ye
An easier way than this, or else lose ye.

Wit.   What aileth this way? Peril here is
    none.
Inst.   But as much as your life standeth upon ;
Your enemy, man ! lieth here before ye :
Tediousness, to brain or to gore ye !
Wit.   Tediousness ?   Doth that tyrant rest
In my way now ?   Lord ! how am I blest
That occasion so near me stirs,
For my dear heart's sake, to win my spurs !
Sir ! would ye fear me with that foul thief,
With whom to meet my desire is chief?
Inst.   And what would ye do, you having
    nought
For your defence ? for, though ye have caught
Garments of Science upon your back,
Yet weapons of Science ye do lack !   [have ?
Wit.   What weapons of Science should I
Inst.   Such as all lovers of their loves crave :
A token from Lady Science whereby
Hope of her favour may spring, and thereby
Comfort ; which is the weapon doubtless
That must serve you against Tediousness.
Wit.   If hope or comfort may be my weapon,
Then never with Tediousness me threaten ;
For, as for hope of my dear heart's favour—
And thereby comfort—enough I gather.
Inst.   Wit, hear me !   Till I see Confidence
Have brought some token from Lady Science,
That I may feel that she favoureth you,
Ye pass not this way, I tell you true.
Wit.   Which way then ?
Inst.   A plainer way, I told ye,
Out of danger from your foe to hold ye.
Wit.   Instruction, hear me !   Or my sweet-
    heart
Shall hear that Wit from that wretch shall start

One foot, this body and all shall crack!
Forth I will, sure, whatever I lack!

   Dil. If ye lack weapon, sir, here is one!

   Wit. Well said, Diligence, thou art alone!
How say ye, sir? is not here weapon?

   Inst. With that weapon your enemy never
     threaten;
For without the return of Confidence
Ye may be slain, sure, for all Diligence!

   Dil. Good, sir! and Diligence, I tell you
     plain,
Will play the man or my master be slain!

   Inst. Yea, but what? saith Study no word
     to this?

   Wit. No, sir! ye know Study's office is
Meet for the chamber, not for the field—
But tell me, Study, wilt thou now yield?

   Study. My head acheth sore; I would we
     return.   [burn!

   Wit. Thy head ache now? I would it were
Come on! walking may hap to ease thee.

   Inst. And will ye be gone, then, without me?

   Wit. Yea, by my faith, except ye hie ye after,
Reason shall know ye are but an hafter.

          Exeat WIT, STUDY *and* DILIGENCE.

   Inst. Well, go your way! When your
     father, Reason,
Heareth how ye obey me, at this season,
I think he will think his daughter now
May marry another man for you.
When wits stand so in their own conceit,
Best let them go; till pride, at his height,
Turn and cast them down headlong again:
And ye shall see proved by this Wit, plain.
If Reason hap not to come, the rather
His own destruction he will sure gather;

Wherefore to Reason will I now get me,
Leaving that charge whereabout he set me.
                              Exeat INSTRUCTION.

TEDIOUSNESS *cometh in with a visor over
                his head.*

[*Tediousness.*]   Oh, the body of me !
What caitiffs be those
That will not once flee
      From Tediousness' nose ;
But thus disease me
      Out of my nest,
When I should ease me
      This body to rest !
That Wit, that villain,
      That wretch—a shame take him !
It is he plain
      That thus bold doth make him,
Without my licence
      To stalk by my door
To that drab, Science,
      To wed that whore !
But I defy her ;
      And, for that drab's sake,
Or Wit come nigh her,
      The knave's head shall ache ;
These bones, this mall,
      Shall beat him to dust
Or that drab shall
      Once quench that knave's lust !
But, ha ! methinks
      I am not half lusty ;
These joints, these links,
      Be rough and half rusty ;
I must go shake them,
Supple to make them !

Stand back, ye wretches !
Beware the fetches
Of Tediousness.
These caitiffs to bless,
Make room, I say ;
Round every way—
This way, that way !
What cares what way ?
Before me, behind me,
Round about wind me !
Now I begin
To sweat in my skin ;
Now am I nemble
To make them tremble.
Pash head ! pash brain !
The knaves are slain,
All that I hit !
Where art thou, Wit !
Thou art but dead !
Off goeth thy head
At the first blow !
Ho, ho ! ho ho !   WIT *speaketh at the door.*
  [*Wit.*]   Study !
  Study.   Here, sir !
  Wit.   How, doth thy head ache ?
  Study.   Yea, God wot, sir ! much pain I do
  Wit.   Diligence !   [take !
  Dil.   Here, sir, here !
  Wit.   How dost thou ?
Doth thy stomach serve thee to fight now ?
  Dil.   Yea, sir, with yonder wretch — a
    vengeance on him
That threateneth you thus.   Set even upon him !
  Study.   Upon him, Diligence ?   Better nay !
  Dil.   Better nay, Study ?   Why should we
    fray ?

Study.   For I am weary; my head acheth
    sore.
[*The last three lines are, in the manuscript, scored
            through.*]
    Dil.   Why, foolish Study! thou shalt do no
    more
But aid my master with thy presence.
    Wit.   No more shalt thou neither, Diligence!
Aid me with your presence, both you twain;
And, for my love, myself shall take pain!
    Study.   Sir! we be ready to aid you so.
    Wit.   I ask no more, Study! Come then, go!
                        TEDIOUSNESS *riseth up.*

    [*Ted.*]   Why, art thou come?
    Wit.   Yea, wretch, to thy pain!
    Ted.   Then have at thee!
    Wit.   Have at thee, again!
                Here WIT *falleth down and dieth.*
    [*Ted.*]   Lie thou there!   Now have at ye,
    caitiffs!
Do ye flee, i' faith?   A, whoreson thieves!
By Mahound's bones! had the wretches tarried,
Their necks without heads they should have
        carried!   [them,
Yea, by Mahound's nose! might I have patted
In twenty gobbets I should have squatted them,
To teach the knaves to come near the snout
Of Tediousness!   Walk further about
I trow, now, they will!   And, as for thee,
Thou wilt no more now trouble me.
Yet, lest the knave be not safe enough,
The whoreson shall bear me another cuff.
                                Striketh him.
Now, lie still, caitiff! and take thy rest
While I take mine, in mine own nest.
                        Exeat TEDI[OUSNESS].

Here cometh in HONEST RECREATION, COM-
FORT, QUICKNESS, *and* STRENGTH, *and go
and kneel about* WIT ; *and at the last
verse raiseth him up upon his feet, and so
make an end.*

*Give place, give place to Honest Recreation ;
Give place, we say now, for thy consolation.*

*When travels great, in matters thick,
Have dulled your wits and made them sick,
What medicine then your wits to quick ?
If ye will know, the best physick
     Is to give place to Honest Recreation ;
     Give place, we say now, for thy consolation !*

*Where is that Wit that we seek than ?
Alas ! he lieth here, pale and wan.
Help him at once now, if we can :
O Wit ! how doest thou ?   Look up, man !
     O Wit, give place to Honest Recreation !
     Give place, we say now, for thy consolation !*

*After place given, let ear obey ;
Give an ear, O Wit ! now we thee pray ;
Give ear to that we sing and say !
Give an ear, and help will come straightway !
     Give an ear to Honest Recreation !
     Give an ear now for thy consolation !*

*After ear given, now give an eye !
Behold ! thy friends about thee lie :
Recreation I, and Comfort I,
Quickness am I, and Strength, hereby.
     Give an eye to Honest Recreation !
     Give an eye now for thy consolation !*

WIT   10

After eye given, an hand give ye !
Give an hand, O Wit ! feel that ye see !
Recreation feel ! feel Comfort free !
Feel Quickness here ! feel Strength to thee !
     Give an hand to Honest Recreation !
     Give an hand now for thy consolation !

Upon his feet, would God he were !
To raise him now we need not fear.
Stay you his hands, while we him bear ;
Now, all at once, upright him rear !
     O Wit, give place to Honest Recreation !
     Give place, we say now, for thy consolation !

     And then HONEST RECREATION *saith as*
               followeth :

[*Honest Recreation.*]   Now, Wit ! how do ye ?
     Will ye be lusty ?
Wit.   The lustier for you needs be must I.
Hon. Rec.   Be ye all whole yet, after your
     fall ?
Wit.   As ever I was, thanks to you all !

     REASON *cometh in, and saith as followeth* :

[*Rea.*]   Ye might thank Reason that sent
     them to ye ;   [do ye
But since the[y] have done that the[y] should,
Send them home soon, and get ye forward !
Wit.   Oh father Reason ! I have had an hard
Chance since ye saw me !
Rea.   I wot well that.
The more to blame ye, when ye would not
Obey Instruction, as Reason willed ye.
What marvel though Tediousness had killed ye ?
But let pass now, since ye are well again.
Set forward again Science to attain !

Wit. Good father Reason, be not too hasty!
In honest company no time waste I.
I shall to your daughter all at leisure.
 Rea. Yea, Wit, is that the great love ye
  raise her?
I say, if ye love my daughter, Science,
Get ye forth at once, and get ye hence!
 Here COMFORT, QUICKNESS, STRENGTH *go out.*
 Wit. Nay, by Saint George! they go not
  all yet.
 Rea. No? will ye disobey Reason, Wit?
 Wit. Father Reason! I pray ye, content ye!
For we part not yet.
 Rea.   Well, Wit! I went ye
Had been no such man as now I see.
Farewell!   *Exeat.*
 Hon. Rec. He is angry.
 Wit.   Yea, let him be!
I do not pass!
Come now, a bass!
 Hon. Rec. Nay, sir, as for basses,
From hence none passes
But as in gage
Of marriage.
 Wit. Marry, even so!
A bargain, lo!
 Hon. Rec. What, without licence
Of Lady Science?

 Wit. Shall I tell you truth?
  I never loved her.
 Hon. Rec. The common voice goeth
  That marriage ye moved her.

 Wit. Promise hath she none.
If we shall be one,
  Without mo words grant!

Hon. Rec.   What, upon this sudden?
Then might ye plain
      Bid me avaunt!
Nay, let me see
In honesty
      What ye can do
To win Recreation;
Upon that probation
      I grant thereto.

Wit.   Small be my doings,
But apt to all things
      I am, I trust.
   Hon. Rec.   Can ye dance than?
   Wit.   Even as I can.
      Prove me ye must.

Hon. Rec.   Then, for a while,
Ye must exile
      This garment cumbering.
   Wit.   Indeed, as ye say,
This cumbrous array
      Would make Wit slumbering.

Hon. Rec.   It is gay gear
Of Science clear—
      It seemeth her array.
   Wit.   Whosever it were,
It lieth now there!   [*Taketh off his gown.*
   Hon. Rec.   Go to, my men, play!

Here they dance, and in the meanwhile IDLE-
NESS *cometh in and sitteth down, and when
the galliard is done,* WIT *saith as followeth,
and so falleth down in* IDLENESS' *lap.*

Wit.   Sweetheart, gramercys!
Hon. Rec.   Why, whither now? Have ye
   done, since?

   Wit. Yea, in faith ! with weary bones ye
    have possessed me ;
Among these damsels now will I rest me.
   Hon. Rec. What, there ?
   Wit.   Yea, here ; I will be so bold.
   Idleness. Yea, and welcome, by him that
    God sold !
   Hon. Rec. It is an harlot ; may ye not see ?
   Idle. As honest a woman as ye be !
   Hon. Rec. Her name is Idleness.   Wit !
    what mean you ?
   Idle. Nay ! what mean you to scold thus,
    you quean, you ?
   Wit. There, go to ! Lo ! now for the best
    game !
While I take my ease, your tongues now frame !
   Hon. Rec. Yea, Wit ! by your faith, is that
    your fashion?
Will ye leave me, Honest Recreation,
For that common strumpet, Idleness,
The very root of all viciousness ?
   Wit. She saith she is as honest as ye.
Declare yourselves both now as ye be !
   Hon. Rec. What would ye more for my
    declaration
Than even my name, Honest Recreation ?
And what would ye more her to express
Than even her name, too, Idleness—
Destruction of all that with her tarry ?
Wherefore come away, Wit ! she will mar ye !
   Idle. Will I mar him, drab? thou callet, thou !
When thou hast marred him already now ?
Callest thou thyself Honest Recreation,
Ordering a poor man after this fashion,
To lame him thus, and make his limbs fail,
Even with the swinging there of thy tail ?

The devil set fire on thee! for now must I,
Idleness, heal him again, I spy.
I must now lull him, rock him, and frame him
To his lust again, where thou didst lame him.
Am I the root, sayest thou, of viciousness?
Nay! thou art root of all vice, doubtless!
Thou art occasion, lo! of more evil
Than I, poor girl—nay, more than the devil!
The devil and his dam cannot devise
More devilishness than by thee doth rise!
Under the name of Honest Recreation,
She, lo! bringeth in her abomination!
Mark her dancing, her masking, and mumming—
Where more concupiscence than there coming?
Her carding, her dicing, daily and nightly—
Where find ye more falsehood than there?   Not
     lightly!
With lying and swearing, by no poppets;
But tearing God in a thousand gobbets.
As for her singing, piping and fiddling—
What unthriftiness therein is twiddling!
Search the taverns and ye shall hear, clear,
Such bawdry as beasts would spue to hear.
And yet, this is called Honest Recreation!
And I, poor Idleness, abomination!
But which is worst of us twain, now judge, Wit!
     Wit.   By'r Lady! not thou! wench! I judge
        yet.   [that ye
     Hon. Rec.   No? Is your judgment such then
Can neither pe[r]ceive that beast, how she
Goeth about to deceive you, nor yet
Remember how I saved your life, Wit?
Think you her meet with me to compare
By whom so many wits cured are?
When will she do such an act as I did,
Saving your life when I you revived?

And, as I saved you, so save I all
That in like jeopardy chance to fall.   [them,
When Tediousness to ground hath smitten
Honest Recreation up doth quicken them
With such honest pastimes, sports or games,
As unto mine honest nature frames ;
And not, as she saith, with pastimes such
As be abused little or much :
For, where honest pastimes be abused,
Honest Recreation is refused ;
Honest Recreation is present never
But where honest pastimes be well used ever.
But, indeed, Idleness, she is cause
Of all such abuses ; she, lo ! draws
Her sort to abuse mine honest games ;
And, thereby, full falsely my name defames.
Under the name of Honest Recreation
She bringeth in all her abomination,
Destroying all wits that her embrace,
As yourself shall see within short space.
She will bring you to shameful end, Wit,
Except the sooner from her ye flit.
Wherefore, come away, Wit, out of her paws !
Hence, drab ! let him go out of thy claws !
    Idle.   Will ye get ye hence ? or, by the mace !
These claws shall claw you by your drab's face !
    Hon. Rec.   Ye shall not need ; since Wit
       licth as one
That neither heareth nor seeth, I am gone.
                                              Exeat.
    Idle.   Yea, so ? farewell !   And well fare
       thou, tongue !
Of a short peal, this peal was well rung,
To ring her hence, and him fast asleep,
As full of sloth as the knave can creep !
How, Wit ! awake !   How doth my baby ?

Neque vox neque sensus, by'r Lady !
A meet man for Idleness, no doubt.
Hark, my pig ! how the knave doth rout !
Well, while he sleepeth in Idleness' lap,
Idleness' mark on him shall I clap.
Some say that Idleness cannot wark ;
But those that so say, now let them mark !
I trow they shall see that Idleness
Can set herself about some business ;
Or, at the least, ye shall see her tried,
Neither idle, nor well occupied.

                        [She marketh WIT.
Lo, sir ! yet ye lack another toy !
Where is my whistle to call my boy ?

            Here she whistleth, and INGNORANCY
                  cometh in.

  [Ingnorancy.] I come ! I come !
  Idle.   Come on, ye fool !
All this day or ye can come to school ?
  Ingn. Um ! mother will not let me come.
  Idle. I would thy mother had kissed thy bum !
She will never let thee thrive, I trow !
Come on, goose ! Now, lo ! men shall know
That Idleness can do somewhat, yea !
And play the schoolmistress, too, if need be.
Mark what doctrine by Idleness comes !
Say thy lesson, fool !
  Ingn.   Upon my thumbs ?
  Idle. Yea, upon thy thumbs : is not there
    thy name ?
  Ingn. Yeas.
  Idle.   Go too, then ; spell me that same !
Where was thou born ?   [mother said.
  Ingn.   Chwas i-bore in England,
  Idle. In Ingland ?
  Ingn.   Yea !

Idle.   And what's half Ingland?
Here's *Ing*; and here's *land*.   What's 'tis?
  Ingn.   What's 'tis?   [what's 'tis?
  Idle.   What's 'tis? whoreson!
Here's *Ing*; and here's *land*.   What's 'tis?
  Ingn.   'Tis my thumb.   [*Ing, Ing!*
  Idle.   Thy thumb? *Ing*, whoreson!
  Ingn.   *Ing, Ing, Ing, Ing!*
  Idle.   Forth! Shall I beat thy narse, now?
  Ingn.   Um-m-m—   [now?
  Idle.   Shall I not beat thy narse,
  Ingn.   Um-um-um—
  Idle.   Say *no*, fool! say *no*.
  Ingn.   *Noo, noo, noo, noo, noo!*
  Idle.   Go to, put together! *Ing!*
  Ingn.   *Ing.*
  Idle.   *No!*
  Ingn.   *Noo.*
  Idle.   Forth now! What saith the dog?
  Ingn.   Dog bark.   [*ran!*
  Idle.   Dog bark? Dog *ran*, whoreson! dog
  Ingn.   *Dog ran, whoreson! dog ran, dog ran!*
  Idle.   Put together: *Ing!*
  Ingn.   *Ing.*
  Idle.   *No!*
  Ingn.   *Noo.*
  Idle.   *Ran!*
  Ingn.   *Ran.*
  Idle.   Forth now; what saith the goose?
  Ingn.   *Lag! lag!*
  Idle.   *His*, whoreson! *his!*
  Ingn.   *His, his-s-s-s-s!*
  Idle.   Go to, put together: *Ing.*
  Ingn.   *Ing.*
  Idle.   *No.*
  Ingn.   *Noo.*

Idle.   Ran.
Ingn.   Ran.
Idle.   Hys.
Ingn   His-s-s-s-s-s.
Idle.   Now, who is a good boy?
Ingn.   I, I, I! I, I, I!
Idle.   Go to, put together: Ing.
Ingn.   Ing.
Idle.   No.
Ingn.   Noo.
Idle.   Ran.
Ingn.   Ran.
Idle.   His.
Ingn.   His-s-s-s-s-s.
Idle.   I.
Ingn.   I.
Idle.   Ing-no-ran-his-I.
Ingn.   Ing-no-ran-his-s-s-s.
Idle.   I.
Ingn.   I.
Idle.   Ing.
Ingn.   Ing.
Idle.   Foorth!
Ingn.   His-s-s-s.
Idle.   Yea, no, whoreson! no!
Ingn.   Noo, noo, noo, noo.
Idle.   Ing-no.
Ingn.   Ing-noo.
Idle.   Forth now!
Ingn.   His-s-s-s.
Idle.   Yet again; ran, whoreson! ran, ran!
Ingn.   Ran, whoreson, ran, ran.
Idle.   Ran, say!
Ingn.   Ran-say.
Idle.   Ran, whoreson!
Ingn.   Ran, whoreson.

Idle.   *Ran.*

Ingn.   *Ran.*

Idle.   *Ing-no-ran.*

Ingn.   *Ing-no-ran.*

Idle.   Foorth, now !   What said the goose ?

Ingn.   *Dog bark.*

Idle.   Dog bark? *His*, whoreson ! *his-s-s-s-s.*

Ingn.   *His-s-s-s-s.*

Idle.   *I* : *Ing-no-ran-his-I.*

Ingn.   *Ing-no-ran-his-I-s-s-s.*

Idle.   *I.*

Ingn.   *I.* [thy name ?

Idle.   How sayest, now, fool ?   Is not there

Ingn.   Yea.

Idle.   Well then ; can me that same !
What hast thou learned ?

Ingn.   Ich cannot tell.   [well !

Idle.   *Ich cannot tell*—thou sayest even very
For, if thou couldst tell, then had not I well
Taught thee thy lesson which must be taught ;
To tell all, when thou canst tell right naught.

Ingn.   Ich can my lesson.

Idle.   Yea ; and, therefore,
Shalt have a new coat, by God I swore !

Ingn.   A new coat ?

Idle.   Yea, a new coat, by-and-by.
Off with this old coat ! *a new coat*, cry !

Ingn.   *A new coat, a new coat ! a new coat !*

Idle.   Peace ! whoreson fool !
Wilt thou wake him now?   Unbutton thy coat,
Canst thou do nothing?   [fool !

Ingn.   I note how choold be.

Idle.   *I note how choold be !* A fool betide thee !
So wisely it speaketh ; come on, now ! when ?
Put back thine arm, fool !

                   [*Taketh off* INGNORANCY'S *coat.*

Ingn.   Put back?
Idle.   So, lo! now let me see how this
    gear
Will trim this gentleman that lieth here.
Ah! God save it! so sweetly it doth sleep!
While on your back this gay coat can creep,
As feat as can be for this one arm.
       [Putteth WIT's *gown on* INGNORANCY.
Ingn.   Oh! cham a-cold.
Idle.   Hold, fool! keep thee warm!
And, come hither! hold this head here! soft
    now, for waking!
Ye shall see one here brought in such taking
That he shall soon scantily know himself.
Here is a coat as fit for this elf
As it had been made even for this body!
      [Putteth INGNORANCY's *coat on* WIT.
So! It beginneth to look like a noddie!
    Ingn.   Um-m-m-m—
    Idle.   What ailest now, fool?
    Ingn.   New coat is gone!
    Idle.   And why is it gone?
    Ingn.   'Twool not bide on.
    Idle.   *'Twool not bide on?*   'Twould if it
    could!
But marvel it were that it should—
Science['s] garment on Ingnorancy['s] back!
But now, let's see, sir! what do ye lack?
Nothing but even to buckle here this throat,
So well this Wit becometh a fool's coat!
    Ingn.   He is I, now!
    Idle.   Yea; how likest him **now**?
Is he not a fool as well as thou?
    Ingn.   Yeas!
    Idle.   Well, then, one fool keep another!
Give me this, and take thou that, brother!

Ingn. Um-m—
Idle. Pike thee home, go!
Ingn. Chill go tell my moother! [*Exit.*
Idle. Yea, do!
But yet, to take my leave of my dear, lo!
With a skip or twain, here lo! and here lo!
And, here again! and now, this heel
To bless his weak brain! Now are ye weel,
By virtue of Idleness' blessing tool,
Conjured from Wit unto a stark fool!
[*Exit* IDLENESS.

CONFIDENCE *cometh in with a sword by his side;
and sayeth as followeth* :

[*Confidence.*] I seek and seek, as one on no
ground
Can rest; but, like a masterless hound,
Wandering all about seeking his master.
Alas, gentle Wit! I fear the faster
That my true service cleaveth unto thee,
The slacker thy mind cleaveth unto me;
I have done thy message, in such sort,
That I not only, for thy comfort,
To vanquish thine enemy have brought here
A sword of comfort from thy love dear;
But also, further, I have so inclined her
That, upon my words, she hath assigned
her,
In her own person, half-way to meet thee:
And, hitherward, she came for to greet thee.
And sure, except she be turned again,
Hither will she come or be long, plain,
To seek to meet thee here in this coast.
But now, alas! thyself thou hast lost;
Or, at the least, thou wilt not be found.
Alas! gentle Wit, how dost thou wound

Thy trusty and true servant, Confidence,
To lese my credence to Lady Science?
Thou lesest me, too; for if I cannot
Find thee shortly, longer live I may not;
But shortly get me even into a corner
And die for sorrow through such a scorner!
                                                                Exit.

Here they [FAME, FAVOUR, RICHES, *and*
        WORSHIP] *come in with viols.*
    Fame.   Come, sirs! let us not disdain to do
That the World hath appointed us to.
    Favour.   Since, to serve Science, the World
        hath sent us,
As the World willeth us, let us content us.
    Riches.   Content us we may, since we be
        assigned
To the fairest lady that liveth, in my mind!
    Worship.   Then, let us not stay here mute
        and mum;
But taste we these instruments till she come.

    Here the[*y*] *sing " Exceeding Measure."*
Exceeding measure, with pains continual,
    Languishing in absence, alas! what shall I do?
Unfortunate wretch! devoid of joys all,
    Sighs upon sighs redoubling my woe;
    And tears down falling from mine eyes too.
Beauty with truth so doth me constrain
Ever to serve where I may not attain!

Truth bindeth me ever to be true,
    Howso that fortune favoureth my chance.
During my life none other but you
    Of my true heart shall have the governance!
    O, good sweet heart! have you remembrance
Now, of your own, which for no smart
Exile shall you from my true heart!

[Experience *and* Science *entereth while
they sing.*]

Experience. Daughter, what meaneth that
ye did not sing? [thing!
Science. Oh mother, for here remaineth a
Friends! we thank you for these your pleasures,
Taken on us as chance to us measures.

Wor. Lady! these our pleasures, and
persons, too,
Are sent to you, you service to do.

Fame. Lady Science! to set forth your name
The World, to wait on you, hath sent me, Fame.

Fav. Lady Science! for your virtues most
plenty [ye.
The World, to cherish you, Favour hath sent

Rich. Lady Science! for your benefits known
The World, to maintain you, Riches hath
thrown. [three,

Wor. And as the World hath sent you these
So he sendeth me, Worship, to advance your
degree.

Sci. I thank thee, World! but, chiefly, God
be praised!
That, in the World, such love to Science hath
raised!
But yet, to tell you plain, ye four are such
As Science looketh for, little nor much;
For being, as I am, a lone woman,
Need of your service I neither have nor can.
But, thanking the World, and you, for your pain,
I send ye to the World even now again! [me,

Wor. Why, lady! set ye no more store by
Worship? Ye set nought by yourself, I see!

Fame. She setteth nought by Fame;
whereby I spy her—
She careth not what the World sayeth by her.

Fav.   She setteth nought by Favour ; where-
    by I try her—
She careth not what the World sayeth or doeth
    by her.
    Rich.   She setteth nought by Riches ; which
    doth show   [go !
She careth not for the World.   Come, let us
        [FAME, FAVOUR, RICHES, *and* WORSHIP
        go out.
    Sci.   Indeed, small cause given to care for
    the World's favouring,
Seeing the wits of [the] World be so wavering !
    Exp.   What is the matter, daughter, that ye
Be so sad ?   Open your mind to me.
    Sci.   My marvel is no less, my good mother,
Than my grief is great, to see, of all other,
The proud scorn of Wit, son to Dame Nature,
Who sent me a picture of his stature,
With all the shape of himself there opening :
His amorous love thereby betokening,
Borne toward me in abundant fashion ;
And also, further, to make right relation
Of this his love, he put in commission
Such a messenger as no suspicion
Could grow, in me, of him—Confidence.
    Exp.   Um !   [vehemence,
    Sci.   Who, I ensure ye, with such
And faithful behaviour in his moving,
Set forth the pith of his master's loving
That no living creature could conjecte
But that pure love did that Wit direct.
    Exp.   So ?
    Sci.   Now, this being since the space
Of three times sending from place to place,
Between Wit and his man, I hear no more
Neither of Wit, nor his love so sore !

How think you by this, my own dear mother?
    Exp. Daughter! in this I can think none other
But that it is true—this proverb old:
Hasty love is soon hot, and soon cold!
Take heed, daughter! how you put your trust
To light lovers, too hot at the first!
For had this love of Wit been grounded,
And on a sure foundation founded,
Little void time would have been between ye
But that this Wit would have sent or seen ye.
    Sci. I think so.
    Exp.   Yea; think ye so or no,
Your mother, Experience, proof shall show
That Wit hath set his love, I dare say—
And make ye warrantise!—another way.

WIT *cometh before.*

[*Wit.*] But your warrantise warrant no troth!
Fair lady! I pray you be not wroth
Till you hear more; for, dear Lady Science!
Had your lover, Wit—yea, or Confidence,
His man—been in health all this time spent,
Long or this time Wit had come or sent;
But the truth is, they have been both sick,
Wit and his man: yea, and with pains thick
Both stayed by the way, so that your lover
Could neither come nor send by none other.
Wherefore blame not him, but chance of sick-
    Sci. Who is this?   [ness!
    Exp.   Ingnorancy, or his likeness.
    Sci. What, the common fool?
    Exp.   It is much like him.
    Sci. By my sooth! his tongue serveth him
        now trim.
What sayest thou, Ingnorancy?   Speak again!
    Wit. Nay, lady! I am not Ingnorancy, plain,
WIT   11

But I am your own dear lover, Wit,
That hath long loved you, and loveth you yet ;
Wherefore I pray thee now, my own sweeting !
Let me have a kiss at this our meeting.
 Sci. Yea, so ye shall, anon, but not yet.
Ah, sir ! this fool here hath got some wit.
Fall you to kissing, sir, now-a-days ?
Your mother shall charm you ; go your ways !
 Wit. What needeth all this, my love of long
  grown ?
Will ye be so strange to me, your own ?
Your acquaintance to me was thought easy ;
But now your words make my heart all queasy,
Your darts at me so strangely be shot.
 Sci. Hear ye what terms this fool here hath
  got ?
 Wit. Well, I perceive my foolishness now ;
Indeed, ladies no dastards allow ;
I will be bold with my own darling !
Come now, a bass, my own proper sparling !
 Sci. What wilt thou, arrant fool ?
 Wit.   Nay, by the mass !
I will have a bass or I hence pass !
 Sci. What wilt thou, arrant fool ? Hence,
  fool, I say !   [this day ?
 Wit. What ! nothing but fool, and fool, all
By the mass, madam ! ye can no good.
 Sci. Art a-swearing, too ? Now, by my hood !
Your foolish knave's breech six stripes shall
  bear !   [be ye there ?
 Wit. Yea, God's bones ! fool and knave too ?
By the mass, call me fool once again,
And thou shalt sure call a blow or twain !
 Exp. Come away, daughter ! the fool is mad.
 Wit. Nay, nor yet neither hence ye shall gad !
We will gree better, or ye pass hence.

I pray thee now, good sweet Lady Science!
All this strange manner now hide and cover,
And play the goodfellow with thy lover!
   Sci. What good-fellowship would ye of me,
Whom ye know not, neither yet I know ye?
   Wit. Know ye not me?
   Sci.   No! how should I know ye?
   Wit. Doth not my picture my person show ye?
   Sci. Your picture?
   Wit.   Yea, my picture, lady!
That ye spake of.   Who sent it but I?
   Sci. If that be your picture, then shall we
Soon see how you and your picture agree.
Lo, here! the picture that I named is this.
   Wit. Yea, marry! mine own likeness this is.
You having this, lady! and so loth
To know me, which this so plain showeth?
   Sci. Why, you are nothing like, in mine eye.
   Wit. No? How say ye?   [*To* EXPERIENCE.
   Exp.   As she saith, so say I.
   Wit. By the mass, then are ye both stark
    blind!   [find?
What difference between this and this can ye
   Exp. Marry, this is fair, pleasant, and
    goodly;
And ye are foul, displeasant, and ugly.
   Wit. Marry, avaunt, thou foul ugly whore!
   Sci. So, lo! now I perceive ye more and
    more.   [make me
   Wit. What! perceive you me as ye would
A natural fool?
   Sci.   Nay, ye mistake me;
I take ye for no fool natural,
But I take ye thus—shall I tell all?
   Wit. Yea, marry! tell me your mind, I
    pray ye,

Whereto I shall trust.   No more delay ye !
   Sci.   I take ye for no natural fool,
Brought up among the innocents' school ;
But for a naughty, vicious fool,
Brought up with Idleness in her school :
Of all arrogant fools thou art one !
   Wit.   Yea, God's body !
   Exp.   Come, let us be gone !
                               [The two go out.
   Wit.   My sword ! is it gone ?   A vengeance
      on them !
Be they gone, too, and their heads upon them ?
But, proud queans ! the devil go with you
      both !
Not one point of courtesy in them goeth.
A man is well at ease by suit to pain him
For such a drab, that so doth disdain him !
So mocked, so louted, so made a sot—
Never was I erst, since I was begot !
Am I so foul as those drabs would make me ?
Where is my glass that Reason did take me ?
Now shall this glass of Reason soon try me
As fair as those drabs that so doth belie me.
Ha ! God's soul ! what have we here ? a devil ?
This glass, I see well, hath been kept evil.
God's soul ! a fool, a fool, by the mass !
What—a very vengeance !—aileth this glass ?
Other this glass is shamefully spotted,
Or else am I too shamefully blotted !
Nay, by God's arms ! I am so, no doubt !
How look their faces here round about ?
All fair and clear they, everyone ;
And I, by the mass, a fool alone,
Decked, by God's bones, like a very ass !
Ignorance['s] coat, hood, ears — yea, by the
      mass !—

Cockscomb and all ; I lack but a bauble!
And as for this face it is abominable ;
As black as the devil! God, for His passion !
Where have I been rayed after this fashion ?
This same is Idleness—a shame take her !
This same is her work—the devil in hell rake
 her !
The whore hath shamed me forever, I trow !
I trow ? Nay, verily, I know !
Now it is so, the stark fool I play
Before all people ; now see it I may.
Every man I see laugh me to scorn ;
Alas, alas ! that ever I was born !
It was not for nought, now well I see,
That those two ladies disdained me.
Alas ! Lady Science, of all other—
How have I railed on her and her mother !
Alas ! that lady I have now lost
Whom all the world loveth and honoureth most !
Alas ! from Reason had I not varied,
Lady Science or this I had married ;
And those four gifts which the World gave her
I had won, too, had I kept her favour ;
Where now, instead of that lady bright
With all those gallants seen in my sight—
Favour, Riches, yea, Worship and Fame—
I have won Hatred, Beggary and Open Shame !

 SHAME *cometh in with a whip.* [REASON
   followeth him.]

 Wit. Out upon thee, Shame ! what doest
  thou here ?
 Rea. Marry ! I, Reason, bade him here
  appear.
Upon him, Shame ! with stripes enow smitten,
While I rehearse his faults herein written !

First, he hath broken his promise formerly
Made to me, Reason, my daughter to marry ;
Next, he hath broken his promise promised
To obey Instruction, and him despised ;
Thirdly, my daughter Science to reprove,
Upon Idleness he hath set his love ;
Fourthly, he hath followed Idleness' school
Till she hath made him a very stark fool ;
Lastly, offending both God and man,
Swearing great oaths as any man can,
He hath abused himself, to the great shame
Of all his kindred, and loss of his good
    name.
Wherefore, spare him not, Shame ! beat him
    well there !
He hath deserved more than he can bear.

                              WIT *kneeleth down.*

[*Wit.*] Oh father Reason, be good unto me !
Alas ! these stripes of Shame will undo me !
    Rea.   Be still awhile, Shame ! Wit, what
        sayest thou ?
    Wit.   Oh sir ! forgive me, I beseech you !
    Rea.   If I forgive thee thy punishment,
Wilt thou then follow thy first intent
And promise made, my daughter to marry ?
    Wit.   Oh sir ! I am not worthy to carry
The dust out where your daughter should
    sit.
    Rea.   I wot well that ; but if I admit
Thee, unworthy, again to her wooer,
Wilt thou then follow thy suit unto her ?
    Wit.   Yea, sir ! I promise you, while life
        endureth.
    Rea.   Come near, masters ! here is one
        ensureth

> *Here cometh* INSTRUCTION, STUDY, *and*
> DILIGENCE *in*.

In words to become an honest man !
Take him, Instruction ; do what ye can !
> *Inst.* What, to the purpose he went before ?
> *Rea.* Yea to my daughter prove him once
> more !

Take him, and trim him in new apparel,
And give that to Shame there to his farewell !
> *Inst.* Come on your way, Wit ! be of good
> cheer !

After stormy clouds cometh weather clear.
> INSTRUCTION, STUDY, WIT *and*
> DILIGENCE *go out*.

> *Rea.* Who list to mark now this chance
> here done,

May see what Wit is without Reason.
What was this Wit better than an ass
Being from Reason strayed, as he was ?
But, let pass now ! since he is well punished ;
And thereby, I trust, meetly well monished.
Yea, and I like him never the worse, I,
Though Shame hath handled him shamefully ;
For like as if Wit had proudly bent him
To resist Shame, to make Shame absent him,
I would have thought then that Wit had been—
As the saying is, and daily seen—
Past Shame once, and past all amendment :
So contrary, since he did relent
To Shame, when Shame punished him even ill,
I have, I say, good hope in him still.
I think, as I thought—if join they can—
My daughter well bestowed on this man.
But all the doubt now is to think how
My daughter taketh this ; for I may tell you

I think she knew this Wit even as well
As she seemed here to know him no deal,
For lack of knowledge in Science there is none ;
Wherefore, she knew him, and thereupon
His misbehaviour perchance even striking
Her heart against him, she—now misliking,
As women oft-times will be hard-hearted—
Will be the stranger to be reverted.
This must I help ; Reason must now walk,
On Wit's part with my Science to talk.
A near way to her know I, whereby
My son's coming prevent now must I.
Perchance, I may bring my daughter hither ;
If so, I doubt not to join them together
                                        Exeat REASON.

CONFIDENCE *cometh in.*

[*Conf.*] I thank God, yet at last I have
      found him ;
I was afraid some mischance had drowned him,
My master, Wit, with whom I have spoken ;
Yea, and delivered token for token,
And have another to Science again—
A heart of gold, signifying, plain,
That Science hath won Wit's heart forever—
Whereby, I trust, by my good endeavour,
To that good lady, so sweet and so sortly,
A marriage between them ye shall see shortly.
                                        CONFIDENCE *exeat.*

INSTRUCTION *cometh in with* WIT, STUDY, *and* DILIGENCE.

[*Inst.*]   Lo, sir ! now ye be entered again
Toward that passage where doth remain
Tediousness, your mortal enemy ;
Now may ye choose whether ye will try

Your hands again on that tyrant stout,
Or else walking a little about.
    Wit. Nay; for God's passion, sir, let me
      meet him!
Ye see I am able now for to greet him:
This sword of comfort, sent from my love,
Upon her enemy needs must I prove!
    Inst. Then, forth there! and turn on your
      right hand
Up that mount, before ye shall see stand.
But hear ye! If your enemy chance to rise,
Follow my counsel in anywise;
Let Study and Diligence flee their touch—
The stroke of Tediousness—and then couch
Themselves, as I told ye: ye wot how.
    Wit. Yea, sir! for that how, mark the
      proof now!
    Inst. To mark it, indeed, here will I abide,
To see what chance of them will betide;
For here cometh the pith, lo! of this journey.
That mountain, before which they must assay,
Is called in Latin *Mons Parnassus*;
Which mountain, as old authors discuss,
Who attaineth once to sleep on that mount,
Lady Science his own he may count.
But or he come there ye shall see fought
A fight with no less policy wrought
Than strength, I trow, if that may be praised.
    Ted. Oh! ho! ho!
    Inst.   Hark!
    Ted. [*entering*].   Out, ye caitiffs!
    Inst.   The fiend is raised!
    Ted. Out, ye villains! be ye come again?
Have at ye, wretches!
    Wit.   Flee, sirs! ye twain!
    Ted. They flee not far hence!

Dil.   Turn again, Study!

Study.   Now, Diligence!

Inst.   Well said!   Hold fast now!

Study.   He fleeth!

Dil.   Then follow!

Inst.   With his own weapon now work him
   sorrow!

Wit lieth at receipt!

Ted. (*dieth*).   Oh! ho! ho!

Inst.   Hark! he dieth!

Where strength lacketh, policy supplieth.

Here WIT *cometh in and bringeth in the head
   upon his sword, and sayeth as followeth*:

[*Wit.*] I can ye thank, sirs! this was well
   done!

Study.   Nay, yours is the deed!

Dil.   To you is the thank!

Inst.   I can ye thank, all; this was well
   done!   [won?

Wit.   How say ye, man?   Is this field well

CONFIDENCE *cometh running in.*

[*Conf.*] Yea, by my faith, so sayeth your
   dear heart.

Wit.   Why, where is she, that here now
   thou art?

Conf.   Upon yonder mountain, on high,
She saw ye strike that head from the body;
Whereby ye have won her, body and all;
In token whereof receive here ye shall
A gown of knowledge, wherein you must
Receive her here straight.

Wit.   But sayest thou just?

[*Conf.*] So just I say that, except ye hie ye,
Or ye be ready, she will be by ye.

Wit. Hold! Present unto her this head here,
And give me warning when she cometh near.
                              [*Exit* CONFIDENCE.
Instruction! will ye help to devise
To trim this gear now in the best wise?
   Inst. Give me that gown, and come with
   me, all!   [fall!
   Dil. Oh, how this gear to the purpose doth
           CONFIDENCE *cometh running in.*
   [*Conf.*] How, master, master! Where be ye
   now?   [thou?
   Wit. Here, Confidence! what tidings bring'st
   Conf. My lady at hand here doth abide ye;
Bid her welcome! What, do ye hide ye?

> *Here* WIT, INSTRUCTION, STUDY, *and*
> DILIGENCE *sing* "*Welcome, my own,*"
> *and* SCIENCE, EXPERIENCE, REASON
> *and* CONFIDENCE *come in at* L[*eft*],
> *and answer every second verse:*

> *Welcome, mine own!*
> *Welcome, mine own!*

Wit and his Company.   *O lady dear,*
                       Be ye so near
                        To be known?
                       My heart you cheer
                       Your voice to hear;
                        Welcome, mine
                          own!
Sci. and her Company.   *As ye rejoice*
                       To hear my voice
                        Fro me thus blown,
                       So in my choice
                       I show my voice
                        To be your own.

Wit and his Company.	*Then draw we near*
	To see and hear
	    My love long
	        grown !
	Where is my dear ?
	Here I appear
	    To see mine own.

Sci. and her Company.	*To see and try*
	Your love truly
	    Till death be flown,
	Lo ! here am I,
	That ye may spy
	    I am your own.

Wit and his Company.	*Then let us meet,*
	My love so sweet,
	    Half-way here
	        thrown !

Sci. and her Company.	*I will not sleet*
	My love to greet.
	    Welcome, mine
	        own !

Wit and his Company. *All sing :*	*Welcome, mine own !* *Welcome, mine own !*

And when the song is done, REASON *sendeth* INSTRUCTION, STUDY, *and* DILIGENCE, *and* CONFIDENCE *out ; and then, standing in the middle of the place,* WIT *sayeth as followeth :*

   Wit.   Welcome, mine own ! with all my whole heart,
Which shall be your own till death us depart !
I trust, lady ! this knot even since knit.
   Sci.   I trust the same ; for since ye have smit

Down my great enemy, Tediousness,
Ye have won me forever, doubtless,
Although ye have won a clog withal !
   Wit.   A clog, sweetheart ? what ?
   Sci.   Such as doth fall
To all men that join themselves in marriage,
In keeping their wives ; a careful carriage !
   Wit.   Careful ?   Nay, lady ! that care shall
      employ
No clog, but a key of my most joy.
To keep you, sweet heart ! as shall be fit,
Shall be no care, but most joy to Wit !
   Sci.   Well, yet I say—mark well what I
      say !—
My presence bringeth you a clog ; no nay !
Not in the keeping of me only,
But in the use of Science chiefly ;
For I, Science, am, in this degree,
As all, or most part, of women be :
If ye use me well, in a good sort,
Then shall I be your joy and comfort ;
But if ye use me not well, then doubt me,
For sure ye were better then without me !
   Wit.   Why, lady ! think you me such a wit,
As being affianced by you, and yet
Would misuse ye ?   Nay, if ye doubt that,
Here is one loveth thee more than somewhat :
If Wit misuse ye at any season,
Correct me then your own father, Reason.
   Rea.   Ho, daughter ! can ye desire any more ?
What need these doubts ?   Avoid them, there-
      fore !
   Exp.   By' lakyn, sir ! but, under your favour,
This doubt our daughter doth well to gather
For a good warning now, at beginning,
What Wit, in the end, shall look for in winning.

Which shall be this, sir ! if Science here,
Which is God's gift, be used mere
Unto God's honour, and profit both
Of you and your neighbour, which goth
In her, of kind, to do good to all :
This seen to, Experience ! I, shall
Set you forth, Wit, by her to employ
Double increase to your double joy ;
But if you use her contrariwise
To her good nature, and so devise
To evil effects to wrest and to wry her,
Yea, and cast her off and set nought by her,
Be sure I, Experience, shall than
Declare you so before God and man ;
That this talent from you shall be taken
And you punished for your gain forsaken.
    Wit.   " Once warned, half-armed," folk say,
        namely when
Experience shall warn a man, then
Time to take heed.   Mother Experience !
Touching your daughter, my dear heart, Science,
As I am certain that to abuse her
I breed mine own sorrow, and well to use her
I increase my joy ; and so to make it
God's grace is ready if I will take it :
Then—but ye count me no wit at all—
Let never these doubts into your head fall ;
But, as yourself, Experience, clearing
All doubts at length, so, till time appearing,
Trust ye with me in God ; and, sweetheart,
While your father, Reason, taketh with part
To receive God's grace as God shall send it,
Doubt ye not our joy till life's end [end] it !
    Sci.   Well, then, for the end of all doubts
        past,
And to that end which ye spake of last,

Among our wedding matters here rendering,
Th' end of our lives would be in remembering ;
Which remembrance, Wit, shall sure defend ye
From the misuse of Science and send ye
The gain my mother to mind did call :
Joy without end—that wish I to all !　　　　[it,
　Rea.　Well said ! and as ye, daughter ! wish
That joy, to all folk in general,
So wish I, Reason, the same ; but yet
First in this life wish I here to fall
To our most noble King and Queen in especial,
To their honourable Council, and then to all
　　the rest,　　　　　　　*[All say Amen.*
Such joy as long may rejoice them all best !

Here cometh in four with viols and sing, " Re-
　　member me," and, at the last, choir all make
　　curtsey, and so go forth singing.

　Thus endeth the Play of Wit and Science,
made by Master John Redford.

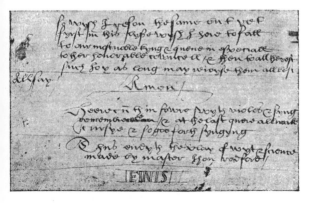

RESPUBLICA

A.D. 1553

A DRAMA OF REAL LIFE IN THE
EARLY DAYS OF QUEEN MARY

A Merry Interlude, entitled

RESPUBLICA

Made in the Year of our Lord 1553, and
the First Year of the most Prosperous
Reign of our Most Gracious
Sovereign Queen Mary
the First

The Parts and Names of the Players:

The Prologue, a Poet
Avarice, *alias* Policy, the Vice of the Play
Insolence, *alias* Authority, the Chief Gallant
Oppression, *alias* Reformation, another
 Gallant
Adulation, *alias* Honesty, the third Gallant
People, representing the Poor Commonalty
Respublica, a Widow
Misericordia,
Veritas,
Justicia, } four Ladies
Pax,
Nemesis, the Goddess of Redress and Cor-
 rection, a Goddess

RESPUBLICA.

THE PROLOGUE.

First, health and success, with many a good
    new year,
Wished unto all this noble presence here!
I have more t' entreat you of gentle sufferance
That this our matter may have quiet utterance.
We, that are th' authors, have ourselves dedicate
With some Christmas devise, your spirits to
    recreate;
And, our poet trusteth, the thing we shall recite
May, without offence, the hearer's minds delight;
Indeed, no man speaketh words so well fore
    pondered,   [construed.
But the same, by some means, may be mis-
Nor, nothing so well meant but that, by some
    pretence,   [sense.
It may be wrong interpreted from the author's
But, let this be taken no worse than it is meant,
And I hope nor we, nor our poet, shall be shent.

But now, of th' argument to touch a word or
    twain:
The name of our play is Respublica, certain.
Our meaning is—I say not, as by plain story,
But as it were in figure by an allegory—

To show that all commonweals ruin and decay
From time to time hath been, is, and shall be
    alway,
When Insolence, Flattery, Oppression,
And Avarice have the rule in their possession.
But, though these vices, by cloaked collusion,
And by counterfeit names hidden their abusion,
Do reign for a while to commonweals' pre-
    judice,
Perverting all right, and all order of true justice ;
Yet time trieth all, and time bringeth truth to
    light ;   [right.
That wrong may not ever still reign in place of
For, when pleaseth God such commonweals to
    restore
To their wealth and honour, wherein they were
    afore,
He sendeth down His most tender compassion,
To cause truth go about in visitation.
Verity, the daughter of sage old Father Time,
Sheweth all as it is, be it virtue or crime ;
Then doth Justice, all such as commonwealth
    oppress—
Tempered with mercy—endeavour to suppress ;
With whom, anon, is linked tranquillity and
    peace,
To commonweals' joy and perpetual increase.

    But shall boys, (saith some now), of such high
      matters play ?   [say :
No ! not as discussers ; but yet, the book doth
Ex ore infantium perferisti laudem.
For, when Christ came riding into Jerusalem,
The young babes, with th' old folk, cried out
    all and some :   [doth come ! "
" Blessed be the man that in the Lord's name

So, for good England's sake, this present hour
  and day,
In hope of her restoring from her late decay,
We children, to you old folk, both with heart
  and voice,
May join all together to thank God, and rejoice
That He hath sent Mary, our sovereign and
  queen,
To reform th' abuses which hitherto hath been ;
And that ills which long time have reigned
  uncorrect
Shall now, for ever, be redressed with effect.
She is our most wise and most worthy Nemesis ;
Of whom our play meaneth, t' amend that is
  amiss ;   [and space,
Which, to bring to pass, that she may have time
Let us, both young and old, to God commend
  her grace !
Now, if you so please, I will go and hither send
That shall make you laugh well, if ye abide th'
  end.

FINIS.

RESPUBLICA.

ACTUS PRIMI, SCENA PRIMA.

[AVARICE.]

Avarice. Now, godigod! everyone, both
    great and small,
From highest to lowest, Godigod to you all!
Godigod! what should I say? even or morn,
If I mark how the day goeth—God give me sorrow!
But, godigod! each one, twenty and twenty
    score   [more?
Of that ye most long for—what would ye have
Ye must pardon my wits, for I tell you, plain,
I have a hive of humble bees swarming in my
    brain;   [must fetch,
And he that hath the compass to fetch that I
I may say, in counsel, had need his wits to stretch.

    But now, what my name is, and what is my
    purpose—   [disclose.
Taking you all for friends — I fear not to
My very true, unchristian name is Avarice,
Which I may not have openly known, in no wise;
For, though to most men I am found commodious,
Yet, to those that use me, my name is odious.

For, who is so foolish that the evil he hath
    wrought
For his own behoof, he would to light should
    be brought ?
Or, who had not rather, his ill doings to hide,
Than to have the same bruited on every side ?
Therefore, to work my feat, I will my name
    disguise ;
And call my name Policy instead of Covetise.
The name of Policy is praised of each one ;
But, to rake gromwell-seed, Avarice is alone ;
The name of Policy is of none suspected—
Policy is ne'er of any crime detected.
So that, under the name and cloak of Policy,
Avarice may work facts, and scape all jealousy.
And, now is the time come that—except I be a
    beast,   [nest—
E'en to make up my mouth, and to feather my
A time that I have waited for, a great long space;
And now may I speed my purpose, if I have grace.

For, hear ye, sirrah ! our great, grand lady
    mother,
Noble Dame Respublica, she and none other—
Of the offals, the refuse, the rags, the parings ;
The baggage, the trash, the fragments, the
    sharings ;
The odd ends, the crumbs, the driblets, the
    chippings ;
The patches, the pieces, the broklets, the
    drippings ;   [strays ;
The flittance, the scrapings, the wild wai[f]s and
The skimmings, the gubbings of booties and
    preys ;   [escheats ;
The gleanings, the casualties, the blind
The forging of forfeit[s], the scape of extreats ;

Th' excess, the waste, the spoils, the super-
    fluities ;
The windfalls, the shreddings, the fleecings, the
    petty fees ;
With a thousand things more, which she may
    right well lack—
Would fill all these same purses that hang at
    my back.
Yea ! and ten times as many more bags as these,
Which should be but a flea-biting for her to lese ;
That, if I may have the grace and hap to
    blind her,
I doubt not, a sweet lady I shall find her.
To her it were nothing ; yet, many a small
    maketh a great ;
And all things would help me whatever I may
    geat :
Full little know men the great need that I am in.
Do not I spend daily of that that I do win ?
Then, age cometh on ; and what is a little gold
To keep a man by drede that is feeble and old ?
No man, therefore, blame me though I would
    have more :   [no sore.
The world waxeth hard, and store, (they say), is
Now, the chance of thieves, in good hour be it
    spoken—
Out, alas ! I fear I left my coffer open.
I am surely undone ! alas ! where be my kays ?
It is gone, that I have sweat for all my live-days !
Woe worth all whoreson thieves, and such
    covetous knaves !
That, for their winding sheet, would scrape
    men out of their graves !   [*Exeat*.

ACTUS PRIMI, SCENA SECUNDA.

Adulation. Insolence. Oppression.

Intrant Canta[n]tes.

Adulation. Oh, noble Insolence ! if I could
  sing as well,
I would look in heaven among angels to dwell.

  Insolence. Sing ! now, do I sing but as other
    many do ?

  Adul. Yes, an angel's voice ye have, to
    hearken unto.

  Insol. Yea ! but what availeth that to high
    dignity ?   [as I can see !

Oppression. By His arms ! not a whit, as far

  Insol. Or, what helpeth that thing to set a
    man aloft ?

  Oppr. By His wounds ! not a straw ; so have
    I told you oft.

  Adul. No ! but ye are one of such goodly
    personage,
Of such wit and beauty, and of sage parentage,
So excellent in all points of every art—

  Insol. Indeed, God and nature in me have
    done their part—

  Adul. That, if ye will put yourself forward
    to the most,   [the roste—
Ye may, throughout the whole land, rule all
How say you, Oppression ? is it not even so ?

  Oppr. Thou sayest sooth, Adulation ! so
    might I go :
If he were disposed to take the charge in hand,
I warrant him a chive to rule all the whole land.

  Adul. So, Master Insolence ! ye hear Oppres-
    sion ?   [Adulation !

  Insol. I thank both him and thee, good

And long have I dreamed of such an enterprise ;
But how, or where to begin, I cannot devise.

    Oppr. Wherefore serve friends, but your
    enterprise to allow?

    Adul. And then must you support them, as
    they must maintain you.

    Oppr. And, wherefore do friends serve, but
    to set you in?   [ye begin.

    Adul. Ye shall have all my help whenever

    Insol. But we may, herein, nothing attempt,
    in no wise,

Without the counsel of our founder, Avarice.

    Adul. He must direct all this gear by his
    holy ghost.

    Oppr. For he knoweth what is to be done
    in each coast ;

He knoweth where, and how that money is to
    be had—   [half mad !

And, yonder he cometh ! methinketh more than
                      [*Intrat* AVARICE.

ACTUS PRIMI, SCENA TERTIA.

AVARICE. INSOLENCE. OPPRESSION. ADULATION.

    Avarice. It was a fair grace that I was not
    undone clean ;   [I ween.

Yet my key was safe locked under mine locks,

But e'en, as against such a thing my heart will
    throb,   [rob.

I found knaves about my house, ready me to

There was such tooting, such looking, and such
    prying ;

Such hearkening, such stalking, such watching,
    such spying.

"What would ye, my masters?" "We look after
   a cat."   [a rat."
"What make ye hereabout?" "We have smelled
Now, a weal on such noses! thought I, by and by,
That so quickly can scent where hidden gold
   doth lie.   [fails,
But had I not come when I did, without all
I think they had digged up my walls with their
   nails!   [chafing talk.
   Insol. Let us speak to him, and break his
   Avar. Such greediness of money among men
   doth walk   [crook!
That, have it they will, either by hook or by
   Oppr. Let us call to him that he may this
   way look.
   Avar. Whether by right, or by wrong, in
   faith! some care not: [spare not!
Therefore, catch that catch may, hardely, and
   Adul. All hail our founder and chief, Master
   Avarice!   [flyce.
   Avar. The devil is a knave, an I catch not a
   Adul. When ye see your time, look this
   way, your friends upon!
   Avar. I doubt not to scamble and rake as
   well as one.
   Adul. Here be that would fain be disciples
   of your art.   [part.
   Avar. I will not be behind to get a child's
   Adul. Now, if ye have done, I pray you
   look this way back.
   Avar. Who buzzeth in mine ear so? what?
   ye saucy Jack!
   Adul. Are ye yet at leisure, with your good
   friends to talk?
   Avar. What, clawest thou mine elbow,
   pratling merchant? walk!

Ye flatterabundus, you ! you flearing clawback,
     you !
You the-crow-is-white, you ! you the-swan-is-
     black, you !   [clock, you !
You John-hold-my-staff, you ! you what-is-the-
You *ait-aio* you ! you *negat-nego* you !

    Adul.   I marvel you speak to me in such
     fashion.

    Avar.   Why troublest thou me then in my
     'contemplation ?

    Adul.   I came of right good love, not mind-
     ing you to let.

    Avar.   Thou ne'er camest to any man of
     good love yet.   [so do.

    Adul.   And these men's minds it was I should

    Avar.   As false wretches as thine own self,
     and falser too !

    Insol and Oppr.   We have been loving to you,
     and faithful alway.

    Avar.   For your own profits, then ; and not
     mine, I daresay ;   [none,
And e'en, veray! you three it was, and others
That would have robbed me, not yet half an
     hour gone.

    Insol., Oppr., Adul.   We never robbed any
     man, later or rather.

    Avar.   Yes, many a time and oft, your own
     very father.

    Oppr.   And to you have we borne hearty
     favours alway.

    Avar.   And, I warrant you hanged for your
     labours one day.

    Oppr., Adul.   And, as our god, we have alway
     honoured you.

    Avar.   And, e'en as your god, I have aye
     succoured you.

Oppr.   We call you our founder, by All Holy
   Hallows !

Avar.   Founder me no found'ring ; but beware the gallows !

Insol.   I pray you leave these words, and
   talk friendly at last.

Avar.   Content! at your request, my fame
   is now well past ;   [tion?
And, in faith! what saith our friend, Adula-

Adul.   I wonder at your rough communication,   [ence.
That ye would to me use words of such vehem-

Avar.   Faith, man! I spake but even to
   prove your patience,
That if thou hadst grunted or stormed thereat.

Adul.   Nay! few times do I use such loud
   manner as that.

Avar.   Come! shake hands! for ever we
   two be at one.

Adul.   As for grudge in me, there shall never
   remain none.   [ghostly purpose !

Avar.   Now, Master Insolence! to your

Insol.   We accorded a matter to you to dis-
   close.   [accord ;

Avar.   I understand all your agreement and
For, I laid in your bosoms when ye spake the
   word ;
And I like well the advice of Oppression,
And eke of Flattery, for your progression.

Insol.   If there were matter whereon to work,
   I care not.

Avar.   Ye shall have matter enough ; be
   doing, spare not !

Insol.   What! to come to honour and
   wealth for us all three?   [out me !

Avar.   Ah then! ye could be content to leave

Insol. No! for I know ye can, for yourself
well provide.

Avar. Yea! that I can; and for twenty
hundred beside.

Adul. Oh, would Christ, good founder! ye
would that thing open.

Avar. Bones, knave! wilt thou have it ere
it can be spoken?

Oppr. For the passion of God! tell it us
with all speed!

Avar. By the cross, not a word! here is
haste made indeed.

Insol. Yes, good, sweet Avarice! dispatch,
and tell at once!

Avar. Nay then, cut my throat! ye are
fellows for the nonce—

Will ye have a matter before it can be told?

If ye will have me tell it, ye shall your tongues
hold.   [clatter cease!

Whist! silence! not a word! Mum! let your

Are ye with child to hear, and cannot hold
your peace?

So sir! now Respublica, the lady of estate,

Ye know, now lately, is left almost desolate.

Her wealth is decayed; her comfort clean ago;

And she at her wit's end what for to say or do.

Fain would she have succour, and easement of
her grief;   [relief;

And highly advance them that would promise

Such as would warrant her spirits to revive

Might mount to high estate, and be most sure
to thrive.

Insol. So!

Adul.   Well said!

Opp.   Ha!

Avar.   What is this hum, ha, hum?

Insol.   On forth !
Adul.   Go too !
Oppr.   Tell on !
Avar.   Body of me !
Adul.   Mum !
Avar.   What say ye ?
Insol.   Haik !
Adul.   Tuff !
Oppr.   Hem !
Avar.   Who haiken, tuffa, hum—what say ye ?
Oppr.   Nothing !
Insol.   Not a word ?
Avar.   Nor you, neither ?
Adul.   Mum !
Avar.   Did ye speak or not !
Insol.   No !
Oppr.   No !
Adul.   No !
Avar.   Nor yet do not ?
Insol.   No !
Oppr.   No !
Adul.   No !
[*Oppr.*   No !]
Insol.   No !
Adul.   No !
Avar.   That, that, that ! that, that, that !
Sir, I intend Dame Respublica t'assail ;
And, so to creep in to be of her counsel ;
I hope well to bring her in such a paradise
That herself shall sue me to have my service ;
Then shall I have time and power to bring in
      you three.
   Oppr.   Do this out of hand, founder ! and
      first, speak for me ;
Bring me in credit that my hands be in the
      pie :

An I get not elbow room among them, let me
    lie.   [elf,

    Avar. Nay! see an Oppression, this eager
Be not since more covetous than covetous self!
Soft! be not so hasty, I pray you, Sir! soft
    awhile!   [stile.
You will over the hedge ere ye come at the

    Oppr. I would fain be shouldering and
    rumbling among them.

    Avar. Nay! I will help javels as shall
    wrong them.

    Adul. I pray you, good founder! let not
    me be the last.

    Avar. Thou shalt be well placed where to
    thrive very fast.

    Adul. I thank you, Master Avarice! with
    all my heart.

    Avar. And when thou art in place, see thou
    play well thy part.

When ye claw her elbow, remember your best
    friend;

And let my commendations be ever at one end.

    Adul. I warrant you!

    Insol. And what! shall [I] be left clean out?

    Avar. No, sir! ye shall be chief to bring all
    things about;

Ye shall among us have the chief pre-eminence;
And we to you, as it were, owe obedience:
Ye shall be our leader, our captain, and our
    guide;   [side.
Then must ye look aloft, with hands under the
I shall tell Respublica ye can best govern:
Be not ye, then, squeamish to take in hand the
    stern.   [trust,
Then shall we assist you, as friends of perfect
To do and to undo, and command what ye lust,

And, when you have all at your own will and
    pleasure,   [measure ;
Part of your livings to your friends ye may
And punish the proudest of them that will resist.

    Oppr.   He that once winceth shall feel the
       weight of my fist.

    Adul.   Yea! we must all hold and cleave
       together like burrs.

    Avar.   Yea! see ye three hang and draw
       together like furze.

    Oppr.   And so shall we be sure to get store
       of money

Sweeter than sugar !

    Avar.   Sweeter than any honey !

    Insol.   Very well spoken! this gear will
       right well accord.   [lord?

    Adul.   Did not I say ye were worthy to be a

    Avar.   I will make Insolence a lord of high
       estate.

    Insol.   And I will take upon me well, both
       early and late.

    Oppr.   But, Insolence! when ye come to the
       encroaching of lands,

Ye may not take all alone into your hands ;
I will look to have part of goods, lands, and
    plate.

    Insol.   Ye shall have enough. each body
       after his rate.

    Adul.   I must have part, too ; ye must not
       have all alone.

    Insol.   Thou shalt be laden till thy shoulders
       shall crack and groan.

    Adul.   I pray you, let me have a good lord-
       ship or two.

    Insol.   Respublica shall feed thee till thou
       wilt say, ho !

Resp.   13

 Adul. And I must have good manor places,
  two or three.   [remain to me.
 Insol. But the chief and best lordship must
 Oppr. Mass! and I will look to be served
  of the best;   [small rest.
Or else some folk, somewhere, shall sit but in
 Insol. I must have castles and towns in
  every shire.
 Adul. And I, change of houses—one here,
  and another there.
 Insol. And I must have pastures, and town-
  ships, and woods.
 Oppr. And I must needs have store of gold
  and other goods.
 Insol. And I must have change of farms,
  and pastures for sheep;
With daily revenues my lusty port for to keep.
 Avar. I would have a bone here, rather
  than a groat,   [other's throat!
To make these snarling curs gnaw out each
Here! be eager, whelps! lo! to it Boy! box
  him Ball!   [will snatch all.
Poor I may pick straws; these hungry dogs
 Oppr. Each man snatch for himself; by
  gosse! I will be sped.
 Avar. Lack who lack shall: Oppression
  will be corn fed!
Is not Dame Respublica sure of good handling
When these whelps, ere they have it, fall thus
  to scambling?   [since forgot.
And me, their chief founder, they have e'en
 Insol. Thou shalt have gold and silver
  enough to thy lot:
Respublica hath enough to fill all our laps.
 Adul. Then, I pray you, sir! let our founder
  have some scraps!

Avar. Scr[a]ps? ye doltish lout! feed you
    your founder with scraps?
If you were well served your head would have
    some raps.
    Adul. I spake of good will.
    Insol.   Nay, fight not, good Avarice!
    Oppr. What any of us getteth, thou hast
    the chief price.
    Avar.   Then, whatever ye do, ye will
    remember me?
    Insol. Oppr. Adul. Yea!   [all three.
    Avar. Well, so do then; and I forgive you
    Insol. But, when do we enter, every man
    his charge?   [large
Avar. As soon as I can spy Respublica at
I will board her; and, I trow, so win her
    favour   [labour.
That she shall hire me, and pay well for my
Then will I commend the virtues of you three
That she shall pray and wish under our rule
    to be;
Therefore, from this hour, be ye all in readiness!
    Oppr. Doubt not of us! thou seest all our
    grediness.   [first call.
    Insol. If it be at midnight, I come at the
        [*They go forward, one after other.*
    Adul. Do but whistle for me, and I come
    forth withal.   [toward twig.
    Avar. That is well spoken; I love such a
        [*He whistleth.*

    Adul. I come, founder!
    Avar. That is mine own good spaniel, Rig—
And come on! back again, all three! come back
    again!
    Insol. Our founder calleth us back.
    Oppr.   Return then, amain.

ACTUS PRIMI, SCENA QUARTA.

Avarice. Adulation. Insolence. Oppression.

Avar. Come on, sirs, all three! And first
    to you, best be trust:
What, is your brainpan stuffed withal? wool
    or sawdust?
    Adul. Why so?
    Avar.   What is your name?
    Adul.   Flattery!
    Avar.   E'en so, just!
    Adul. Yea! or else Adulation, if you so lust:
Either name is well known to many a body.
    Avar. An honest mome! ah, ye dolt! ye
    lout! ye noddy!
Shall Respublica hear your commendation
By the name of Flattery or Adulation?
Or, when ye commend me to her, will ye say
    this:
Forsooth! his name is Avarice or Covetise?
And you, that should have wit, is't your
    discretion
Bluntly to go forth, and be called Oppression?
And you, Insolence! do ye think it would well
    frame
If ye were presented to her under that name?
    Insol. I thought nothing thereupon, by my
    halidom!
    Oppr. My mind was another way, by my
    christendom!
    Adul. That thing was le[a]st part of my
    thought, by Saint Denis!
    Avar. No marry! your minds were all on
    your halfpenny.

But, my masters ! I must on mine honesty pass,
And not run on 'head, like a brute beast or an
    ass.
For is not Oppression eachwhere sore hated ?
And is not Flattery openly rebated ?
And am not I, Avarice, still cried out upon ?
    Adul. Yes ! I could have told you that, a
      great while agone ;
But I would not displease you.
    Avar.   And you, Insolence !
I have heard you ill-spoken of a great way hence.
    Adul. In my conscience ! the devil himself
      doth love you.
    Avar. But changing your ill-name, fewer
      shall reprove you—
As I, mine ownself, where my name is known
Am right sore assailed, to be overthrown.
But doing, as I will now, counterfeit my name,
I speed all my purposes, and yet escape blame.
    Insol. Let us then have new names, each
      man, without delay.
    Avar. Else will some of you make hanging
      stuff one day.
    Oppr. Thou must new christen us.
    Insol.   First, what shall my name be ?
    Avar. Faith, sir ! your name shall be
      Mounsire Authority.   [tion ?
    Oppr. And, for me, what is your determina-
    Avar. Marry, sir ! ye shall be called
      Reformation.   [honest name.
    Adul. Now, I pray you, devise for me an
    Avar. Thou art such a beast, I cannot, for
      very shame !   [Policy.
    Adul. If ye think good, let me be called
    Avar. Policy — a rope ye shall ! nay,
    Hypocrisy !

Adul.   Fie! that were as slanderous a
name a[s] Flattery.   [Policy.

Avar.   And I keep for myself the name of
But, if I devise for thee, wilt thou not shame me?

Adul.   Nay! I will make thee proud of me;
or, else, blame me!

Avar.   Well, then, for this time, thy name
shall be Honesty.   [Honesty!

Adul.   I thank you, Avarice! Honesty,

Avar.   Avarice, ye whoreson! Policy, I tell
thee!   [Honesty!

Adul.   I thank you, Policy! Honesty,
How say you, Insolence? I am now Honesty.

Avar.   We shall at length have a knave of
you, Honesty!   [Authority?

Said not I, he should be called Mounseer

Adul.   Oh, friend Oppression! Honesty,
Honesty!   [brain?

Avar.   Oppression? ha! is the devil in thy
Take heed! or, in faith! ye are Flattery again.
Policy! Reformation! Authority!

Adul.   Hypocrisy! Defamation! and Authority!   [dull ass!

Avar.   Hypocrisy? ha! Hypocrisy? ye

Adul.   Thou named'st Hypocrisy even now,
by the Mass!

Avar.   Policy, I said; Policy! knave Policy!
Now say as I said.

Adul.   Policy, knave! Policy!

Avar.   And what callest thou him here?

Adul.   Defamation!

Avar.   I told thee he should be called

Adul.   Very well!   [Reformation.

Avar.   What is he now?

Adul.   Deformation!

                    [*A line is probably lost.*]

Avar. Was ever the like ass born, in all
    nations? [Asians.
Adul. A pestle on him, he comes of the
Avar. Come on! ye shall learn to solfe
    Reformation!
Sing on now: *Re*.
    Adul.   *Re*.
    Avar.   *Refor*.
    Adul.   *Reformation*.
    Avar. Policy, Reformation, Authority!
    Adul. Policy, Reformation, and Honesty!
    Avar. In faith, ye ass! if your tongue make
    any mo trips,
Ye shall both be Flattery and have on the lips.
And now, Mounsire Authority! against, I you
    call;
Ye must have other garments; and so must ye
    all—
Ye must, for the season, counterfeit gravity.
    Insol. and Oppr. Yes! what else?
    Adul.   And I must counterfeit honesty.
    Avar. And I must turn my gown in and
    out, I ween;
For these gaping purses may in no wise be seen.
I will turn it e'en here—come help me, Honesty!
    Adul. Here, at hand! [Honesty!
    Avar. Why, how now? play the knave,
Help! what doest thou now?
    Adul.   I counterfeit Honesty.
    Avar. Why, then, come thou! help me, my
    friend Oppression!
What help call you that?
    Oppr.   Fit for your discretion!
    Avar. Oh, I should have said: help, sir
    Reformation! [tion.
    Oppr. Yea, marry, sir! that is my nomina-

Avar. And when you are [in] your robe,
keep it afore close.   [purpose?
Oppr. I pray you, Master Policy! for what
Avar. All folk will take you, if they peep
under your gown,
For the veriest caitiff in country or town.
Now, go! and when I call, see that ye ready be!
Insol. I will.
Oppr.   And I will.
Adul.   And so will I, Honesty!
                                        [*Exeant.*
Avar. Well, now will I depart hence, also,
for a space;
And, to bourd Respublica, wait a time of grace.
Wherever I find her a time convenient,
I shall say and do that may be expedient!
                              [*Exeat* AVARICE.

ACTUS SECUNDI, SCENA PRIMA.

[RESPUBLICA.]

Resp. Lord! what earthly thing is perman-
ent or stable?
Or, what is all this world but a lump mutable?
Who would have thought that I, from so
florent estate,   [of late?
Could have been brought so base as I am made
But, as the waving seas do flow and ebb by
course,   [worse.
So all things else do change to better and to
Great cities and their fame, in time, do fade
and pass;
Now is a champion field where noble Troy was.

Where is the great Empire of the Medes and
    Persians?
Where be th' old conquests of the puissant
    Grecians?
Where Babylon? where Athens? where Corinth
    so wide?   [pride?
Are they not consumed with all their pomp and
What is the cause hereof? man's wit cannot
    discuss;   [thus.
But, of long continuance, the thing is found
Yet, by all experience, thus much is well seen:
That, in commonweals, while good governors
    have been,
All thing hath prospered; and, where such men
    do lack,
Commonweals decay, and all things do go
    back.
What marvel then, if I, wanting a perfect stay,
From most flourishing wealth be fallen in decay?
But, like as by default, quick ruin doth befall,
So may good government at once recover all.
    Intrat AVAR[ICE] *cogitabundus et ludibundus.*

ACTUS SECUNDI, SCENA SECUNDA.

AVARICIA.   RESPUBLICA.

    Avar.   Alas, my sweet bags! how lank and
    empty ye be;   [me.
But, in faith and troth, sirs! the fault is not in
    Resp.   Well, my help and comfort, oh Lord!
    must come from Thee.
    Avar.   And my sweet purses here, I pray
    you all, see, see!

How the little fool[s] gasp and gape for grom-
    well-seed !

  Resp.   If it be Thy will, Lord ! send some
    redress with speed.

  Avar.   But, in faith, good sweet fools ! it
    shall cost me a fall.   [all.

But I will shortly fill you, and stop your mouths

  Resp.   Oh, that it were my hap, on friendly
    friends to light !

  Avar.   Ha, ha ! who is that same, that
    speaketh yonder in sight ?

Who is't ? Respublica ? yea, by the Mary mass !

  Resp.   Then might I be again as well as ere
    I was.

  Avar.   Hide up these pipes ! now, I pray
    God she be blind ;

I am half afraid lest she have an eye behind.

We must now change our copy: oh, Lord !
    how I fray,   [say !

Lest she saw my toys, and heard what I did

  Resp.   Is there no good man that on me will
    have mercy ?

  Avar.   Remember now : my name is Master
    Policy :

All thing, I tell you, must now go by Policy.

  Resp.   Hark ! methink I hear the name of
    Policy.   [Policy !

  Avar.   Who calleth Conscience ? here am I,

  Resp.   I pray you come to me, if you be
    Policy !

  Avar.   Yea, forsooth ! yea, forsooth ! my
    name is Policy.   [Policy.

  Resp.   I am sore decayed through default of

  Avar.   Yea, most noble Respublica ! I know
    that well ;

And do more lament it than any tongue can tell.

For, an if good Policy had had you in hand,
Ye had now been the wealthiest in any land :
But good Policy hath long been put to exile.

    Resp.   Yea, God wot! ye have been barred
    from me a great while.

    Avar.   Yea! I have been put back, as one
    clean off-shaken ;

And, what can a man do till he be forth taken ?

    Resp.   Well, I feel the lack of your helping
    hand, by the rood !

    Avar.   Alack, noble lady ! I would I could
    do you good.   [you lust.

    Resp.   Yes, Policy ! ye might amend all, if

    Avar.   Yea, faith ! I durst put myself to
    you of trust.   [make.

But, there be enough that, for you, could shift

    Resp.   Yet, none like to you! if you would
    it undertake—

And I will put myself wholly into your hands :
Metal, grain, cattle, treasure, goods and lands—

    Avar.   Well ! I will take some pain ; but
    this to you be known :   [own.

I will do it, not for your sake, and not for mine

    Resp.   How say ye that, Policy ?

    Avar.   This to you be known :
I will do all for your sake, and not for mine own.

    Resp.   I thank you, Policy !

    Avar.   Nay, I thank you, lady !

And I trust ere long to ease all our malady—
Well, ye put yourself now wholly into my hands?

    Resp.   Order me as you will.

    Avar.   Treasure, goods, and lands ?

    Resp.   Yea, every whit !

    Avar.   Well ! I thank you once again.

But, now that you may think my dealing true
    and plain,

And, because one cannot do so well as many,
Ye must associate me with mo company :
And first, by my will, ye shall set up Honesty.

    Resp.   Marry ! with all my very heart—but
      where is he ?

    Avar.   Very hard to find : but I think I
      could fet him.

    Resp.   Call· him straightways hither ! see
      that nothing let him !

    Avar.   It were best if I shall go fet men
      for the nonce ;   [once.

To make but one viage, and bring them all at

    Resp.   Whom more than him ?

    Avar.   Ye must stablish Authority.

    Resp.   That must needs be done.

    Avar.   And eke Reformation—

We four will rule things of another fashion.

    Resp.   Policy ! I pray you go fet all these
      straightway.

    Avar.   Yes ! for this your present case may
      bide no delay.

I will go and come with all festination.

                              [Exeat.

    Resp.   I like well this trade of Administra-
      tion :

Policy for to devise for my commodity ;
No person to be advanced but Honesty ;   [make ;
Then Reformation, good wholesome laws to
And Authority see the same effect may take ;
What commonweal shall then be so happy as I ?
For this, (I perceive), is the drift of Policy.

        [Intrat AVARICE, *adducens* INSOLENCE,
          OPPRESSION, *and* ADULATION.

And, behold ! where he is returned again since :
He showeth himself a man of [much] diligence.

ACTUS SECUNDI, SCENA TERTIA.

ADULATION. AVARICE. RESPUBLICA. INSOL-
ENCE. OPPRESSION.

Adul. I will do her double service to another!

Avar. Ye double knave, you! will ye never
be other?

Adul. She shall have triple service of me,
Honesty.

Avar. Ye quadrible knave! wi[ll] ye ne'er
use modesty?

Thou drunken whoreson! dost thou not see
nor perceive

Where Respublica stands, ready us to receive?

Resp. What talk have they yonder, among
themselves together?

Adul. I have spied her now, shall I first to
her thither?

Avar. Soft! let me present you.

Resp. I ween they be in fear— [near.

Policy, approach! and bring my good friends

Avar. Come on, my dear friends! and
execute with good will

Such office as each of you shall be put until.

Dame Respublica it is that for you hath sent.

Come on, friends! I will you unto her grace
present.

Insol. [*and*] *Oppr.* To serve her, we are
pressed with heart and whole intent.

Avar. Madame! I have brought you these
men for whom I went.

Resp. Policy! I thank you; ye have made
speedy speed;

Therefore, ye be double welcome, and welcome
friends, indeed!

Avar.   Madame! your grace to serve we all
   are fully bent.   [diligent.
Adul.   And, Madame! ye shall find me double
Resp.   That is spoken of a good heart: but
   who be ye?
Adul.   Forsooth, Madame! my name is
   Master Honesty.
Resp.   Honesty? well said!
Avar.   Madame! this is Honesty.
Adul.   Yea, forsooth! and please your grace,
   I am Honesty.
Avar.   Madame, he is for you: on my word,
   regard him!   [reward him.
Resp.   Yes, and with large preferment I will
Adul.   I thank your grace; and, I will, for
   you, take such pain
That, ere I deserve one, ye shall give me twain.
Avar.   Honesty! your tongue trippeth!
Resp.   How said ye? take such pain—
Adul.   That ere ye give me one, I will de-
   serve twain—   [mote.
By your licence, Madame! to take away this
Avar.   Nay! Honesty will not see a wem
   on your coat.
Now unto you I commend Reformation.
Resp.   Of him is no small need now, in this
   nation.   [redress,
Oppr.   Well, now that ye bid me abuses to
I doubt not all enormities so to repress,
As shall redound to your wealth and honour at
   length.
Resp.   Thereto shall authority aid you with
   his strength.   [fit.
Avar.   Yea! for Authority to govern is most
Insol.   If ye, Dame Respublica! do me so
   admit,

I doubt not to hamper the proudest of them all.

   Resp.   And among you, destroy Avarice!

   Adul.   Hem!

   Insol. and Oppr.   We shall!

   Resp.   Vanquish Oppression and.Adulation!

For those three have nigh wrought my desolation.

   Avar.   Hem, sirs! hem! there, keep your gowns close afore, I say!

Have ye forgotten now what I told you one day?

There is another, too, that would be chased

   Resp.   Who is that?   [hence.

   Avar.   Lucifer's son, called Insolence.

   Resp.   Ye say truth, and many naughty ones mo than he.

   Insol. and Oppr.   If ye dare trust us!

   Insol.   All!

   Oppr.   All shall reformed be!

   Resp.   I thank you; and, I trust you for my maintenance,

To be administere[d] for your good governance.

   Insol.   Then, without fear or care, ye may yourself repose.   [as those.

   Oppr.   And let us alone with all such matters

   Resp.   Then, I leave you here, on our affairs to consult.   [*Exeat* RESP[UBLICA.]

   Insol.   When you please, in God's name!

   Oppr.   We must both sift and bolt.

   Adul.   She is gone.

   Avar.   Well then, sirs! let us make no delay;

But, about our market depart, each man his way.

   Adul.   Nay! first let us sing a song to lighten our hearts.

   Avar.   Then are ye like, for me, to sing but of three parts.

Can Avarice['s] heart be set on a merry pin,
And see no gain, no profit at all coming in ?
    Insol.   We shall have enough to drive away
      all sorrow.
    Avar.   Then sing we *On bowne viage!* and
      Saint George thee borrow!

[*Cantent*: "*Bring ye to me and I to ye,*" etc. et
    sic exeant.

ACTUS TERTIA, SCENA PRIMA.

[Respublica.]

    Resp.   The good hope, that my masters have
      put me in,
To recover ruin that in me doth begin,
Hath so recomforted my spirits and mine heart,
That I feel much easement of my great grief
    and smart,
Now, I do less wonder that lost men, life to
    save,
Far from land do labour, against the roaring
    wave ;
For hope, I see, hath mighty operation
Against the mortal sting of drooping despera-
    tion.
Now, if I might but hear what Policy hath
    wrought,
Or some one good thing that my friends to
    pass had brought,
I would put no doubts but all thing should soon
    be well—
Lo ! where cometh Honesty : he will the truth
    tell.

ACTUS TERTII, SCENA SECUNDA.

Adulation. Respublica.

Adul. Three hundred pound by year, and a
    good manor place— [space !
Well, it is metely well, in so short time and
More will come right shortly ; this gear doth
    gaily walk. [ta[l]ke ?
Bones ! here is Respublica, what use I such
I seek lady Respublica !
Resp. Lo, I am here ! [most dear ?
And welcome, Honesty ! what do my friends
    Adul. Certes, Madame ! we rest nor day,
    nor night, nor hour,
[To] practise and travail for your wealth and
    honour.
But, O Lord ! what a prudent man is Policy !
What a deep head he hath to devise and to spy !
    Resp. He is fine, indeed !
    Adul. Also Reformation—
How earnest he is in his operation !
    Resp. I think of him no less.
    Adul. Now, then, Authority,
The stoutest in his office that ever I did see—
I will no farther praise them, Madame ! for,
    doubtless,
They far surmount all praise that my tongue
    can express : [bc ;
Ye may bless the time ye met with such as they
And I do my poor part.
    Resp. I doubt not, Honesty ! [pain.
And condign reward shall ye all have for your
    Adul. I have scarce an house wherein my-
    self to maintain.
    Resp. Honesty shall not lack.
Resp. 14

Adul.   I do not crave nor care ;
We shall take but scraps and refuse, that ye
    may spare ;
We will not encroach the people's commodity ;
We shall take only that may come with honesty.
    Resp.   Christ's blessing have ye ! but, lo !
    yonder cometh People.
    Adul.   I had thought as soon to have met
    here Paul's steeple !

ACTUS TERTII, SCENA TERTIA.

People. Adulation. Respublica.

People.   Where's   Rice - Puddingcake ?   I
    pray God she be in heal.
Adul.   Who ? Rice-Puddingcake ?
People.   Yea ! alise dicts commonweal.
Adul.   I know her not.
People.   Mass ! you liest valeslie in your
    heart !
She is this way, che wa'r't—a false harlot you
    art !
Adul.   I know Respublica.
People.   Yea, marry ! where is she ?
Adul.   She is busy now.
People.   Mass ! ere ich go, chill her zee,
For this way she came.
    Resp.   Let my people come to me !
    Adul.   God forbid, else !   Come on, People !
    is this same she ?
People.   Yea, malkin is't !
    Resp.   People ! what would you with me
    now ?

    People.   Marry, mustress, madame, my lady !
    how do you?

    Resp.   Even so so, People ! I thank you with
    all my heart :

And I hope for better.

    People.   Then let poor volk ha zome part ;

Vor we ignoram people, whom itch do perzent,

Wer ne'er zo i-polld, zo wrong, and zo i-torment.

Lord Jhese Christ, when he was i-pounst and
    i-pilate,   [late.

Was ner zo i-trounst, as we have been of years

    Adul.   How so? who hath wrought to you
    such extremity?

    People.   Nay ! to tell how zo passeth our
    captivity.

    Resp.   It passeth any man's imagination.

    People.   You zai zouth ; it passeth any man's
    madge mason ;

Vor we think ye love us well as e'er ye did.

    Resp.   My love towards you, my people,
    cannot be hid.

    People.   And we think ye would we zelie
    poor volk did well.

    Resp.   And better than e'er ye did ; if how,
    I could tell.

    People.   And we think ye would we zelie poor
    volk should thrive.   [alive !

    Resp.   Yea, doubtless, as any like creature

    Adul.   What need ye of her good will,
    towards you, to doubt?

    People.   Peace, thou, with zorow ! and let
    me tell my tall owt.

    Resp.   Say on, my good People ! let me hear
    your mind.

    People.   Bum vai ! we ignoram people beeth
    not zo blind

But we passeive there falleth of corn and cattle,
Wull, sheep, wood, lead, tin, iron and other
    metal,
And of all things, enough vor good and bad,
And as commediens vor us, as e'er we had ;
And yet, the price of everything is zo dear,
As though the ground did bring vorth no such,
    nowhere.

    Resp.   Indeed ! I have enough, if it be well
    ordered ;
But few folk the better, if I be misordered.

    People.   Nay ! now you zai zouth ; e'en
    this same way goeth the hare :
Ill ordering 'tis hath made both you and we
    threadbare.

    Adul.   What naughty folks were they ? can
    you their names read ?

    People.   Yea ! that I scan ; a whole mess of
    om for a need.
There is vorst and vormost Flattery—ill a thee !
A slipper, sugar-mouthed whorecop, as can be.
He fleareth on you, and beareth us fair in hand ;
And, therewhile, robbeth both you and we of
    our land.
Then cometh the sour, rough, crabbed child
    Oppression :
He tumbleth whom a lust out of possession.
Then is there the third—I scannot member his
    name—
What call ye this same, fellows !—God give
    them a shame—
That beeth still climbing up aloft for promidence,
And cannot be content with their state !

    Adul.   Insolence ?
    People.   Yea, this same is he, Zoriless !
    Resp.   Nay, Insolence !

People. Well, he'll roil all the roast alone,
  cha hard it zaid ;
Or else, make the best of them aghast and
  afraid.
And zuch good men as could, and would, order
  you well,
He is so copped, he will not suffer to mell.
If they will not be rold, then hence, out of
  favour ;
[Yea, and per]haps corrupt om zore vor their
  labour !   [vice
Yet he, and th' other twain work all after the
Of cha-forget-tone-name, t'other is Covetise.
This hungry whorecop hath such a policate
  wit,
That he teacheth them to rake and scrape up
  each whit.
And zo these vowre—but it shall never come
  out for me—
Volk think will never cease to spoil both you
  and me.
Vor, sometime they face us, and call us peason
  knaves ;
And zwareth : God's bones ! they will make us
  all slaves.
Therevore, chwas besirance your ladydom to
And to give you warning.   [zee,
  Resp.   Hear ye this, Honesty?
  People. Well, and God amend all, and a be
    zo good a clerk—
  Resp. Hear ye this, Honesty?
  People. —though tinkers should lack work.
  Resp. I am put in comfort all shall shortly
    amend—
  Adul. It is in good way already ; else, God
    defend !

Resp.   Lo, People ! hearest thou this ? be of
good cheer !

People.   Yea ! ich hear his vair words : but
what beeth we the near ?

Resp.   People ! understand ye that this is
Honesty ?

People.   Where a be, trow ? mass ! cha zeen
zome as zmothe as he,

Have be a trial, be vound valse flatterers to be.

Resp.   I take this man for no such : this is
Honesty !

People.   A gay smoult smirking whorecop
'tis ; zo mot I thee !

Resp.   Well, credit my words, People ! this
is Honesty.

People.   When Is[e] find it, chil believe it !

Resp.   'Tis Honesty !

People.   I scry him mercy, then !

Resp.   He and Authority,

Joining with Policy and Reformation,

Travail to restore th' old wealth to this nation.

People.   Whough ! then chil wa'r't all within
two years as plenty

As 'twas any time within these years twice
twenty :

But how may we know, and see, that this thing
is true ?

Adul.   Ye shall prove, at length, by th' effect
that shall ensue.

People.   Nay ! and we shall alway be served
but with shales ;

Then chil believe, e'en still, that vain words
beeth but tales.

Adul.   The thing, already, to such forward-
ness is brought,

That much to your benefit is already wrought.

People.   Yea? what any good act have ye
  already done?

Adul.   It is but young days yet ; things are
  but now begun :

The fruit of our doings cannot so soon appear.

But, People ! ye shall feel it within seven year :

Ye know it is no small work, from so great
  decay—

Resp.   People ! he saith truth.

Adul.   —to set all in good stay.

Therefore, be ye quiet, and hope for a good
  end !

People.   Yes ! chil tarry laisure, and take
  what God shall send.

Resp.   Then, People ! let us twain depart in
  quietness ;

For, this talking here may hinder their business.

People.   Come on ! I chil wait avore you, and
  be your man.   [*Exeant.*

Adul.   And I will to my fellows as fast as I
  can.

Be they gone? farewell, they ! God send them
  both the pip !

But, in faith, People ! I will have you on the
  hip ;

I will be even with you for your broad carping—

Ah, ye peasant wretch ! on us four to be harping !

And yet, must we our matters handle discreetly ;

Or else, I fear, it will end not very sweetly.

But now, I would Avarice, or else Insolence,

Or Oppression were here rather than sixpence.

And lo, where Avarice cometh ! a wolf in the
  tale,

(As the proverb saith)—what doth he after him
  hale ?

ACTUS TERTII, SCENA QUARTA.

AVARICE. ADULATION. OPPRESSION.

Avar. Come on, sweet bags of gold! come
on, with a good will!
I, on you so tender, and ye so froward still?
Come forward, I pray you, sweet bags! ah,
will ye so?   [no.
Come! or I must draw you, whether ye will or
I know your desire; ye would fain be in my
chest—   [rest!
When the belly is full, the bones would be at
Be content, awhile! I will couch you all up
soon   [moon.
Where ye shall not be spied, neither of sun nor
What now, brother Honesty! what pry ye
this way?   [say?
Is there anything here that is yours—can ye
Look off from my bags! it is a pretty matter:
Ye can see no green cheese but your teeth will
water!
 Adul. *In nomine Patris*, hast thou got all
this sens?
 Avar. Why, thinkest thou I have sat idle
since I went hence?
Nay! I have filled my little purses too, each one.
 Adul. Hast thou so indeed? thou art a
fellow alone.
 Avar. With old angelots and Edwardes I
think I have.
Come forth! how say ye, sir? peep out, ye little
knave!
How think you by this bunting? is he full or no?
And his fellows all, doth not their skin stretch
for woe?

Now these little buttons, no bigger than two
    nuts,   [their guts?
Have they not played gluttons, and filled well
    Adul.   But look! who cometh yonder, puffing
    and tuffing?
    Avar.   Come the devil, if him lust, staring
    and snuffing!

ACTUS TERTII, SCENA QUINTA.

OPPRESSION. AVARICE. ADULATION.

    Oppr.   In all my whole life was I never
    wearier.
    Avar.   Come near, on God's half! the
    mo knaves, the merrier!
Where have ye lost your breath? in some
    coffer diving?
    Oppr.   Shouldering among them for a piece
    of a living.
    Adul.   And what, are you now in any good
    hope to thrive?
    Oppr.   Faith! if I lust, I may wear mitres
    four or five;
I have so many half bishoprics, at the least.
    Adul.   By th' arms of Calais! then am I a
    very beast.
    Avar.   Why, what hast thou gotten to thy
    share in this space?
    Adul.   Three hundred pound by the year, and
    one manor place.
    Avar.   Ah, the passion of God! three hundred
    pound! and no more?
    Adul.   Is not that fair for him that had
    nothing before?

  Avar. What, three hundred pound by years !
  call thee Honesty ?
Call thee a knave ! thou shamest our fraternity !
Three hundred pound ! if some man had been
  in thy room,
A thousand pound a year, ere this time, might
  have come.
Three hundred pound a year ! against our next
  meeting
Get more ! or, I shall give a homely greeting.
  Adul. He here hath flitched the bishoprics
  already.
  Avar. Yea ! I can him thank ; he hath been
  somewhat speedy.
  Oppr. But yet have I left many a good
  gobbet loose :   [goose !
Change thou for the rest ! give a feather for a
  Adul. Didst thou with any one of them make
  such exchange ?
  Oppr. Yea ! I almost left them never a farm
  nor grange.
I told them, Respublica at their wealth did
  grutch ;   [much.
And, the fifth penny they had was, for them, too
So Authority and I, did with them so chop
That we left the best of them a threadbare
  bishop.
To some we left one house, to some we left
  none ;
The best had but his see place, that he might
  keep home.
We informed them, and we deformed them ;
We conformed them, and we reformed them !
  Adul. And what gave ye them in your per-
  mutations ?
  Oppr. Bare parsonages of appropriations,

Bought from Respublica, and first emprowed ;
Then at the highest extent to bishops allowed,
Let out to their hands for fourscore and
    [nineteen] year.
    Avar. Lo, cousin Honesty ! lo ! do ye hear
      this gear ?   [Lammas !
Faith ! your marsship will thrive at the latter
    Adul. I now grant myself to have been a
      very ass ;   [luck.
But all is not yet gone, in case I have good
    Oppr. No ! there is yet enough left for a
      better pluck.   [not die ;
For some of them were aged, and yet would
And some would, in nowise, to our desires apply.
But we have rods in piss for them everyone,
That they shall be fleeced, if we reign, one by one.
    Avar. And how did all frame with our
      Mounsire Authority ?
    Oppr. At length he won the full superiority.
    Adul. But the rude gross People at him
      repineth sore ;
And against us, all four, with a wide throat
    doth he roar.
But soft ! peace ! methinketh I hear him hem
    and hake ;   [take.
If we meet here, all four, we shall some order

ACTUS TERTII, SCENA SEXTA.

INSOLENCE. ADULATION. OPPRESSION. AVARICE.

    Insol. What, mine old friends, all three ? by
    my truth, sirs, well found !
    Adul. and Oppr. Faith, sir ! most heartily
    welcome into this ground.

Insol.   Bones! what have we here?

Avar.   Aha!

Insol.   Bags of money, I trow!

Avar.   Have we? Nay! I have; but none
   for you, that I know!   [harms;
Lo, sir! thus might an honest man come to his
I will lie down on them, and keep them in mine
   arms.

Insol.   Hast thou got all this? I myself have
   not so much.

Avar.   Then have ye whole towns and castles;
   I have none such.
Yet will ye not deny, I judge, in my fancy,
That ye got them by the drift of me, Policy.

Insol.   I confess that.   [worth.

Oppr.   All my lands are scarce so much

Avar.   They were less when I, Policy, first
   set you forth.

Adul.   He hath purses with gold; would I
   had so many!   [have any.

Avar.   It were pity that such a goose should
Your good marsship appointed me to crumbs
   and scraps;
But Policy will live by his neighbours, perhaps!
But thus, I see, you would poll me, an ye wist
   how;   [vow!
Therefore, I will go hoard it, I make God a
I will make it sure under mine doors and mine
   locks;   [stocks!
And, who but looketh that way, shall sit in nine

Insol.   Nay! first declare to us how thou
   didst all this get.   [tacle set;

Avar.   For your learning I will you a spec-
But first get ye from me, and stand a good
   way hence;   [licence!
This shall not lie within your reach, by your

Nay, yet farther! lest ye take my bags for
    bloodings;   [puddings.
For, such hungry dogs will slab up sluttish
  Adul. Is it well now?
  Avar.   Yea! now hardely stand there still,
And the names of my bags to you declare I will.
First and foremost, this bag is my very clear
    gain
Of leases encroached, and forthwith sold again.
This bag is mine interest of this year's usury;
And this is of matters bolstered up with perjury.
This is bribes above my stipend in office;
This fifth I have by selling of benefices.
This is my rents that my clerks yearly render
    me,
To be and continue in office under me.
This same I got by sectorship of my mother—
A vengeance on her, old witch, for such another!
This bag have I kept of other sectorships whole,
Which the mad knaves would have scattered
    by penny dole.   [law;
This is of church goods, scraped up without a
For which was as quick scambling as ever I
    saw: [them louts,
Of their plate, their jewels, and copes, we made
Stopping People's barking with linen rags and
    clouts.
They had th' altar cloths, th' albs, and amices,
With the sindons in which were wrapt the
    chalices.
This ninth hath beguiled the king of his custom;
This tenth of selling counterfeit wares hath
    come.
Now this eleventh is of tallow, butter, cheese,
Corn, rawcloths, leather—by stealth sent be-
    yond seas.

This twelfth is of grain, bell-metal, tin and
    lead—
Conveyed out by creeks when Respublica was
    in bed.   [daws,
This thirteenth I filled through facing out of
Both from lands and goods, by pretence of the
    laws.   [Policy ;
Thus, these thirteen small jobs are mine by
All men must shift for a poor living honestly.
If e'er I bestow them it shall be, the next Lent,
To the prior of Prickingham and his co[n]vent.
> *Adul.* Well now, we may come near ; may
>   we not, if we lust ?
> *Avar.* Ye are near enough: out of my reach
>   I dare you trust.
> *Adul.* Well now, let us sing, if it please
>   Authority ;

To refresh our spirits it is restority.
> *Insol.* I reck not, for company sake, to sing
>   once [more].
> *Avar.* I have less mind to sing now than I
>   had before :

Then had I no lust to sing, because I was bare;
And now, how to keep that I have got, I do
    care.
> *Oppr.* Solace we must needs have, when
>   that we are weary.
> *Adul.* It prolongeth life of man to be
>   merry.
> *Avar.* An if ye sing so much, Honesty !
>   without fail,   [battle.

Christ and you, at length, I fear, will make a
But go to ! sing on ! if there be no remedy—
An ye look at my bags ye mar my melody.
> > *Cantent:* " *Hey, nony, nony, ho for
> > money !* " etc.

Oppr. Now, about profit devise we ourselves
abroad.
Avar. Yea, and hear ye, masters! while
time is, lay on load!
Consider! ye have but a time of haymaking;
And harvest is not mowed without painstaking.
Now, time will not tarry; and, therefore, take
good heed!
Despatch while time serveth, and all your
matte[r]s speed!   [apace!
Time hath no rein nor bridle, but renneth
    Insol. Mark Policy's words, sirs! excellent
in our case.   [property:
    Avar. And time hath this one ungracious
To blab at length, and open all that he doth see.
Then, a daughter eke he hath, called Verity;
As unhappy a long-tongued girl as can be:
She bringeth all to light; some she bring[eth]
to shame;   [blame.
She careth not a groat what man hath thank or
If men be praiseworthy, she doth so declare
them;   [them.
And, if otherwise, in faith! she doth not spare
    Oppr. We will feather our nests ere time
may us espy;
Or Verity have power, our doings to descry.
    Avar. Remember this verse: *Ut sint omnia
salva*,
Fronte capillata, post hec occasio calva.
    Oppr. Make me understand that fine rag of
rhetoric!   [bishopric!
    Avar. Lo! here a fine fellow to have a
A verse of Latin he cannot understand;
Yet, dareth he presume, boldly to take in hand,
Into a deanery or archideaconry to chop;
And to have the livelood away from a bishop!

Oppr.   A mercy! show thy verse, and leave
this persuasion!

Avar.   Forsooth, sir! it was of the goddess
Occasion!

She weareth a great long tuffet of hair before;

And, behind, hath not one hair, neither less
nor more!

Whereby is taught you that, when Occasion is,

Ye must take it betime, or of your purpose miss.

Adul.   Then, while Occasion doth now serve
so well,   [tell.

I pray you, give ear to one thing that I must

Insol. and Oppr.   What is that?

Adul.   Mounsire! if ye hear People mumbling,

Ye must storm, and sharply take him up for
stumbling.   [since,

Ye would not think what he said, a little while

Of us, to Respublica, in mine own presence!

Insol.   When I meet them next I shall tell
them both my mind.

Avar.   And Policy, to help you, will not be
behind.

Adul.   Gentle Respublica was soon pacified;

But People was sturdy, and would not be
qualified.

Avar.   Alas! good, poor, silly soul! bear
her fair in hand,   [land.

And ye may win her, as you lust, to use her

Oppr.   But of goddess Occasion one little
more.   [before:

Avar.   Marry, sir! even as I would have said

She standeth with winged feet on a rolling wheel,

To take flight or any grass may grow on her heel.

And, even while we stand, jangling in this
presence,   [hence.

I dare say she is flown twice twenty score mile

Oppr. Yea? Cock's bones! then adieu!
Insol. Farewell!
Adul. And I am gone!
[*Exeant currentes.*
Avar. Faith! and have after, as fast as I can, anon!
Now, my godamighties! as I did hither tug you,
So will I, on my back, to your lodging lug you;
And sure, if ye can be quiet there, and lie still,
I will shortly bring you mo fetlows; so I will.
I have a good benefice of an hundred marks:
It is small policy to give such to great clerks:
They will take no benefice but they must have all—
A bare clerk can be content with a living small!
Therefore, Sir John Lack-Latin, my friend, shall have mine;
And, of him, may I farm it for eight pounds or nine.
The rest may I reserve to myself for mine own share;
For, we are good feeders of the poor, so we are!
And we patrons are bound to see, (I do you tell),
The church patrimony to be bestowed well.
Other odd corners, besides these, I have many;
Which, with all good speed shall increase your comp[any].
Come on now, therefore! in faith! I do great wrong
To promise you lodging, and keep you thence so long. [*Exeat.*

RESP. 15

ACTUS QUARTI, SCENA PRIMA.

[RESPUBLICA.]

Resp.   O, Lord! what may it mean to be
thus borne in hand;
And yet, none amendment to feel, nor under-
stand?
People doth daily and hourly to me resort,
Challenging my promise of relief and comfort.
I report to him, as my rulers do to me:
People still affirmeth that they devourers be.
The more I do him cheer, the more he doth
despair.
I say, his wealth doth mend; he saith, it doth
appair,
What should I judge of this? may it be
credible,
Or, by any reason, may it be possible
That such four as those, in whom I have put
my trust,
Showing such face of friendship, should be men
unjust?
I will know if People feel yet any redress
Of his former sores, and of his rueful distress.
We shall meet soon, I doubt not, and talk
together.

[*Intrat* PEOPLE.

And lo! as I would wish, he approacheth hither.

ACTUS QUARTI, SCENA SECUNDA.

Respublica. People.

Resp. Well met, People! what place go ye
    now unto?

People. I cham at the farthest to zee how
    you do.

We twain must oftwhiles come physic either
    other;

Vor, we beeth your children, and you beeth our
    mother.

Resp. And how do you mend now, in your
    thrift and your purse?

People. As zour ale in summer; that is, still
    worse and worse!

Resp. People, what should I say?

People. Nay, mass! I scannot tell:

But we ignorams all would fain ye should do
    well.

And how feel you yourself? better than ye did,
    trow?

Resp. Till God send better hap, rather decay
    than grow:

This bringeth me in a conceit of jealousy—

Rather than much good would I speak with
    Policy.

People. Was not he drowned, trow, last
    year, when Conscience was?

Resp. I see him yonder appear; this cometh
    well to pass.

People. Is this same he?

Resp. Yea!

People. An ich heard not you zo zai

Chould zware a had be dead, or else clean
    run away!

ACTUS QUARTI, SCENA TERTIA.

[AVARICE.] RESPUBLICA. PEOPLE.

Avarice. O most noble lady! that I have
not, of late,
Made to you relation how ye stand in state,
Hath not been of negligence, nor to wo[r]k by
stealth ;   [wealth.
But of my deep studies, devising for your
  Resp. To hear the truth thereof, I wished
you to see.
  People. Doth you stud your brains, mas
gentman!—pray you tell me!—
For our lady Ricepudding-cake's commodity?
  Avar. I devise what I can for the prosperity
Of this Lady Respu[b]lica and her people.
  People. That lie, ere this, is flown as far
hence as Poule steeple !
I spray God, ye stud not, as cha hard of zome
elves   [selves !
That study for the common profit of their own
  Avar. To study for both your wealths, I
am a debtor.
  People. Vay, then! as good ne'er a whit, as
ne'er the better.   [without doubt.
  Avar. I do nothing but compass therefore,
  People. I vay, then! thee vent too far a
compass about,
Vor zome good might ha' be doon in all this
season.   [reason !
  Avar. So there is, if to perceive it ye had
  Resp. Truly! I feel myself, hitherto, worse
and worse.
  People. And I svele the same, both in my
ground and my purse ;

Vive or zix year ago chad vowre kine to my pale ;
And, at this prezent hour, cham scarce worth
    a good cow tail ;
And that time chad a widge, and her vole and
    ten sheep ;
Now, I scan geat nothing, myzelf and my wife
    to keep.   [stable,
Then an chad, I be with the king's mass con-
Chould zet myself vorth prettily, and zo chwas
    able ;   [need,
Now, vor lack of a sallet, when my liege hath
Cham vain to take an hat of God's good on my
    head.
And vor God !—my dame, this is but small
    amendment !   [ment?
I scomport me to you : how thinketh your judg-
Compassing ? ka ! ɡentman ! call ye this same
    compassing ?
And, whom shall we twain thank ? you, for this
    compassing ?
    Avar.   No, sir !   [passed !
    People.   Now, by the compass that God com-
    Resp.   Blame have they of God and man,
    that this compassed !
    People.   A small compass more, now, may
    zoon compass, by th' rood !
To make fowerty thousand volks hair grow
    through their hood !
    Avar.   That is their own fault ; not the fault
    of Policy.
    Resp.   God above, He knoweth whose fault
    it is, and not I.   [ing?
    People   But did not ich, daily, give you warn-
    Resp.   Doubtless !
    People.   And did not ich plain me to you ?
    Resp.   I grant no less !

People.   And when ich made my mone, what
      would [ye] me tell?
Resp.   As my hope was; that, at length, all
      thing should be well.
People.   Compassing? ka!
Resp.   People! I put trust in other.
People.   Valse bezeivers of zembity, by God's
      mother!   [tion,
Avar.   Well, suffer me then, for my declara-
To set Authority and Reformation;
That ye may both hear, and charge them as
      well as me.   [it so be.
Resp.   With all my heart, good Policy! let
I pray you call them hither, if they may be got.
People.   Anch hear om; I scan tell whe'er
      they say true or not!

ACTUS QUARTI, SCENA QUARTA.

AVARICE.   INSOLENCE.   RESPUBLICA.
OPPRESSION.   PEOPLE.

Avar.   The foulest   open-mouthed   wretch
      that e'er ye heard!
Insol.   Could thou, by no means, make the
      peasant afeard?
Avar.   No! but anon, I trow! we shall his
      masship trim—   [him.
Convey her away; and then all we three chide
But, whist! and come apace!
Resp.   I hear Policy's voice.   [rejoice:
Avar.   That I met you, so well, I do much
Lady Respublica! would you come her before?
Insol.   Madame, God ye save!
Oppr.   And preserve for ever more!

   Resp. This is happy hap ye come so soon
    together?

   Avar. As I went I met them, both twain,
    hasting hither.

   Resp. Never in better time!

   Insol. Madame! what is your will?

   Oppr. Is there any thing that you would
    say us until?

   Resp. People crieth out, and I am much
    aggrieved

That we feel ourselves in nothing yet relieved.

   Oppr. No? that is not true; many declare
    I can—

   Resp. Even in brief words, I pray you, do
    it than.

   People. Pray you let me spose with this
    same new come gentman.

   Insol. No, sir!

   People. Mass! but chil speak anch can
    spy my time whan?

   Oppr. First, your priests and bishops have
    not as they have had.

   Resp. [When] they had their livings, men
    were both fed and clad.

   Oppr. Yea! but they ought not, by scrip-
    ture, to be called lords.

   Resp. That they rule the church, with scrip-
    ture well accords.

   Oppr. They were proud and covetous, and
    took much upon them.

   People. But they were not covetous that
    took all from them!

   Oppr. The coin also is changed.

   People. Yea! from silver to dross—

'Twas told us vor the best: but poor we bear
    the loss!

When chad with zwet of brows got up a few
        small crumbs,   [sums.
At paying of my debts ich could not make my
My landlord, vor my corn, paid me zuch sums
        and zuch ;
When he should ha't vor rent, it was but half
        zo much.
Zix pence in each shilling was i-strike quite
        away ;
Zo, vor one piece ich took, che was vain to pay
        him tway.
One would think 'twere brass, and zorow have
        I else ;
But, ich ween most part on't was made of our
        old bells !
    Insol.   Yet, if ye mark it well, for one piece
        ye have three ;
Which, for your People is no small commodity.
    People.   Well, I will meddle in this same
        matter no more ;
But Is reck not an 'twere zilver, as 'twas avor.
    Oppr.   People ! ye shall, at length, find it
        all for the best.
    People.   Cha hard our parish clerk say :
        Diuum este, justlum weste.
    Resp.   Undoubtedly, I feel many things are
        amiss !
    People.   Yea ! I scan tell more things yet,
        an me lust, by Jis !
They have all the woods throughout the realm
        destroyed,
Which might have served long years, being well
        employed.
And then, the great cobs have zo take the rest
        to hire,   [fire.
That poor volk cannot get a stick to make a

Then their great grazing hath made flesh so
    dear, I wot,
That poor volk, at shambles, cannot bestow
    their groat.   [may I do?
   Resp. I lament it, People! Alack! what
I, myself, I fear, shall come to ruin too.
Policy! what comfort? when will you ease my
    smart?
   Avar. Ye are as safe, even now, but for
    your false heart,
As any lady of your name in Christendom.
   People. If ich had zo zaid, chad lied, by my
    halidom!
   Resp. Ye hear what People saith, which
    feeleth as I do?
   Avar. But rude People's words, will ye
    give credit unto?   [ling?]
Will ye judge yourself after his foolish [jang-
Ye were well enough till he began his wrangling.
   Insol. Will ye believe People, that hath no
    manner of skill   [ill?
To judge, or to discern what thing is good or
He is so headstrong, he must be bridled with
    laws.
   People. Though zome be stark bedlams, yet
    wise volks beeth no daws!   [obedient
   Insol. We have oft found People most dis-
To orders most requisite and expedient.
Who such a maintainer of wrong opinions
As People, in all countries and dominions?
Ye ought, therefore, to rebuke him, at all hours,
For discouraging any minister of yours.
   Oppr. Ye must tarry time, ere we can your
    purpose serve.
   People. Ye[a], and then, while the grass shall
    grow, the horse shall sterve.

    Insol. Do ye not see this, by all experience
plain,

That men, from diseases recover[ed] again

Do, after sickness passed, remain a long time
    weak ?

    Resp. People, hark! Authority doth good
    reason speak.

    Insol. So ye, though oppressed with long
    adversity,   [perity.

Yet, doubt not! are toward wealth and pros-

    Resp. Lo! People! to hope a while longer
    shall be best.

    People. Well, then cham perswaged to do
    at your inquest.

    Insol. Madame! mistrust not us, your pain-
    ful ministers!

    Avar. Never had lady more watchful officers!

    Oppr. For my part, I will swear the gospel
    book upon,

That if the laws I have made should, everyone,

Redound to mine own singular commodity,

They could not be friendlier framed than they be.

    Insol. Therefore, repose yourself, Madame,
    awhile, and wink!

Ye are in better case toward than you can think.

    Avar. We shall here remain, and give
    People good counsel ;

Quiet for to be, till Policy may prevail.

    Resp. He will do well with your good in-
    formations.

    People. Yea, vay! chil volow their good
    exaltations.

    Resp. Then I leave you all here to God: I
    will depart.   [*Exeat* RESP[UBLICA].

    People. Now, ho! destructions to member
    in my heart?

Avar.   Destructions? ye miser!
Insol.   Ye peasant!
Oppr.   Ye lout!
Insol.   [Can ye naught] else do but rage, and
rave, and cry out?
Oppr.   And cannot tell on whom?
Avar.   No more than can a daw!
Oppr.   Crow against your betters!
Insol.   And murmur against the law!
Let me hear thee prate as thou hast done here-
tofore!
Avar.   Or trouble Lady Respublica any more!
Oppr.   Thou canst not see, thou wretch!
canst thou, when thou art well?
Avar.   Is't part of thy play with such high
matters to mell?
Insol.   Doth it become thee to bark with
such a wide throat?
Avar.   And to have an oar in everybody's
boat?
Insol.   If thou do so again, it shall with thee
be worse.
Oppr.   We shall wring and pinch thee, both
by belly and purse.
Insol.   I would advise you, friend! to grunt
and groan no more.
Oppr.   Do the like again, and thou shalt
rue it full sore!
Avar.   It were best for you, friend! all
murmuring to cease.
People.   Bum vay, then! chil e'en go home,
and vair hold my peace.
Insol.   Do so by my rede, and fall to honest
labour.
Avar.   Hence home, and be quiet! and thou
shalt find favour.

People.   Then chil bid you varewell !
Oppr.   No words, but hence, apace !
This was done as should be.
    Avar.   This was done in right place.
    People.   But ho ! one word erch go ; ye'll
        give volk leave to think ?
    Oppr.   No, marry ! will we not, nor to look,
        but wink !
    People.   Yes, by Gis ! but chil lo[ok] ; nay,
        lo there ! thought is free,
And a cat, they zaith, may look on a king,
        pardy !   [*Exeat.*
    Insol.   Now, where do we be come ? I,
        home !   [*Exeat.*
Oppr.   And I abroad !   [*Exeat.*
    Avar.   And I must see what feet about my
        door have trod.   [*Exeat.*

ACTUS QUINTI, SCENA PRIMA.

[MISERICORDIA.]

Miser.   Wherein appeareth the graciousness
    of God
More than, infinitely to exceed man's goodness,
But that He keepeth back the sharp stroke of
        His rod   [ness ?
When man would rage in most furious wood-

Scarce any amends may man's eagerness
        appease ;   [forget ;
Yea, and though he forgive, he will not soon
Towards true penitence God's wrath forthwith
        doth cease,
And He, their past sins, behind His back doth set.

Of long sufferance He is with weakness to bear,
While any hope of amendment doth remain ;
And though He plague sinners, to call them
　　　home by fear,
Yet His mercy and grace are aye ready again.

His grievous displeasure dureth not for ever.
And why ? *quia miserationes ejus* ;
Which to show He chiefly delighteth ever,
Manent super omnia opera ejus.

It grieveth Him sore when He must needs take
　　　vengeance ;
His delight and glory is mercy to practise ;
His tender compassion, on true repentance,
He hath still, from the beginni[n]g, sought
　　　t' exercise.

The mass of this world in His mercy did He
　　　frame :
The sky, earth, and sea His mercy replenished ;
In His mercy did He after redeem the same,
When else, remediless, it must have perished.

In His mercy was Israel delivered
From the 'gyptian thraldom and captivity ;
In His mercy the same through the Red Sea
　　　was led ;
And through wilderness to a land of liberty.

Sith that time all commonwealths He hath
　　　protected ;
And to such as, with earnest prayer, have made
　　　moan,
Me, Compassion, He hath amically directed
To revive and recover them every one.

Now, lastly, hath he heard the most doleful
    lament
Of woeful Respublica, his darling most dear!
Therefore me, Compassion, with speed he hath
    sent,   [cheer.
Her most sorrowful heart to recomfort and

I tarry her coming that I may her salute:
And lo! methinketh I see her appear in place;
Of friendship devoid, and of succour destitute—
I will hear her, and then give words of solace.

ACTUS QUINTI, SCENA SECUNDA.

Respublica. Misericordia. Avarice. Adulation.

Resp. O Lord! hast Thou for ever closed
    up Thine ear?   [hear?
Wilt Thou never more the desolate's prayer
Wilt Thou still turn away Thy face from my
    distress?
Wilt Thou clean forsake me and leave me
    comfortless?   [heart,
The secret sighs, and sobs, and prayers of mine
Shall they not forever Thine eyes to me convert?
I grant that mine offences have so much
    deserved;   [served?
But for whom, save sinners, is this mercy re-
[Thou reservst it] so, which hitherto hath been
    just;   [mistrust.
Despair, Lord! I will not; nor Thy goodness
Lo[ok] down on my distress! and for Thy glory
    sake,
Though I be ill worthy it, mercy on me take!

Miser.   Now will I speak to her.
Resp.   Who maketh me afeard?
Miser.   No, I will thee comfort: God hath
    thy prayer heard ;   [trust !
And now, Respublica, be of good hope and
Resp.   O Lord ! now do I see that Thou art
    ever just.   [lica !
Miser.   I am sent to recomfort thee, Respub-
Resp.   O Lady Compassion ! Misericordia !
Miser.   What say ye to me? What, woman !
    can ye not speak?   [break.
I am come down, all your sorrows at once to
Speak, woman !
Resp.   Misericordia !
Miser.   Out, comfortably !
Ye shall have now no more cause to speak
    despairably.
Resp.   My heart, in God's mercy, is so dilated,
That my very spirit to heaven is elated.
O Lady Compassion ! welcome, verament !
Ever be God praised that you, to me, hath
    sent !
Miser.   Now that I have put you in sure
    hope of relief,
I must go fet Verity to try out all your grief.
Verity shall oper how your decay hath grown;
And then, the causers thereof shall be over-
    thrown.
Resp.   Who be the causers thereof I cannot
    discern :
But yond cometh one of them that do me govern.
Miser.   What is his name?
Resp.   Policy !
Miser.   Policy is good ;
He doth work you many good things of likeli-
    hood.

Avar.   A vengeance upon him! and God
   give him His curse!
I am besieged now of every cutpurse;
I can go nowhere now; in city, neither town,
But Piers Pickpurse playeth at organs under
   my gown.
   Miser.   What talketh he?
   Avar.   Who speaketh yond, Respublica?
   Resp.   What of the pickpurse?
   Avar.   Forsooth, dame Respublica!
I said, an we had two pillories mo, 'twere no
   the worse;
For it is a light thing now to meet Piers Pick-
   purse.
God preserve you, right fair lady! and Christ
   you save!   [have?
Who are you? and what would ye in this country
   Resp.   This same is the Lady Misericordia,
Sent from God purposely.
   Avar.   Unto you, Respublica?
   Miser.   Yea!
   Avar.   Then must ye needs be most heartily
   welcome: [dom!
We had ne'er more need of you, by my hali-
There be in this country which, but ye comfort
   [send],   [end.
Are full like to make both a mad and a short
   Miser.   I will go to do that I said, Respublica!
And return with speed.
   Resp.   Sweet Misericordia!
                     [*Exeat Mi*[*sericordi*]*a.*
   Avar.   Good Misericordia, now! and lady
   most dear!—   [here?
Christ blister on your heart! what make you
   Resp.   Come back, Policy!
   Avar.   I come!

Resp.   Whither would ye now?

Avar.   Convey myself hence honestly, if I
   wist how.

Resp.   When come ye, Policy? what look
   ye? something lost!   [cost.

Avar.   Anon! if I tarry, it will turn to my

Resp.   Ah, friend, Policy!

Avar.   Yea!

Resp.   Now shall I be in bliss.

Avar.   Thanks to God!—we must find provision for this.

Resp.   Ha!   [you save?

Avar.   Did not I e'er tell you that God would
Ye may see now what it is, good rulers to have.

Resp.   Ye say truth; but look! yonder cometh
   Honesty.

Avar.   Pray God, amen!

Resp.   Yes, look else!

Avar.   What news bringeth he?

Adul.   I should speak a word in th' ear of
   Policy;
If I may not so, I will speak it openly.

Resp.   I have not seen you a great while,
   Honesty.   [be?

Adul.   O noble Lady Respublica! well you

Resp.   All shall be now, such news I have
   to me brought.

Adul.   I hear it told for truth, Policy, all
   will be nought.

Resp.   Hearest thou any joyful news abroad,
   or not?

Adul.   Yea! I have certain news, which are
   both brim and hot.
There is new start-up, a lady called Verity.

Resp.   Then am I all safe, and sure of prosperity.

RESP.   16

How was it spoken?

    Adul. This is Latin, gross and blunt :

Misericordia et Veritas sibi obviaverunt ;

That is, Mercy and Truth are both met together.

    Resp. Then will it not be long ere they both
come hither.

    Avar. Hither? how so?

    Resp.   Yea, both Mercy and Verity.

    Avar. A pestle on them both, saving my
charity !   [it :

But soft, brother Honesty ! ye might mistake

Of which Verity was 't, trow you, that they
spake it?   [daughter.

    Adul. Of the general Verity, Old Time's

    Avar. Faith ! they were not our friends that
first hither brought her.

Old Time's daughter? that shuttle-brained,
tall, long man !

That ne'er standeth still, but flyeth as fast as
he can,

Much like as he swimmed or glided upon ice?

    Adul. Yea !

    Resp. For all that, of wise men, he is
thought most wise.   [his head ;

    Avar. I know him ; he carrieth a clock on

A sand glass in his hand, a dial in his forehead.

    Resp. Ye say truth, Policy : the same is
very he.

    Avar. Old Time, the eavesdropper : I know
him, pardy !

An ancient turner of houses upside down,

And a common consumer of city and town.

Old Time's daughter, (quod he?), I shrew his
naked heart !

Many of my friends hath he brought to pain
and smart.

Compassion and that Truth come hither to you?

   Resp.   Mercy, before ye came, promised so
   right now.

   Avar.   It is no time now, Honesty, to be idle.

   Adul.   Something breweth?

   Avar.   It is time for us to bridle.

Well, go your ways, afore, in all haste,
   Honesty:

And tell Reformation and Authority

That both these ladies, in all goodly fashion,

Must be entertained here in this nation.

Madame Respublica! is't not your pleasure so?

   Resp.   What else? in all the haste, Honesty,
   see ye go:

   Avar.   Say further, that I would we four,
   anon, might meet

Here, or where they will, save in the open street.

And hear you, Honesty!

   Adul.   What now?

   Avar.   A little near!

Provide in any wise that Verity come not here:

Let Insolence and Oppression keep her hence.

   Adul.   We shall, all three, therein do our
   best diligence.

   Avar.   Bid them well remember the world
   will wax quaisy;

Some of us, ere long, may hap leap at a daisy;

Or put out the *i* of Misericordia,

And without an *i* play e'en plain trussing corda.

                    Exeat ADUL[ATION].

   Resp.   Policy, what is it that ye talk there
   so long?   [do wrong.

   Avar.   I send instructions that they may not

   Resp.   Send ye aught to him that may not
   be told to me?   [trouble ye?

   Avar.   Should we with ery trifling trifle

Well then, ye look for these two ladies, [I am
    sure].   [their cure.
    Resp. I trust they will not fail on me to do
    Avar. I told you ever, did I not, that your
      wealth would frame?
    Resp. I shall reward your pains : or else I
      were to blame.
    Avar. Then best I go now straight to my
      fellows and see—   [unready be ;
    Resp. That things needful for us may not
Do so, I pray you !
    Avar.   Fare ye well, Respublica,
Till I see you next !   [*Exeat.*
    Resp.   Now, Misericordia !
When shall be thy pleasure ? bring hither
    Verity ?
Behold ! e'en with the word speaking, where
    they both be.
            Intrant MI[SERICORDI]A *and* VERITAS.

ACTUS QUINTI, SCENA TERTIA.

MISERICORDIA.   VERITAS.   RESPUBLICA.

    Miser. I daresay Respublica thinketh the
    time long.
    Ver. Who can blame her, having endured
    so much wrong ?
But as meat and drink, and other bodily food
Is never found to be so pleasant, nor so good,
As when fretting hunger and thirst hath pinched
    afore ;   [more,
And as health after sickness is sweeter ever-
So, after decay and adversity overcome,
Wealth and prosperity shall be double welcome.

Miser. How now, Respublica? have I not
been long hence?

Resp. Come ye first or last, ye bless me
with your presence.

Miser. As I was commanded, I bring you
Verity,

To help you, your people, and their posterity.

Ver. Dear jewel Respublica! I do you
embrace.

Resp. I thank your goodness, and submit
me to your grace.

Miser. Embrace Verity for ever, Respublica,
And cleave fast to her!

Resp. Yes, Misericordia! [Verity!

Miser. Now please it you to declare, sister
How she may recover her old prosperity;
Her honour, her wealth, her riches, her sub-
stance, [her puissance.
Her commons, her people, her strength, and

Ver. All this will be recovered incontinent;
And, to better state also, by good government.

Resp. No lady of my name upon earth, I
esteem, [been:
Hath had better administers than mine have
Policy, Reformation, and Authority.

Miser. These three be very good.

Resp. And the four[th], Honesty.

Ver. But what if these, which have had you
and yours to keep, [sheep?
Have been ravening wolves in the clothing of

Resp. If I heard not you, Verity, such
sentence give,
By no man's persuasion I could it believe.

Ver. Ah, good Respublica! thou hast been
abused;
Whom thou chosest are vices to be refused.

Whom thou callst Honesty, is Adulation ;
And he that in pretence was Reformation,
Is indeed Oppression and huge violence ;
Whom thou callst Authority, is proud Insolence;
Then he that was Policy, the chief man of price,
Indeed is most stinking and filthy Avarice.
He first inveigled thee, and his purpose to
     frame,
Cloaked each of these vices with a virtuous
     name.

  Resp.   Benedicite ! is this a possible case?
  Ver.   Ye shall see it proved true before your
     own face ;
They shall be convinced before you, one by one.
  Resp.   O Lord ! what marvel if my thrift
     were well nigh gone?
But what redress shall I have hereof? and
     when ?
  Miser.   Such as may be most fit, and as soon
     as we can.
Justice and peace are appointed to descend ;
Th' one to keep you quiet ; the other you to
     defend.
As soon as we four sisters together shall be
     met,
An order for your establishment shall be set :
By the eternal providence it is decreed so.
  Resp.   O most merciful Lord, all praise be
     thee unto !
  Miser.   I will leave you here with my sister
     Verity,
And learn of their coming with all celerity.
  Ver.   Ye need not ; for I know they be now
     very near ;
And, behold ! they begin already to appear.

ACTUS QUINTI, SCENA QUARTA.

PAX. JUSTITIA. VERITAS. MISERICORDIA.
RESPUBLICA.

Peace. Now, once again, in God let us two
    sisters kiss,
In token of our joining to make a perfect bliss.
Justitia. And now, let us never be sundered
    any more
Till we may Respublica perfectly restore.
Ver. Let us meet them, sister Misericordia!
Miser. And unto their sight present Res-
    publica.   [and Verity!
Just., Pax. All hail, most dear sisters, Mercy
And, all hail, Respublica, with all sincerity!
Resp. O ye ladies celestial! how much am
    I bound   [ground,
With thanks to fall flat before you on the
That ye thus vouchsafe a forlorn creature
By your heave[n]ly protection to recure.
Just. I, Justice, from heaven am come you
    to visit.   [inhabit.
Pax. And I, Peace, for ever with you to
Miser. And all we four sisters, to th' utmost
    of our power,
Shall restore, establish, and defend your honour.
Just. We shall first restore your most happy
    estate,   [late.
And suppress all them that had made you deso-
Ver. Verity shall all truth open as it is.
Just. I, Justice, shall redress whate'er is
    found amiss.
Miser. I, Mercy, where the member may
    recured be,
Shall temper the rigour and slake extremity.

Pax. I, Peace, when th' uncurable is clean
cut away   [aye.
And th' ill made good, shall flourish for ever and
Resp. And I, which cannot otherwise your
goodness deserve,
Shall your wholesome directions duly observe.
And what if Insolence shall come, or Avarice?
Ver. Detest them, abhor them, and refuse
their service.
I doubt not but they will be still haunting hither,
Till we four shall them four take here altogether.
Miser. Now, sisters! go we, and Respublica
with us,
To be new apparelled otherwise than thus.
Just. Come on, Respublica! with us to
wealth from woe:
God hath given us in charge that it must be so.
Ver. The blissful renovation ye shall reign in
Must, from henceforth, now immediately begin.
Cantent: " The mercy of God,"
et exeant, etc.

ACTUS QUINTI, SCENA QUINTA.

AVARICE. ADULATION.

Avar. Such greedy covetous folk as now-of-
days been,   [seen;
I trow, before these present days were never
An honest man can go in no place of the street
But he shall, I think, with an hundred beggars
meet.   [Charity!"
"Give for God's sake!" "Give for saint
"Give for our Lady's sake!" "Give for the
Trinity!"

"Give in the way of your good-speed!" "Give,
　　give!" "Give, give!"
Find we our money in the street, do they believe?
If I had not a special grace to say Nay,
I were but undone amongst them, in one day.
But who cometh yond? Honesty? he cometh
　　in haste.

Adul. I seek Policy.

Avar. 　　　　　　　Here, boy!

Adul. 　　　　　　　　　　All is in waste!

Avar. How so? 　　　　　　　　[we do.

Adul. We strive against the stream, all that

Avar. Wherein?

Adul. That Verity come not this place unto.
For wot ye what?

Avar. I shall when he have spoke the word.

Adul. Justice, and Peace too, with full con-
　　sent and accord
Are come down from heaven and have kissed
　　together.

Avar. God give grace that they twain also
　　come not hither!

Adul. As Mercy and Truth *sibi obviaverunt*,
So *Justicia et Pax osculatae sunt.*

Avar. Is it true? are they come?

Adul. 　　　　　　And have kissed together.

Avar. Then carry in apace for fear of foul
　　weather.
Have they kissed together?

Adul. 　　　　Yea!

Avar. 　　　　　　　What needeth that?
Men should kiss women—and what point be
　　they at?

Adul. All the four sisters, I do you t' under-
　　stand,
Have already taken Respublica in hand.

They four progress with her in every border,
And mar all that ever we have set in order.

> *Avar.* And what doth Insolence, or what
> saith he to that?
>
> *Adul.* He stampeth, he stareth, and snuffeth
> sore thereat.
>
> *Avar.* I advise him to storm, and to show
> himself stout:

They be women and perchance may be faced
out ;
And Peace is an honest lady and a quiet.

> *Adul.* Verity and Justice are not for our diet.
>
> *Avar.* Then Mercy is a good one ; I like her
> well.
>
> *Adul.* Yet oft turneth she her face away,
> and will not mell.
>
> *Avar.* Well—fall back, fall edge—I am once
> at a point,

If Respublica come, t' adventure a joint.

> *Adul.* She is fresh and gay and flourisheth ;
> who but she?
>
> *Avar.* Who brought it to such pass, will I
> tell her, but we?

Or else, making these new ladies of her weary,
We should triumph and reign.

> *Adul.*   Oh, never so merry !
>
> *Avar.* Well, go to our company, I will
> remain here ;

I may perhaps see Dame Respublica appear :
I will in hand with her, and make a good face.

> *Adul.* And what shall I do?
>
> *Avar.*   Give warning, in the mean space,

That Insolence shrink not, but play the stout
man.

> *Adul.* That I know, he will do ; for once I
> know he can.

Avar. And that you, all three, be pressed to
   come hither ;   [together.
When need shall require, we lay our heads
Why, art thou here yet ?
   Adul.   I am gone with all my might.
                              Exeat.
   Avar. And, lo ! where Respublica appeareth
   in sight.

                    Intrat RESP[UBLICA].

She is now at [hand,] her nymphs bearing up
   her train ;
I will stand aside, and listen a word or twain.

ACTUS QUINTI, SCENA SEXTA.

RESPUBLICA. AVARICE.

   Resp. O Lord ! Thy mercies shall I sing
   evermore
Which dost so tenderly Thy handmaid restore.
But what creature would suspicion have had
That my late administers had been men so bad ?
Or, who would have thought them counterfeits
   to have been
That had heard their words, and their counten-
   ance seen ?
And chiefly Avarice, which did the matter break ?
   Avar. That word toucheth me : now is time
   for me to speak.   [as steel.
   Resp. I thought him Policy, as just and true
   Avar. I am glad that by me ye do such
   goodness feel.
   Resp. And that my wealth did grow, as it
   hath grown of late.   [this estate.
   Avar. I ever told ye you should grow to

Resp.   Thou tell me?

Avar.   Yea! I told you so in very deed;
And highly I rejoice it doth so well succeed.
And *salva festa dies* upon you, Madame!
I am glad ye have got a new robe, so I am:
What saint in the calendar do we serve to-day,
That ye be so gorgeously decked, and so gay?

Resp.   In rejoicing that I shall be clean rid of
thee.

Avar.   Nay, by this cross! ye shall never be
rid for me.

Resp.   And of thy compeers.

Avar.   Well, let them do as they lust!
I will ride upon Jill, mine own mare; that is just.
Other ways I shall do you service of the best.

Resp.   Thou wicked wretch! darest thou
with me to jest?   [*mores,*

Avar.   What? I now see, *honores mutant*
But, as seemeth here, *raro in meliores.*

Resp.   Thee, and all thy service I do from
me exile.

Avar.   Is that the high reward ye promised
me erewhile?
Is not this a wise woman, and minded to thrive,
That would me, Policy, out of the country drive?

Resp.   Thee and thy complices from me I
shall outcast.

Avar.   Then, I pray you, pay us for our pains
that are past.

Resp.   Ye shall be paid.

Avar.   Once I have done the best I can;
Authority also, he hath played the man;
Reformation hath done his part, I can tell.
If ye mistrust Honesty, faith! ye do not well.
And as for Avarice, he is conveyed quite:
I bade him get him hence, or I would him indite.

I, Policy, have made him to pluck in his horns:
I sware I would else lay him on prickles and
    thorns,   [night;
Where he should take no rest, neither day nor
So he had as lief be hanged as come in sight.
    Resp.   I may say with Job, how vainly do ye
    cheer me,   [disagree;
When all the words ye give, from truth doth
And with the wise man, I may most justly say
    this:
Just[ici]a tamen non luxit in nobis.   [mood,
Or else, with the prophet, in most sorrowful
The fruit of our justice is turned into wormwood.
Well, the best of you is a detestable vice;
And thou, for thy part, art most stinking
    Avarice.
    Avar.   Jesu! when were you wont so foul-
    mouthed to be,
To give such nicknames?   Ah, in faith! dame
    Verity
Hath had you in schooling of late; well, in
    God's name!
I am sorry for you, e'en sorry, that [I am].
I wis I have wrought to set you in good state,
And watched for that purpose, both early and
    late.
And I wis, if you would abide my framing,
And not thus to have fall to checking and
    blaming,   [work
I would, ere long, of you made such carpenter
That ye should have said, Policy had been a
    clerk;
Nay! you should have seen, how I would have
    you compact.
    Resp.   Yea, no doubt! ye would have done
    some great and fine act.

    Avar.   I would have brought half Kent into
      Northumberland ;
And Somersetshire should have raught to
    Cumberland.   [Warwick
Then would I have stretched the county of
Upon tenter hooks, and made it reach to
    Berwick.   [ward—
A piece of the bishopric should have come south-
Tut, tut ! I tell you, I had wondrous feats
    toward.
    Resp.   God hath placed me already in the
      best wise.
    Avar.   Yea ! but yet not half so well as I
      could devise—   [me ?
But no force ; well then, I see ye will none of
    Resp.   No !   [ye ?
    Avar.   Then ye can be content I depart from
    Resp.   Yea !   [still.
    Avar.   Well ! yet and ye pray me, I will tarry
    Resp.   No !
    Avar.   Well, speak me fair, and woo me yet,
      and I will.
    Resp.   No ; hence, avaunt !
    Avar.   Have I had of you such a clog,
And now [you] bid me avaunt and make me a
    Resp.   Hence, at once !   [dog ?
    Avar.   Nay, tut ! and ye will ha' us, ha' us.
    Resp.   Out of my presence !
    Avar.   Well then, ye will not ha' us ?
    Resp.   No, avoid, I charge thee !
    Avar.   Then needs depart I must. [trust !
Adieu ! in faith, I would have served ye of
But, since Respublica hath put me to exile,
Where may I go keep myself secret for a while ?
Is there never a good chaplain in all this town,
That will, for a while, hide me under his gown ?

Never a good farmer ? never a good merchant-
 man ?
Well, I will go pick out some corner, if I can.
But, first will I monish my fellows of this gear ;
And we stay this plunge, I care not for the
 next year.   *Exeat.*
 Resp. Now will I to Justice and th' other
 ladies three,   [be.
And pray that these vices may all suppressed
        Intrat PEOPLE.
But lo ! here cometh People ; I will now turn
 again,   [twain.
And first know of his good state by a word or

ACTUS QUINTI, SCENA SEPTIMA.

RESPUBLICA.   PEOPLE.

 Resp. What standeth he prying ? dareth he
 not enter ?
 People. Chould vain zee my lady : but I
 sdare not venter.
 Resp. Shrink not back from me, but draw
 to me, my dear friend !
 People. Chill virst know an ye be alone, zo
 God me mend !   [me believe.
 Resp. Come ! here be none but thy friends,
 People. Well then, chill be zo bold to peak
 in, by your leave.
 Resp. How happeneth that thou hast so
 long been me fro ?   [ye were ago,
 People. Marry ! chill tell you : as soon as
Hither came a zort of courtnals, hard men and
 zore :   [avore.
They shaked me up, chwas ne'er zo rattled

They vell all upon me, catch a word that might
    catch ;   [snatch.
Well was him that at me, People, might get a
Could have been at home rather than a new
    groat ;
Ich may zedge to you, Is feared pulling out
    my throat.
They bade me pike me home, and come at you
    no more.
An ich did, they zware, Is should be corrompt
    therefore.
Zo this prowt whorecop—what call ye him ?
    Resp.   Insolence !
    People.   Yea ! even this same, he vair popt
    me to silence.
    Resp.   And how is it with you now ? better
    than it was ?
    People.   All beginneth now to come gaily
    well to pass.
We hear of your good vortune that goeth
    about ;   [prout ;
How ye beeth permounted, which maketh all us
And ich am able since to buy a new coat ;
And, Is thank God, chave in my purse a zilver
    groat.
I wis ich could not zo zai these zix years afore ;
Whoever caused it, ill thank have they there-
    fore.
    Resp.   They will be here soon ; bide you them
    here for a train.
    People.   Mass ! but I ninnat ; would ye have
    om squat out on's brain ?
    Resp.   They shall not do thee harm the value
    of a point.
    People.   Then, an you zai the word ichill
    jeopard a joint.

Resp. If they but offer thee wrong, they shall smart therefore.

People. Nay! will ye be zo good to tie om up avore?
And what shalche zai to om?

Resp.　　　　　　Nothing ; but be abate,
Till take them all here suddenly I may await.
　　　　　　　　　　Exeat.

People. Well, it shall be do, chould laugh and both my hands clap,
To zee Ricepuddingcakes envies take in a trap.
And azee, pray! if zome of om come not yonder ;
Chould my lady had bide ne'er zo little longer.

ACTUS QUINTI, SCENA OCTAVA.

INSOLENCE. ADULATION. OPPRESSION.
PEOPLE. AVARICE.

Insol. Where is Avarice? Ho! He doth not now appear.

Adul. He bid me monish you that we might all meet here.

Oppr. But see where People standeth !

Adul. What doth he here now?

Oppr. About little goodness, I dare my word avow!

Insol. Let us speak unto him. People! wherefore and why,
Like a loitering losell, standest thou here idly?

Oppr. Thou comest to Respublica to make some mone?

Adul. Or else some complaint.

People.　　　　You all see cham here alone.

RESP.　　　　　　　　　　17

Insol.   Ye must have silver money, must ye,
    gentleman?   [can?
You cannot be content with such coin as we
    Oppr.   Ye must burn wood and coal, must
    ye, all of pleasance?   [vengeance!
Burn turves, or some of thy bedstraw, with a
    Adul.   Ye must eat fresh meat bought from
    the shambles, must ye?
Eat garlic and onions, and roots or grass, and
    lust ye !
    Insol.   In faith !   I will whip you for this,
    peasant lout !
    Adul.   And twig you !
    Insol.   Ere another year come about.
    Adul.   But, see !   where Avarice cometh,
    running very fast.
                         Intrat AVARICE.
    Avar.   I have trod and scud till my wind is
    almost past,
Yet my mates are not where.
    Insol. and Adul.   We be here come of late.
    Avar.   Be there not, trow we, honester men
    in Newgate ?   [I rede you.
    Insol.   No words of reproach, brother mine !
    Avar.   None but godigod eve, and godigod
    speed you.
Fare ye well again, an ye be falling out now.
    Insol., *Adul.*   We mind it not.
    Avar.   'Twere more need to look about you.
    Insol.   How goeth all? tell us !
    Avar.   My lady is waxed froward ;   [ward.
Our names be all known, so there is array to-
    Insol., *Oppr.*   God speed us well !
    Avar.   Once I am thrust out of service.
    Adul.   Alas ! what may I do?
    Insol., *Oppr.*   Tell us thy best advice.

Avar. Nay! I cannot have you, when I
would none of you all ;
Therefore, shift for yourselves, each one, for
me, you shall.
Adul. Nay, for the pash of God! tell us
what best to do ;
Ye know I was ne'er slack to restore you unto.
Avar. These ladies that are come for
commonweal's relief,
Prepare to work us woe, and do us all mischief.
Insol. Nay, by His precious populorum! I
swear
Not the proudest of them all can hurt me a hair.
Oppr. If they offer, of us, to make them
gauds or toys
They shall [find], I trow! we are no babes nor
boys.
Avar. To prevail against them with force I
do despair.
Insol. Be that as be may.
Adul.   I will fall to speaking fair ;
But, of all this trouble, we may thank People,
this wretch.
Oppr. Faith, villain! if we scape, thou
shalt an halter stretch.
Adul. But what remedy therewhile?
Avar.   Faith! all will be nought.
Adul. Tell us what to do.
Avar.   I will—they come—we are caught.
Adul. Whither shall I run?
Avar.   Now sing a song, Honesty!
Adul. I am past singing now.
Avar.   Yes, one song, Honesty!
Hay! hay! hay! hay!
I will be merry while I may.

ACTUS QUINTI, SCENA NONA.

VERITY. JUSTICE. AVARICE. RESPUBLICA. ADUL-
ATION. MISERICORDIA. PEACE. PEOPLE.
INSOLENCE. OPPRESSION.

Ver. Here they be, all four! this is a
happy chance.

Avar. Take each man a lady, sirs! and let
us go dance!

Resp. I left People here for a train, to hold
them talk :   [walk!

Alas, that I could tell which way best hence to

Avar. What be these fair ladies? and
whither will they, trow?

Just. We arrest you, sirs! all four, as ye
stand in a row ;   [say.

Not so hardy in your hearts, our arrest to gain-

Avar. Nay! we are content, if ye let us go
our way.

Just. No, not a foot! we must first your
reckoning take.

Avar. I ne'er bought nor sold with you,
reckoning to make ;

Nor I know not who you be.

Just.   Justice is my name.

Avar Where is your dwelling?

Just.   In heaven ; and, thence I came.

Avar. Dwell ye in heaven and so mad to
come hither?

All our hucking here is how we may get thither!

Just. I bring heaven with me, and make it
where I am.

Avar. Then I pray you let me be your
prentice, Madame!

I will be at your beck.

Just.   Ye shall, ere ye depart.

Avar.   I would learn how to make heaven,
with all my heart.

Well, as for Lady Misericordia,

I remember I saw you with Respublica.

Adul.   You, if you so please, may do much
good in this land ;   [hand.

Many, at this hour, do need your good helping

Avar.   And ye came down from heaven too,
I judge ?

Miser.   Yea, sure !

Avar.   Why, what folk are ye that cannot
heaven endure?

And what may I call you, lady ?

Pax.   My name is Peace.

Avar.   Ye have long dwelt with us ; we have
been long in peace.

Peace.   Call ye it peace, sirrah ! when brother
and brother

Cannot be content to live one by another?

When one for his house, for his land, yea, for
his groat,   [throat?

Is ready to strive and pluck out another's

I will in all such things make perfect union.

Avar.   Then, good-night ! the lawyers gain,
by Saint Tronnion !   [to pass.

Westminster Hall might go play, if that came

Faith ! we must serve you with a supersedeas.

Ver.   Well ! leave vain prattling, and now
come answer to me.

Avar.   I must hear first what ye say, and
who ye be.

Ver.   I am dame Verity.

Avar.   What? the daughter of Time?

Ver.   Yea !   [afine.

Avar.   I know my master, your father, well

Welcome, fair lady! sweet lady, little lady,
Plain lady, smooth lady, sometime spital lady;
Lady Long-tongue, lady Tell-all, lady Make-
    bate:
And, I beseech you, from whence are ye come
    of late?

    Ver.   I am sprung out of the earth.
    Avar.   What, ye do but jest!   [*est.*
    Ver.   The book sayeth: *Veritas de terra orta*
    Avar.   Happy is he which hath that garden
      plat, I trow!   [grow;
Out of which such fair blossoms do spring and
Yet this one thing, I say.
    Ver.   What?
    Avar.   Ye are friend to few, [to show.
Pressed to open all things, and men's manner
    Ver.   If ye be true and just, that is your benefit.
    Avar.   True or untrue, just or unjust, it is
      your spite;
And glad ye are to take other folks in a trip.
[Yes! ye do it no]w and then, your ownself,
    on the whip.   [would.
Well, ye might be honest of your tongue, if you
    Ver.   If your acts were honest, ye did but as
      ye should.
    Avar.   Who chargeth me with the crime of
      any vice?   [Avarice.
    Ver.   Thou callst thyself Policy, and art
    Avar.   Nay, I defy your malice, I am Policy—
Ask of my fellows here! am not I Policy?
    Ver.   Ladies! will ye all see him openly tried?
    Just.   If he be an ill one, let him be descried.
    Ver.   What hast thou in thy bosom?
    Avar.   Nothing, I, truly!   [openly.
    Ver.   Nothing truly got, say! show it forth
    Avar.   What should I show forth?

Ver.   That bag in thy bosom hid.
Avar. It lieth well, I thank you; as much
 as though I did.
Ver. Nay, come on! out with it!
Avar.   Lo! here 'tis, for your fancy.
Ver. Give it me!
Avar.   Yea, nay; I defy that Policy!
Ver. Open it!   [ing:
Avar. Yea, that each body might be catch-
Some's teeth, I think, water e'en since to be
 snatching.
Ver. We must needs see what it is.
Avar.   'Tis a bag of rye!
Ver. Rye, what rye?
Avar. A bag of rye [. . . . .]
Ver. . . . . . such as men do eat?
Avar. A bag of rye flour, a great deal
 better than wheat.   [in haste!
Ver. Let us see what rye it is! pour it out
Avar. Yea, shall? I trow not! indeed, so
 might we make waste.
Ver. There is no remedy; pour it out in
 my lap!
Avar. Nay! if there be no choice, I will
 use mine own cap.
Ver. So! a bag of rye, quod thou?
Avar.   Yea, so God me speed!
Ver. Thou sayest even truth; 'tis a bag of
 rye indeed:
Usury, perjury, pitchery, patchery;
Pilfery, bribery, snatchery, catchery;
Flattery, robbery, cloutery, botchery;
Trumpery, harlotry, misery, treachery!
Avar. There is too, an please you, a little
 sorcery,
Witchery, baudery, and such other grossery.

Ver. And how gottst thou all this in thy
  possession?

Avar. Pardon me! and I will make my
  confession :   [small ;

The world is hard, and the bag is but very

I got it where I could, to go on beg[ging]
  withal—   steal ;

A plain true dealing man that loveth not to

And I durst not be bold to crave of commonweal.

Ver. Now, do off thy gown, and turn the
  inside outward !   [reward !

Aver. Let me alone, and an angel for a

Ver. Come, off at once ! when? come off !
  no more gaudies [n]or japes.

Avar. Must I needs whip over the chain
  like Jack-a-napes?

Resp. Out ! in the virtue of God ! what do
  ye here see?

Avar. All this had been lost, Respublica,
  but for me !

Resp. O Lord ! where hast thou dragged up
  all these purses?

Ver. Where he hath had for them many
  thousand curses.

Resp. Where hast thou gotten them? tell
  truth, and do not lie !

Avar. Where no honest man could have
  gotten them but I.

In blind corners, where some would have
  hoarded them,

Had not I take them with the manner and
  burdened them.

Resp. And whither was it thine intent to
  convey them now?

Avar. I hid them that I might bring them
  safely to you.

I durst not bear them openly, to God I vow!
I wis ye have heard me blame pickpurses or
    now—
And this is all yours.
   Ver.   It is hers, in very deed!
   Avar. With sufferance I could get mo to
   help her need.
   Ver. How say ye, Respublica! now to
   Policy?   [jealousy.
   Resp. I ne'er suspect him nor had him in
   Ver. In such like counterfeits shall all
   the rest appear.
Sirs! do off your utmost robes, each one even
   here.   [stration.
Now, what these are, ye see plain demon-
   Resp. Insolence, Oppression, Adulation!
O Lord! how have I be used these five years
   past!
   People. Nay, Is ne'er thought better of
   om, ich, by God's vast.   [these
Vey! madame, my lady! such strussioners as
Have oft made you believe the moon was a
   green cheese.
   Ver. Now ye see what they are; the
   punishment of this
Must be referred to the goddess Nemesis:
She is the most high goddess of correction;
Clear of conscience, and void of affection;
She hath power from above, and is newly sent
   down
To redress all outrages, in city and in town;
She hath power from God all practice to repeal
Which might bring annoyance to lady Common-
   weal;
To her office belongeth the proud to overthrow,
And such to restore as injury hath brought low;

'Tis her power to forbid and punish in all
    estates
All presumptuous immoderate attemptates.
Her cognisance, therefore, is a wheel and
    wings to fly,
In token her rule extendeth far and nigh ;
A rudder, eke, she beareth in her other hand,
As directri[c]e of all things in every land ;
Then pranketh she her elbows out, under her
    side,
To keep back the heady, and to temper their
    pride.
To her, therefore, dear sisters ! we must now
    resort,
That she may give sentence upon this naughty
    sort ;
She knoweth what is fittest for their correction ;
Nemesis must, therefore, herein give direction.
    Just.   Then, People ! while we lady Nemesis
    do fet
All these offenders in this custody we set ;
Them to apprehend and keep till we come
    again.
    People.   An ye give me tority, chill keep om,
    that is plain.
    Insol., *Oppr.*   Shall People keep us, of whom
    we have been lords ?
    People.   Stand still, or by Jis ! [chill] bind
    you vast with cords.
Nay, sirs ! ich ha' you now in my custodity.
    Avar.   Mass, I will be gone for my mine own
    commodity.
    People.   Zoft ! whither wilt thou ? wilt thou
    not be roiled ?
Stand still, skitbrained thief, or thy bones
    shall be coiled !

Yond be they coming now, che war't that
will tame ye.
A, zee! art thou gone too? come back, and
evil a thee!

ACTUS QUINTI, SCENA DE[CIMA].

NEMESIS. RESPUBLICA. MISERICORDIA. VERITAS.
JUSTICE. PAX. PEOPLE. INSOLENCE.
OPPRESSION. ADULATION. AVARICE.

Nem.   Come forth, Respublica, our darling
most dear!
Resp.   At your word, most gracious lady! I
am here.
Nem.   Are these your trusty men that had
you in government?
People.   The skitb[r]ains nold not be roiled
ne'er, since ye went.
Nem.   People! why art thou bashful and
standest so far?
Be of good cheer now; and, I warrant thee,
come near!
People.   I will come no near: cha not be
haled up with states,
But I scannot be fichant enough amongst my
[mates].
Nem.   Come near, when I bid thee
People.   Marry! but I ninnat;
I namnot worthy to perk with you, no, I nam
not.
Nem.   Well, Respublica! are these your late
governors,   [sellors?
Whom ye took for faithful and trusty coun-
Resp.   Yea, forsooth, Madame!

    Avar.   These three be, but I am none ;
For I was discharged nigh half-an-hour agone.
    Nem. Come ! first stand forth here, thou
        Adulation !
    Adul. Speak a good word for me, lady
        Compassion !
    People. Nay ! she shall not need, I chill
        speak for thee myself—   [elf.
Madame, take good heed ! for this is a naughty
    Adul. Nay, Madame ! the cause of all this
        was Avarice ;
He forged us new names, and did us all entice.
    Oppr. We neither did nor could work, but
        by his advice.
    Adul. Because I got no more, he chid me
        once or twice.
    Insol. Madame ! only Avarice made us all
        to fall.
    Avar. Yea ? Fall to preaching ? Nay !
        then will I tell all.
Madame ! ere I had taught these merchants
    any while,
They were cunninger than I, all men to beguile.
And Verity saw mine were small purses and
    bags,
Tottering loose about me, like wind-shaken rags.
But he that should have bagged that Insolence
    did win,   [in ;
Must have made a poke to put five or six shires
He must have made wide sacks for castles,
    towns, and woods :
The canvas to make them of, were worth ten
    times my goods.
Then Oppression here, to feather well his nest,
Cared not, of their livelood whom he dispos-
    sest.

Bishops, deans, provosts, the poor folk from the
    spital,
Lands with church and chapel, all was for him
    too little.
Poor I did not so ; I scraped but little crumbs ;
And, here and there, with odd ends, patched
    up my sums.
Flattery got his thrift by counterfeit honesty ;
Yet, by these ten bones ! I bid him use modesty.
Therefore, spare not him ; he will ne'er come
    to good pass ;
But I may well be mended, by the Mary Mass !
    Miser. Lady Nemesis ! now have ye occasion
And matter to show your commiseration.
[It is much] more glory, and standeth with more
    skill,
Lost sheep to recover, then the scabby to spill.
    Just. But how shall this redress be well
    persecuted,
If justice with mercy shall be executed ?
Straight Justice must such great enormities
    redress ;
Severity must put men in fear to transgress ;
Justice must give each man that he doth deserve.
    Miser. If offenders were not, wherefore
    might mercy serve?
    Avar. Stick hard to it, good, sweet lady
    Compassion !   [sion !
We are all else undone, by Cock's bitter pas-
    Miser. Verity ! how say you? have I not
    spoken well?
    Ver. Mercy in one place with Justice some-
    time may dwell,   [Peace ?
And right well agree together—how say you,
    Pax. Where all thing is well amended, I do
    increase.

    Nem.   Ladies, we have heard all your discreet
      advises ;
And each one shall have some part of your
    devises.
Neither all nor none shall taste of severity
But as they are now known through lady Verity ;
So shall they receive our mercy or our ire,
As the wealth of Respublica shall best require.
Now, Adulation ! what sayeth you in this case ?
    Adul.   Nought in mine excuse, but submit
      me to your grace.
Only this : I promise, if I may Mercy find,
Utterly for ever to change my wicked mind ;
I ne'er sought afore mine own private gain so
    much,   [much.
But I will further Commonweal's ten times so
    Nem.   Well, thou mayest become a worthy
      subject, it is plain.
    Adul.   Else ye know at all times how to
      reach me again.
    Nem.   Thou mightest swerve of frailty, thou
      might'st do to please ;
Thou might'st do for fear, thou might'st do to
    live in ease ;   [thee.
Well, upon thy promise, for once we pardon
Go, and see that from henceforth thou be per-
    fect Honesty !
    Adul.   So long as shall please God to give
      me life and heale,   [weal.
I shall most duly serve God and the Common-
    Now to thee, Avarice ; have at thy petti-
    coat !
    Nem.   Now the plague of commonweals,
      as all men do note :   [boot ;
Come forth, Avarice ! to spare thee will be no
Thou must be plucked up, e'en by the very root,

Because thou scraped'st up whatever thou
    might'st get.   [my debt!
    Avar.   Indeed, I thank God there is no man in
    Nem.   And, because thou caught'st it by
    wrong contribution,
Thou shalt first and foremost make restitution.
    Avar.   Let me then, with pardon, go hence
    about it lightly.   [uprightly.
    Nem.   No! ye shall have help to see it done
People, take this fellow—
    Avar.   God save me from this plunge!
    Nem.   —that he may be pressed as men do
    press a sponge;
That he may drop aught, t' every man his lot,
To the utmost farthing that he hath falsely got.
    People.   An ye bid me, chill squeeze him as
    dry as a kyx.
    Avar.   Nay, the pash of God! I shall then
    die of the flix.
    Nem.   Nay! thou shalt deliver him to the
    head officer
Which hath authority, justice to minister.
    People.   Chil 'liver him to the constable, and
    come again.
    Nem.   Now, Justice, for these two that do
    here remain: [great—
Because the fault of Insolence is heinous and
Lucifer's own fault t' aspire to the highest seat—
And because Oppression hath wronged men so
    sore   [more,
That he spoiled innocents of all they had and
People shall deliver them unto safe custody,
Where they may no farther annoy anybody.
When the time may serve t' examine and try
    their cause,   [the laws.
Call them both before you, and judge them by

People.   And shalche carry away these same
    two men also?

Nem.   Yea; go deliver them to an officer, go !
Now, darling Respublica ! ye are in th' old
    good estate ;
And they taken away that spoiled you of late.
Now cleave to these ladies, from heaven to you
    direct ;
They from all corruption will you safe protect.
Well, I must go hence to another count[r]y now,
That hath of redress the like case that was in
    you.   [give
I leave you for this time, immortal thanks to
To God, and your Sovereign, which do you thus
    relieve.

Resp.   Thanks be to Thee, O Lord ! which
    hast this world wrought,
Andhast me to this state from utter ruin brought.

Pax.   Now let us all together, both with
    heart and voice,
In God and in Queen Mary most joyfully rejoice.

Ver.   Praying that her reign, most graciously
    begun,
[May] long years endure, as hitherto it hath
    done.

Just.   Pray we for her Council, to have long
    life and health,
Their sovereign to serve.

Pax.   And to maintain Commonwealth.

Omnes.   Amen !

                              Cantant et exeant.

FINIS.

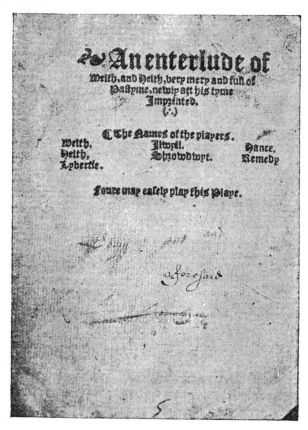

[*A reduced Facsimile of the Title-page of "Wealth and Health" from the unique recently recovered copy of the Play now in the British Museum.*]

An Interlude of

WEALTH AND HEALTH

VERY MERRY AND FULL OF PASTIME, NEWLY
AT THIS TIME IMPRINTED

The Names of the Players:

WEALTH	ILL-WILL	HANCE
HEALTH	SHREWD WIT	REMEDY
LIBERTY		

Four may easily play this Play

———

EXTRACT FROM THE STAT. REG. 1557 [ARBER I. 75]

To master **John wally** these bokes Called *Welth and
helthe | the treatise of the ffrere and the boye | stans puer
ad mensam* another of *youghte charyte and humylyte* an
a b c for cheldren in englesshe *with syllabes* also a boke
called *an hundreth mery tayles.* . . . . **ij**[s]

[WEALTH AND HEALTH.]

A2,r. Here entereth WEALTH *and* HEALTH
  *singing together a ballat of two parts, and
  after speaketh* WEALTH.

  Wealth. Why is there no courtesy now I
    am come?
I trow that all the people be dumb;
Or else, so God help me and halidom!
They were almost asleep.
No words I heard, nor yet no talking;
No instrument went, nor ballats singing;
What ails you all, thus to sit dreaming?
Of whom take ye care?
  Of my coming ye may be glad;
Therefore, I pray you be not sad,
For all your desire shall be had:
I can amend your cheer.
  By God! I think ye have forgotten me.
I am Wealth of this realm; look upon me!
For I am to every man loving and friendly:
For Wealth hath no peer.
  Health. Brother Wealth! have ye not yet
    done?
Ye praise yourself above the moon.
Every man may perceive thereby, soon,
That you lack discretion.   [too much.
  Wealth. Wherefore? by God! I cannot say

I am so wealthy of substance and rich ;
In all the world where is one such
As I am of comparison?

Health.   Wealth is good, I cannot denay ;
Yet praise yourself too much ye may ;
For wealth, oftentimes, doth decay :
And wealth is nothing sure.

Wealth.   Wealth hath been ever in this
      country ;   A2,*v.*
And here I purpose still for to be ;
For this is the land most meet for me,
And here I will endure.

Health.   Therein ye speak full lovingly ;
For, in this realm, wealth should be ;
Yet, no displeasure, I pray you heartily !
But in the way of communication,
    And for pastime, I would speak some ways,
Of no comparison, nor to you no dispraise—
I do not intend that manner always—
But for a recreation.

Wealth.   Brother ! whatsoever ye say to me
I will hear you patiently.
I am content, and I thank you heartily ;
Begin, and say your pleasure.

Health.   I thank you heartily ; then will I
Somewhat unto my purpose apply :
Though Wealth be praised marvellously,
Yet to mine understanding
Wealth is mutable, and that in shame ;
And Wealth is haughty and proud of name ;
Wealth is cruel and in great blame ;
For Wealth is ever wavering.

Wealth.   To whom have I done any harm—
      can ye say?
Ye slander me now ; yet I trust I may
Answer for myself in every manner way ;

Ye will not deny that?

    Health.   God forbid but ye should do so!

And ye may do it whether I will or no.

In like wise I must answer you, also,

When ye say not true.

Though I be but to you a poor man,   A3,*r.*

Yet Health I hight; the same I am:

That is desired universally than—

Some calls me as good as you!

    Wealth.   As I? marry! there, indeed, ye do compare;

Such words might bring you soon in care.

Lewd person! thou art not ware

Of what substance I am.

    Health.   Yes! I can tell what you are; be not displeased.

Wealth is of great substance; that cannot be denied.

Yet, show your commodities, and ye shall be answered:

I promise you wealth is fugitive.

    Wealth.   What sayst thou? am I a tagetive?

I was never so taken up in my life,

Nor called unsure—well! I will make no strife.

Yet, whereas thou dost say

    That I should show my commodities always,

The best for myself, whereof I ask praise,

If I should stand here all my life days

Yet I could not say.

    Nor half the benefits that cometh of me,

It cannot be told nor recited shortly.

Wealth is the flower of all thing earthly—

That you cannot deny.   [Queen;

    First, God save our sovereign lady, the

With all the Council, and all that with them been.

Am not I, Wealth, with them ever at ene?
Who should be there but I?

Men of the law, and jolly rich merchants
There be, wealthy both; of goods and lands,
Without comparison, is in their hands:
I, Wealth, have all treasure.

    Health. O good sir! of whom cometh all
      this?   A3,*v.*
Of God only: to you no thank, I wis.
And yet man's wealth stands not all in riches:
I dare say that boldly.

When a man hath a competent living,
With the grace of God that passeth all thing,
Love of his neighbour, and good reporting:
Then is he wealthy.

Wealth of goods is but a fame;
He is wealthy that hath a good name;
Every wise man will covet the same:
For other wealth I not rech.

If a man have never so much good name
Every wise man will covet the same;
If his dispositions be nought and wood,
Then he is but a wretch.

    Wealth. Nay! thou art a wretch, and a fool
      unwise,
Wealth of riches thus to despise;
Dost thou not see all the world arise
By goods and substance?

He that hath plenty of silver and gold
May have all thing, whatsoever he would.
When can Wealth lack, seeing all thing is sold,
And Wealth is of assurance?

    Health. I deny that; your saying is nought:
Grace, heaven, nor cunning cannot be bought
Without great pain, and good deeds wrought;
Else man cannot them have.

Wealth. Stop thereat, and hold thy peace !
May not men buy heaven with richesse,
As to build churches and make by-ways ?
Such deeds man's soul doth save.

    Health. Yea ! but yet ye must mark one
      thing,   A4,*r.*
If these goods came with wrong-doing
Shall ye have heaven for so spending,
Or yet any meed?

Nay, nay ! except that man himself do meek,
And make resistance the right honour to seek,
Else all such good deeds is not worth a leek.
Wealth ! hereof take heed !

    Wealth. Why thinkest thou that all men
      which hath wealth
Getteth their goods with bribery and stealth ?
Thy report is nought ; therefore, Health,
I counsel thee to say the best.

    Health. So I will ; but yet, I must say true.
And now a little more I will say to you :
Much sorrow and care wealth doth brew ;
He is seldom in rest.

When a man is a little hite and wealthy,
And hath in his chest treasures plenty,
Then will he wrangle, and do shrewdly
By his power and might.

With his neighbours he will go to law ;
And a-wreak his malice for value of straw :
Wealth is fickle and out of awe,
Wilful in wrong or right.   [tongue,

    Wealth. Thou speakest with a slanderous
All of evil will ; and yet, it is wrong :
Wealth in this realm hath been long ;
Of me cometh great honour.

Because that I, Wealth, hath great port,
All the world hither doth resort ;

Therefore I, Wealth, am this realm's comfort,
And here I will endure.

 Health. So I would ye should, and I shall
  do the same.   A4,*v.*

Health I am called, and that is my name ;
If I would not abide here I were to blame,
For here I am well cherished.

 Yet say yourself now, indifferently,
And if every man do not love me,
Health, as well as Wealth? yes, verily !
Thereof I dare be reported.

 Wealth. Why should they love thee—that
  would I know—

As well as me? I pray you, show !
I am the superior of high and low ;
No man may compare with me.

 Health. To show why, I will not be afraid ;
For, I can bide by that I have said :
If wealthy men be very well apaid,
Or much they set you by.

 But of wealth, if they have never so much—
Goods, treasure, and gold—and be called rich,
Yet, if they lack health, their pain is such
That they were better die.

 A man to wear gold and be in pain,
What joy hath he ? None ! but would be fain
To give all his treasure for health, plain ;
Or else he were very mad.

 For, if a man be never so poor,
Yet if he have health, that is a treasure ;
Then, for his living, he may labour,
And in his heart be glad.

 Wealth. I never marked thus much, nor
  understood

That health was such a treasure, and to man so
  good ;

Wherefore, I am sorry, and will change my
    mood :
Now, I pray you, forgive me!
    Health.   I will forgive, or else I were to
    blame ;   B1,*r.*
And I pray you to forgive me the same ;
I love you heartily, and will praise your name
If it please you to keep my company.

    Here entereth LIBERTY *with a song, and after*
               speaketh.   [going?
    Liberty.   Why tarry, sirs! whither are ye
I see well ye looked not for my coming.
Lo! out of sight, out of remembering ;
Absence is cause of strangeness.
    What look ye on? wherewhy are ye so
    strange?   [change?
From your fellow, Liberty, doth your minds
In your company I was wont to range ;
What needs all this business?
    Wealth.   By Liberty, now, I do not set
Seeing that Health and I am met,
As felloweth together ; no man shall let
Me for to love him best.
    Lib.   Let me hear what ye do say :
Then ye are about to cast me away!
How haps this?   Marry! then I may
Go pick straws and take me rest.
    I pray you, tell me whom I have offended ;
If I have made a fau[l]t it shall be amended ;
With so short warning let me not be voided :
I trow yet ye do but jest.
    Health.   Why do ye make this cavillation?
We intend to make no alteration ;
Wealth and I have had communication :
He is my friend of old.

Lib.   What was the matter?   I pray you
Methinks, I ought to be of counsel;   [tell!
Or else, I promise you, ye do not well:
With you I should behold.   B1,*v.*

Wealth.   The matter is done; we are agreed;
To reason it more it shall not need.
O, brother Health! thou art, indeed,
More preciouser than gold.

Lib.   God's body! how cometh this gear to
   pass?
I am cast out at the cart's arse;
The world is nothing as it was
For I am here refused.   [agree?

Health.   Why be you angry that we do
Then are ye not wise; for, if ye love me,
I will love him again; so it should be;
Or else, I were misadvised.

Lib.   Then of my love ye set no store;
My company, I see well, ye looked not for.
Farewell! I will get me out of the door;
Yet I am your betters, and so am I called.

Wealth.   Such presumptuous words will
   have a fall;
Your comparison is but feeble and small:
What can ye do? nothing at all
As you have reputed!

Lib.   What were ye both two, were not I?
Wretches and caitiffs! look not so high;
Think no scorn hardly,
For I may be your peer.

If Wealth have never so much substance,
Lacking Liberty and were in durance,
Within a whit—I am in assurance—
Ye would pray me come near.

If Health be never so lust and strong,
Yet, if Liberty were kept from him long,

Then sorrow and care would be his song:
It would abate your cheer.   B2,*r*.
　　Fie of Wealth, which lacketh Liberty!
Fie of Health, and be in captivity!
Fie of Riches, and lack good company!
Liberty hath no peer!
　　Health.　Will ye hear how he doth clatter?
What need ye to rehearse all this matter?
Ye know that we twain, afore any other,
Liberty must needs have still.
　　Liberty on us is glad to wait;
Ye stand too far in your own conceit:
I wis, Liberty, ye can make no bate
To catch us at your will!
　　Lib.　Now, there ye lie! I can suffer no
　　　　longer:
Wealth for Liberty doth labour ever;
And Health for Liberty is a great store;
Therefore, set me not so light.
　　Wealth.　Liberty! I pray ye, reason no
　　　　more!
Ye are welcome to us as ye were before;
Indeed, of Liberty it is great suitor:
Therefore welcome, by this light!
　　Lib.　Now, I thank you both, full kindly!
Your strange words a little did grieve me;
And now, at your commandment, I am ready,
And at your own will.

　　　Here entereth with some jest ILL WILL.

　　Ill-Will.　Marry! I am come at the first call:
Will, your own man, have me who shall;
For I am Will, servant to you all;
Ye shall not need to send for me.
　　Wealth.　Who is acquainted with this man?
He is very homely, and little good he can B2,*v*.

To come in here so boldly ; then
Drive him away quickly !
   Ill-W.   Why, I came not till I was called.
Your own Will openly ye named ;
Then I came apace, lest I should be blamed :
Therefore, I pray you, let me bide still.
   [*H*]*eal*[*th.*]   Whose will, or what will, doth
   he mean?
Thou art not my will, I forsake thee clean ;
My will and their wills is often seen :
Our wills can none ill.
   Ill-W.   Alas, good masters ! I can none ill.
Yet, by my troth ! I am your evil will—
Your will, and your will, and your will ; there-
   fore, keep me :
I love ye, by God's mother !
   Lib.   This is a strange saying unto me :
My will, your will, and his will—this cannot
   be ;
For in our wills is great diversity ;
For one is not like another.
   Ill-W.   Yet, by Christ ! your own will I
   am ;
The maddest will, and the merriest than.
For God's sake ! now let me be your man
Till ye have better acquaintance.
   Wealth.   I perceive this fellow is kind,
And oweth to us good will and mind ;
Some kinds again then let him find :
Let him have some furtherance.
   Ill-W.   By God, sir ! and I durst be so bold,
Acquaintance of this man claim I would,
And kindred, too ; if the truth were told
We be of one consanguinity.
   Health.   How so? let me hear that, I pray
   thee heartily !

Ill-W. Will and Liberty is of ancestry old: B3,*r*.
Without Liberty, Will dare not be bold ;
And where Will lacketh, Liberty is full cold ;
Therefore, Will and Liberty must needs be of
  kin.
  Lib.   Indeed, as he saith, it may well be ;
For Will ever longeth unto Liberty :
Therefore, good friend, welcome to me !
I pray you all be good to him.   *And goeth out.*
  Wealth.   For your sake he is welcome to
    us all ;
Let him come to our place, and then he shall
Have succour of us and help withal :
And now we will depart.

                    And WEALTH *and* HEALTH *goeth out.*
  Ill-W.   Will ye go hence ?   I thank ye,
    masters, with all my heart !
I will seek you out, I warrant you ! fear not !
Now they be gone ; I am glad, by Saint
    Mary !
A little while here I purpose to tarry :
How to deceive Wealth, Health, and Liberty
Now must I devise.
  For I am a child that is past grace ;
Ill-Will—I am called that in every place—
Doth much mischief ; this is a plain case :
Virtue I do utterly despise.
  But if they wist what I were,
Then of my purpose I should be never the
    near :
I will keep my tongue lest that I mar
My whole intent and will.
  But now I marvel, by this day !
Where Shrewd Wit is gone astray ;
Some crafty touch is in his way—
I hear him ! peace ! stand still !

Entereth SHREWD WIT *with a song*.

Dieu vous garde playsaunce !
On seven or on mumchance, what yonkers dare
To play a groat or twain ?   [avance B3,*v*.
   Lo ! here I have in store
Two or three groats, and no more ;
I take great thought, therefore,
For to keep it ; it is much pain.
   I come now out of a place
Where is a company of small grace :
Thieves and whores that spends apace—
They were drunken all the sort.
   One of their purses I did aspy
Out of his sleeve, where it did lie ;
And one winked on me with his eye :
But there began the sport.
   There False Falsehood, and I, Crafty Wit
Got the purse : lo ! here I have it.
I came my way and let him sit,
Smoke and shitten arse together.
   And if that I had Ill-Will here,
With this money we would make good cheer.
Gentle brother Will ! I pray thee, appear !
For thou art in some corner.
   Ill-W. [*from without.*] I would come in, but I
Lest that I be taken by the beard   [am afeard
With some catchpoll ; I have heard
How thou hast stolen a purse.
   Wit.   Thou whoreson ! art thou mad ? come
     in, I say !   [ILL-WILL *comes in.*]
This is not the first hazard that I have scaped ;
If I make an hand to deck myself gay,
What am I the worse ?
   Ill-W.   From thy company I cannot abide ;
I must needs hold upon thy side :

Ill-Will and Shrewd Wit, who can hide? B4,*r*.
For they will be together.
   Wit.   Now welcome, Will! and what cheer?
By God! I thought for thee a thousand year.
Peace! for God's body! who cometh there?
Hance Beerpot, a scon router!

     Entereth HANCE *with a Dutch song.*

  [*Hance.*] Gut, mynen scone rutters, by the
    moder Got!
Ic heist nowne schon, for stave ye nete
De qusteke man, iche bie do do?
Van the groate bumbarde well ic wete
Dartyck dowsant van enheb it mete
Ic best de manikin van de keining dangliter
De grot keyser kind ic bene his kusketer.
   Ill-W. Hear ye not drunken Hance, how he
    begins to prate?
The malapert Fleming is a little too checkmate.
   Wit. Let the knave alone! for his name is
    War:
Such drunken Flemings your company will
    mar.
   Hance. Ic best nen einond; ic best in soche;
Ye fecte nete vell; ic forstave ye in doche.
   Ill-W. Com'st here leyt with your gound?
    stand near!
It becomes you better to handle a pot of beer.
   Hance. Dat maght ic vell dan, ic can skynke
    frelyck;
Tab bers frew; ic bringes brore, begotts
    nemerick!
   Wit. The whoreson knave, by the mass! is
    drunk
A winking, for deep his eyen be clean sunk.
   Hance. Ic forave ye vell ye seg dac ic slepe

Nenike, nenike, ic compta hore for an audor
    cepe.
    Ill-W.   Well coppin, I pray thee, heartily
    tell us true   [sue?
Wherefore comest thou hither for anything to
    Hance.   Ye icke feger en bumbardere van de
    koyning wei it be   [culveryn.
Heb twe skelling de dagh ic con scote de
    Wit.   Nay! ye shall walk, a Fleming knave!
    will ye not see   B4,*v.*
We have English gunners enow? there is no
    room empty.   [spreken
    Hance.   Ic best en bomberde mot ye to me
What segge ye? bones! it sal ye yode staen.
    Ill-W.   We speak not to thee; thou art a
    scon man,   [thee can.
But go thy way! they be not here that promote
    Hance.   Cant ye me a de house dragen van
    de grot here?
    Wit.   Hance! ye must go to the court, and
    for Wealth inquire.
    Hance.   What segte ye, Wealth? nenyke he
    is net hore;   [dore.
Wealth best in Flanders; ic myself brought him
    Ill-W.   Beshrew your whoreson Fleming's
    heart, therefore!   [wealth.
Indeed, as he saith, by war in Flanders there is
    Hance.   Segt ye dat brower? by the moder
    Got dan!
Gut naught ic mot watt, to sent Cafrin, to mi
    lamnan store.   *And goeth out.*
    Ill-W.   Is he gone? farewell, Hanijkin
    Bowse!
I pray God give him a hounded drouse;
For I trow a knave brought him to house.
But now, Brother Wit!

We must devose how that we may
Be in service with Wealth alway ;
Let me hear what thou canst do, or say,
To help for to contrive it.
 Wit. For thy pleasure that I shall.
This will I do first of all :
Flatter and lie, and evermore call
Them my good masters still.

 Then with swearing, lying, and polling,
Bribery, theft, and privy picking,
Thus I, Shrewd Wit, will ever be doing,
I warrant thee, Ill-Will !
 Ill-W. I can thee thank ; this is well
  devised ;
And I, Ill-Will, would have every man despised.
But now, another thing must be contrived, C1, *r.*
Or else all will be nought.

 There is one they call Good Remedy
In this realm ; he hath great authority ;
He is a noble man, and much worthy :
Many things he hath wrought.

 He is called lust, discreet, and indifferent,
Willing to fulfil his sovereign's commandment ;
He is not 'fraid to do right punishment ;
Therefore of him I am afraid !   [sad.
 Wit. So am I, too ; this maketh me very
Yet, oftentimes, I have been hard bestrad ;
Now that I am warned of him I am very glad :
S[ome crafty wile] for him [shall ye] had.
 Ill-W. Peace ! no mo words ; but mum !
Methink I hear mast Wealth come.
Kneel down and say such devout orison
That they may hear us pray.
Now, Jesu save Wealth, Health, and Liberty !
   LIBERTY *and* HEALTH *returneth back*
    with WEALTH.

WEALTH   19

Wealth.   Sirs! you will have both God's
        blessing ;
So are ye worth for your praying ;
Ye are well disposed, and of good living—
I will love you the better alway.

Ill-W.   Sir ! this do we use every day ;
For Wealth, Health, and Liberty to pray.
This same is my brother to you I [say] :
He is an hard honest man !

Wit.   Forsooth, master ! I am his brother ;
To be your servant was my coming hither ;
As long as we could be together
Ye shall not perish than.

Health.   To have you both to service I am
        content.   C1,*v.*
How say you, Liberty? will you thereto consent?
Will and Wit God hath us lent :
We may be glad of them.

Lib.   If we should refuse Will and Wit
We were to blame ; for they be fit.
Therefore, by my will they shall not flit :
They be welcome to me.

Ill-W.   God thank you, masters, all three !
Ye shall find us poor, but true we cannot be—
My tongue stumbles, I cry you mercy !—
We will be true, I should say.

Wealth.   Sirs, go your way home, unto one
        place !
And we will hie us after a-pace ;
And when we come, we shall set you in case
To have a living alway.

Health.   Then look ye do both truly and just ;
For we must put you in great trust ;
All our household guide ye must :
Behave you[r]self well.

Wit.   Masters, fear not ! for I have wit enough

To beguile myself, and to beguile you ;
I have beguiled many one, I may say to
    you :
I pray you keep that in counsel.
    Lib. Beware of that ! what doth he say?
Beguile us all? yet I charge thee, Nay !
Ye shall not beguile us : if I may,
I will beware betime.
    Ill-W. Sir, be not angry ! I you pray ;
The fool wotteth not he doth say ;
He meaneth that he will be profitable alway,
And save you many things.
    Health. What he meaneth I cannot tell, C2,*r.*
But his saying is not well.
Depart hence, sirs ! by my counsel,
And tarry us at our lodging.
    Wit. Now and it please ye, will ye hear
    any singing ?
Therein, I tell you, I am somewhat conning ;
Ye shall hear and ye list.
    Lib. Sir ! I pray you sing and ye can.
    Ill-W. Now will I begin like a lusty blood
than.   *They sing and go out.*
    [*Health.*] Sirs ! now go your way, of you I
    am glad
As of any servants that ever I had ;
For these can do both good and bad :
We must needs have such men.
    What were we if we lacked Will ?
And without Wit we should live ill ;
Therefore, Will and Wit I will keep still :
I promise you I love them.
    Here cometh REMEDY *in and to him saith—*
    Wealth. Sir ! your mastership is heartily
    welcome ;
Take your place here above, as it is reason.

    Health.   I pray you pardon us, we know not
      what ye be ;
Ye seem a man of honour and of great authority.
    Lib.   Sir ! to know wherefore ye come we
      are desirous.   [known
    Remedy.   I am he that ought for to be well
Of you three specially ; and of duty
Great pain and business, as for mine own,
For you I have taken because I love you
      heartily ;
To maintain you is all my desire and faculty ;
Yet hard it is to do, the people be so variable ;
And many be so wilful : they will not be re-
      formable.
    Wealth.   Sir ! I pray you pardon us of our
      ignorance now ;
I see well ye know us better than we do you.
    Rem.   I pardon you for I do know you well,
      both ;   C2,*v*.
Wealth and Health is your right names :
The which England to forbear were very loth.
For by Wealth and Health cometh great fames ;
Many other realms, for our great wealth,
      shames
That they dare not presume, nor they dare not
      be bold
To strive again England, or any right withhold.
    Health.   Sir ! ye be welcome ; I beseech you
      show us your name.
    Rem.   Good Remedy, forsooth ! I am the
      same.
    Lib.   If I durst be so bold I would pray you
      heartily
To show us a part of your great authority.
    Rem.   My authority is given to me, most
      special,

To maintain you three in this realm to be :
What mine intent is I will tell, but not all,
For that were too long to rehearse, of a surety ;
And I desire you all for to be loving to me,
For your own ease, come wealth and profit.

    Wealth.   Good Remedy ! then we must desire
      your aiding ;
For by Good Remedy cometh all our preferring.

    Rem.   All that I do intend, if ye will thereto
      agree,
And to be reformable for your own ease,
It is not the thing that lieth only in me.
But my good will, therefore, I will not cease,
To have your love and favour ; and thereby
    to please
All the world over, and to promote this realm :
That you three may prosper—ye perceive what
    I mean?   [estates :
   The chief part of all wealth lieth in great
Their substance and lands is right commend-
    able.
Prelates of the church is wealthy of riches ;
Merchants hath merchandise and goods incom-
    parable,   [laudable :
Men of law and franklins is wealthy, which is
                  [C3,*r.*
Thus wealth of riches is divided diverse ways ;
And to these many charges come now-a-days.

    Health.   My heart rejoiceth to hear your
      good reporting ;   [thing.
Much are we bound to God which provideth all

    Rem.   Forsooth ! here is not half that I
      could rehearse   [Wealth.
The benefits of God that He showeth to you,
Consider Englishmen, how valiant they be
    and fierce ;

Of none nations none such when they have their
    health ;

No land can do us harm but with falsehood or
    stealth.

Remember what number of men, or artillery,
    and good ordinance ;

Specially the grace of God which is our chief
    furtherance.   [do

   If there be any that will grudge, surmise, or

Again Wealth, Health, and Liberty, then must
    I, for the same,   [it, so

Show mine authority and power, for to remedy

That none of you shall diminish, nor amiss be
    tane.

I, Good Remedy, therefore, may and will
    speak without blane

For the commonwealth, and health both of
    the soul and body :

That is my office and power ; and therefore
    I have my authority.

    Wealth. Our Lord continue ye, and we
    thank you heartily

Both for your good instruction, and for your
    kindness

That you intend so well for us, Good Remedy.

When we have need, we will desire your good-
    ness.   [body,

    Health. When we be infect in the soul or

Then will I seek Good Remedy for succour.

As yet, I thank God, I have no need greatly ;

If I have, then will I seek to have your favour.

    Lib. Sir ! now we will depart hence, with
    your license,   [together.

For other divers business that we must have

    Rem. Sirs ! I am content ; now, when ye
    will depart,

To God I commit you; I will not make you
tarry.
But yet, I pray with all my mind and heart,
Take heed! in any wise eschew ill and shrewd
company.
If a man be never so . . . . . . [*original
is illegible*] C3,*v*.
He shall lose his name, and to some vice they
will him tempt;
Therefore beware of such people, and from
them be exempt.

    Health. Yes, yes, I warrant you! of such
I will beware—
Farewell, Good Remedy, and well to fare!
                     And goeth out.
    Rem. I pray God be your speed, and pre-
serve you from pain!
It is my mind ye should prosper; I would
have it so, fain.
           [ILL-WILL *and*] WIT *returneth.*
    Ill-W. Here is none of our acquaintance:
We have made too long tarriance—
That will ye say, perchance;
And they be gone home, come away apace.
    Wit. Nay, by God! not so hasty;
A little while we will tarry.
Good even, sir, to you, marry!
Dwell ye in this place?
    Rem. Nay, good fellow! I dwell not here:
Wherefore dost thou that inquire?
Holdest thou aught with any here?
Speak! be not afraid!
    Ill-W. By God! I would I had your gown,
And were a mile without the town;
Thereon I would borrow a crown,
It is I that so said.

Wit.   How, lookest thou on him half a-scorn?
I promise you he is a scant gentleman born:
What sayest thou in his face?

Rem.   For somewhat in his face I look;
Indeed, his mastership stands a-crook:
For false shrews both of you I took,
And children that be past grace.

Ill-W.   I will swear for him, as for these
        years twenty,
That he hath been ever as true as I;
Yet sometime he will steal and make a lie. C4,*r.*
He is of my alliance.

Rem.   In good faith, the same think I,
That ye be both like, full unthrifty.
Sirs! how do ye live? show me quickly,
Or I shall put you in durance.

Wit.   How live we? marry, our meat!
Comest thou hither for to threat?
So lordly sir Wittam doth speak!
From whence doth he come—can ye show?

Ill-W.   What dost thou ail? Canst thou
        tell?
Hast thou anything with us to mell?
By the mass! thy hands doth tickle—
Thou shalt bear me a blow.

Rem.   You false thieves! I know ye well:
I shall let your purpose every deal,
Ill-Will and Shrewd Wit, the devil of hell
Take ye both, for me!

Wit.   Marry, thou liest! our names be not
        so:
Call us but Wit and Will—add no more thereto.
If thou dost, thou were as good know
We shall handle you shrewdly.   [abide:

Rem.   Sirs, farewell! here I will no longer
For you both, shortly, I will provide

That all your false craft shall be outtried,
And your subtilty known.   *And goeth out.*
   Wit. To go so soon, the whoreson was wise ;
Therefore some now I must devise
That each man may Wealth, Health, and
    Liberty despise ;
Or else he will mar all our matter.
Brother wat ! let me alone :
When they come you shall see me anon ;
Complain of him unto them, each one,   C4,*v.*
And put him out of favour.   [yonder.
   Ill-W. Peace ! no mo words, for they come
    [WEALTH, HEALTH, *and* LIBERTY *cometh in.*]
   Wealth. Sirs ! I am glad that you be here.
How doth all our household ? with them what
Is everything in order there,   [cheer ?
After our intent ?
   Ill-W. Yea, Sir ! they be all merry and glad ;
With revel and rout sometime they be mad—
Pipe whore, hop thief, every knave and drab
Is at our commandment.
                HEALTH *turneth him.*
   Health. What do ye say ? then ye are to
    blame,
And we put you in trust for the same ;
To keep such rule, it is a shame ;
It is not for our honour.
   Wit. By the mass ! the whoreson doth lie ;
There is no such rule, by God's body !
A man may break his neck as lightly
As his fast in your kitchen or cellar, truly !
               LIBERTY *turneth him.*
   Lib. With that neither I am not content ;
I would there should be liberality competent ;
And, with honesty, it is convenient
That our neighbour fare the better.

Ill-W.   You be angry with all that we have
  done?
Come away, brother! let us go hence soon;
I know a new master where we shall be welcome.
God be with you, gentle master!
  Wealth.   Why, will ye be gone for a word?
Peradventure, we did but bord;
Methink ye should your master ford
For to speak my mind.   D1,*r*.
  Wit.   Nay, nay! I can tell what was the
    matter:
Remedy was here, and he did flatter;
Ye trust he more than us, and better;
But, mark the end! what ye shall find.
  Health.   With Good Remedy we spake,
    indeed;
To follow his counsel we had need.
He warned us that we should take heed
Of excess and prodigality.
  Wit.   I marvel ye speak so of Good Remedy:
It is I that can do more than he.
Wit can make shift at necessity
When Remedy cannot be heard.

  I know some that hath, this thousand year,
Sought Good Remedy, and yet never the near;
Wit can put Remedy by, yea, this is clear;
For Wit is a crafty lad.
  Ill-W.   And Will is an ungracious stay;
Will hath done many things men say;
And if ye let Wit and Will go his way,
Ye will repent it soon.
  Lib.   Why, what cause have you to go your
    way?
Ye shall abide with us, though you say, Nay;
I will follow Will and Wit alway;
And so I have ever done.

Wit. If I wist all my masters would so do,
Then from your service I would not go ;
Speak now ! whether ye will or no,
And let us know your mind.
    Health. Sirs ! ye be welcome to me, plain ;
And for your company I am full fain ;
I had liever suffer great pain
Than to leave my Wit and Will.
    Ill-W. Then, let us go hence ; with kindness
    my heart do kill.   D1,*v.*
    Health. I pray you, let us go ; wherefore
    do we bide still ?

        And goeth out. [REMEDY *cometh in.*]
    Rem. As touching my first purpose, hither
    I am come again.
I trow ye know me ; Good Remedy is my name ;
That every day doth take great labour or pain
To amend all faults : I am chosen to the same.
If any man's conscience here doth grudge or
    shame,
Having in himself remorse, and mends in time
    and space,
I am Good Remedy, and God is full of mercy
    and grace.   [remain,
Therefore I will stand aside, and a little while
Of Wealth, Health, and Liberty for to inquire
How they be ordered ; and if any man complain
I will be glad to show my remedy—methink I
    see one appear !   [HANCE *cometh in.*]
    Hance. Be Got's drowse ! ic myself bin
    cumpt heye scon lansman ;
Ic mot in ander land lopen, all is quade dan.
    Rem. Thou Fleming ! from whence comest
    thou, and what dost thou here ?
    Hance. Ic myself cumt from sent Katryn's
    doxe, mot ic skyne de can beer.

Rem. Get thee thither again, and tarry
here no longer!

Hance. Sir! ic mot mid ye spreken; ic
myself be en scomaker.

Rem. What and thou be? therewith I have
nothing ado.

Hance. Ic dest al forlore; copin is dod, ic
maght not do thereto.

Rem. I pray thee, go hence, for thou dost
trouble me ill.

Hance. Nen ic seker, ic wil not gon, ic
wold fain live hore stil.

Rem. There is too many aliants in this
realm; but now I,

Good Remedy, have so provided that Englishmen shall live the better daily.

Hance. What segt ye? by Got's drowse!
dai is de quade man;   [man.

Be de moro goi, ic myself love de scone English-

Rem. Fie on thee, flattering knave! fie on
you aliants all, I say!

Ye can, with craft and subtle figure, Englishmen's wealth away.

Hance. O, skon mester! ic heb hore bin
this darten yeore.   [broer.

Ic can skote de culverin, and ic can be de beare

[*A line (or lines) apparently missing here.*]

[*Rem.*] Trust see so provide that Wealth
from you have I shall.   D2,*r*.

Hance. Ic seg to you dat Wealth is lopen
in an ander contry;

Wat hebegy dar brough forstan ye net, segt me.

Rem. I understand thee well; yet, thou
liest, like a knave.

Wealth is here in England, and Wealth still I
trust we shall have.

Hance. Ic ment no quad, ic love de English
    man, by min bere!

Cump by sent Katrin, and ic shal ye geven
    twe stope bere.

Rem. Get thee hence, drunken Fleming!
    thou shalt tarry no longer here.

Hance. Mot it net mare herebin woder sal
    ic gewest kiskin;

Ic wil to de kaizer gan, dar sall ic wal skinkin.
                     And goeth.

Rem. Is he gone? I pray God the devil
    go with him!

Where is Wealth, Health, and Liberty? I
    would see them come in.   [*head.*

    HEALTH *cometh in with a kercher on his*

Health. O, good Lord, help me! by your
    license, my Sovereign!

I am homely to come here in your presence,
    thus diseased.

Need constraineth me, for Remedy I would have
    fain;

I am infect, both body and soul, I pray you
    be not displeased.

Rem. Why, what ail you? show me! yet,
    you I do not know;

Glad I am to remedy any man that is affirmity;

I perceive by your phisn'amy that ye are very
    weak, feeble, and low;   [*gladly.*

Yet show me your grief, and I will help you

Health. Gracious Remedy! I thank you;
    yet I am half ashamed

To show you my malady and my name—I was
    called Health;   [blamed

Therefore, I am well worthy to be punished and

Because I have not followed your counsel, but
    all thing may be suffered save Wealth.

    Rem.   Are you Health? this maketh me very
    pensive and sad :   [infect ;
Yet be of good cheer, and show how you were
To remedy you and succour you, I would be
    very glad ;   [detect.
For God will punish the people when they be
    Health.   Sir! I thank God therof; for well
    worthy I am,   [must ;
My conscience doth judge ; some trouble have I
Amends I will make to God, and if I can.
Wit and Will hath deceived me : in them I put
    my trust.   D2,*v.*
    Rem.   If thou have done amiss and be sorry
    therefore,
Then half amends is made, for that is contrition.
Let that pass! now will I axe you one thing
    more :   [disposition?
Where be Wealth and Liberty? be they of good
    Health.   As for Wealth [he] is fallen in decay
    and necessity   [Shrewd Wit ;
By waste and war, through Ill-Will and
And Liberty is kept in durance and captivity.
God help us all, and send us good remedy for it !
    Rem.   For to hear this tale, it maketh my
    heart heavy ;
Yet, be of good comfort! God is full of grace,
    and I am good.
    Health.   Sir! then I beseech you, help us in
    the way of charity !
    Rem.   I would fain, but I cannot tell which
    way to begin,
Except I might catch Will and Wit ; then, I
    trow, I could
Tie them shorter ; for they destroy Wealth,
    Health, and Liberty by sin.   [would.
If I had the thieves, punish them extremely I

Health.　You may soon catch them if ye will
　　stand aside ;
From this place they two will not long abide.
　Rem.　Methinketh I hear them come ; help
　　to hold them fast.

ILL-WILL *turneth.*

　Ill-W.　Come in, Wit ! for here is nobody ;
We may be bold, and talk largely
Our hearts to ease, and show plainly
What we have done.　[SHREWD WIT *comes in.*]
　Wit.　I must needs laugh, I cannot forbear
To remember War, that knave ! Will ye
　　hear ?
The whoreson Fleming was beshitten for fear,
Because he should void so soon.　　　[bread !
　Ill-W.　Hark ! now do I marvel, by this
For I ween, surely, that Health be dead !
I saw him go with a kercher on his head,
As he should go to hanging.　　　　[hap
　Wit.　Hark, in thine ear !—if the whoreson
To complain to him that wears the red cap,
I fear then shortly he will us clap　　　D3,*r.*
By the heels from our living.
　Ill-W.　Nay, nay ! there is no doubt ;
By him I have reported, all about,
That he doth not well his good name to put out :
Ill-Will cannot say well.
　Rem.　Friend ! therein thou art the more to
　　blame,
To slander me wrongfully and undeserved ;
But, or thou depart thou shalt answer for the
　　same.
Where is Wealth and Liberty ? how hast thou
　　them ordered ?
　Ill-W.　Qury cisis quest is un malt ombre ;
Me is un Spyanardo compoco parlavere.

Health.   Thou false thief! is thine English
   tongue gone?
As mischievous Ill-Will and Shrewd Wit ye
   have destroyed many one.
   Wit.   Sir! hurt not me, and I will tell you
   truth, anon :   [Saint John's.
This same is as false a knave as ever came within
   Ill-W.   Per amor de my as pica un poco
Eo queris andar pour lagtaunt creae so.
   Rem.   I cannot tell what thou dost mean,
   babbler !
But thou shalt speak English, and confess
   another matter.
   Health.   Sir! I beseech your lordship, in the
   way of charity,
Let not these thieves escape your hands : they
   have destroyed us utterly.
   Wit.   Sir! believe him not! he speaks but
   of malice only.   [witness,
We be true men ; thereof we shall fetch good
An honest man that shall be bound for him
   and me.
The law saith plain : *Nulla fides contra testes*.
   Rem.   That is truth ; but who will be witness
   or bound for thee?   [house.
   Ill-W.   There is three among you in this
   Wit.   I will go to fetch them quickly.
   Rem.   They will come unsend for, I warrant
   you, if they wist.
What be their names ? tell me what they be !
   Ill-W.   That one is John Irische and John
   Sholer :
But full these be honest men, all three.   D3,*v*.
   Health.   Trust not their words ! they will
   dissemble still ;   [ill.
They are so false and crafty, all their intent is

Ill-W.   Ye lie falsely ! I speak but right and
    reason ;
And by the law of arms, ye must needs be tane.
You are called Good Remedy which, at all season,
Should lean to man's life, and maintain the
    same.   [accused by defame :
We be here both your prisoners, wrongfully
Keep one of us fast ; let him lie for all ;
That other for friends and witness go shall.
    Wit.   Sir ! let him not go, and leave me
        behind ;   [mind.
He will ever be a false knave, for I know his
    Ill-W.   Hold thy tongue, foolish knave ! I
        do not mean so.
    Rem.   I hear now ye cannot agree which
        of you should go.   [go but I.
    Ill-W.   No, by God's body ! there shall none
    Wit.   Thou playest the knave ! it must needs
        be I !
    Health.   Keep them safe, I pray you ; for if
        they scape again   [pain.
Many men shall repent it : it shall be to our
    Rem.   They be here yet ; to keep them fast
        is mine intent.
Have them away, both to prison, incontinent !
    Ill-W.   Lo, false knave ! this is for thy
        crafty wit ;
Now fast by the heels we are like to sit.
    Wit.   I am content so that I may have
        company ;
If I should be hanged I would be hanged honest.
                              And goeth out.
    Rem.   Go hence with them, and bring
        Wealth and Liberty.
    Health.   Come away, ye thieves ! now I
        shall keep you surely !   *And goeth out.*
WEALTH   20

Ill-W. Lock us up, and keep us as fast as
ye can,   [a man.
Yet Ill-Will and Shrewd Wit shall be with many
Rem. I am half ashamed that long it
hath been said   [deceived.
That noble men by such wretches hath been
They did rejoice and jest, and were very well
apaid,   [reigned.
Trusting to scape clear and still for to have
But now, they shall not so ; let them be well
assured
That Ill-Will and Shrewd Wit shall have but
ill rest ;   D4,*r.*
For wheresoever they be I will break their nest.
Wealth. In the honour of God we ask you
forgiveness, all three ;   [face.
We ought to be ashamed to look you in the
By our folly and negligence we have done so
unwisely ;   [grace :
We were foully deceived ; we put us to your
This shall be a good warning for us a long
space ;   [ware ;
When man is well punished then he will be-
Who that knoweth what need is, will after
dread care.
Rem. I may not blame you greatly, for by
mine own reason
I know Ill-Will and Shrewd Wit deceiveth great
and small.   [season,
If ye can remember this, and beware another
This is a good example and learning to you all :
Now serve God and love Him, and for grace
ever call,   [abstain :
And Ill-Will and Shrewd Wit from you I shall
Ye have used them too long to your damage
and pain.

Health.   Forsooth, sir! ye say truth; they
    did us great displeasure;   [Will,
Full hard it is to vanquish the ungracious Ill-
He is so crooked by flattery, dissimulation, and
    such other.   [ill,
Man's mind is so variable, and glad to report
I fear many one yet would have him reign
    still;
For some unto their own will hath so much
    affection:
Yet the devil and Ill-Will is both of one com-
    plexion.   [Wit;
Lib.   Ill-Will is nought, but worse is Shrewd
For he contriveth all subtle imagination;
It were unpossible for a man else to do it.
Shrewd Wit breweth mischief, and false con-
    spiration;
He hath put me, Liberty, in prison and great
    tribulation;
If it had not been for your good remedy and
    furtherance,
I, and other that hath liberty, should have been
    in durance.
Rem.   Be all of good cheer, and have no
    mistrust!
The end of Ill-Will and Shrewd Wit is but
    shame.   [unjust,
Though they reign awhile, wrongfully and
Yet Truth will appear, and their misdeeds
    blame;   D4,*v.*
Then wrong is subdued, and good remedy
    tane;   [all,
Though falsehood cloak and hide his matters
Craft will out, and deceit will have a fall.
   Whereas ye are now in distress, all three,
Near were ye brought in case like to mar;

Now, have ye no doubt! if ye will be ruled
 after me   [were.
I shall restore ye again as well as ever ye
Wealth! keep still this realm; look ye stray
 not far!
And Health! be of good cheer! your disease
 I can soon mend.   [offend!
Liberty! now ye be released, do no more
  Wealth. Now let us all thank God, that
 Good Remedy hath send;
Trust to Him only for His grace and goodness.
We axe forgiveness of our trespass; I trust
 we will amend,
And clean forsake sin, folly, and unthriftiness.
Thus we will here conclude. Sovereign!
 of your graciousness,
We beseech you to remit our negligence and
 misbehaviour:
There we have said amiss, we commit all to
 your favour.
  Health. And for your preservation heartily
 we will pray;
Your realm to increase with joy and tranquillity;
That Wealth, Health, and Liberty may con-
 tinue here alway,
By the oversight and aid of him that is Good
 Remedy;
Which willingly doth his duty under your
 authority,   [tain:
As part here appeareth, your purpose to main-
God continue his goodness, that long he may
 reign.
  Rem. Jesu! preserve Queen Elizabeth, the
 noble princess worthy!
Jesu! continue her health long for to endure!
Jesu! endue her in virtue, grace, and honour!

Jesu! maintain the Lords of the Council to
    execute good remedy ever!
Jesu! speed and help all them God's honour
    to further!
Jesu! increase the commonalty to prosper
    and do well!

FINIS.

[The printing of this play in the original is atrocious—
à la Cock-Robin shop: type worn and battered; bad
spelling; turned letters—b, d, f, long s, k, l—all long
"stamps" used interchangeably; throughout a monu-
ment of bad Caxtonship.]

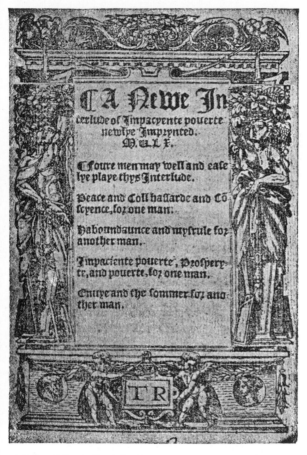

¶A Newe In
terlude of Impacyente pouerte
newlye Imprynted.
M.U.LX.

¶foure men may well and ease
lye playe thys Interlude.

Peace and Coll haſſarde and Cõ
ſcyence, for one man.

haboundaunce and myſrule for
another man.

Impacyente pouerte, Proſpery
te, and pouerte, for one man.

Enuye and the ſommer for ano
ther man.

T R

*[Reduced Facsimile of the Title-page of "Impatient Poverty"
from a copy now in the British Museum.]*

A New Interlude of

IMPATIENT POVERTY

newly Imprinted, 1560

Four men may well and easily play
this Interlude

Peace, and Colhazard, and Conscience	} for one man
Abundance and Misrule	} for another man
Impatient Poverty Prosperity, and Poverty	} for one man
Envy, and the Sumner	} for another man

Imprinted at London, in Paul's Churchyard
at the Sign of the Swan, by John King

[IMPATIENT POVERTY.]

Peace. The puissant Prince and Innocent
    most pure,   [piternal,
Which humbly descended from the seat sem-
Illumine his beams of grace to every creature;
To withstand the conflict of our enemies mortal;
The devil, the world, and the flesh, these three
    in special,   [the body;
Which setteth division between the soul and
In like wise envy setteth debate between party
    and party.
    I speak for this cause: daily ye may see
How that, by envy and malice, many be
    destroyed;   [humility,
Which, if they had lived in peace with patient
Riches and prosperity with them had been
    employed.
For thereas is peace, no man is annoyed;
For by peace men grow to great richesse;
And by peace men live in great quietness.
    I am named Peace, which Envy doth expel.
Envy with me shall never rest;
For Envy is one of the pains of hell.
When that he sojourneth within a man's breast,
Like the burning Phœnix in her own nest,
Though she can none other hurt, ne grieve,
Yet she doth not cease herself to mischieve

Envy. A, sir! here was a long predication:
Methought ye said, in your communication,
To every man peace was most behoved.
    Peace. Forsooth! and so said I.
    Envy. That shall be proved contrary, by
        and by;
For by peace much people are undone.
    Peace. What people are tho[se]?   [bowyer,
    Envy. The armourer, the fletcher, and the
Mariners, gunners, and the poor sowdyer;
Yea, and also many another artificer
Which I do not rehearse by name.
    Peace. I say the universal people doth best
        obtain   A2,*v.*
Whereas Peace is ever abiding.   [halidom!
    Envy. Thou liest! so God me help and
For then were surgeons clean undone.
Of them that will fight, and break a pate,
They get good living, both early and late;
And what sayest thou by men of law?
Their living were not worth a straw
And every man should live in peace!
    Peace. That is not for the commons
        increase;
For by peace they profit in many a thing.
Peace setteth amity between king and king;
In time of peace merchants have their course
To pass and repass.
    Envy. Thou liest, knave! by the mass!
For under colour of peace much subtlety hath
        been wrought;
And ships are taken the merchants dear have
        bought—
Was that for their promotion?
Nay, in time of war,
Such a knave durst not stir.

By the mass ! were it not for shame thou shouldst
    bear me a blow.
  Peace.   Hold thy hands, thou lewd fellow !
Thou art of evil disposition
Thus against peace to repugne ;
The which from heaven descended down
To bring man out of captivity.
  Envy. A, whoreson ! why dost thou lie ?
When were thou in heaven ? tell me by and by !
How camest thou down ? with a ladder or a
    rope ?
  Peace. It were no sin to hang thee by throat ;
Thy words be envious, not grounded on charity.
  Envy. Sir ! one thing, I pray you, tell me.
  Peace. What is that ?
  Envy. Have ye any wife, or no ?   A3,*r.*
  Peace. Wherefore ask ye so ?
  Envy. Because ye say peace is most ex-
    pedient :   [present,
If your wife made you cuckold, you being
What would ye do ?
  Peace. Give her such punishment as longeth
    thereto.
  Envy. A false, flattering whoreson, lo !
Now thou sayest against thine own declaration :
If thou fight, where is then peace become ?
  Peace. I break not peace with doing due
    correction ;
For correction should be done charitably—
Irascemini et nolite peccare.
  Envy. I shall meet that at *omnium quare* :
Peace should forgive, and not be revenged.
Hence, whoreson ! by our Lady of Wolpit,
I shall rap thee of the pate !
  Peace. Go hence, wretch ! thou makebate !
It were alms to set thee in Newgate.

Ho, Master Constable, come near !
Here is a wretch without reason ;
Take and put him in prison,
With as many irons as he may bear !
 Envy. By our lady ! I will come no near.
A constable, quod ha! nay, that will I not abide ;
For I am loth to go shorter tide.
Yet long, whoreson ! for all thy pride,
I shall meet with thee another day,
When one of us two shall go a knave away.
 Peace. O, thou wretch ! thou ought to
  remord
That so far art exiled from charity.
Lo ! he thinketh not how meekly his Maker
  and Lord
Suffered reprefe, and died upon a tree,
Giving us example that with humil[it]y
Every man should follow his trace,   A3,*v.*
That in heaven will claim a place.

   [*Enter* IMPATIENT POVERTY.]

 Imp. Pov. Keep, keep, for Cock's face !
 Peace. Why art thou so out of patience?
 Imp. Pov. A knave would have rested me :
  I owe him but forty pence—
He shall abide, by God's dear blest ! [text :
 Peace. Take heed, my friend ! thus saith the
In little meddling standeth great rest.
Therefore, pay thy duty well and honestly,
With few words discreetly ;
Another time ye shall be the better trust.
 Imp. Pov. That will I never do while I live ;
  let him do his best.
I had liever lay all my good to pledge
To get a writ of privilege ;
So may I go by his nose at large,

Spite of his teeth, whosoever say Nay.
    Peace. This is but a wilful mind : if thou
      wilt not pay
Thy very duty, which cannot be denied,
Getting of thy writ and expense in the law
Will cost more than thy duty—this well I knaw.
Thy debt therewith cannot be paid ;
It is only a deferring of the payment. [intent.
    Imp. Pov. Yet the knave shall not have his
    Peace. Thou shalt pay by rightful judgment,
For the law is indifferent to every person.
    Imp. Pov. I see thou holdest on his opinion.
Yet, I set not by you both a rish :
And I meet the knave I shall hew his flesh ;
Help him, thou old churl and thou can !
    Peace. I see thou art an evil-disposed man :
I utterly forsake thy condition.   [whoreson !
    Imp. Pov. Marry ! avaunt, long, precious
I set not by thee nor him, I make God avow !
                                [A4,*r.*
I am as good a man as thou, for all thy good :
Let it be tryd by manhood, and thereto I give
      thee my glove.
    Peace. All such warriors I do reprove,
For peace loveth not to fight.   [might ;
    Imp. Pov. No, old fool ! thou hast lost thy
For in age is nought else but cowardise.
    Peace. Youth with his courage light,
Nor strength with multitude, I do thee plight
Are not only the cause of victory.
    Imp. Pov. No, good sir ! what then ?
    Peace. Grace and good governance of man.
For with good discretion they began
That were the great winners of victory.
    Imp. Pov. Then victory is gotten by dis-
I pray you, sir, show me this lesson :   [cretion ;

How to come to richesse, for that is all my care.
For I am ever in great necessity ;
Meat and drink with me is scarcity ;
No man will trust me of a penny ;
And, also, my clothes are but bare.
Good sir ! what say you therein ?

    Peace.   I hold it punishment for thy sin :
Show me what is thy name !

    Imp. Pov.   I am named Impatient Poverty.

    Peace.   Forsooth ! that may full well be :
Thou art so full of wrath and envy
In thee can grow no grace ;
But if thou wilt forsake sensuality,
And be governed by reason, as I shall induce
    thee,
Thou shalt come to richesse within short space.

    Imp. Pov.   Show me that now, in this place,
And thereto I will agree.

    Peace.   Thou must love thy neighbour with
    charity ;   A4,*v.*
Do unto him no manner of disease ;
Look how thou would he did to thee,
Do to him no worse, in no degree ;
And then thou shalt Our Lord please.

    Imp. Pov.   Shall I love him that loveth not
    me ?
Those that trouble and rebuke me shamefully ?
That will I never do, while I live !

    Peace.   Thou must charitably all faults forgive ;
Whatsoever any man to thee say
Let as thou heard it not ; turn thine ear away ;
Thou shalt please God if thou so do.

    Imp. Pov.   Nay, by God ! there ho !
What is he, in all this place,
That will do as this man said ?
Show me or I go !

If a man do you a great offence
Will ye keep your patience?
Nay, by God, not so!
I put case: I break your head—
Will ye suffer that in very deed?
    Peace. To suffer, for Christ's sake, I shall
      have meed.   [bread!
    Imp. Pov. That shall I know, by God's
    Peace. Hold thy hand, and keep patience;
Think what Christ suffered for our offence!
He was beaten, scourged, and spit on with
    violence,
And suffered death for our sake.
Yet He took it patiently;   [enemies:
He forgave His death, and prayed for His
Pater dimitte illis, His saying was; truly
An example for us to take
To be meek in heart: *beati pauperes spiritu*
Shall Christ say full even;   [B1,*r.*
Et venite benediciti, come my blessed children
To the kingdom of heaven!
    Imp. Pov. Sir! I thank you for your ghostly
      instruction;
Unto your saying I can make no delayance;
I put me under your governation,
And, for m' ill-deeds, I take great repentance.
    Peace. Then, to my saying take good re-
      membrance:
Exercise yourself in virtue from this time hence;
And, unto peace, evermore be obedient;
Set before every sharp word a shield of suffer-
    ance;
And when time is of your concupiscence,
Then pacify it with benign resistance.
    Imp. Pov. Sir, gramercy that ye have
      brought me to this estate;

By your advertisement I am willing to live in
    Christ's law ;
Thereas I have offended Him, both early and
    late ;
I served Him not for love, nor for awe ;
Therefore, now right well I know
That poverty and misery that I my life inlead
It is but only punishment for my misdeed.
    Peace.   Now, or we any further proceed,
Hold this vesture, and put it on thee ;
From henceforth thou shalt be called Prosperity.
    Prosperity.   I thank God, and you ! I am in
    felicity.
    Peace.   Now, unto you I shall here shew
Of such things as ye shall eschew.
First, your soul look that ye keep clean ;
Beware of misrule in any wise ;
Play not at cailes, cards, nor dice ;
Also from miswomen, for by them mischief
    may rise,
As it doth often ; this daily is seen ;
Haunt no taverns, nor sit not up late ;
Let not hassard nor rioter with you be check-
    mate ;
For then will Envy come, and make debate,
The which shall cause great trouble.   B1,*v.*
Be plentiful of such as God hath sent ;
Unto the poor people give with good intent ;
For every penny that so is spent
God will send thee double—
Take heed and do as I have said.
    Pros.   Sir ! therewith I hold me well apaid ;
As ye have commanded me, it shall be done.
    Peace.   Then let us depart for a season ;
If ye need, I will be your protection.
                               Exeunt ambo.

[*Enter* ABUNDANCE *and* CONSCIENCE.]

Abundance. Joy and solace be in this hall!
Is there no man here that knoweth me at all?
I am beloved, both with great and small;
Abundance is my name.
I have all things as me list:
Meat, drink, and cloth of the best;
Gold and silver, full is every chest—
In faith! I will not layne.
I think ye know not my ways,
How I get goods, now-a-days,
By a proper mean.
Think you that I wold
Lend either silver or gold?
That day shall not be seen.
But I will lend them ware,
That shall be both bad and dear,
Not worth the money he shall pay;
And if he can no surety get,
Of my ware he getteth right nought
Without a good pledge he lay.
Then will I, for mine avail,
He shall make a bill of sale;
To me full bought and sold.
If the day be expired and past,   B2,*r.*
Then will I hold it fast;
He shall not have it though he would.
Thus, craft I have long used;
And some men do not yet refuse it:
This is be openly known.
What is he, in all this town,
That will lend without singular commodum?
Should I lend without a profit?
Nay, then I hold nought worth my wit.   [ence.
Conscience. All this ye say is against Consci-

Abun.   Conscience, quod a? Nay, then shall
   we never thrive!
For I know him not alive
By conscience that cometh to substance.
I have all manner of marchandy;
I sell for long days to them that are needy,
And for the payment I have good surety,
Bound in statute marchant.
Because I may forbear,
I sell my ware so dear;
I make forty of twenty in half a year:
Other men do so as well as I.

Cons.   Evensine very shame! marry, fie!
These goods are gotten untruly;
Many a man is undone thereby,
To take this ware so dear.

Abun.   They seek to me both far and near;
Methink it is a good deed
To help a man at his need.
Yet have I other means
Whereby I get great gains:
I think ye know not that.

Cons.   I? no, God wot!

Abun.   No, ye are but an idiot!   B2,*v.*
I sold a man as much ware as came to forty
   pound,
And in an obligation I had him bound
To pay me at a certain day;
And when the bargain was made plain,
Mine own servant bought the same ware again
For the third penny it cost—ye wot what I
   mean!
But was not this a wise way?

Cons.   Thou shalt repent it another day;
I charge thee, as far as I may,
Such false ways never begin.

Abun.   Wherefore? this is no sin:
It is plain buying and selling;
Lawful it is for a man to win,
Else rich shall he never be.   [ciance,
   Cons.   Winning, to be had with due suffi-
In true buying and selling is not to discommend;
But for thy false usury thou art cursed in the
      sentence.
I pray God give thee grace for to amend.
   Abun.   Is every man accursed that doth buy
      and sell?
Then shall no man with merchandise mell:
How shall the world then be uphold?
   Cons.   Nay, sir, amiss ye do understand me:
All those that occupy false usury,
And transgresseth the laws of God by iniquity,
All such are accursed I you told;
As for buying and selling needs must be;
And God commandeth to lend to them that are
      needy,
So it be not to their injury
For lucre to them sold.
   Abun.   How should I sell? show me your
      ways!
   Cons.   Ye may not sell the dearer, for days;
If ye do, it is contrary to God's laws.
   Abun.   It is used in our country.   B3,*r.*
   Cons.   It is the more pity;
One such is able to destroy a city.
And God show not His great mercy,
All such are damned by His equity.
   Abun.   God forfend that should be!
How shall men do that be of great reputation,
Which kept their goods on this same fashion,
By usury, deceit, and by extortion?
I do so myself: wherefore should I lie?

Cons.   Thou mayst be the more sorry.

Abun.   It is so now—what remedy?

Cons.   To make restitution.

Abun.   What call ye restitution?

Cons.   Restore such goods as ye have gotten
Wrongfully, by oppression.   [sion :

Abun.   Then shall I have little in my posses-
I will make God amends another way.

I will fast, and I will pray,

And I will give alms every day,

That I have done amiss, I am sorry, therefore.

Cons.   This is not sufficient; thou must
     restore ;

Quia non dimittitur peccatum
Nisi restituatur ablatum :

Ye must restore to them ye have offended unto.

Abun.   Then I shall show you what I shall
I will put it in my testament   [do!
That my executors shall pay and content ;

For while I live I will not have my good spent,

For if I do, I am but spilt.

Cons.   Make amends, man, for thy guilt ;
Rather spoil thy body than spoil thy soul.

Abun.   Men of substance are ashamed to fall.

Cons.   That causeth them to rest in their
     sin.   B3,*v.*

Abun.   Yet ever with thy strongest part
     renneth the ball.

Cons.   Yesterday thou canst not again call.
When thou art dead the gate of mercy is shut ;
     you cannot come in.

Abun.   Then let him stand without.

Cons.   So of thy soul thou hast no doubt?

Abun.   When thou seest my soul torn, set
     on a clout.   [rout,
If falsehood, usury, and extortion should not

Thousands in this realm should be put out ;
The third part should not bide, by Saint Paul !
    Cons.   Yet often falsehood hath a great fall :
An example, by King Achab, which is soth,
Desired the vineyard of that poor man Naboth,
By counsel of Jezebel that king's wife.
Because he would not sell his possession,
Of two false witnesses he was peached of high
        treason ;
And, through the mouth of a false quest, it rave ;
Which caused the poor man to lose both land
        and life.
After that, of God's own bidding,
Came Helias the prophet to Achab the King ;
Saying he should have evil ending.
And so he had ; for by the way as he rode,
He fell and brake his neck where dogs lapped
        his blood.   [thinketh me,
This example, to all usurers and oppressors, as
Should cause them of God sore adread to be.
    Abun.   Sir, ye preach very holily, but our
        deeds be often contrary ;
Ye be so acquainted with covetise and simony
That maketh us to take the same way.
    Cons.   So every evil disposed person doth say.
The frailty of man doth often offend ;
Then call for grace, and shortly amend ;
Therefore I counsel thee to pretend
To repent, and be sorry for thy misdeed.
    Abun.   Yet thus I will my life lead ;   B4,*r*.
For of your saying I take no heed.
Ye will mucker up both gold and treasure ;
Ye have riches without measure ;
And of the flesh ye have your pleasure ;
Ye can find no ways to amend yourself, I you
        insure.

Therefore rebuke not me for my sin ne good :
God be with you ! ye shall not rule me.

    Cons.   O dull wit ! plunged by ignorance,
Regarding nothing of ghostly instruction,
Setting more his mind on worldly substance
Than on the everlasting life that is to come !
God will strike when He list ; ye know not how
    soon.
Therefore to every man this counsel I give :
To be sorry for your sin and do penance while
    ye live.

        Here cometh ENVY *running in, laughing,*
          and saith to CONSCIENCE.

    Envy.   Now, in faith ! I would ye had be
    there.
    Cons.   Where should I have be ?
    Envy.   A better sport ye never see.
    Cons.   Whereat laugh ye so fast ?
    Envy.   He to go, and she after ;
And, within a while, he caught her.
He took of her an incroke,
And chopt her on the heel with his foot ;
Anon he whipt her on the back.
A, whoreson ! quod she ; playest thou me that ?
And with her heel she gave him a spat,
That he was fain to go back again.

    Cons.   Good fellow, thou art to blame
Such words to have : no good thou can.

    Envy.   I said it to make you sport and game.
I cry you mercy ! I was to blame :
I see ye are some virtuous man.   B4,*v.*

    Cons.   Shortly hence, that way thou came !
For here thou shalt not be.   [me,

    Envy.   Good Lord ! some succour Thou send
That I be not outcast !

    Cons.   What is thy name ? shortly, show me !

Envy. I dare not, sir, by Christ Jesu,
Except ye keep it privily.

   Cons. Fear not ; say on, heartily !

   Envy. Sir, my right name is Charity.
Sometime beloved I was with the spiritualty ;
But now covetise and simony doth them so
    avance   [ordinance ;
That good institution is turned to other
And *bonum exemplum* is put to such hindrance
That here I dare not appear.

   Cons. Simony is not now in the spiritualty :
Bonus pastor ovium thereto will see ;
Therefore methink this is a lie :
In holy church simony cannot abide.

   Envy. He goeth in a cloak, he cannot be
    espied ;
And coveteous so craftily doth provide   [see.
That *bonus pastor ovium* is blind, and will not

   Cons. This that ye speak is upon Envy ;
Therefore, I think ye be not Charity,
For Charity alway will say the best.

   Envy. Amongst them can I have no rest.

   Cons. How do ye with the temporalty?

   Envy. There is pride, sloth, and lechery,
Which putteth me from that place.

   Cons. Then be ye with the commonalty?

   Envy. They despise me utterly.
One of them love not another ;
The sister cannot love the brother ;
Ne the child the father, ne mother :   C1,*r.*
There I dare not show my face.

   Cons. This is to me a strange case :
What hear ye by Conscience ?

   Envy. Spiritual and temporal set against
    him, marvellously ;   [degree ;
Merchants, men of law, and artificers of every

They will hang him and they him espy.
Such exclamation goeth through this realm,
    round.
    Cons.   Why what fault have they found
With him, so to do?
    Envy.   His wit is nought, they say; also,
Every man putteth his will thereto,
To banish him for ever.
    Cons.   I know well it is not as ye say;
For I am Conscience, the high judge of the
    law.
    Envy.   Be ye Conscience? alas! that ever
    I this day saw!
If ye be taken, ye shall be hanged and draw;
For they have utterly put you down,
And set Covetise in your room,
Subtilty the scribe, his own cousin,
And Falsehood the Sumner, for the Court's
    promotion.
    Cons.   I marvel wherefore this was done.
    Envy.   When riches came before you, that
    much will pay—
There he had lived in sin many a day—
Ye should for money let him go quit away,
And put him to no shame.
Let poverty do penance for a little offence:
He is not able to promote you of twenty
    pence.
Then should ye have kept your residence,
And gotten yourself a good name.
    Cons.   Who so doeth they are to blame
In misordering them in such wise.
    [*Envy.*]   Y-wys, cousin! I show you as now
    is the guise;
For by covetise much people doth uprise,   C1,*v.*
Which is against both you and me.

Cons.   Charity, I pray you show what remedy
In this matter, for me, may be found.
   Envy.   Shortly, get you to wilderness, or
     some other region ;
For they will hang you up at the Tyborn
If they find you in this place ;
And I must depart also.
   Cons.   This is to me much sorrow and woe ;
I will go into some far country.
Farewell, gentle cousin, Charity !
   Envy.   I shall pray for you : pray ye for me !
This is an heavy departing,   *Et plora.*
I can in no wise forbear weeping.
Yet kiss me or ye go ;
For sorrow my heart will break in two.
Is he gone? then have at laughing !
A, sir ! is not this a jolly game
That Conscience doth not know my name ?
Envy, in faith ! I am the same :
What needeth me for to lie ?
I hate Conscience, Peace, Love and Rest ;
Debate and Strife, that love I best,
According to my property.
When a man loveth well his wife,
I bring them at debate and strife—
This is seen daily ;
Also, between sister and brother ;
There shall no neighbour love another
Where I dwell by.
And now I tell you plain,
Of one man I have disdain ;
Prosperity men do him call.
He is nigh of my blood ;   *C2,r.*
And he to have so much worldly good,
That grieveth me worst of all.
   Pros.   Jesus, that is both steadfast and stable,

Ever perseverant, and never mutable —
He save this congregation!   [passion!

Envy.   Welcome, Poverty! by Cock's
How have ye done this many a day?

Pros.   I thank God, as well as any may.
Ye call me wrong: my name is Prosperity.

Envy.   Prosperity, with an evil hap!
How the devil fortunest that?
I knew thee Impatient Poverty.   [pass,

Pros.   Whatsoever I was, let that matter
And take me as I am.

Envy.   I cry you mercy! I was to blame
To call you by your old name;
Yet all these people think ye are the same
Impatient Poverty, as I said before.   [bore;

Pros.   Avaunt! I tell thee, I am gentleman
If I hear thee report such words any more,
Thou shalt be punished like a knave.

Envy.   A knave, quod a? by Cock's passion!
I am your own cousin,
And nigh of your consanguinity.

Pros.   Thou and I are not of one affinity.

Envy.   If I were a rich man ye would not say
       so by me;
Ye would then say, I were your next kinsman
       on live.   [strife:

Pros.   I say, go hence, and make no more
I set not by such a poor haskard.

Envy.   Sir, do not ye know my name?

Pros.   I know thee not, by Saint Jame.

Envy.   Charity, in faith! I am the same:
What needeth me for to lie?   C2,*v.*
I am your cousin, and so will I die;
Ye may be glad such a kinsman to have.

Pros.   Shall we have more ado yet, thou
       knave?

I charge thee, never know me for your kin!
   Envy.   I pray you, one word or I go.
   Pros.   Say on, shortly; then have I do.
   Envy.   Sir, I have of gold three hundred
    pound,
In a bag fast i-bound,
At home locked in my chest.
I purpose to go to Jerusalem;
Ye shall keep it till I come again:
I put you best in trust.
   Pros.   Cousin, I would fain do the best
Because ye are near of my blood.
   Envy.   What! are ye now in that mood?
Now I am your kinsman, because of my good;
Before of me he had disdain!
   Pros.   As for that, I was to blame;
I knew you not—be not angry.
Ye are welcome to me, cousin Charity.
   Envy.   Then all these matters let be!
I come hither with you to dwell;
Ye must have more servants, I do you tell,
Such as were necessary for your person.
   Pros.   I am content after your provision;
In every thing let it be done
As ye think most expedient.
   Envy.   Sir, I shall do mine intent
To get you servants mo.
   Pros.   I pray you heartily it may be so:
A little season I will from you go,
To solace me with some recreation.   [*Exit.*
   Envy.   He that sitteth above the moon   C3,*r.*
Evermore be in your protection!
Aha! here is sport for a lord,
That Prosperity and I be well at accord!
I shall bring his thrift under the board,
I trust, within short space.

For it grieveth my heart right sore
He hath so much treasure in store,
And I have never the more.
I must find some proper shift
That from his good he may be lift ;
To bring him to Misrule I hold it best,
For he can soon bring it to pass.

   Here MISRULE *singeth, without coming in.*
How ! what rutterkin have we here ?
I would he were our subchanter
Because he can so well sing. [*Enter* MISRULE.
 Misrule. *Venir avecque vous gentyl com-*
   paygnon
Faictes bone chere pour lamour de sainct John
Mon coeur iocund is set on a merry pin—
By my troth ! I am disposed to revelling.
 Envy. So methinketh, by your coming in.
What, Misrule ! where hast thou been many
  years ?
 Mis. By my troth, even amongst my peers.
I came now straight from the stews,
From little pretty Jone—
Lord ! that she is a pretty one !
 Envy. Hold thy peace ; let that alone.
Hark ! a word or twain to thee :
I dwell now with Prosperity,
Which hath much worldly treasure ;
If thou can contrive, in thy thought,
How that he may be brought to nought,
In all this world I desire no more.
 Mis. Tush ! take no thought therefore ; C3,*v.*
I can provide for that in the best wise.
 Envy. Then let me hear thy device. [dice,
 Mis. I will bring him to clash, cards, and
And to proper trulls, that be wanton and nice,
Which will not be kept with a small price.

How thinkest thou? will not this do well?
   Envy.   Yes; but hearken in counsel;
Thou must change thy name.
   Mis.   I will say I hight Mirth.
   Envy.   And I will say the same.   [PERITY.
Peace! whist! I see him come.   [*Enter* PROS-
   Pros.   God save all this honourable company.
   Envy.   Sir, you be welcome, by our blessed
I have thought for you full long.   [lady!
Here is a gentleman; I pray you, for my sake,
Say he is welcome, and into your service him
     take,
For great courtesy he can.   [hand,
   Pros.   Sir, you be welcome; give me your
And show me what is your name.
   Mis.   Sir, my name is Mirth;
Beloved with lords and ladies of birth,
At every triumph I am them with:
They can me not once forbear.
   Envy.   And ye had sought this thousand year
Such another ye shall not find;
Wherefore I counsel you, in my mind,
Let him dwell with you for one year.
   Pros.   At your request, I am content;
Such a pretty man for me were expedient;
And of his counsel fain would I hear.
   Mis.   Ye must sing and dance, and make
     good cheer:
I would ye had some proper wench
That were young and lusty; at a pinch,   C4,*r.*
Her heel were not so broad as an inch,
She would quicken your courage.
   Pros.   Peace hath forbid all that outrage.
   Envy.   He would set you at dotage
Because he is old, and nature is past;
He would now every man should fast.

If ye do so ye do but waste,
And unto you no meed.

   Mis.   A straw for him ! ye have no need
Of him to stand in awe or dread ;
A merrier life now may ye lead :
Therefore, be at your own liberty.

   Pros.   By my troth ! I may say to thee
Sith I to him did assent
Had I never merry day ;
But lived in fear and dread alway,
Nothing to mine intent.
Another while I will me sport,
Sing and dance, to my comfort.

   Envy.   And among merry company do resort ;
For that shall length your life.

   Mis.   Spare neither maid, ne wife ;
Take both and they come in your way.

   Envy.   Off with this lewd array !
It becometh you nought, by this day !

   Pros.   By my troth ! even as ye say.
Yea, marry ! now am I well apaid ;
Methinketh I am properly arrayed.
If I had a proper trull, she should be assayed
In the worship of the new year.

   Envy.   Rush up mutton, for beef is dear !
Have, and revel, and chance !

   Mis.   Now let us both sing and dance.   C4,*v.*
Will ye have a French round ?

   Pros.   And thou shalt see me bounce above
     the ground :
Hey, with revel dash !

Peace *entereth.*

   Peace.   What, Prosperity ! is it come hereto ?
   Pros.   What devil of hell hast thou to do ?
Shall I not make merry when me list ?

Peace. Yet I say, beware of Had I wist !
Envy. Hence, ye knave ! or else thou shalt
  lick my fist :
I trow thy head would have some knocks.
Pros. Go, set him in a pair of stocks,
That I him no more see.
Peace. Yet, man ! I say, remember thee,
And think what I to thee have said :
Eschew evermore these rioters' company,
And be ruled by reason, as I thee bade.
Put from thee these two persons, by whom thou
  art lade—   [abusion,
Envy and Misrule, with their sinful and great
Which, if thou wilt not forsake, will be thy
  confusion.   [conclusion :
Pros. Avaunt, lorel ! and take this for a
These men from me thou shalt not separate.
Go ! out of my sight ! or, by Cock's passion !
I shall lay thee fast in Newgate.
Peace. It is better to forsake them betime
  than too late.
Mis. This knave would have a broken pate ;
Let me alone, by God's bread !
This same sword shall strike off his head.
Pros. I pray you, hence that he were rid—
Shortly have him out of my sight !
Peace. A little while give me respite,
And take heed what I do say :
Remember in what condition thou was
When I first met thee in this place—
Full simple, in poor array.   B1,*r*.
Now, by the grace of God and counsel of me,
Thou art come to great prosperity ;
And so mayst continue, until thou die,
If thou wisely take heed.
Let not sensuality lead the bridle ;

Be occupied in virtue, and be not idle ;
The better shalt thou proceed.
These wretches will thy goods spend and waste ;
Then shalt thou be taken for an outcast,
And mocked and scorned with most and least ;
Then will no man thee help at need.

 Envy. A, sir, evil mote thou speed,
That so can read his destiny !

  Mis. Will ye suffer this knave in your company ?

Then God be with you ! I will forsake you.

  Pros. Go hence ! or in faith I shall make you !

  Peace. Then to almighty God I betake you.

  Envy. Let me come to that bragger !
I shall thrust him through the arse with my dagger.

   And here they face PEACE *out of the place.*
How say ye ? was not this a good face,
To drive a knave out of the place ?

  Mis. In faith, thou made him run apace !
Thou looked as thou had been mad.

  Pros. Now, by my troth ! my heart is glad ;
Some minstrel now I would we had,
To revel and dance ; for, by saint Chad !
I am so light methink I flee !

  Envy. Yea, marry ! so should it be ;
For now I hold you wise.

  Mis. Sir, and ye will do mine advice,
Let us go straight to the Fleur de Lys ;
There shall ye find a man will play at dice D1,*v.*
With you for an hundred pound.

  Pros. What man is he ?   [sea,

  Mis. Colhazard ; came late from beyond the
Ragged and torn, in a garded coat ;
And, in his purse, never a groat ;

And now he goeth like a lord!
   Pros. I pray thee tell me at one word—
Is he a gentleman bore?
   Envy. Tush! take no thought therefore!
For be he gentleman, knave, or boy,
If he come hither with trifle or a toy,
He can no money lack.
   Pros. Now by the bread that God brake!
I think long till I him see!
Mirth! go before and ordain a good dish;
One of flesh and another of fish.
   Envy. Nay, let all be flesh!
A young pullet, tender and nesh,   [thou go!
That never came on broach—have with thee or
   Mis. What shall I have?
   Envy. Four quarters of a knave,
Roasted upon a spit!   *Exit* MISRULE.
   Pros. Now, by my troth! and Colhazard
   will sit,   [last.
I will play as long as an hundred pound will
   Envy. And ye will play an hundred pound
   at a cast,
He will keep you play.
   Pros. Then let us go our way;
I sit on thorns till I come there.
   Envy. That shall make your thrift full bare.
   Pros. What will it do?
   Envy. I say, we shall have good cheer
When we come there.   *Exeunt ambo.*
                [PEACE *entereth.*
   Peace. When Phebus draweth into the oc-
   cidental,   D2,*r.*
And obscured with clouds misty and dark,
Then trees, herbs, and grass, by course natural,
Want their chief comfort: thus saith many a
   clerk.

IMPATIENT   22

And, likewise, that a man in his wark
Is destitute of reason following sensual opera-
   The last time I was in this place   [tion.
Prosperity unto Misrule put his whole con-
   fidence.
He regarded not my counsel ; he lacked grace ;
Which, in time coming, shall turn him to
   inconvenience.   [ence
With hazarders and rioters he keepeth resid-
At clash and cards, with all unthrifty game ;
Which, in continuance, shall bring him shame.
To him yet I will resort :
If he be brought in poverty
I shall do him all the comfort
And all the help that lieth in me ;
I will never rest till I him see.
But seek about, from place to place,
And bring him to some better grace.   *Exit.*

        [*Enter* MISRULE.]

  Mis. Colhazard ! art thou there ?
Whoreson knave ! wilt thou no appear ?
By my troth ! I had went to have found him here ;
I hold him gone some other way.
And where is Envy ? I cannot him espy :
I trow he is with Prosperity.   [*Enter* ENVY.
Prosperity ? Nay ! I may call him Foolish
   Poverty,
As wise as a drake.
I have brought him to dice, cards, and clash ;
And ever on his side ran the loss,
That he is not worth a handful of moss,
Neither hath not a whole brat to his back !
  Envy. Passion of God ! is it come to
   that ?   D2,*v.*
These tidings maketh my heart glad.

Mis. In faith! he has neither gold, silver,
 ne plate:
Colhazard and I be both at one.
He promised me to have half the game ;
That everything shall be divided in twain—
He to have the one half, and I the other.
 Envy. Then let us be partners, as brother
 and brother.
 Mis. I cannot say till Colhazard come ;
Then shall we know, both all and some.
       [*Enter* COLHAZARD.
 Col. Here is a bag of gold so round,
Herein is two thousand pound ;
Of Prosperity me it won.
What man is able with me to make comparison ?
Now shall I take a merchant's place
To occupy ; I trust, within short space,
To be in credence with English men ;
And when I am so well betrust,
I may borrow so much as me lust.
A subtle craft then find I must
To convey under colour, like free men.
 Envy. Hark, this knave ! so proud and stout,
That had not to his arse a whole clout
When he came to this land ; and now hath
 brought about
To compare with a state.
 Mis. Now must I have half money, and
 half plate.   [late ;
 Col. Nay, by God ! there thou spake too
None thereof from me shall scape :
Then had I lived too long.
 Mis. Thou promised me, when thou began,
Half thy winning I should have.
 Col. Hold thy peace, lewd knave !
Knowest thou to whom thou dost speak ?

Mis. A, whoreson, thy head shall I
    break!   D3,*r.*

Envy. For the passion of God, sober your
I fear shedding of knave's blood.   [mood!
    *Here they fight and run all out of the place,
    and then entereth* PROSPERITY *poorly* [*clad*]
    and saith.

Pov. O Jesu! what may this mean?
My goods are spent and wasted away!
Also my men are from me clean;
I see them not this seven nights' day.
As long as I might spend and pay,
They held me up with false dissimulation;
And now they forsake me in my most tribula-
    tion. [ENVY *returneth followed by* MISRULE.

Envy. Come! for Cock's bones! why tarry
    ye so long?

Mis. In faith! I come as fast as I can;
I am so angry, I wot not what to do,
That yonder knave scaped from me so.

Envy. What knave is this? I hold him
    some spy.

Pov. I am your master; know ye not me?

Envy. Thou art come alate out of Mar-
    shalsea.   [hood!

Mis. Methink his hair groweth through his

Pov. Alas! Colhazard hath won all my
    good,
And left me never a groat.

Envy. Marry! so methink; ye have
    changed your coat;
But now ye have one vantage.

Pov. What is that?

Envy. Your executors shall not strive for
    your goods another day;   [way:
Nor thieves shall not rob you, going by the

Thus ye shall stand out of doubt.

   Mis. Hence, ragged knave! or thou shall
     bear me a clout:

His clothes smell all of the smoke.   [bishop!

   Envy. Now, by saint Hugh, that holy

This matter is well brought to pass:

He is now a knave as he was—

First a knave, and then a man;   D3,*v.*

And now he is a knave again.

   Pov. Why say ye so? ye be to blame:

I am your master, Prosperity!

   Mis. Avaunt, lorel! and evil to thee!

Get thee out of this company!

Beginnest thou now to make comparison?

   Envy. Let him be your under page;

Give him meat and drink, but no wage;

Go! brush his gown and make clean his shoon!

   Mis. Well, knave! canst thou no courtesy?

   Envy. He hath such a disease in his knee

He cannot chance a main groat:

It is not as ye ween.

   Mis. Come and see my shoon made clean!

   Envy. By my faith! he shall wipe mine.

   Mis. This knave is not meet for me;

It grieveth my heart when I him see;

I will go hence, and leave you twain;

For Envy, thou mayest with Poverty reign.

                        Exit.

   Envy. Nay, I had liever he were slain:

I am gone as soon as ye.   [*Exit.*

   Pov. Abide still with me, gentle Charity!

O, to whom should I sue, to whom should I
    plette?

O mortal worm, wrapped all in woe!

As a man all mortified, and mased in my wit,

I, a captive in captivity, lo, fortune is my foe!

I am in endless sorrow ; alas ! what shall I do ?
These caitiffs, through their counsel and false
    imagination,
Have brought me to nought that was of great
    reputation.
Woe worth the time that I them knew !
I may well sigh, and say Alas !
For now I find these words full true
That Peace showed me here in this place. D4,*r.*
I regarded not his counsel ; I lacked grace ;
Wherefore needy poverty on me doth blow his
    horn,   [scorn.
That every man and woman doth laugh me to
Example to all young men, when they take in
    hand
To occupy in the world : for your behoof
Look wisely before, and also understand
Evil company destroyeth man—on me ye see
    the proof.
Make a sure foundation or ye set up the roof.
Of a good and virtuous beginning cometh a
    good ending ;   [ing !
And evermore beware of unmeasurable spend-

Here entereth the SUMNER.

    Sumner.   I ascite you in our court to appear !
    Pov.   I pray you tell me wherefore ?
    Sum.   Ye be great slanderer, and full of envy.
    Pov.   There will no man say so but ye.
    Sum.   What wilt thou give me and thou shalt
    go quit ?
    Pov.   By my troth, I have not one mite !
    Sum.   Then open penance and thou art like.
    Pov.   By my troth, I slander no man !
    Sum.   Then come and secule thyself as well
    as thou can.   [*They go out.*

ABUNDANCE *entereth.*

Abun. What man is he that can me dismay?
For I obtain all thing at my will.
Or who dare anything against me say,
Whatsoever I do, be it good or ill?
For if he do, he were better be still;
I shall him punish be it right or wrong,
For with my purse I can both save and hang.
To repugn against me he were better be still.
I have a proper trull for my pastance;
In my chamber I her keep, both night and day;
My neighbours therewith taketh great griev-
    ance;
Yet I keep her still, whosoever say nay. D4,*v.*
Howbeit, there is one, a poor caitiff, I hear say,
Hath me accused in the court spiritual.
And it cost me a hundred pound, punish him I
    shall.   [*The* SUMNER *returneth.*
Sum. Open sin must have open penance;
God speed, my master Abundance!
Abun. What knave art thou, with a very
    mischance,
That cometh in so homely?
Sum. Sir! I pray you be not angry.
I am an officer of the spiritualty.
There is upon you a great slande[r];
Ye keep another man's wife in your chamber,
And live in great advoutry.
Abun. What wretches doth so say by me?
Sum. It is openly known everywhere.
Before my master I charge you to appear;
Upon a book there shall ye swear
Whether it be so, or no.
Abun. What is the best for me to do?
Rather than I to the court will go

I had liever spend twenty pound.

    Sum. Sir! of such a way may be found

To excuse you ; what will ye then say?

    Abun. Now thereof heartily I thee pray!

    Sum. Ye shall come home to my master's place

And say that ye be put up of malice ;

Thrust money in his hand apace ;

And so shall ye go quit away.

    Abun. For thy counsel, gramercy! Hold! here is forty pence !

    Sum. Come on, sir! I will do my diligence.

                          Exeunt ambo.

    Here entereth the SUMNER *again, and* POVERTY
       followeth him with a candle in his hand
       doing penance about the place. And then
       sayeth the SUMNER :

    Sum. Room, sirs! avoidance !

That this man may do his penance.   E1,*r.*

    Pov. Now have I my penance done.

    Sum. Nay! thou shalt about once again.

    Pov. The poverty and trouble that I endure

I cannot to you in few words express.

If it should be unto God no displeasure

I would desire death, my pain to release ;

Such is my penury and troublesome heavi-
        ness,

That I could, in no wise, suffer it patiently

But that I trust to win heaven thereby.

                    [PEACE *entereth.*

    Peace. What man art thou that maketh such lamentation ?

    Pov. Master Peace! I desire you of pardon ;

I am your servant, sometime called Prosperity.

    Peace. How came thou to this perplexity ?

Pov. Colhazard, Misrule, and false Envy
Brought me to this distress.

Peace. I showed thee before, plain, express:
Then of my words thou haddest disdain?

Pov. Therefore now it is to me great pain.

Peace. What persons are those that did him
accuse?

Sum. Sir! he is put up by suit of office.

Peace. Suit of office? then it is so
There hath been credible persons, three or two,
Such articles to the judge did show.
He ought thereto to have good respect;
And do swear these persons upon a book—
For love, ne dread, they say but true—
For it is not leeful for a callet, a caitiff, or a
knave   [have,
Against honest persons such matters for to
To put a man to open penance, without due
proof.   [was my oath:

Sum. Sir! when I entered mine office this
To hearken about and hear
For backbiters, slanderers, and false jurors,
Schismatics, homicides, and great usurers, E 1, *v.*
Bawds, advouterers, fornicators, and escheaters:
All such must penance do.

Pov. I know one such came never thereto.

Peace. Who is that?

Pov. His name is called Abundance,
Which hath done many a great offence;
For he keepeth another man's wife.
No manner of penance ye make him do,
But redeemeth with money, and let him go;
So in advoutry still he leadeth his life.

Sum. He made his purgation upon a book,
Or else redeemed with the silver hook.

Peace. Silver hook? that I deny!

For it is a plain decree
That open sin must do open punishment ;
There can be no such judgment
That money shall stop the law.

    Pov.   Nay, there stop, and lay a straw !
Where see ye any man a substance
Put to open penance,
But punished by the purse ?
A poor man, that hath nought to pay,
He shall be punished : this ye see every day ;
But if he be obstinant, and will not obey,
Anon they will him curse.

    Sum.   Well, for thy saying another day thou
       shall fare the worse.   *Exit* SUMNER.

    Pov.   Sir, I beseech you comfort me with
       some solace !

    Peace.   Thou art well punished for thy tres-
       pass.
By thine own sensual and undiscreet operation
Hath brought thee to all this tribulation.
Stand up ! with this vesture I shall thee renew.

    Pov.   Sir ! I thank you, and will do at your
       reformation ;   E2,*r.*
And for my time mispent I am sore ashamed.

    Peace.   If ye do as I you bid, ye shall not be
       blamed.   [peers ;
Forsake Envy and Misrule with all their old
Be conversant with good men ; goodness thereof
       will grow.   [*eris ;*
Follow the saying of David : *Cum sancto sanctus*
For wicked men evermore wicked seed do
       sow.   [doth know ;
What cometh of evil company, now thyself
Print it well in thy memory, and do it not
       forget :   [wit.
Many a man doth decay for lack of good fore-

Pros. Sir! your sayings is full true ; I have
   perceived it ;
And for the virtuous counsel that ye to me
   have give,
I shall be your orator while I have a day to
   live.
   Peace. Sovereigns! here may ye see proved,
   before you all,
Of this wanton world the great fragility ;
Ever mutable of the turning, as a ball.
Now, flood of riches ; now, ebb of poverty :
What should men set by this world's vanity ?
Think on this lesson, and do it not forget :
The gayest of us all is but worms' meat.
   Pros. With the supportation of this noble
   audience,
We have here showed this simple interlude ;
Beseeching you of your benevolence to take
   patience.
It is but a mirror vice to exclude.
The maker hereof, his intent was good,
No man to displease, old nor young ;
If any fault be therein we desire you of pardon.
   Peace. Let us pray all to that Lord of great
   magnificence
To send among us rest, peace, and unity.
And Jesu preserve our sovereign Queen of
   preclair pre-eminence,
With all her noble consanguinity ;
And to send them grace to the issue to obtain,
After them to rule this most Christian realm.

$E2,v.$

O good Lord! as Thou art omnipotent,
Have regard unto my petition !
Conserve this noble realm, and all that are
   present,

Of thy eternal Deity grant them all thy fruition;
And from our mortal enemies be our protection.
Jesu! as Thou us redeemed, bring us to the
    bless
Thereas angels sing: *Gloria in excelsis.*

AMEN.

Thus endeth the interlude called
Impatient Poverty.

[*Here follow two ornaments and between them*
the colophon as on page 312.]

[*Reduced Facsimile of the Title-page of "John the Evangelist" from a unique copy, recently recovered, now in the British Museum.*]

THE INTERLUDE OF

JOHN THE EVANGELIST

[The Names of the Players:

ST. JOHN THE EVANGELIST

EUGENIO   ACTIO

IRISDISION   EVIL COUNSEL

IDLENESS]

Imprinted at London, in Foster Lane,
by JOHN WALEY

[SAINT JOHN
THE EVANGELIST.]

A2,*r*. St. John the Evangelist.

Domine, ante te omne desiderium meum,
Et a te gemitus meus non est absconditus.
The sweetest life, Sovereign, in this world with
    some
Is to have meditation of our Lord Jesus,
Very contemplative God worshipped thus,
Bethinking in the soul without any speech.
God tendeth right more the prayer with the
    heart of us   [teach
Than the prayer of the mouth.   The text doth
In meditation whoso hath forfence,   [heart.
The mouth cannot express the thoughts of the
That holiest fruition is of so high intelligence
As it ravisheth the soul into a blessèd desert ;
It feeleth no earthly thing unto the time it revert.
Thus fared Magdalen when Martha complained :
She heard her not, in God her heart was so
    expert ;   [strained—
Nor the angel at the sepulchre, love so her con-
The cause why I rehearse you, the holy medita-
    tion,
For it is mine exercise express.   [tion,
Whoso will labour in this must see His habita-
Be solitary in soul, of great quietness.

Therefore ever to the church I do me dress ;
Rest, reverence, and worship therein should be,
With crying on Christ, and our sins confess.
Beati qui habitant in domo tua, Domine!

Eugenio. *Qui cum Deo Patri*—granted by
the pope
A thousand four hundred, and never a day less—
That hath heard this noble sermon, and thereon
doth hope,
A pœna et culpa here I them release.
Is it not pity such a pulpit man to lose?
I pray you, sir, let us hear more of your pope
holiness,
For methink I have heard you preach or this
at Paul's Cross. A2, *v.*

Irisdision. Whom call you pope-holy?

Eug. Such a fool as thou art, that clappest
ever in divinity.

Iris. All virtuous people to commend is my
property.

Eug. Then is Caton false, and that he
indites,
For he saith "*Nec te collaudas nec te culpaberis
ipse.*"
Great laudations loveth these hypocrites!
Qui se collaudat, etc.
No more to you at this time.
But understand you this Latin?

Iris. Yea, sir, I trow.

Eug. *Responde, tunc, domine, doctor clericorum.*
But sir, know you any justice of quorum?

Iris. Why so?

Eug. A fellow of mine was take[n] with a
cuculorum
For a couple horses he stole in an evening.

Iris. What would ye have me do in that case?

Eug. *Sursum corda* for him to sing,
Ye should have [? known] well why.

Iris. I cannot sing.   [spring A3,*r.*

Eug. No, sir, ye should but make a
Under a perch looking up toward the sky.

Iris. Without God be thy friend, that same death thou shalt die.

Eug. Marry, I beshrew his heart that so can prophesy!

Iris. What is thy name?

Eug.   A, read!

Iris.   Eugenio, I trow; the same!

Eug. A, sir; the devil strike off thy head!
Whoreson, who taught thee so right to read?
I trow some evil spirit be within thee.

  [*The continuation seems imperfect.*]

Iris. In the city of Jerusalem, that is so called.
I fear thou wilt never come to that holy Sion
That with twelve precious stones is surely walled.
Full strait is the way thither to gone,
And into that castle entering is none   [before:
Without thou acquaint thee with two porters
Hope is the first, and Faith the other one.

Eug. Lo! so ghostly he prateth evermore;
Ye dare not cough, your conscience is so holy!
But I pray you show me before
Which is the way to yonder castle ye praise
    so greatly?   [the way;

Iris. Over the Mead of Meekness mark thou
Then to the Path of Patience shalt thou pass
Into the Land of Largeness; hold for the
    lay,   A3,*v.*

SAINT JOHN   23

And in the Lane of Business look thou not bash;
Then measure in a marsh a fair manor hasse ;
Rest there hardely, and abide all night.
   Eug.   Nay, that I will not, by this light !
But what callest thou this way ?
   Iris.   *Via recta*, leading to life ;
So David named it in his day—
Spes mea stetit in via recta.
      Eug.   Passeth all men by this journey ?
      Iris.   Nay, and the more pity, verily, I say.
      Eug.   What be they that go that way most?
      Iris.   They that be inspired with the Holy
      Ghost,
As innocents and virgins.
      Eug.   Marry, I know none such in all this
      coast !   [*electi.*
      Iris.   They that go thither must be *gratia*
      Eug.   Why, is there no other way but this ?
      Iris.   Yes, on the left side another there is,
That is called *via obliqua et via circularis.*
      Eug.   And whither draweth this ?
      Iris.   Even right to death ; A4,*r.*
Whoso walks that way, himself he slayeth.
      Eug.   Sir, who goeth that way so ill ?
      Iris.   All they that worketh the devil's will,
As *omnes iniquo in circuitu impii ambulantes.*
      Eug.   Thou art a lowler, by my troth, I
      warrants !
How many by-paths be in that way ?
      Iris.   Six score and odd, I say.
      Eug.   Then one cannot fail where he go by
      night or day.
But may a man go to the stews that way
At his pleasure, if he list to play ?   [array ;
      Iris.   It brings men to the seat of rueful
The lady of confusion lieth therein,

That Babylon is called ; she is the end of all sin.
  Eug.   Which way coasteth that country?
  Iris.   To an isle in the north, I say ;
Ab aquilone pandetur omne malum.   [assay,
  Eug.   That is the first place that men should
Whether it be hedged or walled.   [paled.
  Iris.   With boughs and trees it is marvellously
There groweth the elders of envy,
Staked with pride full high,
And the briars of backbiting with wrath
    wreathed about,   A4,*v.*
Full of slouthy bushes and lecherous thorns dry,
With gluttonous posts and covetise railed
    throughout,
And at Mischief's Gate many doth in run.
  Eug.   And where do they all become?
  Iris.   Down to the dungeon where the devil
    dwelleth,
Lucifer, that loathly lord, that is in bale blisses.
There is woe upon woe, as Christ us telleth ;
All that may disease and nothing please, ever
    restless.
There is frost, there is fire,
Hope is lost and her desire ;
There care hath no recover ;
Without pity there is pain ;
To cry for mercy it is in vain,
For grace is gone for ever.
Fumus tormentorum suorum
Ascendit in secula seculorum.
Lo ! thus hath lost wedded confusion,
Lucifer's daughter damnation
In hell to have heritage.
Septum dominium peccati est mors.
  Eug.   In faith, that is a knavish way to walk.
Now awhile of some mirth let us talk,

For I forsake that passage.

    Iris.   Now farewell, sir, and have good day,
For I must go another way;
Forget not my reasons sage!

    Eug. What! will ye go your way?   B1,*r*.
Ye have done a fair journey to-day.

    [*Iris.*] It is time for to be walking,
For I am weary of your talking.   [*Exit.*

    [*Eug.*] Lo! sirs, he spake full holily,
But yet I beshrew him for all his clergy;
He may well be called witless Sir Will,
For I trow his brain is steadfast as a windmill.
But now well remembered, by books Amromes

    [*Here again something appears to be missing.*]
I would have a plaster for all harms,—
Some fair wench to lie in mine arms;
That would avoid all strifes.
It were to me *administrate nos,*
Et restaurate nos, also *comfortate nos.*
Yea, and sometime I will take men's wives;
For cuckold-makers have merrier lives
Than they that do all the cost   [sworn.
As to wed at the church-door, and there to be
Perhap her husband should have an horn;
Then may he curse the time that ever he was
    born,
For all the love is lost.   [knit;
Clerks say that of wedlock God that knot doth
And yet women do venture to break it.
For though their souls should lie in hell pit,
They will use that sorry work;
And if they so die,
Atropos cometh full suddenly,
And or they beware, full slily
He leadeth them all down in the dark.
The courtesy of England is oft to kiss,

And of itself it is lechery where pleasure is.
All young folk remember this—
Intentio judicat quenquam. B1,*v.*
So great delight thou mayst have therein
That afore God it is deadly sin.
But farewell! yonder cometh Sir William of
    Trentram. [*Exit.*] [principal,
  St. John the Evangelist. That lord which is
Conserve and keep this congregation,
And cover you with his mantle perpetual.
After that ye do pass with death's visitation,
This prince bring you to that holy nation
Where love doth dwell with virginity.
And to give you plain information,
In that realm dwelleth the Holy Trinity.
I am that John that presently doth appear,
Called " the grace of God " by interpretation,
And of my doctrine if ye list to hear,
Much can I show you of Christ's incarnation,
And of His passion ; for verily I was there.
I saw Him hang on the Cross, on high, on high ;
His mother and I stood there under,
And I heard when He cried " Eli, Eli,"
And saw Lungis smite His heart asunder.
His laws to the people will I preach,
And all that ever do follow me in peace,
The kingdom of heaven their souls shall reach,
There having joy that never shall cease. [owe,
But now the true love, that we should to God
Men giveth it to richesse that is mutable ;
Full sore they will it repent, I trow,
That ever they were of mind so unstable.
If any man will have richesse ghostly, B2,*r.*
I will hastily again be here,
And thereof he shall have gladly ;
At all times I will him cheer.

My coming hither was for your furtherance,
And now I leave you in God's governance.
                    [*Exit, Enter* ACTIO.
    Actio.   Now merry might you be !
Who was that that callèd me
So early to-day ?
One resided me with a bowl of water ;
Here was a shrewd matter,
Suddenly one to affray !
It was some knave, my brother :
Beshrew him and none other
For that array !
I was fast asleep ;
Till I felt the wet
Full still I lay.
He brake mine old custom,
For I would have lain till noon,
And then have risen to play.
But now to the purpose ;
For by the faith that now goes
I love to go gay !
And with other men's wives
That be wanton of lives
Oft do I run away.
And wheresoever I go
One good condition have I so —
I use never truth to say.
Also I have a great disease, if ye will me leave,
Even here, sirs, in the bottom of my sleeve. B2,*v.*
                    [*Enter* EUGENIO.
    Eug.   By God, sir, and I do lay a plaster to
        your coat
I will heal it, I dare lay a groat !
    Actio.   Eugenio, from whence come you ?
    Eug.   From thence that ye were spoke of
        right now ;

Ye shall have an office.

 Actio. What is that? I pray you tell me!

 Eug. By my faith, ye shall be hangman of
  Calais;

Thereto ye be appointed, verily!

 Actio. Then the first man that shall be
  hanged shalt thou be,

For I tell thee I will begin with thee. [say.

 Eug. Nay, sir, but hark what I shall thee

Here was one late this same day

That dispraised richesse worldly.

He said he that doth forsake prosperity,

And take him to wilful poverty,

He shall have joy eternally.

 Actio. What was he?

 Eug. A doctor, as seemed me;

He spake as holily

As though God had been his cousin. [crisy?

 Actio. Yea, but was he not mired with hypo-

 Eug. No, man; he spake so ghostly B3,*r.*

He had almost changed my mood.

I had thought to give away my good

And then ask myself for charity.

 Actio. Why, wouldest thou have been so
  witty?   [egging

Nay, thou art a fool and thou wilt for any

Give away thine own good, and go thyself a-
  begging,

For so will not I do yet, trust me!

 Eug. Sir, he promised most largely

That I should in joy live ever,

Where I shall die never.

Thus also he said verily,

That I should feel there' no ill,

And have all that I desire will,

And see God in His majesty.

Also he promised me a greater hire
That I should have all that I would desire.
 Actio. I rede thee lay that thought away ;
For mayst thou not see all day
That they that useth sport and play
Liveth at ease merrily ?
They have most heartiest rest
And fareth of the best
That thus spendeth their lives in jollity.
 Eug. Well, then, my wit I will renew,
For I trow thou sayest full true.
If I do it, and afterward rue it
As to give away my good,
I trow I should it forethink.   B3,*v.*
Without a cup then might I drink,
For that purse that sowneth not trink
His master weareth a thread-bare hood.
 Actio. Yea, yea, man, that is true indeed.
But let us go walk a space,
For Evil Counsel hither will speed ;
That person, I trow, he be void of all grace.
 Eug. Go we hence then in time ;
Hastily we will come again,
For John will be here by prime ;
His sermon would I hear fain.
   [*They go out and* Evil Counsel *entereth.*
 Evil Counsel. By your leave, let me come
  near.
What doth all this company here ?
Whereafter is your gaping ?   [far ;
By our lady and master ! I have sought nigh and
For sith I came from Rochester
I have spent all my winning.
By our lady ! I will no more go to Coventry,
For there knaves set me on the pillory,
And threw eggs at my head

So sore that my nose did bleed
Of white wine gallons thirty.
Some time in London did I dwell ;
I was prentice with Evil Counsel,
And so men calleth me.
I hope again to go thither,
If summer were come and fair weather,
And live full merrily.   [B4,*r.*
I have sought England through and through,
Village, town, city, and borough ;
With many a thousand bequainted I am,   [man,
As ill-tongued churls and many a proud gentle-
That shrewdly roundeth many a pistle
When they in young wives' ears doth whistle
Of matters pertaining to Venus' acts ;
With fair flattering words and pretty knacks
Both men and women they bring to lechery,
Through me, Evil Counsel, to live in advoutry.
In Cornwall I have been and in Kent,
Westminster, St. Catherine's, and in Unthrift's
There I rested very lately.   [Rent,
Now fain would I have a master
                              [*Enter* IDLENESS.
That would do by my counsel,
For though he spend and be a waster
To get money I can teach him the craft well.
    Idleness. What art thou, tell me, that
        speaketh this ?   [a service ;
    Evil C. Marry, sir, a man that would have
Great need have I thereto.
    Idle. Why, what service canst thou do ?
    Evil C. Both steal and lie, and on your
        errand go
To fet another man's wife to your bed.
    Idle. If I of such things may be sped,
I am glad that we be met.

Evil C.   In England shall nothing me let.
With you will I bide for ever.   B4,*v.*
But master, have ye any wife?
    Idle.   Yea, more than twenty-five, by my life ;
But some other men keepeth them for me.
    Evil C.   Marry, sir, no force ; it costeth you
      the less money,
But you have good cheer when you come.
    Idle.   Yea, at meat I am merry, and at bed
      if I list to play.   [way,
    Evil C.   Then their husbands be out of the
Or else ye come not there.
    Idle.   Yes, yes, daily! and make good cheer,
And not spied at all, I have such policy.
    Evil C.   I am glad that ye be so witty ;
And sir, if you will have a fresh lusty trull
I will get her you, or a house-wife that can spin
      a pound of wool.
    Idle.   Then will we drink wine at the full,
In one place if thou canst help me.
    Evil C.   I pray you tell me ; what is she?
    Idle.   An artificer's wife—a pretty woman.
    Evil C.   Sir, I will go to my brother Tempta-
      tion
And then to Wanton Youth I will make a station;
For between us three
Of her your pleasure ye shall have hardely.
    Idle.   Shall I go with you also?   C1,*r.*
    Evil C.   Yea, sir, and it please you so to do.
How say you?   Have not they merry lives
That may kiss and bass other men's wives.
Lo! youth is full of jollity.
But when saw you your brother Sensuality?
    Idle.   Sir, I left him on the plain of Salisbury.
He told me that he would lift
Some good fellow from his thrift ;

And as I trow somewhat he will get
To make with the penny.
Many one for their good do labour and
    sweat ;
But he doth not so ; he getteth it lightly.
    Evil C.   Sir, he did me a shrewd turn, as I
    you tell.
    Idle.   I pray thee show me how it befel.
    Evil C.   The last day, sir, I wist
The puttock that he ware on his fist
Would have trod my hen,
And up I caught a rottock
And hit him on the buttock
That there lay in a thenne.
    Idle.   Whereby knowest thou that it was he ?
    Evil C.   For he had a bell about his cue,
And thereby each him knew.
I bid him hold in the wind,   C1,*v.*
Till at the last he had his mind ;
God give him an ill pew.
    Idle.   And what meat did thou give him ?
Say on hardely !
    Evil C.   Sir, a fair piece of bacon,
And a black bowl full of barley.
    Idle.   By Jesu, this is a gentle meat for a
    hawk ;
To keep birds thou art very conning.
Thy thrift, I trow, is laid a sonninge ;
But tell me now where is thy wonning ?
    Evil C.   Sir, at the stews is my most abiding ;
Otherwise going and sometime riding ;
And if the ground be slipper and sliding,
In faith I fall down mosellinge.   [pears ;
    Idle.   What, some pleasure then there ap-
Beshrew your head between your ears !
    Evil C.   Nay, sir, it shall be yours and theirs ;

For when a man hath enow
Let him part with his neighbours.
　　Idle.　It is thy destiny, I trow,
For to be clad all in briars,
And ride the horse with four ears.
　　Evil C.　Nay, sir, not afore you
For I love ill to walter ;　　　　　　　　　　C2,*r.*
A ride in a saddle, but ye shall ride in a halter.
　　Idle.　In good faith, knave, thou shalt bear
　　me a stripe.
　　Evil C.　And thou shalt have another an I
　　can hit thee aright.
　　Idle.　Why smitest thou not ? Come off !
　　Evil C.　Nay, I trow ye do but scoff.
But I would not for an hundred pound fight
　　with thee.
　　Idle.　Why so ? Tell me !
　　Evil C.　For I never fought with man but
　　he died ;　　　　　　　　　　　　　　[abide.
And so should you and ye did my strokes
　　Idle.　Marry, I had liever thou were tied ;
Thou art as manly as ill chieving ;
Thou were a good bold fellow to go a thieving.
　　Evil C.　Well, let us go to Unthrift's a while
　　hence,
And let some other keep residence ;
For I dare lay thereon forty pence
We shall have a sermon or night.
　　Idle.　I trow then he will come hither
That laid first *In principio* together.
　　Ambo.　Go we, for we two will go thither,
Thereas we will make merry, by this light !
　　　　　[*They go out.　Enter* ACTIO *and* EUGENIO.
　　Actio.　A, sir, I have been long away ;
I said I would see you by the light day.　C2,*v.*
　　Eug.　There hath be a fair array.

Where we two have be,
There was laying of the law,
And all was not worth a new straw,
So God help me!

 Actio. Sir, I saw the wench that did your
  neck claw,
That bare in her hand a gay gewgaw;
Methought it was like a paw
Of a whiting;
She held me with a tale of titmary tally,
Till my thrift was gone as quit as a dally.
God wot, it is a nice thing.   [i-fashion

 Eug. Peace, man! ye shall hear a sermon
Of the eagle that riseth full high;
If he do hear thy exclamation
He will make thee to fly.

 Actio. Not in a string, I trow.
Peace! for he is come now. [*Enter* St. John.

 St. John. O men unkind, wretched and
  mortal,
Hearken to this parable that I shall tell.

 Eug. The hearing thereof give you I shall.

 Actio. And I to do by your counsel, if ye
  say well.

 St. John. Now I begin; give good audience!
            [pray, C3,*r.*

Two men ascended once to a temple to
Their conversation having great difference.
It was the Pharisien and the Publican, I say.
Two ensamples by them perceive we may.
The great pride of the Pharisee:
Other men's faults he dispraised aye,
And his own counsel hid under false hue.
In the Publican's prayers there was than
A great excellence of meekness;
He despised himself, a wretched man,

Thinking each creature exceeded him in good-
    ness.
His faults he did confess
With great sorrow for his transgression.
And in the Pharisee's prayer did express
Of full pride and adulation.
He prayed not, but praised himself there,
Standing upright with a pert face.
The mass beginneth with *Confiteor,*
And endeth with *Deo gratias.*
Even the reverse he did in this case.
There the mass endeth, he began proudly,
Making no confession of his trespass,
But said *Deo gratias ago tibi,*
In that he thanked God he was not to blame,
But in that he thanked Him not with very
    meekness.
Three species of sin he rehearsed by name
In which all sins be comprehended express.
By raveners is understand covetise ;
In unrightful to say pride of him than ;
In advoutry all lechery that men can rehearse.
And thus he excused himself, and slandered the
    publican.
I pay my tithes, he said also ;   C3,*v.*
And so he did, but not of the best.
In that cayme he was like to,
For he tithed alway of the worst.
Twice in the week, he said, he did fast ;
From meat and drink he did, but not from
    deadly sin ;
And that is the fast that pleaseth God best.
But thereat hypocrites will not begin.
Against God he sinned grievously,
In that he justified himself so,
And his even Christian slandering maliciously.

Tu testimonium perhiberis de teipso,
Et testimonium tuum non est verum—I say so.
Wherefore God did him divide
From the nine parts of angels the tenth, so
There Lucifer is falle[n] for his pride.
The Gospel said, who doth hie him shall be
    ho.
All they that praiseth themself do sin, be
    you sure.
And so, you curséd men, do your cure ;
For by God's judgment,
If ye forsake not your sin, be you sure
You go to hell. Wherefore, repent !
  Ambo. I cry God mercy for mine offence ;
My wicked life I do defy.
  Eug. Also I am sorry of my negligence ;
Your doctrine I will follow full meekly.
  St. John. This sample God sayeth us to,
That we should consider it wisely.
Who deemeth himself good is far therefro,
And he that thinketh himself sinfullest is blessed
    hardely.   [edly, C4,*r.*
Think now that your purpose was set curs-
In sin thus to lead lives vain
Under colour of virtue, deeming yourself
    good.
You and all they that it doth sustain
Be worlde than the Pharisee ; men's laws are
    wood ;
Remember this for the reverence of Him that
    died on rood ;
And to the laws of the Church abide every
    man,
And ye shall be partners of Christ's precious
    blood,
And blessed of God, as was the Publican.

Thus if ye will be stedfast and true
Jesus will then with His grace you renew.
To that Lord's bliss ye shall come all a
Qui vivit per infinita seculorum secula.   Amen.

FINIS.

Thus endeth the Interlude of ST JOHN THE EVANGELIST.

Imprinted at London in Foster Lane by JOHN WALEY.

A NOTE-BOOK AND WORD-LIST

INCLUDING

CONTEMPORARY REFERENCES, BIBLIOGRAPHY, VARIORUM READINGS, NOTES, &c., together with a GLOSSARY OF WORDS AND PHRASES now Archaic or Obsolete; the whole arranged in ONE ALPHABET IN DICTIONARY FORM

A FOREWORD TO NOTE-BOOK AND WORD-LIST

Reference from text to Note-Book is copious, and as complete as may be; so also, conversely, from Note-Book to text. The following pages may, with almost absolute certainty, be consulted on any point that may occur in the course of reading; but more especially as regards

    Biographical and other Notes,

    Contemporary References to Author and Plays,

    Bibliography,

    Variorum Readings,

    Words and Phrases now obsolete or archaic.

The scheme of reference from Note-Book to text assumes the division, in the mind's eye, of each page into four horizontal sections; which, beginning at the top, are indicated in the Note-Book by the letters a, b, c, d following the page figure. In practice this will be found easy, and an enormous help to the eye over the usual reference to page alone in " fixing " the " catchword." Thus 126a = the first quarter of page 126; 40c = the third quarter of page 40; and so forth.

Abbreviations.

    M.   *Mankind.*

    N.   *Nature.*

  WS.   *Wit and Science.*

    R.   *Respublica.*

  WH.   *Wealth and Health.*

   IP.   *Impatient Poverty.*

   JE.   *John the Evangelist.*

NOTE-BOOK AND WORD-LIST
TO RECENTLY RECOVERED
"LOST" TUDOR PLAYS

With Some Others, viz.:

*Mankind—Nature—Wit and Science—Respublica—
Wealth and Health—Impatient Poverty—John
the Evangelist*

A, (*a*) (*passim*), of varying usages : *e.g.* (1) I : " to God
a vow"; (2) " *a* be " (R213,*d*)—" He tumbleth whom
a lust" (R212,*c*)=he ; (3)=one ; (4) " a potful *a*
worts " (M13,*c*)=of ; (5)=on ; (6)=have ; (7) sometimes used to lengthen a line, to accent a syllable, or
to make a rhyme-ending : also merely pleonastic.
For examples see other volumes of this series.
(*b*) "azee " (R257,*b*)—" A, zee ! " (R267,*a*),
look ! see !

ABAND, " if thou *aband* thee " (N48,*c*), forsake,
abandon. " And Vortiger enforst the Kingdome
to *aband*."—Spenser, *Fairy Queen* (1590), ii. v. 63.

ABLE, " zo chwas *able* " (R229,*b*), fit, proper,
" fettled " : in original *hable*—cf. *habile*. " Noye, to
me thou arte full *able*, And to my sacrifice acceptable."—*Chester Plays* (*c.* 1400), i. 55.

ABRY, see Jack Noble.

ABUSION, " hidden their *abusion* " (R180,*a*), abuse,
malpractice. " The vtter extirpation of false
doctrine, the roote and chief cause of all
abusions."—Udall, *Pref. to St. Mark.* " To print

such *abusion.*"—*Albion Knight*, Anon. Pl. 2 Ser. (E.E.D.S.), 131,*d.*

ADJUTORY, "God will be you[r] *adjutory*" (M12,*a*), properly an adjective=helpful; the exigencies of the rhyme has, however, apparently led to its use substantively: the original manuscript, as indicated, has " be yow *adiutory.*"

ADVENTURE, see Joint.

AFFEED, "*affeed* with them" (N70,*a*), hired, engaged with for profit: cf. *fee* (A.S.)=property, money, annual salary, reward. "There is not a thane of them but in his house I have a servant *feed.*"— Shakespeare, *Macbeth* (1606), iii. 4.

AFFERE, "With his company myself *affere*" (N63,*d*), belong, be identified with, "of a kidney with." "He was then buryed at Winchester in royall wise, As to suche a prince of reason should *affere.*"— Hardyng, *Chronicle* (*d.* 1465), f. 106.

AFFIANCE, "Company of my *affiance*" (N78,*a*), close connection, affinity, trusted advisers or servants: see other volumes of this series.

AFINE, "well *afine*" (R261,*d*), perfectly, thoroughly; *i.e.* well a (=and) fine: a generic intensive. "Till grapes be ripe and well *a-fine.*"—Chaucer, *Romaunt of the Rose* (1360), 3690.

AGAINST, "*against* I you call" (R199,*b*), again: the converse usage (*again*=against) was also common enough in old writers.

AGED, "some of them were *aged* . . . one by one" (R219,*b*). Mr. Magnus thinks that in these lines there must be some hint at the treatment of Bishops Gardiner and Bonner, who were imprisoned and their lands seized: see Respublica.

ALBS, "th' *albs* and amices" (R221,*d*), a long white linen garment or robe worn by officiating priests of the Roman communion. It reached nearly to the feet, and differed from the modern surplice (Rev. H. J. Tod), inasmuch as it was worn close at the wrists, similar to a bishop's lawn sleeves nowadays. "They (the bishops) shall have upon them in time

of their ministration, besides their rochet, a surplice
or *alb*, and a cope or vestment."—*Rubric of K.
Edw. VI.* (1548).

ALE, " mend . . . as zour *ale* in summer " (R227,*b*),
i.e. not at all : see Heywood, *Works* (E.E.D.S.),
II., 91*b*.

ALGATE, " hath pleased thy noble grace *algate* "
(N48, *a*), always.

ALIANTS, " too many *aliants* in this realm " (WH
300,*b* and *c*), aliens.   Foreign immigration seems
to have become a burning question early enough :
how dealt with history informs us ; and posterity
has, in the main, confirmed the generally judicious
and far-sighted policy of welcome extended to
refugees and others, with its consequent introduction
of new blood, new ideas, new crafts, and the benefits
arising therefrom.

ALISE DICTS (R210,*b*), *i.e. alias dicta.* People's
manglement of both English and Latin phrases is
a noteworthy characteristic of the play—see Divum,
Captivity, Commediens, Enquest, Policate, etc.

ALL, " then am I *all* safe " (R241,*d*), quite, entirely.
" Woe to the bloody city ! it is *all* full of lies and
robbery."—*Nah.* iii. 1.   *Bible*, Auth. Vers. (1611).

ALLECTUOUS, " *allectuous* ways " (M33,*d*), alluring,
enticing : *allective* is a commoner form.   " Woman
yfarced with fraude and disceipt, To thy confusion
most *allective* bait."—Chaucer, *Rem. of Love*, ver. 14.

ALLOW, " these words be greatly to *allow* " (N59,*a*),
approve, sanction : American by survival.   " First,
whether ye *allow* my whole device—And if ye like it,
and *allow* it well."—Norton and Sackville, *Gorboduc*
(1570. 1),   94,*a* and *b* (E.E.D.S.).

ALL THING, " *all thing* hath prospered (R201,*b*)—
"*All thing* I tell you " (R202,*c*)—"*all thing* should
soon be well " (R208,*d*), everything.

ALOFT, " look *aloft* with th' hands under the side "
(R192,*d*), *i.e.* Insolence when presented to Respublica
as the captain of the marauding crew is to assume
a butter-will-not-melt-in-my-mouth expression.

AMICALLY, "he hath *amically*' directed " (R237,*d*), amicably, in a friendly fashion. "An *amical* call to repentance and the practical belief of the Gospel."— W. Watson, M.A., 1691," in A. Wood, *Ath. Ox.*, 2nd ed., vol. ii., col. 1133.

AMICES, "th' albs and *amices*" (R221,*d*), a piece of fine linen worn by officiating priests : it was oblong-square in form, folded diagonally. It covered the head, neck, and shoulders, and was buckled or clasped before the breast, and when the altar was reached was thrown back upon the shoulders. It forms the uppermost of the six sacerdotal garments, the others being the alb, cingulum, stole, manipulus, and the planeta. The amice is still worn under the alb.

AMONG, "follow his appetite *among*" (N49,*c*), in company—elliptical : see other volumes of this series.

AMROMES, "books *Amromes*" (JE356,*b*), so in original. I can suggest nothing beyond a misprint for "amorous" ; but, in that case, why the capital *A* ? A line (or lines) may also be missing at this point, the connection being not at all obvious. However, there is nothing to suggest a break, the printing being unusually regular and clear at this point in the original.

ANCH, "*anch* hear om" (R230,*b*)—"*anch* can spy my time" (R231,*c*). for *an ich*=if I.

ANGEL, (*a*) "an *angel* for a reward" (R264,*b*). Mr. Magnus thinks that here is enshrined a play on the proper meaning of the word, and *angel*=a coin of the realm.
(*b*) see Angelot.

ANGELOT (R216,*d*). Mr. Magnus in his note (E.E.T.S. ed., p. 67, line 768) seems to identify this coin with the angel. He may be right ; but on the other hand, it is not out of place to point out that in numismatics an angelot is generally regarded as an ancient French coin first struck at Paris when that capital was in English occupation (1420). It bore on it the figure of an angel supporting the escutcheon of England and France. The angel of Edward VI.

was a gold coin, named from the fact that on one
side of it was a representation of the Archangel
Michæl in conflict with the Dragon (Rev. xii. 7).
The reverse had a ship with a large cross for the
mast, the letter E on the right side and a rose on
the left ; whilst against the ship was a shield with the
usual arms.   Angels were first struck in France in
1340, and were introduced into England by Edward
IV. in 1465.   Between his reign and that of Charles
I. it varied in value from 6s. 8d. to 10s.   The last
struck in England were in the reign of Charles I.
—H. Noel Humphreys, *Coins of England*, 5th ed.,
1848 ; and other authorities.   *Angelots* (*i.e.* half the
value of an angel), were also struck by Edward VI.
in 1550 : see Edwards.

ANNEXION, " the soul hath his *annexion* " (M38,*c*),
conjunction : Shakespeare in *The Lover's Complaint*
employs it in the sense of *addition*.

ANOINTED, " two knaves *anointed* " (N113,*d*), thorough-
paced, " out-and-out " ; a double pun is intended
the references being to *anointed*=beaten, with an eye
on *anointed*=consecrated by the pouring on of oil.
" Then thay put hym hout, the kyng away fly,
Which so well was *anoynted* indede, That no sleue ne
pane had he hoe of brede."—*The Romans of Partenay*
(ed. Skeat), 5652–4.

APAID, " very well *apaid* " (WH280,*c*), glad, satisfied,
pleased, paid.   " They buy thy help : but sin ne'er
gives a fee, He gratis comes ; and thou art well
appay'd, As well to hear as grant what he hath
said."—Shakespeare, *Rape of Lucrece* (1594), l. 913.

APPAIR, " I say his wealth doth mend, he saith it
doth *appair* " (R226,*b*), becomes worse, degenerates.
" All that liveth *appaireth* fast."—*Everyman*, Anon.
Pl. 1 S. (E.E.D.S.), 94,*d*.

APPLE (19,*d*), in original *a nappyl*.

APPLIED, " to Him should be *applied* " (M3,*b*), given,
rendered, one's heart or mind fixed upon : the only
sense of *apply* in the English Bible.

APPLY, see Aged.

APPREHENSIBLE, "was not *apprehensible*" (M33,*a*), competent.

APPROPRIATIONS, "bare parsonages of *appropriations*" (R218,*d*), technically, at law (according to Blackstone, I. 11) an *appropriation* is the transference to a religious house, or spiritual corporation, of the tithes and other endowments designed for the support of religious ordinances in a parish; also these when transferred. When the monastic bodies were in their glory in the Middle Ages they begged, or bought for masses and obits, or in some cases even for actual money, all the advowsons which they could get into their hands. In obtaining these they came under the obligation either to present a clergyman to the church, or minister there in holy things themselves. They generally did the latter, and applied the surplus to the support and aggrandisement of their order. On the suppression of the monasteries in the reign of Henry VIII. the appropriated advowsons were transferred to the king, and were ultimately sold or granted out to laymen, since called *impropriators*. See Respublica.

ARRAY, (*a*) "*array* toward" (R258,*d*), *i.e.* preparations in progress. (*b*) "nice in their *array*" (M14,*b*), dress, equipment, outward appearance. "But for to telle you of his *aray*, His hors was good, but he ne was nought gay."—Chaucer, *Cant. Tales* (1383), Prologue, 73-4.

ASCITE, "I *ascite* you . . . to appear" (IP342,*c*), summons, call. "Hun answered that the infant had no propertie in the shet, wherupon the priest *ascited* him in the spiritual courte."—Hall, *Henry VIII.*, f. 50.

ASPEN-LEAF, "tir-tremmeleth as the *aspen-leaf*" (M32,*c*), an early example of a common simile. The text, "tir-trimmeleth," etc., is as in original.

ASSAY, *subs.* and *verb*, "*assay* him I will" (M11,*a*),— "*at all assays*" (M7,*c*), as *verb*=try, tempt, essay; as *subs.* =at all points, in every respect. "I will *assay* ere long."—*Jacob and Esau*, Anon. Pl. 2 Ser. (E.E.D.S.), 15*d*; "at all *assays*" (*Ibid.* 53*b*).

ASSEMBLE, " I *assemble* the life " (N89,*b*), compare, liken : cf. Shakespeare's use of *assemblance*.—" Care I for the limb, the thewes, the stature, bulk, and big *assemblance* of a man ! "—Shakespeare, 2 *Henry IV.* (1598), iii. 2.

ASSIEGE (N89,*b*), siege : see Halliwell, *s.v.* Assege.

ATAME, " almsdeed I can *atame* " (N86,*d*), commence, begin : Fr. *entamer*. " Yes, hoste, quod he, so mote I ride or go, But I be mery, y-wis I wol be blamed ; And right anon his tale he hath *attamed*."—Chaucer, *Cant. Tales* (1383), 14824.

ATTEMPT, " Ye must *attempt* the world " (N59,*d*), try, " sample," experience : cf. Shakespeare, *Lear*, ii. 2.

ATTEMPTATES, " immoderate *attemptates* " (R266,*a*), attempts, endeavours : specifically to commit a crime. Puttenham, in 1589, said this word was a recent importation, but it had already been in use half a century at least. " To forbear that *attemptate*."—Sadler (A.D. 1543), in Froude, *Hist. Eng.*, vol. iv. p. 241.

AVENT, " *avent* thee ! Nature compels " (M25,*b*), *i.e.* relieve the bowels.

AVOID, " *Avoid*, good brother ! " (M5,*d*)—" *avoid !* I charge thee " (R254,*d*), begone, make room, depart, " get out." " I shall make you *avoid* soon."—*Youth*, Anon. Pl. 2 Ser. (E.E.D.S.), 94,*b*.

AVOIDANCE, " as for mine *avoidance* " (N52,*a*), departure : see Avoid.

AVORE, " I chil wait *avor* you " (R. *passim*), afore : there are numerous examples of *v* for *f* in this play : also of *z* for *s*.

AVOUTRY, " taken in *avoutry* " (*passim*), adultery : see other volumes of this series.

AYENST, " *ayenst* thy sores " (N121,*d*), against. ". . . whan he wente in batayle *ayenst* them . . ." —*Invention of the Holy Cross* (ed. Morris), p. 159.

BA, " *ba* me " (M19,*d*), kiss : cf. *basse* or *buss*.

BADGE, " bear on my bryst the *badge* of mine arms " (M15,*b*), badge. Princes, noblemen, and other gentlemen of rank had formerly, and still retain, distinctive badges, and servants and dependants wore these cognisances on their liveries. Douce, in his *Illustrations of Shakespeare* (1839), pp. 205–7, says : " The history of the changes which badges have undergone is interesting. In the time of Henry IV. the terms *livery* and *badge* seem to have been synonymous. A badge consisted of the master's device, crest, or arms on a separate piece of cloth, or sometimes on silver in the form of a shield fastened to the left sleeve. In Queen Elizabeth's reign the nobility placed silver badges on their servants. The sleeve badge was left off in the reign of James I., but its remains are still preserved in the dresses of porters, firemen, and watermen, and possibly in the shoulder-knots of footmen. During the period when badges were worn the coat to which they were affixed was, as a rule, blue, and the blue coat and badge still may be seen on parish and hospital boys."

BAGGAGE, " the *baggage*, the trash," etc. (R183,*c*), rubbish, refuse, trumpery, scum. " Fill an eggshell newly emptied with the juice of singreen, and set it in hot embers ; scum off the green *baggage* from it, and it will be a water."—Lupton, *Thousand Notable Things* (1579).

BAGS, " the names of my *bags* " (R221,*a*), purses : those carried by Avarice were probably, for the sake of " business," more like small sacks ; he is represented as hugging them (216,*a*), as hauling them (215,*d*), and as dragging them out (225,*d*). " . . . see thou shake the *bags* Of hoarding abbots ; imprison'd angels Set at liberty."—Shakespeare, *King John* (1596), iii. 3.

BALE BLISSES (JE355,*c*), probably blisses which are evil, and the reverse of blisses ; with an eye on A.S. *bale*=" fiery " ; as in *bale*-fire, etc. " . . . bring me forth toward *blisse* with se *bale* here."—*MS. Cott., Titus*, D. xviii., f. 146 *b*.

BALES, " lay on with your *bales* " (M6,*a*). " Scared us with a *bales* " (M35,*d*), in the first example the manuscript has *ballys*, in the second *bales*, but I think the context in each case shows the meaning to be the same. *Bales*=a rod or scourge, and specifically a bow: at 6,*a* it is the minstrels who are charged to " lay on."

BALL, " to it Boy, box him *Ball* " (R194,*c*), a dog: cf. 195,*d*. Halliwell says the name was given to various animals : " it is mentioned as the name of a horse in Chaucer and Tusser, of a sheep in the *Promptorium*, and of a dog in the Privy Purse Expenses of Henry VIII., p. 43."

BANKET, see Junkery.

BAUDERY, " sorcery, witchery, *baudery* " (R263,*d*), the manuscript has *bandery*, but ? *baudery* as in present text. If *bandery*, plotting is doubtless meant.

BASH, " look thou not *bash* " (JE354,*a*), *i.e.* timidly, or with too much inattention. " No, Leonato, I never tempted her with word too large, But, as a brother to his sister, shew'd *Bashful* sincerity and comely love."—Shakespeare, *Much Ado* (1600), iv. I.

BAST, " begat the whoreson in *bast* " (N68,*b*), fornication, adultery. " For he was bigeten o *baste*, God it wot."—*Artour & Merlin*, 7643.

BE (*passim*), been.

BEDLAMS, " stark *bedlams* " (R233,*c*), madmen: see other volumes of this series.

BEES, " hive of humble *bees* swarming in my brain " (R182,*c*), proverbial: cf. modern " bee in the bonnet." Here=restless, whimsical, full of projects: see Heywood, *Works* (E.E.D.S.), II. 385 ; *s.v.* Head.

BEFORN, BEFORNE (*passim*), before.

BELLS, " one would think 'twere brass, most part on't was made of our old *bells* " (R232,*b*). People states an historical fact, and refers to the reformation of the coinage which occurred in the previous reign. Under Edward VI. (1547–53) the Protector Somerset reduced the coinage to its true value and the export of bell-metal was forbidden (2 & 3 Edw. VI., c. 37). The pence of the coinage of 1552 (the fourth of the reign, other issues having been made in 1546–47, 1548, and 1550: see Respublica) was both of fine and base metal. The *fine* penny has (on the obverse) the king seated, with arms and cross on the reverse. The *base* penny has a full-blown rose (the Tudor rose) instead of the enthroned king. Half-pence are nearly the same as the pence.

BELLY, " when the *belly* is full the bones would be at rest " (R216,*b*), proverbial : see Heywood, *Works* (E.E.D.S.), II. 55,*b*.

BENEFICES, " the fifth I have by selling of *benefices* " (R221,*b*). " I have a good *benefice* of a hundred marks " (R225,*b*)—" they will take no *benefice*, but they must have all " (R225,*b*), references apparently to the prevalence of simony. Although a bill had been passed by a parliament of Edward VI., it did not receive the royal assent ; and it was not until 1588–89, under Elizabeth, that any serious attempt was made to remedy the evil.

BERWICK (R254,*a*), in original *Barwicke*, to rhyme with " Warwicke."

BESENE, " so well *besene* " (N117,*b*), good appearance, comely. " And sad habiliments right *well beseene*." —Spencer, *Fairy Queen* (1590), I. xii. 5.

BESIRANCE, " chwas *besirance* your ladydom to zee " (R213,*c*), desirant.

BET, " could not a counselled us *bet* " (M35,*c*), better. " Perhaps he shall be *bet* advisde within a weeke or twayne."—" Romeus and Juliet," *Supp. to Sh.*, i. 292 (Nares).

BEZEIVERS, " valse *bezeivers* " (R230,*a*), deceivers.

BIDE, " had *bide* ne'er so little longer " (R257,*b*) bided.

BIRD'S ARSE, " clean as a *bird's arse* " (M22,*b*), a proverbial simile not uncommon in old writers : Heywood varies it—" as bare," etc. (*Works*, E.E.D.S., II., 89,*a*).

BLANE, " without *blane* " (WH294,*b*), ceasing.

BLENCH, " to *blench* his sight " (M23,*d*), deceive, hinder, obstruct. " The rebels besieged them, winning the even ground on the top, by carrying up great trusses of hay before them, to *blench* the defendants' sight, and dead their shot."—Carew, *Survey of Cornwall* (1602).

BLEST, " God's dear *blest* " (IP316,*c*), *i.e.* happy or blessed, " people " being understood. Also bliss, happiness.

BLIN, " of thy prayer *blin* " (M25,*b*), cease, stop. " How so her fansies stop—Her tears did never *blin*." " Romeus and Juliet," *Supp. to Sh.*, i. 287 (Nares).

BLOODINGS (R221,*a*), black (or blood) puddings.

BLOTTIBUS, etc. (M30,*b*), kitchen Latin.

BOARD, BOURD, " I will *board* her " (R195,*b*)—" to *bourd* Respublica " (R200,*b*). Mr. Magnus says " to engage in tilting," but is not the sense that of Fr. *aborder*=to accost, address, woo. The spelling in the present text should, of course, have been uniform. " I am sure he is in the fleet ; I would he had *boarded* me."—Shakespeare, *Much Ado*, ii. 1. " . . . for, sure, unless he knew some strain in me, that I know not myself, he would never have *boarded* me in this fury."—Shakespeare, *Merry Wives of Windsor*, ii. 1.

BOAT, " an oar in everybody's *boat* " (R235,*c*) : see Heywood, *Works* (E.E.D.S.), ii., 24,*b* ; 207,*a* ; 417,*c*.

BOLT, " my *bolt* is shot " (M34,*d*), an arrow : for examples of the proverb, see Heywood, *Works* (E.E.D.S.), ii. 58,*d* ; 91,*a* ; 205,*d* ; 332,*d* ; 370,*c*.

BOLT, " sift and *bolt* " (R207,*d*), the legal sense is probably intended rather than redundancy for the rhyming's sake. Oppression means that matters must be gifted and discussed privately in order to improve their opportunities for rascality. " And having performed the exercises of their own houses called *boltes, mootes,* and putting of cases, they proceed to be admitted and become students, in some of these four houses or innes of court, where continuing by the space of seven yeares (or thereaboutes) they frequent readings, meetings, *boltinges,* and other learned exercises."—Stowe, *Survey of London,* p. 59. " The judge, or jury, or parties, or the counsel, or attornies, propounding questions, beats and *bolts* out the truth much better than when the witness delivers only a formal series."—Sir M. Hale (*d.* 1676).

BONES, see Belly.

BOOT, " he will be my *boot* " (M11,*a*), help, remedy, cure. " Ich haue *bote* of mi-bale."—*William of Palerne* (*c.* 1300), 627. " God send every trewe man *boote* of his bale."—Chaucer, *Cant. Tales* (1383), 13,409.

BORD, " we did but *bord* " (WH298,*a*), jest : see other volumes of this series.

BORROW, (*a*) " I shall be your *borrow* " (M   ), security, pledge, surety, protector. " Their *borrow* is God Almighty."—Piers Plowman (1363), 37,*b*.
  (*b*) see St. George.

BOURD, see Board.

BOY, see Ball.

BOYS, " shall *boys* . . . of such high matters play " (R180,*d*). Mr. Magnus asks whether this reference to " boy-chorister-actors " may not " have some special reference to Edward VI.'s theological precocity.

BRAST, " the halter *brast* asunder " (M27,*c* ; also 28,*d*), burst. " But with that percing noise flew open quite, or *brast*."—Spenser, *Fairy Queen* (1590), I. viii. 4.

BRAT, " a whole *brat* to his back " (JP338,*d*), cloak, mantle. " Ne had they but a shete Which that they might wrappen hem in a-night, And a *bratt* to walken in by day-light."—Chaucer, *Cant. Tales* (1383), 16,347.

BREADIBUS, " *breadibus* . . . ˉhorsibus . . . firibusque " (M5,*b*), for bread, for horses, and for fires : a form, of dog-Latin which has always been, and still is, popular : see Misericordia.

BRETHEL, " and thy own wife *brethel*, and take thee a leman " (M27,*a*), *brethell* in original : the E.E. text editors suggest [*be*] *brethell*, that is, " if thy own wife be adulterous." This, however, seems beside the mark of the context, as why should Mankind be counselled to take a whore because his

wife is unchaste ?   May *brethel* not be a mis-script
for A.S. *betelle* (Halliwell)=to deceive ? The
meaning is then clear enough and the reading sound.
On the other hand, I fail to find any authority for
Halliwell's suggestion *betelle*=deceive, mislead, in
either Anglo-Saxon or M.E. dictionaries, and the
r in the word brethel, perhaps precludes the adoption
of betelle, *r* being a highly characteristic letter.
An alternative suggestion is that brethel is meant
for *brechell*, from *breken*, to break, to injure, to vex,
harass, torment, or destroy.   " Breken " has among
its derivatives " brac," " brake," " brek," " breche,"
" briche," " bruche," " bruchel."

BRENNING, " hot and *brenning* " (N122,*a*), burning :
also *brent*=burnt : see other volumes of this series.

BREST, " till his belly *brest* " (M6,*a*), burst.

BRIARS, " all in *briars* " (JE364,*a*), in trouble, mis-
fortune, difficulty, doubt : see *Anon. Plays*, 2· Ser.
(E.E.D.S.), 341,*a*.

BRIM, " *brim* and hot " (R241,*d*). Magnus glosses
this " brimhot " : but cf. *brim*=well-known, spoken
of, public.   " That thou dost hold me in disdain,
Is *brim* abroad, and made a gibe to all that keep
this plain."   Warner, *Albion's England* (1586–1606).

BROKLETS (R183,*d*), crumbs ; cf Scots *brock*.

BRONT, " Titivilly would assay you a *bront* " (M39,*b*),
brunt, charge.

BROTHERN, " ye *brothern* " (M4,*b*), an old plural : cf.
childern still in dialect use.

BUM VAY (R211,*d*), by my faith : original spelling *vei* :
cf. Fr. *foi*.

BUNTING, " how think you by this *bunting* " (R216,*d*),
Mr. Magnus glosses this " swelling " ; but is it
not a term of endearment, perhaps with an eye
on the diminutive form of *bunt*=" a swelling part,
an increasing cavity, the bagging of a fishing net
or the like " (*Ency. Dict.*).

BURRS, " cleave together like *burrs* " (M193,*a*), proverbial.

BY AND BY (*passim*), immediately.

CAILES, "play not at *cailes*, cards, nor dice" (IP320,*b*), ninepins (Minshew).

CALAIS, *arms of Calais* (R217,*c*), a common oath of the period. The French citadel was lost to the English in 1558, after an occupation lasting for upwards of two centuries : see other volumes of this series.

 (*b*) "*hangman of Calais*" (JE359,*a*), this mention (*see supra*) may have some bearing on the date of the play. Halliwell in *Old Plays* gives 1566 as the date of printing, but does not state how he arrives at the figures : see John the Evangelist.

CAN (*passim*), able to do ; does.

CAPAX, "tractable and *capax*" (WS137,*d*), capable, sharp, knowing : Latin. "I am a trew flie ; sure I can no false knackes ; Alas ! master spyder, ye be to *capackes.*" Heywood, *Works* (E.E.D.S.), III., *Spider and Flie*, 1556.

CAPPER, "the scald *capper*" (N67,*c*), a cap-maker. "*Cappar*, bonnettier."—Palsgrave, *Lang. Franc.*

CAPTIVITY, "passeth our captivity" (R211,*b*), capacity : part of People's mumble-jumble.

CAREFUL, "a *careful* carriage" (WS173,*a*), full of care : cf. Painful, Hateful. "By him that raised me to this *careful* height."—Shakespeare, *Rich. III.* (1597), i. 3.

CAREN, "as *carene*" (M32,*d*), carrion. "I felte the stench of *caren* here present."—*Wisdom* (E.E.T.S.), 71, 1103.

CARONOUS, "*caronous* body" (N89,*c*), rotten : cf Shakespeare (*Julius Cæsar*, iii. 1), "That this foul deed shall smell above the earth With *carrion* men, groaning for burial."

CASSE, "I hung upon the *casse*" (M27,*d*), apparently a frame of some sort.

CAT, "a *cat* . . . may look on a king" (R236,*b*); see Heywood, *Works* (E.E.D.S.), II., 340, *s.v.* Cat *a*.

CATCH, "Catch that *catch* may" (R187,*b*). An early example of this proverbial saying.

CATON (JE352,c), Cato, the Roman Censor : the pattern of sternness and austere manner, he stabbed himself at Utica 46 B.C. because, considering freedom as alone sustaining the dignity of man, he felt himself unable to survive the independence of his country. He was frequently quoted by writers of this period —" *Caton*, the grete clerke "—*Cast. Persev.* (E.E.T.S., 103, 868).

CAVEATIS, " I say *Caveatis* " (M21,d ; 22,b), Beware !

CAVILLATION, " make this *cavillation* " (WH281,d), frivolous objections, cavilling. " I might add so much concerning the large odds between the case of the eldest churches in regard of heathens, and ours in respect of the Church of Rome, that very *cavillation* itself should be satisfied."—Hook.

CAYME, " in that *cayme* he was like to " (JE366,c), in original *Cayme*. I can make nothing of it except that it is a misprint for Cain.

CEPE, " speak to the sheriff for a *cepe* coppus " (M34,d), *i.e. cape corpus* for *capias corpus*, a writ of attachment.

'*Ch* (*passim*)=I : *e.g.* cha=I have (ich 'a') ; chad= I had ; cham=I am, etc.; see Dialect.

CHA, CHE, " *Che* wa'r't " (R210,c),—" *Che* was vair " (R232,b),—" *Cha* not be haled up " (R267,c). I.

CHAD (*passim*), I had—'ch 'ad.

CHAM (*passim*) I am—'ch am.

CHAMPION, " now is a *champion* field " (R200,d), *i.e.* champagne=flat open country. " Fra the thine thay went fourty dayes, and come intille a *champayne* cuntree that was alle barayne, and na hye place, ne na hilles mighte be sene on na syde."—*MS. Lincoln*, A. i. 17, f. 31. " . . . the Canaanites, which dwell in the *champaign* over against Gilgal, beside the plains of Moreh ? "—*Bible*, Auth. Ver. (1611), *Deut.* xi. 30. " The verdant meads are drest in green, The *champion* fields with corn are seen."—*Poor Robin* (1694).

CHARITY, see St. Charity.

WORD-LIST, L.T.P.   25

CHAVE (*passim*), I have—[i]ch 'ave.

CHECK, " let us con well our neck-verse that we have
not a *check* " (M23,*c*), *i.e.* be hung.

CHERY - TIME, " but a *chery-time* " (M12,*a*), a short
time, " like cherry blossoms " (Furnivall and Pollard).

CHE[VI]SANCE, " the new *che*[*vi*]*sance* " (M29,*a*),
chesance in original : usually *chevisance* = treaty,
agreement, bargain ; but here, as Mischief is speaking of the food and other cheer he has stolen,
the meaning may be gain, booty, plunder, spoil.
" Eschaunges and *chevysaunces*, with swich chaffare
I dele."—Langland, *P. Plowman* (1363), 2969.

CHILL (*passim*), I will—'ch 'ill.

CHIVE, " I warrant him a *chive* " (R185,*d*), a chip,
fragment : a small standard of value. " If any
chive, chip, or dust skip into the eye, . . . then can
you not cure the eye but by removing and drawing
the said *chive*.—Barrough, *Method of Physick* (1624.)

CHOP, CHOPE (*a*) " in nomine Patris, *chope* . . . Ye
shall not *chop* my jewels " (M20,*a*), in both cases the
original has *choppe* ; but as Nought and New Guise
were funning and punning, I have preserved the
play on the words which I think was intended—
chope=ch'ope (I hope) and *chop*=cut off ; but the
student can choose, and regard the first *chop* also
to mean " cut ! " " strike ! " " *Chope* you'll consider my pain."—*Misogonus*, Anon. Plays, 2 Ser.
(E.E.D.S.), 210*b*.
    (*b*) " Into a deanery . . . to *chop* " (R223,*d*).
Mr. Magnus glosses this as " snap " ; but is it not
used in the closer sense of *to pop* ? cf. *chop-church*
=(1) one who exchanges livings, or (2) such an act
of barter. " As flise at libertee in and out might
chop."—Heywood, *Spider and Flie* (1556), *Works*, III.
(E.E.D.S.).

CHOULD (*passim*), I would—'ch 'ould.

CHRISTENDOM, " by my *christendom* " (R196,*d*).
See E.E.D.S., *Anon. Plays*, Series 2 and 3, Note-
Books, *s.v.*

CHRISTMAS DEVICE (R179,*b*), Christmas was better
kept as a festival in olden times than in modern
days, lasting at this period from Christmas Eve to
Old Christmas Day or Twelfth night. At Court,
and in the Inns of Court, high revel was kept ; from
references such as the above it is clear that many
a play was specially written for, and first presented
at, these festivals. The sources of detailed descrip-
tions are too well known to need particular reference.

CHRISTMAS SONG (M15,*d* ; 16,*a* to *c*). Prof. Manly
omits this precious production ; perhaps rightly
in view of his text being prepared for class-room
use ; the E.E.T. Society's issue gives it as a matter
of course, as do I.

CHURCH, " a *church* here beside," etc. (M28,*b*), *i.e.* the
abbey larder should provide the requisite cheer.

CHURCH - STILE, " on the *church stile* " (M26,*a*), a
stile in, or leading to, the precincts of the church.

CHWAS (*passim*), I was—'ch was.

CLARIFY, " This question to *clarify* " (M5,*a*), make
clear or intelligible, answer, clear up. " A word to
you I wold *claryfy*."—*Towneley Myst.*, p. 67.

CLASH, " at *clash* and cards " (IP338,*b*), bawdy
talk, gossiping, tittle-tattle, quarrelling. " Good
Lord ! what fiery *clashings* we have had lately for a
cap and a surplice ! "—Howell, *Lett.* (1644–45), iv.
29.

CLAWBACK, " you flearing *clawback* you " (R188,*a*),
lickspittle, flatterer. The whole passage is a striking early instance of sarcastic vituperation, and the
gradual piling up of the weight of abuse.

CLEAN, " a clean gentleman " (M22,*a*), fair, comely,
noble : a general appreciative. " With the *clennest
cumpanye* that euer king ladde."—*Will. of Paleren*
(*c.* 1360), 1609.

CLEPE, " if I should *clepe* to memory " (N45,*a*), call.
" I shall inwardly *clepe* the Lord." — Wycliffe,
Psalm xvii. 4.

CLERICAL, "*clerical* manner" (M8,*b*),—"a *clerical*
matter" (M26,*a*), clerk-like, scholarly, abstruse,
learned.

CLOTHES, "the *clothes* of thy *shoon*" (M35,*b*), generic
for fabric and material as well as for dress and
apparel.

CLOUTERY, (R263,*d*). Mr. Magnus glosses this as
"mending," and probably he is right. On the other
hand, a glance may be given to the Northern *clouter*
= to do dirty work.

COBS, "the great *cobs*" (R232,*d*), a rich but grasping
person, a person of superior rank and power.
"Susteynid is not by personis lowe, But *cobbis* grete
this riote sustene."—*Occleve, MS. Soc. Antiq.* 134,
f. 267. "But, at leisure, ther must be some of the
gret *cobbes* served likewise, and the king to have ther
landes likewise, as, God willing, he shall have th'
erle of Kildares in possession, or somer passe."—
State Papers, ii. 228 (Nares).

COCK'S (*passim*), God's. Hence *Cock's body sacred* =
God's consecrated body.

COMMEDIENS, "as *commediens* vor us" (R212,*a*),
commodious.

COMMODITY (*passim*), advantage and many allied
senses : see other volumes of this series.

COMPANABLE, "such as be *companable*" (N62,*a*),
affable, sociable, companionable. "Frendly to ben
and *compaygnable* at al." *MS. Fairfax* 16.

CONFORMED, see Respublica.

CONGY, "a little pretty *congy*" (N60,*d*), bow of
salutation.

CONVERT, "thine eyes to me *convert*" (R238,*c*), turn,
move.

CONVERTIBLE (M33,*b*), unstedfast, changeable.

CONVICT, "*convict* them" (M19,*a*)—"Mercy shall
never be *convict* of his uncurtess condition"
(M34,*a*), conquer, persuade.

CONVINCED, " they shall be *convinced* " (R246,*b*), convicted : cf. convict. " Which of you *convinceth* me of sin ? "—*Bible*, Auth. Vers. (1611), *John* viii. 46.

COPED, (*a*) " Christ's *coped* curse " (M36,*a*); in original *coppyde* : cf. *copie, copy*=abundance, plenty (Trevisa, i. 301), and *copped, coppyd* = rising to a point, heaped-up as a measure ; hence " Christ's *copious*, abundant, overflowing malediction." " This Spayne . . . hath grete *copy*, and plente of castelles."—*Trevisa*, i. 301.

(*b*) " he is so *copped* " (R213,*a*), apparently a variant of *coppet*=saucy, impudent, overbearing.

COPY, " change our *copy* " (R202,*b*), manner.

CORROMPT, " Is should be *corrompt* therefore " (R256,*b*); punished is meant, but the usual sense is " corrupted."

COUCH, " I will *couch* you all up " (R216,*b*), conceal, hide away, put in safe keeping. " In the seler of Juppiter ther ben *couched* two tunnes."—Chaucer, *Boethius*, p. 35.

COURTESY, " the *courtesy of England* is oft to kiss " (JE356,*d*). In *The English Historical Review* (vol. vii., p. 270) there is an article by Major Martin A. S. Hume on " Philip's visit to England " in 1554. The article is founded on a Spanish account written by Andres Muñoz, a servant in the household of Don Carlos, Philip's son, then a child. Muñoz did not himself go to England, but probably got his account from someone, much in the same position as himself, who did go. The writer describes how Philip met Queen Mary at Winchester, " *and kissed her on the mouth, in the English fashion.*" On taking leave Philip was introduced to Mary's ladies, all of whom he kissed " *so as not* (says Muñoz) *to break the custom of the country, which is a very good one.*" This no doubt explains the passage in the play, but there was at law another *courtesy of England* with which, in the origins, it may have some obscure connection. Cowel, in his *Law Dictionary* (1607), describes a tenure by which, if a man marry an inheritrix, that is, a woman seised of land, and getteth a child of her that comes alive into the world, though both the child and his wife die forthwith, yet, if she were in possession, shall he keep the land during his life, and is called tenant *per legem Angliæ*, or by the *courtesy of England*.

COURTNALS, " a zort of *courtnalls* " (R255,*d*), courtiers : in contempt (Halliwell).

COURT SPIRITUAL (JP343,*b*), Abundance was accused of fornication, and so came under ecclesiastical jurisdiction. These courts were made separate to the Secular or Civil Courts in 1085, but until the establishment of the Divorce and Probate Courts in 1857 the Ecclesiastical Courts took cognisance of blasphemy, apostasy, heresy, schism, ordinations, matters pertaining to benefices, matrimony, divorces, bastardy, tithes, incest, fornication, adultery, probate of wills, administrations, and similar matters (Haydn).

CREANCE, " chief of His *creance* " (N45,*d*), ordinarily faith, belief, credit, payment : I subjoin examples of each usage, but neither seem to fit the sense. There is an alternative which is nearer the mark, in the Latin *creans*, pr. p. of *creo*, to create ; but I find no authority beyond *creant*, which, as far as I know, is modern : see last example. " This mayden tauzte the *creance* Unto this wyf so perfitly."—Gower, *MS. Soc. Antiq.* 134, f. 66. " And with his precyous bloode he wroote the bills Upon the crosse, as general acquytaunce To every penytent in ful *creaunce*."— *Rom. of the Monk*, Sion College MS. " The *creant* word Which thrilled around us."—Mrs. Browning.

CREASETH, " when she *creaseth* again " (N44,*a*), short for *increaseth*.

CREATURE (R. *passim*), throughout a trisyllable.

CROW, see Clawback.

CUCULORUM, " taken with a *cuculorum* " (JE352,*d*), the rhyming exigency no doubt influenced the form of the word, but in any case the use is obscure, probably slang now lost. Whether, however, it originated in *cucullus*, a hood, or *cuculus*, a cuckoo (whence cuckold), or whether the word enshrines a play on both, I cannot say.

CUMBERLAND, see Respublica.

CURIA, etc. (M30,*c*), the proceedings of Manorial Courts were generally headed "*Curia* generalis tenta ibidem," etc. Mischief, with assumed official authority, means that the document was written in an alehouse (or where ale was plenty) with a sham date.

CUSTODITY, " in my *custodity* " (R266,*d*), custody.

CUT, " Call me *cut* " (N54,*b*), properly a gelding or any animal with a short or cut tail, and specifically an intensive reproach. The classical illustration to the present passage is, of course, from Shakespeare, " If I tell thee a lie, spit in my face and call me horse " (*1 Hen. IV.*, ii. 1). Compare again, " cutted whore " (N66*d*): see other volumes of this series.

DAINTY, " men have little *dainty* of your play " (M13,*b*), *i.e.* little that is agreeable or pleasant, small liking for or delight in. " It was *daynte* for to see the cheere bitwix hem two."—Chaucer, *Cant. Tales* (1383), 8983. " . . . and all things which were *dainty* and goodly are departed from thee, . . ." —*Bible*, Auth. Vers. (1611), *Rev.* xviii. 14.

DAISY, " leap at a *daisy* " (R243,*c*), be hanged : see *Anon. Plays*, 3 Ser. (E.E.D.S.).

DALLIATION, " leave your *dalliation* " (M5, *a*), dallying.

DALLY, " quit as a *dally* " (JE365,*b*), what " a tale of titmary tally " (see previous line) or " quit as a *dally* " mean I am unable to discover. The original is, " She helde me with a tale of tytemary tally Tyll my thryfte was gone as quyte as a *dally*."

DA PACEM (M31,*d*), literally " give us peace " ; here slang for a knife or dagger : cf. modern " Arkansas toothpick "=a bowie knife, " Meat-in-the-pot "=a gun, and similar locutions.

DARNEL, see Drawk.

DEAMBULATORY (M37,*c*), a covered walk, cloister, ambulatory.

DELECTABLE, " my talking *delectable* " (M5,*d*), pleasing, delightful.

DELVER (*passim*), delve.

DEPARTED, DEPART, (*a*) "how I *departed* them"
(N80,*b*).
(*b*) "till death us *depart*" (WS172,*d*), *i.e.*
(*a*) left them ; (*b*) till death divides, or parts :
now corrupted in the Marriage Service into "do
part." "We wille *departe* his clothing."—*Towneley
Myst.*, p. 228.

DESTRUCTIONS, "*destructions* to 'member in my heart"
(R234,*d*), instructions : part of People's mangled
English.

DETECTED, "ne'er of any crime *detected*" (R183,*b*),
possibly here=accused.

DEVER, "put me in *dever*" (M24, *d*), duty, service.
"Do the *deuer* that thow hast to done."—*William
of Palerne* (*c.* 1360), 2546.

DEVOSE, "we must *devose* how that we may"
(WH289,*a*), devise.

DIALECT AND JARGON, see Respublica, Wealth and
Health.

DINTY, "no *dinty* to do" (N49,*d*), pleasure, liking :
see Dainty.

DISEASE (*passim*), generic for absence of ease—dis-
comfort, annoyance, trouble, difficulty, sorrow, etc. :
see other volumes of this series.

DISPECTIBLE, "thou art *dispectible*" (M33,*c*), despic-
able.

DISPECTUOUS, "*dispectuous* and odible" (M33,*a*), un-
sightly : see previous entry.

DIVUM, "*Divum este justlum weste*" (R232,*c*), Prof.
Brandl suggests *Divites estis justi fuistis*.

Do, see Way.

DOGS, "hungry *dogs* will slab up sluttish puddings"
(R221,*a*), see Heywood, *Works* (E.E.D.S.),II.14*a* ;
357,*d* (*n*).

DORT, "a shrewd crank *dort*" (N83,*d*), fit of sulks, a
pet, sullen humour.

DOUBLER, " both dish and *doubler* " (M29,*a*), a large dish, plate, or bowl. " A dysche other a *dobler* that dryghtyn onez serued."—*Early Eng. Allit. Poems;* Cleanness, 1145.

DRAFF, " driff, *draff*, mish, mash " (M5,*b*), rubbish, refuse, dregs: see other volumes of this series. *Mish, mash*=mess.

DRAWK, " *drawk* and . . . *darnel* " (M24,*a*), a weed very similar to darnel—*Bromus secalinus; darnel* is *Lolium perenne*.

DRIFF, see Draff.

DRIFFE, " hence I will you *driffe* " (M17,*d*), drive.

DRIVEL, " live thus like a *drivel* " (N61,*b*), a generic reproach; drudge, servant, idiot, dotard, fool; see other volumes of this series.

DROUSE, " a hounded *drouse* " (WH288,*d*), in view of the wretched printing of this play it serves little useful purpose to suggest a correct reading; the most probable would seem to be *hounded*=hundred and *drouse*=douse; *i.e.* a god give him a hundred ducklings.

DUTCH JARGON, see Wealth and Health.

EACHWHERE, " *eachwhere* sore hated " (R197,*a*), everywhere.

EDWARDS, " angelots and *Edwards* " (R216,*d*), see Angelots. I am further inclined to doubt whether the pieces referred to were of current or recent striking. It is true Edward VI. reformed the coinage, but as the angelots (at least) are specifically referred to as "old," and as the angelot is probably that of 1420, the *Edward* is also likely to be the angel of Edward IV. introduced in 1465, which bears an effigy of that king. The angel of Edward VI., of the third coinage of the reign, *does not bear an effigy of Edward VI.* It may not be out of place to detail the various issues, though this cannot, of course, settle the point as to what coin was meant by the *Edward*. Kenyon, on " The Gold Coins of England," says there were four distinct series of *gold* coins issued during the reign of Edward VI. *First Coinage (January* 1546–47):— HALF-SOVEREIGNS (value 10s.). *Obverse*—king in robes

and crowned, enthroned, the figure of an angel on
each arm of the throne; *reverse* — shield bearing
arms of France and England quarterly, supported by
lion and dragon. CROWN (value 5s.). *Obverse*—rose,
crowned; *reverse*—shield with arms, crowned. HALF-
CROWNS (value 2s. 6d.). Type like the crowns.
Second Coinage (1548):—TREBLE SOVEREIGN (value
£3). Type like last half-sovereign, except that king
has no robes, and holds a sword instead of a
sceptre. SOVEREIGN (value £1). Same as £3, only with
different mint-mark. HALF-SOVEREIGN (value 10s.).
Obverse — bust in profile to right; *reverse* — oval
shield, crowned, and garnished. CROWNS (value
5s.). Same as half-sovereign of this coinage.
HALF - CROWNS (value 2s. 6d.). Same as half-
sovereign of this coinage. *Third Coinage* (1550):—
DOUBLE SOVEREIGN (value 48s). *Obverse*—king
seated, holding sceptre and orb; *reserve*—shield
with arms, upon a large double rose. SOVEREIGN
(value 24s.). Same as double sovereign. ANGEL
(value 8s.). Type similar to angels of Henry
VIII. The type seems to have been fixed in Henry
VI.'s reign. The Archangel Michael was on the
obverse, trampling with his left foot upon the dragon,
and piercing him through the mouth with a spear.
Reverse has shield bearing arms of England and
France upon a ship. [*No effigy of Edward VI.*]
ANGELET (value 4s.). Same as angel. *Fourth
Coinage* (1552):—SOVEREIGN (value 20s.). *Obverse*—
three-quarter length of king in profile; *reverse*—same
as sovereign of second coinage. HALF-SOVEREIGN
(value 10s.). *Obverse*—same as sovereign; *reverse*—
square shield crowned between E.R. CROWN (value
5s.). Same as half-sovereign. HALF-CROWN (value
2s. 6d.). Same as crown. Hawkins, on "The Silver
Coins of England," says of Edward VI. SILVER
coinage, there were GROATS, HALF-GROATS, PENNIES,
HALF-PENNIES. *Note* — All silver. SHILLINGS—
Obverse—king's bust in profile, crowned; *reverse*—
arms upon an oval shield. CROWNS—*Obverse*—the
king mounted on a horse; *reverse*—arms, and cross
fleuree. HALF-CROWNS. Same as crowns. SHILLINGS
—*Obverse*—the king on horsebark, galloping; *reverse*
—a square-topped shield, crowned. SIXPENCE,
Exactly the same as the shilling. THREEPENCE.

Same as shilling. PENCE of this coinage (1552)
occur both of fine and base metal. The *fine*
penny has (on the *obverse*) the king seated, with
arms and cross on the *reverse*. The *base* penny has
a full-blown rose, instead of the enthroned king.
HALF-PENCE are nearly the same as pence.

EMPERY, " in this *empery* " (N56,*d*), empire, dominion ;
also more loosely, region. " Ruling in large and
ample *empery* o'er France."—Shakespeare, *Henry V.*
(1599), i. 2. " A lady So fair, and fastened to an
empery, Would make the great'st king double."—
Shakespeare, *Cymbeline* (1605), i. 7.

EMPRISE, " th' *emprise* of all this world " (N46,*a*),
generally an undertaking more or less onerous
or risky. Here = the responsibility of subduing and
righteously governing the material creation. " Then
shal rejoysen of a grete *empryse* Acheved wel."
—Chaucer, *Troilus and Cressida* (1369), ii. 1391.

EMPROWED, " bought . . . and *emprowed* " (R219,*a*),
improved : with an eye to a higher rent.

ENCHESON, " for th' *encheson* " (N43,*c*), reason, cause,
occasion. " Certes, said he, well mote I shame to
tell The fond *encheason* that me hither led."—Spenser,
Fairy Queen (1590), II. i. 30.

ENCROACHING OF LANDS, see Respublica.

ENDRAIT, " live after that *endrait* " (N59,*d*), quality.

ENFORMED, see Respublica.

ENGLAND, see Courtesy.

ENQUEST, see Inquest.

ENTRIKED, " I am wondrously *entriked* " (N55,*c* ; 59*c*),
deceived, entangled, tricked, hindered. " That mir-
rour hath me now *entriked*."—*Romaunt of the Rose*,
1642.

ENTUNES, " *entunes* in silence of the night " (N45,*a*),
songs, tunes, chants, melodies. " So mery a soune,
so swete *entewnes*."—Chaucer, *Boke of the Duchesse*
(1371), 307.

ENURE, " myself to *enure* " (N48,*b*), use, make a habit of,
accustom. " He gan that Ladie strongly to appele

Of many haynous crymes by her *enured*."—Spenser,
Fairy Queen (1596), v. ix. 39.

ENVIES, " to see . . . *envies* take in a trap " (R257,*b*),
enemies.

EQUITY, see Mankind, *Amended Readings*.

ERCH (*passim*), ere I—er' 'ch—ere ich.

ESCHEATS, " thǝ blind *escheats* " (R183,*d*), lands or
tenements which fell to the crown or lord of the
fee through failure of heirs or corruption of blood :
the latter kind was abolished by the Felony Act,
33 & 34 Vict., ch. xxiii. " The last consequence
of tenure in chivalry was *escheat* ; which took place
if the tenant died without heirs of his blood, or if
his blood was corrupted by commission of treason
or felony. In such cases the land escheated or fell
back to the lord—that is, the tenure was determined
by breach of the original condition of the feudal
donation. In the one case there were no heirs of
the blood of the first feudatory, to which heirs alone
the grant of the feud extended ; in the other the
tenant, by perpetrating an atrocious crime, forfeited
his feud, which he held under the implied condition
that he should not be a traitor or felon."—Blackstone,
Commentaries, bk. ii., ch. 3.

EXALTATIONS, " follow their good *exaltations* " (R234,*d*),
exhortations.

EXTENT, " at the highest *extent*," etc. (R219,*a*), sale
under compulsory powers (M).

EXTREATS, " the scape of extreats " (R183,*d*), *i.e.*
estreats, enforced by trick. At law an estreat is an
official copy of the specification of fines or penalties
(such as a forfeited recognisance for use of the
bailiff or sheriff's officer in levying. " A forfeited
recognisance," if taken by a justice of the peace, is
certified to the next sessions ; and if the condition
be broken by any breach of the peace in the one case,
or any misbehaviour in the other, the recognisance
becomes forfeited or absolute ; and being *estreated*
or extracted, taken out from among the other records, and sent up to the Exchequer ; the party and
his sureties, having now become absolute debtors

of the Crown, are sued for the several sums in which they are respectively bound."—Blackstone, *Comment.,* bk. iv., ch. 18. See Respublica for authorities dealing with the systems of extortion referred to in these lines.

FAITOUR, " ye are no *faitour* " (M12,*c*), deceiver, imposter : a generic reproach. " There be many of you *faitours.*"—Gower, *Confessio Amantis* (1393), i. 47.

FALL, " *fall* back, *fall* edge " (R250,*b*), *i.e.* whichever way it turns out I am prepared (edge=aside or sideways).

FARTHING, " I may not change a man a *farthing* " (M18,*b*), in the least or smallest degree. A farthing, the fourth part of a penny, and the smallest copper coin current in Great Britain, is mentioned as far back as Robert of Gloucester. It seems to have become a simile of small value or amount in most early writers. " In hire suppe was no *ferthing* sene Of grese, whan she dronken hadde hire drauht." —Chaucer, *Cant. Tales* (1383), Prologue, 134.

FASHION, see I-fashion.

FEATHER, " *feather* my nest " (R183,*b*); this proverbial saying does not occur in Heywood.

FELL, " the world, the flesh, and the *fell* " (M39,*c*), the devil (Furnivall & Pollard).

FELLOWSHIP, " flee that *fellowship* " (M32,*b*), company, body of associates, confederacy, joint interest. " Parry felle in *felaschepe* with Willyum Hasard at Querles."—*Paston Letters*, i. 83. " Antenor fleenge with his *felowschippe.*"—*Trevisa*, i. 273.

FEOFFED, " *feoffed* thee with all " (N46,*a*), endowed. " May God forbid to *feffe* you so with grace."— Chaucer, *Court of Love.*

FERE, " create to be his *fere* " (N49,*b*), companion, partner, fellow. " He wod into the water, his *feren* him bysyde."—*Political Songs*, p. 217.

FESTINATION, " with all *festination* " (R204,*c*), speed, hurry, expedition. " Sweet Frank, when shall my father Security present me ? " " With all *festina-tion*."—Jonson and Chapman, *Eastward Hoe* (1605), ii. 1.

FETCHES, " beware the *fetches* of Tediousness " (WS143,*a*), stratagems, tricks, contrivances, artifices : the word does not always carry a bad or unworthy meaning.

FICHANT, " Ise cannot be *fichant* enough " (R267,*c*), sufficient ; *i.e.* better received and esteemed.   Mr. Magnus suggests *Je m'en fiche*, as origin.

FIDE, W[illiam] (M22,*d*), so given in the E.E.T.S. text, *Fide* being *Fyde*.

FIERCE, "a likely man and a *fierce* " (M27,*d*)—" how valiant . . . and *fierce* " (WH293,*d*), strong, full of fire and ardour.   " Yet have I *fierce* affections." —Shakespeare, *Antony and Cleopatra* (1608), i. 5. " The ships, though so great, are driven of *fierce* winds ; yet are they turned about with a very small helm."— *Bible*, Auth. Vers. (1611), *James* iii. 4.

FIRIBUSQUE, see Breadibus.

FIST, " a good running *fist* " (M30,*b*), writing :   an early example of a common present-day colloquialism.

FLATERABUNDUS, " ye *flaterabundus* you " (R188,*a*), see Clawback.

FLEAR, FLEARING, FLEERETH (*passim*), mock, gibe, leer, smirk ;   and as *verb*=to grin contemptuously or scornfully, sneer, smirk.

FLEXIBLE, " Mankind is so *flexible* " (M33,*a*), pliant, easily influenced, wavering in disposition.

FLITCHED, " hath *flitched* the bishopricks " (R218,*b*), so in orignal, but ? *filched*.   Mr. Magnus says, " Cut up into strips."

FLITTANCE (R183,*d*), " a ghost word for fleetings, *i.e.* skimmings " (Mr. Magnus quoting Prof. Skeat).

FLIX, " die of the *flix* " (R271,*c*), flux, dysentery. Mr. Magnus glosses this " flyxe [*flixe* in E.E.T.S. text], flick,thief, 62, 1908."   The mistake in giving the text spelling in glossary leads one to suspect that all the rest, save the page and line reference, is wrong also. At all events, how could Avarice " die of the thief " ? Perhaps, however, the E.E.T.S. editor meant the Great Thief of Thieves—Old Age !! " Diseased with the bluddy *flixe*."—Udal, *Matt.* ix.

FLORENT, " so *florent* estate " (R200,*d*), flourishing, prosperous. " Sinopa was a *florent* citee."—Udal, *Apoph. of Erasmus* (1543), p. 77.

FLOUTHY, " full of *flouthy* bushes " (JE355,*b*) ? *slouthy* as in my text and in original: if *flouthy* from flout=mock, jeer, treat with contempt : cf. lecherous thorns, back-biting briars, elders of envy, and other kindred similes in the same passage.

FOND, " each *fond* opinion " (N58,*a*; *et passim*), foolish, silly, unwise.

FONE, " God shield you from your *fone* " (M14,*d* ; *et passim*), foes : an old plural.

FOOT, " I hope to have his *foot met* " (M23,*d*), *i.e.* caught by the foot, tripped.

FOOTBALL, " lend us a *football* " (M32,*c*). Dr. Brandl says this is the earliest mention of the game.

FORBORNE, " it may no longer be *forborne* " (N51,*d*), endured. " I may not certes, though I shulde die, *Forbere* to ben out of your compagnie."—Chaucer, *Cant. Tales* (1383), 10,056.

FORCE, FORCETH (*passim*), as *sub.*=matter, consequence, importance, ground for care or anxiety ; as *verb*=to care, regard, value, to be of importance or signify. " What *fors* were it though al the town bihelde ? "—Chaucer, *Troilus and Cressida* (1369), ii. 373. " It little *forceth* how long a man liue, but how wel and vertuously."—Udal, *Mark* v. " I *force* not argument a straw."—Shakespeare, *Rape of Lucrece* (1594), 1021.

FOR-COLD, " pottage shall be for-*cold* " (M13,*b*)— " when a man is *for-cold* " (M5,*c*), very cold : as a prefix *for-* has (1) an intensive force ; (2) a negative or privative force ; and (3) a deteriorative force. Typical examples of each class are——(1) forlorn= utterly lonely ; for-drunken = beastly drunk ; (2) forbid, forfend ; (3) forshapen=badly formed, etc.

FORMA, see In.

FORTY PENCE, see Jack Noble.

FOUNDER, " our *founder* and chief—*founder* me no foundering " (R186,*b* ; 187*c* ; 189*a*), patron, benefactor : see other volumes of this series.

FOUR EARS, see Horse.

FRAGILITY ? " of your nature and of your *fragility* " (M14,*a*), frailty, weakness, proneness to fall. " Earnestly beseeching the dictatour to forgive this humane *fragilitie* and youthful folly of Qu. Fabius." —P. Holland, *Livius*, p. 307.

FRAY, " how I *fray* " (R202,*c*), fear. " The troubled ghost of my father Anchises So oft in sleepe doth *fray* me, and aduise."—Surrey, *Virgil, Æneis*, iv.

FRAYRY, " the demonical *frayry* " (M8,*d*), friary, conventicle.

FUSION, " God send it His *fusion* " (M15,*d*), ? *foison*, *fusoan*, *fusin*=plenty, abundance : in original, *fusyon*.

GAN, " how God . . . *gan* devise " (N46,*a*), began : auxiliary with force of *did*. " Not with less dread the loud Ethereal trumpet from on high *gan* blow."— Milton, *Paradise Lost* (1667), vi. 60.

GARD, " freshly *gard* " (N77,*c*), trimmed, edged. " Those of the forewarde vnder the Duke of Norffolke, were apparelled in blue coats *garded* with redde."—Stow, *Henry VIII.* (1544).

GAUDIES, " no more *gaudies* or japes " (R264,*b*), trick, jest. " Thynke wel that. it is no *gaude*."— Chaucer, *Troilus* (1369), ii. 351.

GEAR (*passim*), formerly a word-of-all-work=outfit, ornament, dress, accoutrements, arms, harness, tackle, goods, property, tools, implements, material, stuff, matter, business, affair, manners, habits, customs, rubbish, trash—and what not ? See other volumes of this series.

GENERALIS, see Curia.

GENTLE-MEAT, "*Gentle meat* for a hawk" (J.E. 363,*c*), the pun is double-barrelled : *gentle* also=a trained hawk.

GENTMAN (R231,*b*), gentleman : cf. jentman.

GEOFFREY, " farewell, gentle *Geoffrey* " (M9,*a*), apparently a common tag or catch-phrase, or from some song of the period. Heywood (*Works*, E.E.D.S., II. 36*b*) quotes almost the identical words of *Mankind* : " Now, here is the door, and there is the way ; And so, (quoth he), farewell, gentle *Geoffrey* ! "

GERE, read Gear.

GESUMME, "a good horse should be *gesumme*" (M12,*d*). Dr. Bradley (quoted by E.E.T.S. editors) suggests *geason* (A.S. *gœsne*=empty, scarce). The whole passage from the beginning of the speech is obscure and apparently corrupt : at all events, it hardly " reads " as it is. The following suggestion is made with a view to eliciting a re-examination. The original is (E.E.T.S.)—

"Ande my wyf wer*e* yow*u*r hors, sche wolde yow a**ll** to-sa*m*ne

ʒe fede yow*u*r hors in mesure ; ze ar*e* a wyse man.

I trow, & ʒe wer*e* þe kyng*is* palfrey-ma*n*,

A goode horse xulde be gesum*m*e."

Now, take as mis-written the words *yow* and *to-samne* in the first line, and substitute respectively *be* and *to-famen*, and sense is obtained. New Guise has overheard Mercy saying that too much corn for a horse makes it unruly and unmanageable. " Good ! " says New Guise, " you are no liar, for I fed my wife so well that she has given me a clouting—here is the plaster ! . . . If my wife were your horse she would be altogether famished. I trow if ye were the King's palfrey-man a good horse would go empty or be scarce (King's horses, for parade purposes requiring plenty of the best fodder). The misscripts are not unlikely ones, and—well, 'tis but a suggestion. " Steuen wille vs traueile and *famen* vs to dede."— *Robert de Brunne*, p. 122.

GHOST, GHOSTLY (*passim*), soul, breath, spirit, will ; spiritual, not carnal or secular, religious : Ger., *geistlich*. As, his holy *ghost* (of the will of a man), ghostly purpose, *ghostly* enemy, *ghostly* solace *ghostly* comfort, *ghostly*, *ghostly* to our purpose, father *ghostly*, *ghostly* reason.

GINNETH, " when she *ginneth* wane " (N44,*a*), beginneth. " This lessoun thus I *ginne*."—*William of Palerne*, 1929. " Into hyr bedde the boy *gan* crepe." —*Octovian*, 176.

GINST, " *ginst* to err " (N52,*b*), see previous entry.

GIS, " by *Gis* " (*passim*), Jesus : also Jis and Gisse.

GIVE, " *give* the rope just to thy neck " (M35,*d*), put, adjust.

GODAMIGHTIES (R225,*a*), a term applied to any person or thing greatly idolised : also and mostly, nowadays, in sarcasm, *e.g.* a little God-almighty (of a conceited prig), etc. Avarice is speaking of his money bags.

GODIGOD (R182,*c*), " God give you good [day]," a gloss of Prof. Brandl's. Also (R258,*c*), *Godigod eve* and *Godigod speed*.

GOD'S GOOD, " a hat of *God's good* " (R229,*b*), yeast ; *sallet*=helmet (see E.E.D.S., *Anon.Plays*, 1 Ser. 274*a*). People means that instead of being well enough off to get a helmet to serve the king, he is fain to be content with a yeast tub ; probably it was meant also as a bit of " business " for the groundlings' sake.

GOSS, " by *Goss* " (R194,*c*), God.

GOVERNANCE, " this is his *governance* " (M26,*d*), behaviour, manners, conduct, mode of life. " Now schalle I telle you the *governance* of the court of the grete Cham."—*Maundeville*, p. 232.

GOVERNY, " the whole rule and *governy* " (N60,*c*), control, management, guidance.

GRASS, " while the *grass* shall grow the horse shall sterve" (R233,*d*), see Heywood (E.E.D.S., *Works*, II., 378), *s.v.* Grass.

GREEN CHEESE, " Ye can see no *green cheese* but your teeth will water " (R216,*c*), cream cheese, the material of which " the moon is made " : see Heywood, *Works* (E.E.D.S.), II., 97*c*.

GREEN FRIARS (N92,*d*), no such order is known either
to the highest living English authority on monastic
orders, or to Helyot or Dugdale ; *The Catholic Dictionary* likewise makes no reference to Green Friars.
And, in truth, having regard to the context, it seems
tolerably certain that Medwall (a priest himself
was merely satirizing known abuses, with an eye
perhaps on "Friar Tuck" and "Lincoln green":
the "hedge-marriages" alluded to later (93,*c*) would
also support this interpretation.

GROGE, GROGED (N75,*d*), grudge, grudged : as *subs*=
discontent, ill-will, anger, unwillingness to benefit ;
as *verb*=grieve, repine, murmur, raise objection,
feel ill-will.	" Perish they That *grudge* one thought
against your Majesty."—Shakespeare, *1 Henry VI.*
iii. (1592), iii. 1.

GROMWELL-SEED (R183,*b*), properly grey millet ; here
a slang term for money: see other volumes of this
series.

GROSSERY, "such other *grossery*" (R263,*d*), *i.e.*
grossness, enormities, obscurity, with an eye on
" grocery " (fr. O.F. *grossier*, one who sells by the
gross, or wholesale).

GRUTCH (*passim*), grudge : see Groge.

GUBBINGS, " the *gubbings* of booties and preys "
(R183,*d*), properly the parings of haberdine, but
also generic for fragments of any kind.

GUISE, " good new *guise* . . . vicious *guise*," etc.
(*passim*), generic for fashion, style, manner, mien,
conduct.

'GYPTIAN, " the *'Gyptian* thraldom " (R237,*c*),
Egyptian.

HA (*passim*), have.

HAD, see Wist.

HAFTER, " ye are but an *hafter* " (WS141,*c*), wrangler,
caviller ; also a generic reproach ; here specific-
ally a falterer, laggard.	" Of ale he doth so stinke,
That whether he go before, or behynde, Ye shall
hym smell without the winde.	For when he goeth

to it, he is no *hafter*."—*Doctour Double Ale*, 216
(*c.* 1547).

HAIK, HAKE (R191,*b* and *c* ; R219,*c*), " an exclamation, generally a signal of defiance " (Halliwell) :
cf. " hack " (" hawk ")=to clear the throat.

HAIR, see Hood.

HALE, " What doth he after him *hale* " (R215,*d*),
haul.

HALED, see States.

HALFPENNY, " your minds were all on your *halfpenny* "(R196, *d*), *i.e.* with an eye to the main chance,
generally attentive, cautious, or prudent. The
proverb is in Heywood (*Works*, E.E.D.S., II. 14,*c* ;
174,*b*). " *Ri.* : Dromio, looke heere, now is my
hand on my *halfepeny*. *Half.* : Thou liest, thou hast
not a farthing to lay thy hands on."—Lyly, *Mother
Bombie* (1594), ii. 1. " But the blinde [deafe] man,
having his hand on another *halfe-penny*, said, What
is that you say, sir ? Hath the clocke strucken ? "
—*Notes on Du Bartas*, *To the Reader*, 2nd page.

HALSED, " his fair wife *halsed* in a corner " (M28,*d*),
embraced (*hals*=neck) : the special use of the word
is singularly appropriate, as Mischief had just escaped
the halsman (=executioner or jailer) himself.

HANCE BEERPOT (W.H.), *i.e.* Hans, but there was
no object in carrying the modernisation of the
orthography so far as to alter the original Hance :
see Wealth and Health.

HAND, " I bless you with my *left hand* " (M23,*c*), *i.e.*
curse : cf. " over the left "=altogether wrong, or
the reverse of what is said. Such " left-handed "
colloquialisms are by no means rare to express
insincerity, ill-omen, underhandness, or inferiority.
The earliest quotation in the *O.E.D.*, *s.v.* Left, is
1705, so this example carries its use back upwards
of 200 years.

HANDS, see Aloft.

HANGMAN, see Calais.

HANSTON, see Respublica.

HARDELY (*passim*), steadily, boldly, certainly.

HARE, " this same way goeth the *hare* " (R212,*b*), *i.e.* that's the gist, trend, secret, why and wherefore of the matter : in Heywood.

HASSARD, " fet not *hassard* nor rioter " (IP,320,*c*); so in original. It may be a contraction of *hasarder* =gamester, or a misprint for *haskard*=a rough, blustering fellow (Dekker) ; probably, however, the former fits the context best.

HASSE, " a fair manor *hasse* " (JE354,*a*), so in original ; and but for the rhyme-word *bash* being spelt *basshe* one might suspect a misprint, especially as Dr. Murray records no such form as *hasse* for *house*, nor anything like it. The meaning, however, is clear enough.

HAT (*passim*), have it—ha[ve i]t.

HAUT, HAUTY, " his *haut* courage " (N60,*d*), —" Wealth is *hauty* " (WH276,*d*), high, lofty, proud. Also see N53,*c*, where *haut* is misprinted *hawt*.

HAVE (*a*) (*passim*) bears several idiomatic meanings in old writers. Thus *to have after*=to follow ; *to have at* (a person or thing)=to try, attempt, begin, strike, hit ; *to have with* (a person)=to go with, come on. Also, *have at him* (subs.)=a thrust, blow ; and so forth. " *Have after*, to what issue will this come."—Shakespeare, *Hamlet* (1596), i. 4. " *Have at it*, then."—Shakespeare, *Cymbeline* (1605), v. 5. " *Have at thee* with a downright blow."—Shakespeare, *2 Henry VI.* (1594), ii. 3. " I'll venture one *have-at-him*."—Shakespeare, *Henry VIII.* (1601), ii. 2. (*b*) see Petticoat.

HAVIOUR, " a man of your *haviour* " (N85,*b*), conduct, manners, demeanour, as in Shakespearean usage. But possibly it may, and probably does, stand here for the Anglo - Norman *havoir*=wealth, property. The context would seem to indicate this, " Into a *haviour* of less fear."—Shakespeare, *Cymbeline* (1605), iii. 4.

HAWT, see Haut.

HEADIBUS, " your headibus " (M18,*c*), heads.

HEAL (*passim*), health.

HEDGE, " over the *hedge* ere ye come at the stile " (R192,*a*), proverbial: in Heywood (*Works*, E.E.D.S., II. 97,*d* and 443,*c*).

HEELS, see Lead.

HELPEN, " he can be *helpen* thereof " (N122,*a*), helped ; also *holpen*. Still in use.

HEND, " to me full *hend* " (M11,*c*), courteous, civil, polite. " So loveth she this *hendy* Nicholas."— Chaucer, *Cant. Tales* (1383), 3386.

HEY, " *Hey nonny nonny, ho for money* " (R222,*d*), if not a popular song, a popular refrain. The words occur in many old writers, not infrequently with an obscene meaning or reference : see *Slang and its Analogues*, *s.v.* Nonny.

HIE, " *Hie* you forth lively " (M17,*d*), probably a snatch of some old song, which, however, I have been unable to trace. A somewhat similar reference occurs in *Misognus* (Anon. Plays, 2 Ser., E.E.D.S., 185,*d*) during a dancing scene : " O lively with high, child, and turn thee ; ah, this is good sport ! " Although this does not settle the source of the saying, yet it adds force to Mankind's words.

HIGH, " on *high*, on *high* " (JE357,*c*), a duplication necessitated by the rhyme—*Eli, Eli*, but all the same a very striking one.

HIGHT, " Health I *hight* " (WH277,*a*), am called, have for a name : the only passive verb in English : see other volumes of this series.

HIP, " have you on the *hip* " (R215,*c*), to have or get an advantage : see *Slang and its Analogues*, *s.v.* Hip.

HITE, " when man is a little *hite* and wealthy" (WH279,*c*) =idle : in original *hit*. I take the word to be akin to the northern *hite*, to run up and down idly (Halliwell). Still, this may be wrong, and the now obsolete sense of *hit*=to be fortunate or successful may be meant.

Ho (*passim*) is used in varying senses in all old writers. Thus *Ho !* = a command to stop, cease, or refrain from the continuance of any action. Hence, as a verb=to cry out, shout, etc. Whence many colloquialisms. *To be ho* (JE367,*a*)=to be restrained, stopped, delayed ; *out of all ho*=out of all bounds or restraint ; *no ho with*=restive of control, out of hand ; *let us ho*=let us stop ; and so forth. *Ho, ho, ho!* occurs in many old plays, being given to the devil or vice when making an entry.

HOLPEN, " if it be *holpen* " (N54,*b*), helped : see Helpen.

HOLYKE (M16,*c*). From the nature of the song itself it must be inferred that a triple pun was intended, *Holy* (sacred refrain)—*wholly* (holelyche =wholly)—*Hole-lick* (osculare fundamentum) : probably the " roof " was intended to be " raised " by the medley of interpretations thus offered, the business of each of the chorus being different.

HOLY NATION (JE357,*b*), *i.e.* the Saints and redeemed. The reference to love and virginity is apparently founded on a passage in Revelations, attributed by many to St. John the Evangelist : see *Rev.* xi. 4, and John Evangelist, p. 416 *ante*.

HOOD, " his hair groweth through his *hood* " (IP340,*c* ; also R229,*d*), *i.e.* comes to poverty.

HOOK, " by *hook* or by crook " (R187,*b*), by some means or other, by fair means or foul, at all hazards, probably of forestal origin. " Their work was by *hook or crook* . . . to bring all under the emperor's power."—Thomas the Rymer, *On Parliaments* (*d.* 1298).

HORSE, (*a*) " *horse* with four ears " (JE364,*a*), apparently a reference to some form (or rather means) of punishment—the gallows (or mare with three legs), the pillory, or the timber-mare (or horse) for flogging purposes. Probably the latter, as its construction would justify the " four ears " of the text.

(*b*) see Grass.

HORSIBUS, see Breadibus.

HOURS, see Prime.

HUFFA GALLANT, see Rutter.

HYNGHAM, see Macro Plays.

I (*passim*) occurs in several connections now archaic.
(*a*) It is frequently repeated in conversation for the
sake of emphasis, " I am hight Mercy, *I*."

   (*b*) = Ay.

   (*c*) = An augment or prefix to represent the A.S.
ge, the most frequent example being *i-wis = gewiss* :
see *i-fashion* (JE365*b*) = fashioned.

ICH (*passim*), I : see other volumes of this series.

IGNORUM, " we *ignorum* people " (R211,*a*)—" we
ignorams all would fain," etc. (R227,*c*), (*adj.* and
subs. : ignorant, ignoram[use]s.

IMPATIENT POVERTY. The text will be found on pages
311–348. Hitherto little indeed seems to have
been known concerning this interlude. As far as I
can learn no copy has been traceable, at all events
in modern days, until " the Irish find " was put up
at Sotheby's in July 1906. Part of this " recovery "
(see Preface) was a copy of *Impatient Poverty*, which
is now national property, in the custody of the
trustees of the British Museum, the price paid for
the item being no less than £150. It is true that
the title, together with one or two details of the
baldest description, occur in most catalogues of
early English plays, from that of Rogers and Ley
in 1656 down to Mr. W. W. Greg's " hand-list "
prepared for, and issued by, the Bibliographical
Society in 1900. It is, however, an obvious fact
that in each case all the authorities appear to quote
from mention only. Further, though " known "
to a similar extent to latter-day critics—to Collier,
Halliwell, Hazlitt, Fleay, Ward, Gayley, Brandl,
Greg, and Pollard—all these, likewise, quote either
from an early mention, or from one another ; none
seem to have seen a copy of the play. Dyce alone
was explicit. In a note to *Sir Thomas More* (Shakes.
Soc., p. 55) he records *Impatient Poverty* as " non-
extant." After an interval of more than sixty
years since Dyce wrote, and 350 years or more
after publication, the " lost " play has been recovered ; and it is now my good fortune to make
it generally accessible to scholars. The British
Museum Catalogue entry is as follows :

   POVERTY. A new Interlude of Impacyente

> Poverte, newlye Impreynted, M.V.L.X., B.L.
> John Kynge, London [1560], 4°.—c. 34. i. 26.
> The title-page is enclosed in a woodcut border
> bearing the initials T. R.

in which the Museum catalogue has made a slight
blunder in copying from the title-page, which may
be consulted on page 311. *Impatient Poverty*, as
already stated, is mentioned in the old play of *Sir
Thomas More*, itself only extant in a somewhat
mutilated manuscript. The passage is as follows:

> *Moore.* I prethee, tell me, what playes have ye ?
> *Player.* Diuers, my lord ; *The Cradle of Securitie,
> Hit Nayle o' th' Head, Impacient Povertie, The
> Play of Foure Pees, Diues and Lazarus, Lustie
> Juuentus,* and *The Mariage of Witt and Wisedome.*
> —Shakes. Soc. ed., 55–56.

The copy now happily recovered shows the play to
have been " newly " printed in 1560 by John King,
who was in business at the Sign of the Swan in St.
Paul's Churchyard from 1555 to 1561. There is no
entry in the Stationers' Register for the year 1560 or
earlier. The British Museum copy is a tolerably well-
printed black-letter quarto of its kind ; it is also in
excellent preservation. A reduced facsimile of the
title-page is given on page 311, but unfortunately
the paper used in these volumes is not altogether
suitable for illustrative work. The old copy is,
however, announced among *The Tudor Drama
Facsimile Texts,* and will shortly be available in
collotype. The collation is A to Eii in 4s (18 leaves).
The first sheet (A) has no signature, but the others are
regular in notation. *Impatient* (=intolerable, unen-
durable) *Poverty* is by an unknown author, but a very
shrewd attribution might even now be made were not
the time, as yet, hardly ripe for scientific deductions.
The materials are not at hand for anything like a
systematic study of pre-Shakespearean dramatic
effort and achievement ; and the study of isolated
plays can, at best, lead to imperfect and perhaps
erroneous conclusions. Unquestionably, however,
the Tudor drama deserves to be studied, as Shakespeare is nowadays studied : as a whole, and not
piecemeal. But—alack and alack ! — where is the
accessible material for such an inquiry ? Still, if
at present we do not know the author's name, we

can nevertheless learn something of him from his play. He was evidently a sedate man, serious to a degree, with apparently deep-seated religious principles : note the long-sustained exhortations and the general tone of the play. It is also note-worthy that, for the period, the bawdry is "cut" to the lowest limit. There are no women's parts, and the Vice is a watered-down specimen of his class. There is little internal evidence to enable one to form an idea of the date of composition, though this may, I think, be fixed as probably not earlier than 1545, but before 1552. The allusions to usury seem to point to a period anterior to the repeal by Edward VI. in 1552 of the Usury Act of 37 Henry VIII., which was re-enacted by Elizabeth in 1570. Yet the reference to " the Queen " (347,*d*), unless a later interpolation, is obviously to Queen Elizabeth, and not to Queen Mary. The play is too distinctly and settled Protestant—indeed, the tone is even that of " the new learning " victorious —to admit of a Marian chronology. In this latter case the downward limit would be extended at least to 1558. Other allusions are likewise scanty or unilluminating—" Joy and solace be in this hall " (321,*a*), seems suggestive of a College or Inns of Court audience, as distinguished from a purely Court performance ; the joining of simony with covetise (325,*c*) recalls the Edward VI. Act against simony (1552) ; " Conscience, the high judge of the law " (328,*b*), is reminiscent of *Respublica* : cf. 227,*d* ; other references are to Newgate, Tyburn, the Fleur de Lys, etc., but they do not appear to have any special meaning. The present text is transcribed direct from a rotary-bromide copy of the original, and having been twice collated, once with the photo-text, and again finally with the original, it will, I hope, be found as accurate as human care can make it. *Variations and Corrigenda* are as follows : The colophon (312,*d*) is in original given on Eii. v. at the end of the play—The text begins at the top of Aii *r* without title—The stage directions in brackets do not appear in the original—The names of the speakers are in the present text systematised a little, and are consequently, in some cases, slightly different to the original—" What people

are tho[se] " (314,*a*), in original *tho* (A.S.=those)—
" for shame thou *shouldst* bear " (315,*a*), in original
shuls—" that with *humility*" (316,*b*), in original
humyly — " Thy very duty " (317,*a*), in original
They—" this *well* I knaw " (317,*a*), in original
wyll—" Let it be *tryd* by manhood, and *thereto* I
give thee my glove " (317,*c*), in original *tryet* and
thertho—" I pray *you* sir " (317,*d*), in original
your—" I hold it *punishment* " (318,*a*), in original
punisshment—" Nay by *God*! there *ho*! " (318,*d*),
in original *good . . . hoo*—" I break your *head* "
(319,*a*), in original *heed*—" *Pater dimitte illis* "
(319,*b*), in original misprinted *dimitie*—" *beati
pauperes spiritu* " (319,*b*), in original *beaty pauperes
spiritu*—" As it *doth* often " (320,*c*), in original
doeth—" *Exeunt ambo* " (320,*d*), in original *Exiunt
ambo*—[*Enter* ABUNDANCE] (321,*a*), throughout
this is *Haboundaunce* — " *though* he would "
(321,*d*), in original *thought* — " *be* openly known "
(321,*d*), in original *he* — " Singular *commodum* "
(321,*d*), so in original—" to *them* that are needy "
(322,*a*), in original *theym*—" *Because* I may forbear "
(322,*b*), in original *Bycause*—" *Cons. Evensine*
very shame " (322,*b*), in original, *Evensynne*—
" *Cons.* To make restitution " (324,*a*), in original
Doo—" *Make* amends " (324,*c*), in original *Mke*—
" *you* cannot come in " (324,*d*), should be *thou*,
as in original—" Now in *faith* " (326,*b*), in original
fayte—" He goeth in a *cloak* " (327,*b*), in original
clocke—" the *temporalty* " (327,*c*), in original *them-
poraltye* — " pride, *sloth*, and lechery " (327,*c*), in
original *slewth* — " Set covetire in your *room* "
(328,*b*), in original *rowm*—" [*Envy*] Y-wys, cousin
(328,*d*), not in original, but the speech is clearly
to *Envy*—" by *Cocks* passion " (330,*a*), in original
coxs; so also at 330,*c*—" I have of gold three *hundred*
pound " (331,*a*), in original *hundreth*—" I am your
kinsman " (331,*b*), in original *Kyngman*—" Ye must
have *more* servants " (331,*c*), in original *moo* —
" most *expedient* " (331,*c*), original *expedyende*—
" *Because* he can so well sing " (332,*b*), in original
Bycause—" Tush! take no *thought* " (332,*d*), in
original *though*—" at a pinch . . . broad as an
inch (333,*d*), the punctuation may not rightly
interpret the exact sense here, but it seems elliptical

and to require *If* before *her heel* : *i.e.* how little
light-heeled she were she would still serve to inflame
Prosperity ; the whole speech in original is without
a single punctuation mark—" *Because* he is old "
(333,*d*), in original *Bycause*—The signature (335,*d*)
given as *B1,r* should of course have been *D1,r*—
" That so can read his *destiny* " (336,*a*), in original
destanye—" tell me at *one* word " (337,*a*), in original
our — " *obscured* with clouds " (337,*d*), original
obscrued — *Colhazard* (*passim*), this in original is
variously spelt ; Colhasard, Collhasard, Colehazard,
Collhassard, etc.—" *Sober your mood* " (340,*a*),
in original *sobre you mode*—" *won* all my good "
(340,*c*), original *wome*—" Cannot chance a *main*
groat " (341,*c*), original *man*—" for I *obtain* all thing "
(343,*a*), in original *optayne*—" upon you a great
slande[*r*] " (343,*c*), in original *sclaunde*—" and live
in great *advoutry* " (343,*d*), original misprints
aduantrye — " what will ye *then* say " (344,*a*),
original *thed*—" And *then* sayeth the *Sumner* "
(344,*b*), original *them . . . somuer*—" be *unto* God "
(344,*c*), original *into*—" brought me to *this* distress "
(345,*a*), original *his*—" leeful for a *callet* " (345,*b*),
original *called* — " and great *usurers* " (345,*c*), in
original *usures*—" *Bawds*, advouterers " (345,*c*),
in original *Bandes*—" fornicators, and escheaters "
(345,*c*), in original *echeters*—" made his purgation"
(345,*d*), original *is*—" as Thou art *omnipotent* "
(347,*d*), in original *onypotent*.

In, (*a*) *in manus tuas* (M23,*b*), from Psalm xxx. 6 :
in manus tuas commendo spiritum meum=into Thy
hands I commit my spirit. ↓ The *queck* in text
should not have been in italics.

(*b*) " *i*[*n*] *forma juris d'hazard* " (M29,*c*), restored
by Prof. Brandl : in original, " *do yt forma jurys
dasard*.

INCROKE, " He took of her an *incroke* " (IP326,*c*), ?—
As a verb, Murray has *incrook* and *inkroke*=to bend
or bow down ; *e.g.* in Rom. xi. 10, the phrase " and
bow down their back alway " is given by Wyclif as
" in kroke " their back.

INGHAM, see Macro Plays.

INQUEST, " to do at your *inquest* " (R234,*b*), request :
in original, *enquest*.

INSTITUTE, " He hath *institute* you above all His works " (M11,*d*), appointed, set, invested. " Cousin of York, we *institute* your Grace to be our Regent in these parts of France."—Shakespeare, *1 Hen. VI.* (1596), iv. 1, 162.

INSTITUTION, " a beast doth after his natural *institution* " (M9,*b*), nature, established order.

INTERLECTION, " Let us have an *interlection* " (M20,*c*), talk, consultation, conference : not in *O.E.D.* Though regularly formed, probably a nonce word.

INTERMISE, " *intermise* yourself not in their company " (M14,*b*), mix, interfere, interpose, concern, or occupy oneself with : not in *O.E.D.*, but sufficiently indicated (*s.v. Inter-*, p. 381, I. 1 *b* and *Intermise*, subs.).

INVENTUS, " *non est inventus* " (M34,*d*), *i.e.* he is not to be found.

I-PILATE, " he was i-pounst and *i-pilate* " (R211,*b*), pilated=brought before Pilate, " beaked " : see I.

I-POLLD, " were ne'er so *i-polld* " (R211,*a*), fleeced, robbed, cheated. Mr. Magnus, however, glosses it as " pulled about." " And have wynked at the *pollyng* and extorcion of hys unmeasurable officiers." —Hall, *Union* (1548).

I-POUNST, " he was *i-pounst* and i-pilate " (R211,*b*), ? beaten, scourged ; an eastern counties word.

IRISDISION, see Trentham.

IRK, " unlusty and *irk* " (M24,*c*)—" I am near *irk* of both " (M26,*b*), tired, bored, disgusted.

IS (R. *passim*), I ; oftentimes the sibilant is carried to the next word.

I-STRIKE, " sixpence in each shilling was *i-strike* quite away " (R232,*a*), struck : see Respublica.

I-TORMENT, " zo *i-torment* " (R211,*a*), tormented.

I-TROUNST, " so *i-trounst* " (R211,*b*). Prof. Brandl refers to M.E. *trunsioun* and O.F. *tronchon*.

JACK-A-NAPES (R264,*b*), here=a tame ape or monkey. The origin of the term in this and its more usual

sense (=an ape-like, pert, or ridiculous person)
is obscure. Dr. Murray says that so far as yet
found the word appears first as an opprobrious
nickname of William de la Pole, the Duke of Suffolk
who was murdered in 1450, whose badge was a
clog and chain such as was attached to a tame
ape. Thus in contemporary poems (*e.g.*, *Pol. Poems*,
c. 1499 [Rolls], II. 222) several noblemen are desig-
nated by their badges, Suffolk being named the
" ape-clogge." We find *Jack-napes* generic for an
ape in Skelton (1522), and shortly afterwards the
term was current in the present and more common
sense. But the connection between *Jack Napes*
and an *ape* (again to quote Dr. Murray) " is uncertain."

JACK NOBLE, " Hence Forty Pence . . . *Jack Noble*
is a-bed " (N98,*a*), a pun on the value of the coins
(forty pence being half a noble) and the lady's
preference. What *K. q. title* means I cannot
divine. Prof. Brandl suggests *King—Queen*, but
confesses it obscure ; *a bry* appears to signify a
breeze, awkward affair or predicament.

JAKE, " a good *jake* of fence " (M32,*a*), coat of defence ;
a sleeveless tunic or jacket formerly worn by foot-
soldiers and others, usually of quilted leather.
Sometimes=a coat of mail.

JAVELS, " *javels* as shall wrong them " (R192,*b*), a
generic reproach—rascal, good-for-nothing. " How
much more abhominable is that pieuish pride in
a lewde vnthriftye, *iavell*."—More, *Treat. Pass.*
(1534), Introd. Wks., 1272.

JE, *Je nescey* (N97,*b*), *i.e. Je ne sais [pas]*.

JET (*passim*), formerly as hard a worked word as
" commodity " or " cast " ; it signified any device,
contrivance, art, fashion, style, mode, manner, or
custom. As *verb*=to strut, walk with consequence,
and so forth.

JEWELS (M18,*a*), privities : see privity (19,*d*) : New
Guise's and Mankind's " business " seems to have
been not over fastidious.

JIS (*passim*), Jesus : cf. Gis.

JOAN (*passim*), a generic name for an alewife, strumpet, and the like : see *Doctour Double Ale* and next entry.

JOHN, "*Come kiss me, John*" (N93,*c*). Chappell says that nothing remains of the words except " Jon come kisse me now, Jon come kisse me now ; Jon come kisse me by and by, and make no more adow." The music is given in *Citharen Lessons*, 1609 ; *Airs and Sonnets, MS.*, *T.C. Dublin*, etc. It is also mentioned in *Jacob and Esau*, in Heywood's *A Woman Kill'd with Kindness* (1600) ; in '*Tis merry when Gossips meet* (1609) ; in a song in *Westminster Drollery* (1671 and 1674) ; in Burton's *Anatomy of Melancholy* (1611) ; *The Scourge of Folly* (N.D.) ; Brathwayte's *Shepherd's Tales* (1623) ; in Hy. Bold's *Songs and Poems* (1685) ; and in Sir W. Davenant's *Love and Honour*.

WILLIAM BYRD.

Fast

JOHN-HOLD-MY-STAFF (R188,*a*), a parasite, lickspittle. " And here it is the fortune of a man to be married to a woman of so peevish and domineering a temper that she will wear the breeches and the cap too : so that the poor fop at home is like *John-Hold-my-Staff*; she must rule, govern, insult, brawl," etc.— *Fifteen Comforts of Matrimony*.

JOHN IRISCHE (WH304,*d*), the allusion is lost.

JOHN SHOLE (WH304,*d*), see previous entry.

JOHN THE EVANGELIST. The text of this play is given on pages 349–368, together with a reduced facsimile of the title-page. Until recently *John the Evangelist* was looked upon as one of the innumerable "lost" plays of the Tudor period. It has now been recovered under the notable circumstances narrated in the preface to this volume. Curiously enough, *John the Evangelist* was at first, in the sale catalogue, confused with Bishop Bale's *John Baptist's Preaching in the Wilderness*, no copy of which also is now traceable, being known only through the reprint in the *Harleian Miscellanies*. However, there is no doubt that if a choice of "finds" had to be made the lot would fall to the present play, which has been untraceable in any form, save that of mere mention, for hundreds of years. The British Museum Catalogue entry is :

> JOHN SAINT AND APOSTLE. Here begynneth the interlude of Johan the Evangelist [with a woodcut]. B.L. John Waley, London [1560?]. 4°. [c. 34. i. 20.

Greg, in his "notes" to *Early Play Lists* (App. II. lxxix), says : " Neither Langbaine nor any of his followers had seen the piece. The *Biographica Dramatica* gives the date 1566, which, however, appears to be an invention of Chetwood's." The colophon indicates that it was printed by John Waley (or Walley), who was in business in Foster Lane from 1546 to 1586. This, of course, decides nothing as to the date of the play. Moreover, there is, as far as I am at present aware, only one allusion in the play itself that serves the purpose ; even allowing more weight to such evidence than I am inclined to consider safe in the circumstances—Eugenio appoints Actio (359,*a*) "hangman of Calais." It is hardly likely such an allusion to what was at the time regarded as a national " disaster " would have been made after the loss of Calais in 1558. On the other hand, the absence of the concluding prayer for the sovereign—its presence being a pretty certain indication of an Elizabethan play—seems to confirm the downward

limit of date. One other allusion may be pertinent
—" the sweetest life, Sovereign . . . is to have
meditation of our Lord Jesus." A Marian date is,
from the tone of the play, unlikely ; to suppose the
reference is to Henry VIII. is equally incongruous.
Both considerations are, moreover, emphasised by
the fact that had the " Sovereign " been a queen,
regnant or dowager, some qualification indicative
of sex would in such courtly times most assuredly
have been given. We are thus reduced, by the
process of exhaustion, to the days of Edward VI. :
i.e. between 1547 and 1553. Beyond that point I
do not think we can safely go at present. The
play, as now bound by the British Museum authorities, shows no signs of mutilation, and the numbering
of the sheets is consecutive. The type is, for the
most part, clear and good ; nothing obliterated,
very little blurred, and only occasionally is there
exhibited a wrong letter (*e.g.* " laue " for " lane ") ;
but as a whole very correct. The construction of the
play is of the slightest, turning at its most serious
point on the incident of " The Pharisee and the
Publican going up to the Temple to pray." Indeed,
the whole piece seems curiously incomplete and
disconnected. Yet there are no signs whatever,
in the original, of mutilation or of lines omitted.
The text goes straight on, though the relation of one
part to another is by no means obvious. Is it possible that the play as it has reached us is only a draft,
or an imperfect, or a " pirated " copy ? I am inclined on first glance to think this interlude one of
the same class as those that Bishop Bale speaks of
as being played at market crosses on Sunday after-
noons by way of religious instruction—" thin,"
slight moral plays. Indications are not wanting
which point to this conclusion. Such a fact, if
established, would account for the transparent loose-
ness of construction, the deep religious feeling, the
reticence and restraint, the apparent confusion of
one of the players at once with the apostle, the parish
priest, and the actor—and much else. The original
is almost devoid of punctuation ; the modernised text
conforms in that respect to present-day standards.
The names of the speakers are likewise not always
consistently given in the old copy ; they are now

standardised. *Latin Quotations and Origins*: It is
thought convenient, in respect to this play, to group
these as follows:—" *Domine, ante . . . absconditus* "
(351,*b*), " Lord, all my desire is before thee, and my
groaning is not hid from thee" (Psalm xxviii. 9):
in original *a te* is omitted after *Et* in second line—
" *Beati . . . Domine !* " (352,*a*), " Blessed, O Lord,
are they that dwell in Thy house " (Psalm lxxxiv. 4)
—" *Qui cum Deo Patri* " (352,*a*), " Who with God
the Father," the beginning of an ascription or gloria
—" *A pœna et culpa* " (352,*b*), from penalty and
fault : part of the Latin absolution—" *Nec te collaudas . . . ipse* " (352,*c*), the sense is, " You will
not be blamed so long as you don't extol yourself "—
" *Qui se collaudit* " (352,*c*), " Who praises himself " ;
probably from same source as preceding—" *Responde, tunc . . . clericorum* " (352,*d*), " Answer
then, master, doctor of the clergy"—" *Sursum
corda* " (353,*a*), " Lift up your hearts " ; from the
office of the mass—" *Via recta* " (354,*a*), " the right
way "—" *Spes mea . . . via recta* " (354,*a*), " My
hope stood in the right way " (or way of righteous-
ness) : several passages like this in sense appear in
the Psalms, but none exactly parallel—" *gratia
electi* " (354,*b*), " chosen by grace "—" *via obliquia
. . . circularis* " (354,*c*), " the crooked way and
circular way": no doubt scriptural—" *omnes iniquo
in circuitu impii ambulantes* " (354,*c*), *iniquo* in
original reads *iniqui*, which I take to be a misprint :
it now reads, " all the ungodly walking in the ungodly path " (or path of ungodliness): probably from
the Psalms—" *Ab aquilone . . . omne malum* "
(355,*a*), " from the north is spread every evil " :
a parallel passage is found in Jeremiah iv. 6, " I
will bring evil from the north," etc.—" *Fumus
tormentorum . . . secula seculorum* " (355,*d*), in
original *fumus* reads *finit*, most likely a misprint :
the passage as it now stands is intelligible, " The
smoke of their torment ascendeth for ever and ever ;
a quotation from Revelation xiv. 11—" *Septum
. . . mors* " (355,*d*), *Septum* conveys the idea of
a surrounding fence or hedge (cf. 355,*a* and *b*),
" the enclosing (or surrounding) master of sin is
death ; but ?—" *administrate . . . comfortate nos* "
(356,*c*), dog-Latin : " administers, restores, com-

forts " — " *Intentio judicat quenquam* " (357,*a*),
" The intention decides everything " ; no doubt
proverbial—" *In principio* " (364,*d*), " in the beginning " : the first two words of the Latin version
of St. John's Gospel—" *Confiteor* " . . . *Deo gratias*
. . . *Deo gratias ago tibi* " (366,*b*), " I confess . .
thanks be to God . . . God I thank thee " : see
Luke xviii. 11—" *Tu testimonium . . . est verum* "
(367,*a*), " Thou bearest testimony of thyself ; and
thy testimony is not true " ; an adaptation of John
viii. 13—" *Qui vivit . . . seculorum secula* (368,*a*),
" Who lives through the infinite ages of age."
Amended Readings, Corrigenda, Suggestions, &c.
The collation is A to Civ in 4s, with A1,*v* blank.—
Names of Players are not in the original.—The
colophon is transferred from Civ,*v*—Stage directions
and words in brackets do not appear in the original :
this is not further mentioned in these notes—" *Et*
a te *gemitus* " (351,*b*), *a te* not in original—" As it
ravisheth the soul " (351,*c*), original *rauysshet*—
" such a pulpit man to *lose* " (352,*b*), original *lese*—
" *Reponde*, tunc, *domine* " (352,*d*), original *tunice*—
" that same death *thou shalt* die " (353,*a*), erroneously given in my text : the original has *shalt
thou*—[" *The continuation seems imperfect* "], there
may be several causes for this. Certainly here, as
in other places, there are no signs whatever in
original of mutilation or of lines omitted. The
text goes straight on, though the relation of one
part to another is by no means obvious. The
whole play seems curiously incomplete and scrappy,
even for early dramatic effort, oftentimes of the
" thinnest " and crudest. True, the action may be
modelled somewhat on the lines of Heywood's
Pardoner and the Friar, in which the " interruptions " of one speaker with another lead to " business." Or the play may be a mere fragment of the
" book," as it left the author's hands—surreptitious,
unauthorised, or unrevised. In the former case,
especially assuming that it was intended as a kind of
a " dramatic sermon," the action shows order of a
kind : commencing with what is obviously intended as
the commencement of an exhortation and omitting
the " comic " and " lighter " parts, the sermon
would, in a measure, be naturally complete by

" following on " the speeches as follows : *St. John
the Evan.* 351,*b* to 352,*a* ; *Irisdision,* 353,*c* (with asides,
incentives, or interruptions) to 356,*a* ; *St. John the
Evan.* 357,*b* to 358,*a* ; then comes an " interval," and
the discourse is resumed at (JE365,*c* to end) winding
up with the " application " which was soon to form
such an important feature in Puritan worship. So
for the point directly at issue ; but another puzzle
confronts the student and one concerning which at this
early stage I do not pretend to offer a solution.   Per-
sonally, I should have preferred to have deferred pub-
lishing the text, in order to have had an opportunity
of careful and exact comparative study of the piece
in its relation to the Tudor drama as a *whole* as well
as " *play* "-meal.   On the other hand, I felt that
the generous support we have met with at the
hands of the Society's subscribers would be best
repaid by speedy publication—" In the city of
Jerusalem . . . walled " (353,*c*), if the play has
come to us intact, and the lack of continuity is
intentional, the punctuation of this passage must
be altered : delete the full point after *called* and
regard the next line as a parenthesis, and substitute
a semicolon for the period after *walled*—" in the
lane of business " (354,*a*), in original *laue of besy-
nesse*—" Yes, on the left side " (354,*c*), *Ies* in original
—" full of *slouthy* bushes " (355,*b*), this may be *flouthy*
—" *Fumus tormentorum* " (355,*d*), in original *Finit* :
Latin quotations, *supra* (418,*d*) — " [*Iris*].   It is
time for to be walking, &c." (356,*a*), these two lines
are not in original given to Irisdision, but form part
of Eugenios' speech, which proceeds without a break
to " Sir William of Trentram " (357,*a*).   They seem
to me, however, to be rightly restored as now given
—" by books *Amromes* " (356,*b*), so in original : ? a
misprint for *amorous*, which would at least restore
the sense.   There is, moreover, nothing in original
to suggest a break—" *St. John the Evangelist* "
(357,*a*), preceded by ✠ instead of the usual " leaf "
—" plain *information* " (357,*b*) in original *infyr-
macyon*—" I am *that* John that " (357,*b*), in original
" I am John that " : a blunder I carelessly passed
—" saw *Lungis* " (357,*c*), original *Longes* : see (424,*d*)
—" almost changed my mood " (359,*c*), original
mode—" have *been* so witty " (359,*c*), in original

brn—" *Yes*, yes daily " (362,*b*), in original *Ies*—
" some pleasure then there *appears* " (363,*d*), in
original *areres*—" between your ears " (363,*d*), in
original *bytwene*—" make thee to *fly* " (365,*b*), a
mistake : the original is *stye* (=ascend, A.S.)—
" *Deo gratias ago tibi* " (366,*b*), substitute a full
point for the comma—" In *that* he thanked God "
(366,*b*), in original *than*—" By raveners . . . men
can rehearse " (366,*c*), I do not feel sure that the
present punctuation gives the best rendering of the
original, which is entirely unstopped—" In that
cayme " (366,*c*), see *supra, s.v.* Cayme : ? Cain—
" *Against* God " (366,*d*), in original *Agayne*—
" Who doth hie him shall be *ho* " (367,*a*), see *supra,
s.v.* Ho.

JOINT, " *jeopard a joint* " (R256,*d*)—" *t'adventure a
joint* " (R250,*c*), to take a risk or hazard, as of
injury, loss, hanging, etc. " My ten duckets are
like my ten fingers, they will not *jeopard a joynt*
for you."—Decker, *Fortunatus* (1600), Works (1873),
I. 153.

JOLLY, " here is a *jolly* jacket " (M31,*d*), bright, gay,
splendid, in newest fashion. " *Jolye* and gaye
sadeles."—Wyclif, *Sel. Wks.* (*c.* 1380), III. 520.

JUNCTLY, " marred *junctly* together " (M16,*d*) jointly.

JUNKERY, " a banket or a *junkery* " (N95,*c*), banquet,
feast, junket : specifically a merrymaking accompanied by eating and drinking. " Pertrych and
his felaw bere gret visage and kepe gret *junkeryes*
and dyneres."—*Paston Lett.* (1449), IV. 24 (1901).

JURIS, see In.

JUSTICES OF QUORUM (JE352,*d*). According to Mr.
Craigie (*O.E.D., s.v.*), *quorum* was " originally certain
justices of the peace, usually of eminent learning
or ability, whose presence was necessary to con-
stitute a bench ; latterly the term was loosely
applied to all justices." " The Justicez or *Justice
of the* Pease of the *Quorum* yn the same shire."—
Rolls Parlt. (1455), V. 334. I.

JUSTITIA, (*a*) (R. *passim*), as a pertinent comment on

the *motif* of this play it may be remarked that the name *Justitia* was (*O.E.D.*) applied in the eleventh century in a general way to persons charged with the administration of the law, especially to the Sheriffs ; it was subsequently limited to the pre-sident or one of the members of the Curia Regis, out of which the Courts of King's Bench, Common Pleas, and Exchequer were developed : see previous entry.

(*b*) *Just*[*ici*]*a tamen non luxit in nobis* (R253,*b*), see *Book of Wisdom* (*Sap.*, I, 15), where it reads, *Justitiæ lumen non luxit in nobis.* Mr. Magnus earmarks the mistake as "interesting, if, as is probable, the MS. is not the author's ; it is the kind of miscopying which we might expect."

KAYS, "where be my *kays*" (R184,*d*), this seemingly cockney Irish pronunciation of "key" is in truth the correct one, and was the standard down to the close of the seventeenth century. In M.E. the rhyme was with *day, play, say,* etc., and Dryden so employs it. On the other hand, early in the fifteenth century the (northern) spelling *kee* was in vogue, from which it appears that the modern pronunciation *kee* is of northern origin, but it is difficult to say how it came into general English use (*O.E.D.*).

KEEP, " *Keep* your tail " (M21,*a*), *i.e.* keep it out of sight.

KENT . . . NORTHUMBERLAND, etc. (R254,*a*):   see Respublica.

KING, see Cat.

KISS, see Courtesy.

KNIGHT, "Christ's own *knight*" (M12,*a*), soldier. "A *knight* with a spear."—*Youth*, Anon. Plays, 2 Ser. (E.E.D.S.), 97,*d.* "That *knycht* quha peirsit our Lordis syde with the speir."—Winzet, *Four Scoir Thre Quest.* (1563), *Works* (1888), I. 77.

KNIL, "I rang her a *knil*" (N97,*d*), a loud peal on a bell : specifically the passing bell, but frequently used of more or less violent ringing.

K. Q. TITLE, see Jack Noble.

KYX, " as dry as a *kyx* " (R271,*b*) ,a dry, hollow stalk.
" Elders they may bee, which being fullest of
spungie pith, proue euer the driest *kixes*."—*Pappe
w. Hatchet* (1589), Civ.

LADE, " by whom thou art *lade* " (IP335,*b*), led.

LADYDOM, " Chwas besiraunce your *ladidom* to see "
(R213,*c*). Mr. Magnus says " a new formation."
Murray's first quotation is dated 1843.

LADY OF WOLPIT (IP315,*d*), this should have been
Woolpit, near Bury-St.-Edmunds. See Woolpit.

LAMMAS, " at the latter *Lammas* " (R219,*a*), never :
see *Slang and its Analogues*.

LAVATORY, " that blessed *lavatory* " (M3,*c*), a figurative
usage : cf. " the *lavatory* of grace " (*Pilgr. Perf.*,
W. de W. 60*b*, 1526).

LAY, " hold for the *lay* " (JE353,*d*), lake, pool : in
the *O.E.D.* the latest quotation for the literary
use of this word is 1481, later ones being taken from
the early nineteenth century dialect glossaries. This
example is therefore useful.

LEAD, " I have no *lead* on my heels " (M25,*a*), the
" heel of lead " was proverbial for slow, unsprightly
movement : cf. " Love, I am full of *lead* " (Shakespeare, *Ant. and Cleop.*, iii. 11, 72).

LEARN, " Titivillus can *learn* you many pretty things "
(M25,*d*), this present - day vulgarism was formerly
in constant literary use. Wyclif in his first (1382)
rendering of Prov. ix. 7 employed it—" Who
lerneth a scorner," etc. : in the revised text of
1388 he substituted " techith."

LEFT HAND, see Hand.

LEGS, see Titivillus.

LEMAN, " take thee a *leman* " (M27,*a*), mistress,
whore : see other volumes of this series.

LESE, " an open *lese* " (N108,*d*), pasture, meadow-
land, common. " We been his people and scheep
of his *leese*."—*Prymer* (*c.* 1400), 17 (1891).

LESING, " many a *lesing* " (M18,*b*), lie, lying, falsehood.

LET, " not minding you to *let* " (R188,*b*), hinder, obstruct.

LIKELY, " such a *likely* man " (M27,*d*), in original *lygh*[*t*]*ly* ; seemly, becoming, good-looking. " The damoysel beheld the poure knyght, and sawe he was a *lykely* man "—Malory, *Arthur* (1470–85), II. ii. 77.

LIMIT, " a pardon by *limit* " (M8,*c*), in original *bely mett*. Apparently a pardon sold or bestowed by a friar limiter : see other volumes of this series.

LION OF COTSWOLD (N109,*c*), a sheep : an earlier example than the first of the *O.E.D.* quotations.

LIVE, " *on live* " (IP300,*c*), alive : an attributive use.

LIVER, " shall *liver* him " (R271,*c*), deliver.

LONGETH, " that *longeth* to thine office " (M8,*c*), pertains to, is fit and appropriate for.

LOREL (IP335,*b*), a generic term of reproach. " I play the *lorell* or the loyterer."—Palsgrave, *Lang. Fran.* (1530), 659.

LOSELL, " like a loitering *losell* " (R257,*d*), profligate, rake : etymologically, " one who is lost," " a son of perdition."

LOSS, " poor we bear the *loss* " (R231,*d*), see Respublica.

LOUTS, " we made them *louts* " (R221,*c*), *i.e.* caused them to submit to our demands and disgorge. " To whome grete astates obeyde and *lowttede*."—*Elegy on Henry* (*c.* 1500), in *Percy's Releg.*, 45.

LOVE, " Hasty *love* is soon hot, and soon cold " (WS161,*a*) ; Heywood (*Works*, E.E.D.S., II. 6,*d*) has " hot *love*, soon cold."

LOWLER (JE354,*d*), a variant of Loller=Lollard. Originally applied (*c.* 1300) to a charitable fraternity, and subsequently to pretenders to austere piety and humility. Hence in reproach to certain " heretics," followers of Wyclif and similar purists.

LUNGIS (JE357,*c*), in original *Longes*. As this play is, generally speaking, carefully printed the use of the capital seems to point to a proper name, and not to *lunges*=thrusts, stabs. *Lungis* is the apocryphal name of the centurion who pierced our Lord with a spear : L. *longinus*. The *O.E.D.* cites this as the origin of *lungis*=lout, loafer—a generic reproach.

On the other hand, if *lunge*=a stab, it gives an instance of the use of the word some 200 years earlier than Dr. Murray's premier example : in either case the present illustration is useful and interesting.

LURDAN, LURDEN (*passim*), a generic reproach and term of abuse ; examples are numerous.

MACE, see Mass.

MACRO PLAYS AND MANUSCRIPTS (THE). These derive their name from a former owner, Cox Macro, an eighteenth century antiquary, physician, and cleric. From the *Dictionary of National Biography* it appears he was born in 1683, and died in 1767. He was the eldest son of Thos. Macro, grocer and alderman, and five times Mayor of Bury-St.-Edmunds. Thos. Macro married Susan, only daughter of Rev. John Cox, rector of Risby (near Bury-St.-Edmunds). The son received his name from his mother's surname. His name was made the subject of a punning motto for the family—" Cocks may crow." Educated at Bury Grammar School, he matriculated at Jesus College, Cambridge, but migrated to Christ's. In 1703 he entered at Leyden University, where he studied under Boerhave. In 1710 he proceeded to LL.B. degree at Cambridge, and to D.D. in 1717. He was chaplain to George II., but his possession of a large fortune rendered him independent of preferment. Macro was reputed to be master of most modern languages, and his house at Little Haugh contained a large collection of artistic treasures. Macro died 2nd Feb. 1767, and was buried at Norton, near Bury. A catalogue of Macro's treasures was compiled in 1766. Among them were many letters from Protestant martyrs, which came to him through Bishop Cox ; the great register of Bury Abbey ; a ledger-book of Glastonbury Abbey ; and the original MS. of Spenser's *View of the State of Ireland*. Many of his MSS. had previously been the property of Sir Henry Spelman, others formed part of the library of Bury Abbey. The Macro property ultimately came to John Patteson, M.P. for Norwich, who disposed of the old masters (pictures) in 1819, and sold the books and MSS. for no more than £150 (it is said) to Richard Beatniffe, a Norwich bookseller, who resold them at a large profit. They were sold for Beatniffe by Christie in 1820, and realised £700, 41 lots going to Dawson Turner, and the rest to Hudson Gurney. The latter are now in the possession of J. H. Gurney, of Keswick Hall, near Norwich, and are described in the Historical MSS. Commission's 12th Report. Macro's correspondence with literary men and artists forms the additional MSS. at the British Museum, 32556–7. The Rev. Joseph Hunter edited for the Camden Society in 1840 a volume of *Ecclesiastical Documents*, containing 21 charters from Macro's library; and from a MS. formerly in his possession was printed, in 1837, for the Abbotsford Club, a morality called *Mind, Will, and Understanding*. So far generally the D.N.B. : the manuscript of the plays alone concern the present volume. I have not seen the volume myself, though I hope one day to have the satisfaction of reproducing it in facsimile. I have therefore to acknowledge my indebtedness for the *précis* which follows to Mr. A. W. Pollard's exhaustive account as given in the introduction to the Early English Text Society's *Macro Plays* (Extra Series, xci.). Boiled down, the facts are these, so far as they relate to the two Macro Plays included in the present volume, *Mankind and Respublica*. *Mankind* now forms part of a volume which in the eighteenth century contained other plays and treatises in manuscript, with which we need not now concern ourselves, except to remark the strange juxtaposition of old moralities, a Juvenal, a treatise on alchemy, etc. When sold at auction in 1820 the collection was broken up, and three plays, *Mankind, Wisdom*, and *The Castle of Perseverance*, bound afresh in one volume. Other points of interest are given by Mr. Pollard, but which I pass by as not germane to the present purpose. The manuscript of *Mankind* and *Wisdom* are contemporaneous ; and were, says Mr. Pollard, in the same ownership before the end of the fifteenth century. This is in all likelihood a fact ; but that the ownership was a purely personal one is not so clear as appears at first sight, or for the reasons stated by Mr. Pollard. It is now necessary for me to quote Mr. Pollard's own words in order to make my suggestions quite clear. He says : " It is . . . possible that both this play and . . . [*Wisdom*] were written in different parts of a miscellany-book belonging to Monk Hyngham, though the fact that his doggerel inscription of ownership is written after each of them inclines one at first to think that they were separate units among his possessions. As it occurs at the end of this play [*Mankind*], the inscription . . . has been partly erased and partly cut through, the lower part of the leaf being supplied with modern paper. Enough, however, of the inscription remains to make it fairly certain that it reads like that at the end of the next play : O liber si quis cui constas forte queretur Hyngham q*ue* monacho dices super omnia consto. This apparently is to be translated (I owe the suggestion to Dr. Warner): ' O book, if any one by chance asks to whom do you belong, you are to say I belong to Hyngham, above every-thing which a monk can own.' Who Monk Hyngham was we do not know. He may have belonged to Bury-St.-Edmunds, whence some of the Macro manuscripts are said to have come." Thus far also Mr. Pollard.

Now, I am inclined to think the deductions hitherto drawn from the foregoing facts are not altogether of the soundest. In the first place, *Is the inscription rightly translated ?* Secondly, *Does " Hyngham " refer to a person or a place ?* In answer to the first question, I offer an alternative reading for consideration ; in reply to the second, I offer evidence that a place is meant. If I am right in my contentions fresh light is thereby thrown upon several problems, at present unsolved, in respect to these Macro plays. To take the points in order. The inscription as given by Mr. Pollard in his introductory remarks on page xxx, varies somewhat from the text as given on pages 34 and 73 : *que* is *quem* and consto is given as consta[s]. My own text (40,*d*) follows the latter, which for the sake of the ensuing argument I quote again, with contractions, etc., duly indicated :

O liber, si q*ui*s cui constas forte q*ue*ret*ur*,

Hyngham, q*uem* monacho dices, super omnia consta[s].

Now if for qu*em* we read qu*od* and for co*n*sta[s]
we substitute co*n*sta[t], we get on surer ground.
The original hardly conveys the idea that *constas*
occurs twice, though there is evidently a play on
" *constas*," " constat " ; at least that is a possible
reading.   In this instance, too, the verb *constare*
seems to be used in the sense of *value*, and one
hardly sees where Dr. Warner's *belong* comes in.
If *quod* and *constat* are accepted, the translation
would be something like this :

> " O book, if haply anyone should ask to what
> [place] you are precious, tell them Hyngham,
> which [*quod*] to a monk is precious beyond all
> [places]."

That is, the book is precious to Hyngham ; Hyngham is precious beyond all places to the monks.

This brings me to the next point.   Assuming
this translation to be correct (and I invite discussion), it seems pretty clear that the ownership
of the manuscripts of *Mankind* and *Wisdom* was
not to a *Monk* Hyngham, but to a monk or monks
of Hyngham.   Facts again seem to confirm alike
this new view and also the Eastern Counties tradition.   Hyngham, Hingham, or Ingham, as a surname, is not common in the district ; on the contrary, it is uncommonly rare.   It belongs more
to the north, especially to Lancashire and Yorkshire.   Its occurrence nowadays in Leeds, Bradford,
Liverpool, and Manchester, may be regarded as
fifty or sixty to two, or at most three, for other large
towns all over the country ; whilst in the Eastern
Counties it is simply not to be found.   This is
especially and particularly the case as regards
Lincoln, Grimsby, Boston, Stamford, Norwich,
Yarmouth, Ipswich, Bury-St.-Edmunds, Cambridge,
Colchester, Chelmsford, etc.   The facts are at least
significant.

On the other hand, taking Hyngham (or Ingham)
as a place-name, we go, as the kiddies say, from
" cold " to " hot " at once.   There are three places
of this name, all comparatively close to one another.
There is Ingham near Bury-St.-Edmunds, Ingham
near Lincoln, and Ingham 16 miles N.E. from
Norwich.   I have been unable at present to trace
any ecclesiastical connection with the two Inghams

first named. But at Ingham near Norwich, Sir
Miles de Stapleton, of Bedale, in Yorkshire, in
the fourteenth century founded a chantry in the
church of Ingham, with a warden and two priests,
in honour of the Holy Trinity. This foundation
afterwards became a priory of friars of the order
of the Holy Trinity, otherwise known as " Trini-
tarians " or " Mathurines." At the dissolution there
were seven friars, and a revenue estimated at £63
per annum. "Yngham Trynyte" is twice mentioned
in Bale's *Three Laws* [Works, E.E.D.S. 34 and 63].
In Carlisle's *Topographical Dictionary* of England
(1808), Ingham is spoken of as being in the fourteenth
century " a college or priory of the order of the
Holy Trinity." This is as far as I have at present
gone, but I shall not have sought and written in
vain if my remarks lead to further research in
connection with these Macro plays. The new
light certainly tends to confirm Mr. Pollard's dates ;
but how far it affects his argument founded on the
collation of the manuscript, I do not know, and
writing, as I do, far away from the great centres of
antiquarian literary research and reference, my
inquiries have been perforce of the slightest.

MADGE MASON, " it passeth any man's *madge mason* "
(R211,*b*), imagination : People, like Codrus in
Misogonus (Anon. Pl., Series 2), is given to distorting
the " hard words " he hears.

MAHOUND, " by *Mahound's* bones, . . . by *Mahound's*
nose " (WS144,*c*), Mahomed.

MAIN GROAT (IP341,*c*), a term at hazard : an earlier
use than in *O.E.D.*

MAINMISSION, "needest no *mainmission* " (N48,*c*),
manumission : rare, a refashioning after *main*
hand (*O.E.D.*, in which the only example given is
the present one).

MAINPRIZE (N123,*c*), to procure or grant the release
of a prisoner by making oneself surety for his
appearance. " Mede shal nouȝte *meynprise* ȝow
bi the Marie of heuene."—Langland, *Piers Plow.*
(1377), B. iv. 179.

MAISTRY, " no *maistry* yourself to comfort " (N121,*d*),
i.e. it is no achievement (or is easy), to comfort your-

self. " It is no grete *maistre* to gader up that money."
—*Paston Lett.* (1456), 1. 380.

MAKEBATE (IP315,*d*), busybody, breeder of strife
" a discordant element." " They agree better
together, then to fal at variance for ye wild wordes
of suche a malicious *make-bate*."—More, *Suppl.
Soulys* (1529), *Works*, 296, 2.

MALKIN (*passim*), slut, slattern, strumpet : originally
a typical name for a woman of the lower classes.
Hence many colloquial and proverbial expressions—
" no man desireth *Malkin's* maidenhead " ; " mo
maids than *Malkin* " ; " an old mother *Malkin's*
talk " ; " *Malkin*, the May lady " (Maid Marian) ;
a " carter's or swineherd's *Malkin* " ; " some gentle-
man-swallowing (=whorish) *Malkin* " ; " a kitchen
Malkin " ; " trapish . . . petticoats to heels like a
Malkin," etc.

MALL, " this *mall* shall beat him to dust " (WS142.*c*),
a club ; usually of hard wood. " A leaden *maule*,
or suche lyke weapon, to beate downe his enemyes
withall."—Ascham, *Toxoph.* (1545), 70 (Arber).

MANKIND. The text is given on pp. 1–40. This
curious picture of real life and ne'er-do-weels in
late Plantagenet and early Tudor times is one
of the unique Macro plays, and existed, until quite
recently, in manuscript only. With this manuscript and its history I have dealt fully in another
part of this volume (*see* Macro Plays and MSS.).
During the last ten years *Mankind* has been three
times reprinted—by Dr. Brandl (*Quellen*, etc., 1904),
by Prof. Manly (*Specimens of the Pre-Shakespearean
Drama*, 1904), and by the *Early English Text Society*
(Extra Series xci, 1904). The last-named text
in all probability more nearly approaches fidelity
to the original than the others ; but as the amanu-
ensis, to all appearance, was the same for all three,
and was responsible for the confessedly untrust-
worthy texts which Dr. Brandl and Prof. Manly
have been compelled to use without an opportunity
of a new collation with the original manuscript,
one cannot but entertain some misgiving as to
the accuracy of the Early English Text Society's
version. Especially is this the case in view of

the fact that, so far as I can learn, the E.E. text,
as set by the printers from the copy supplied to
them, does not seem to have been compared with
the original MS.   The manifold errors too, alike
in the otherwise admirable introductory sketches,
in the footnotes, and in the glossary, are not re-
assuring.   Quotation after quotation, reference after
reference, are incorrectly given. For example,
in § 2, pp. xi.–xix., there are no less than twelve
errors of this description that have casually come
to my notice ; while, having occasion to use the
glossary references more frequently, I have found
its usefulness much more largely impaired.   Taking
a column here and there at random, these are the
results :—page 196, col. 1, 2 errors ; 199, col. 2,
1 error ; 200, col. 2, 5 references wrong ; 210,
col. 1, 4 errors.   Why, too, Monk *Hyngston* (xix.)
instead of *Hyngham* ?   And, in reference to this
strange inaccuracy, I must add that the same
Society's edition of *Respublica* is no better ; indeed,
it is worse !   One page alone of the Notes (p. 66)
contains no less than four wrong references, and the
weight of Mr. Magnus's argument for an attribution
of the play to Udall is marred by such unaccount-
able misquotation of names as *Mengrade* for *Merry-
greek* and *Mumblecourt* for *Mumblecrust* (both on
page xxi.).   Under the circumstances, and being
unable to obtain access to the original manuscript,
my own text must be taken for what it is ultimately
proved.   I have, of course, always given greater
weight to the E.E.T.S. version, because it is the
copy nearest to the original (the Brandl and Manly
texts are copies of this copy), but in many cases
Dr. Brandl and Professor Manly have done what
service they could, and good service often, in
suggested and amended readings and restorations.
As no good purpose could, under the circumstances,
have been served in dealing with all the minutiæ
of this kind in an uncertain text, I have confined
my remarks in this respect to the more important
points raised.   By punctuation, often and *in toto*,
I differ from all three, jointly and severally ;
varying the interpretation.   These I have noted.
But one conclusion is obvious.   The texts of these
Macro plays as they stand are not all that scholars

can desire ; and it is to be hoped that permission
may be obtained for a collotype facsimile of the
whole of the plays. The cost would be great,
but I have no doubt that consideration can be
satisfactorily solved. *Corrigenda, Suggested Readings,
Restorations, etc.* [In the following pages the attributions are indicated by F=Early Eng. Text Society's
Editors ; M=Professor Manly ; B=Dr. Brandl ; and
Ed. =the present editor.] The "Names of the players"
do not appear in the original manuscript — "our
first creation" (3,*b*), original *syest* or *syrst* (F)—
"to *have* him revived" (3,*c*), original *hade*—"By
meditation of our Lady (4,*a*), read *mediation* (M)—
"make his *avaunt*" (4,*b*), *a-vaunce* in MS.—"that
venomous serpent" (4,*d*), original *vemynousse*—
"leave your *calculation*" (5,*a*), *calcacyon* in F. :
I follow M and B in present reading—[*A leaf of
the manuscript, etc.*] (6,*a*), in the manuscript the
next speech is to Mercy, but I have followed Prof.
Manly's suggestion, also quoted by Dr. Furnivall.
He says : "These lines begin a new leaf in the
MS. They seem highly inappropriate in the mouth
of Mercy. . . . Moreover, it is clear from ["we
three" (7,*a*), and "all three" (7,*c*)] that the entrance
of New Gyse, Nowadays, and Nought was immediately preceded by Mercy's use of the words forming
their names. I therefore suppose that at least
one leaf of MS. (containing their entrance) has been
lost at this point, and suggest that the command
to the minstrels be assigned to New Gyse"—"have
traced somewhat *to fell*" (7,*a*), *to fylde fell* in MS. :
I have followed the Manly text, which is based on
a suggestion of Prof. Kittredge's, that *fylde* was
written by mistake, and that the copyist then,
observing that *fylde* neither rhymed nor made
sense, added the right word, but neglected to erase
fylde—"Christ's curse *have ye*" (7,*b*), *hade* in
MS.=had ye=have ye—"I had the *cup in* my
hand" (7,*b*), MS. has *cup ready in* : so also F and
B ; M as in present text—"Say *no[ugh]t* again"
(7,*c*), I have followed Manly : B and F have *not*
as in MS.—"shall find us *sh[r]ews*" (7,*c*), *schewys*
in MS.—"that brought you *hither*" (7,*c*), *brethern*
in MS., *hither* being M's emendation with a suggestion that possibly *brether* is the right word : F and

B follow MS.—" Ye betray *many men* " (7,*d*),
" *a man* " struck out (F)—" *my* denomination "
(8,*a*), " *by* " written over in MS. (F)—" a little
force " (8,*a*), *faus* in MS.—" full of English Latin "
(8,*a*), a marginal note says : " to have this English
made in Latin : I am a-ferde yt wyll brest : ' It
ram be ' [? MS.], quod the bocher on-to me, ' When
I stale a leg a motun ʒe are a stronge cúnnynge
clerke, I prey,' etc."—" *here is a pardon by limit* "
(8,*c*), I have omitted *lo* before " here " by mistake :
" pardon by limit " is in original, *pardon bely mett*—
" the demonical frayry " (8,*d*), M supposes a line
lost here, but there is no indication of such in the
MS. — " of *their* own Christ " (9,*b*), *her* in MS.
—" Alas ! what was thy fortune " (10,*d*), here a
marginal note in the MS. occurs, " I may both
syth and sobbe ; þis ys a pituose remembrance,
O In my soull, so sotyll in thy substance." Prof.
Manly says " this may be a part of the three lines
necessary to restore the versification." He indicates
a line missing before the line beginning " Alas !
what was thy fortune," and two lines missing
after the line ending " that stinking dunghill "—
" [MANKIND *approaches* MERCY " (11,*a*), F adds
" and kneels to him "—" In *sinful* guiding " (11,*b*),
sympull in MS. which is followed by F ; M has
sinful—"*Vita hominis est* milicia " (11,*d*), nnilicia
in MS.—" Measure yourself," etc. (12,*b*), this
line is in margin in MS.—" *I trow* and ye were "
(12,*d*), *It row* in MS. : the same miscript occurs
at 13,*a*—" *Mo than a* good sort " (13,*b*), M
suggests emending to " Me think a "—" To *them*
ye will go " (13,*b*), *hem* in MS. ; I follow M : B
suggests *hom*—" by Saint *Quintin* " (13,*c*), *Sent
Qisyntyn* in MS. — " I am even *very weary* " (13,*c*),
wery wery in MS.—" be there again to-morrow "
(13,*c*), M, for the sake of the rhyme, suggests
to-morne—" patience of Job *in* tribulation " (14,*a*),
so in M : the MS. has &—" my own sweet son "
(14,*a*), against this line in the margin in another
hand is, " *ita factum est* "—" To pervert *your*
conditions " (14,*b*), *per* in MS. : F suggests for þi ;
M reads your ; B suggests *your* — " all their
means " (14,*b*), *nnenys* in MS.—" *intermise* yourself
not " (14,*c*), scratched through in MS. and " *intro-*

mytt " written over in another hand — " of the
cunning that I can " (15,*a*), *cōmynge . . . kam* in
MS.—" It is written, etc." (16,*a*), this song is
omitted by Manly (*see* Holyke, *ante*) but given
by F and B, the latter in *Quellen*, pp. 50–51, not
page 61 as erroneously given by the Early English
Text editors—" if he will have *compos*[*t*] " (17,*c*),
compasse in MS. : F corrects to *compass*[*t*]*e* ; M
to *compost* ; B to *composte*—" By Cock's body
sacred " (18,*b*), F queries this as being *sakyide* in
MS.—" By the *aid* of His grace " (18,*b*), *syde* in
MS. : F suggests *ayde* and says " MS. ſs crost
there before *syde* . . . see line 400 " [With the
help, &c., 19,*a*]—" *Nec in* hasta " (18,*c*), *hastu* in
MS. : F refers to " Non in gladio, nec in hasta . . .
1 Reg. xvii. 47 "—" Alack, alack ! " (19,*d*), F says
(this commences leaf 127 back), " In another
hand, at top, ' Honorabyll well belouyd frende,
I hertely Recummend me on-to you ' "—" Yea,
Christ's cross " (20,*b*), *Crastes* in MS. : M suggests
Christ's curse, comparing it with " Christ's copped
curse " (36,*a*)—" There ! we're on anon " (20,*b*),
I may have been misled, though the MS. is by
no means clear : " Ther, wher, on & on,"
which *might* be interpreted, " There, ware ! on
anon ! Out ! ye shall not," etc., or " There !
we're one and [*i.e.* to] one. Out ! ye shall not,"
etc.—" Know ye any *aught* " (20,*c*), *out* in MS. : F
and B read *ou*[*gh*]*t*—" with a *flowte* " (20,*d*), *flewte*
in MS. : M queries it for *flowte*, which I have
adopted—" Else *there* shall " (20,*d*) ? *þei* in MS. (F)
—" he is a *worshipful* man " (21,*a*), *worschyppull*
in MS.—" nor pence *nor* two pence " (21,*b*), *of* in
MS. ; F, M, and B read *or*—" Ye say *us* ill " (21,*b*),
as in MS.—" The devil have [*thee*] " (22,*a*), suggested
by M—" *that be* sought " (22,*c*), so in MS. : F and
B read *that* [*yt*] *be* ; though elliptical the passage
reads = that which is to be : my "pointing"
varies from other authorities—" Mischief *hat*[*h*] informed
[*me*] " (22,*d*), *hat* in MS. : [*me*] suggested by F—
" Take *W*[*illiam*] Fide " (22,*d*), suggested by F :
M reads *w*[*ith yow*], and B *w*[*yth yow*]—" begin
at *m*[*aster*] Huntington " (23,*a*), supplied by M
—" Huntington of Sanston . . . Hammond of
Swaffham " (23,*a* and *b*), see E.E.T.S edition—

" *see* well where and whither " (23,*b*), *be* in MS.—
" Let us *con* well our neck-verse " (23,*c*), *com* in
MS.—" I bless you with my *left* hand " (23,*c*),
right struck out in MS.—" enter, I hope, *unreadily* "
(24,*a*), so in M : *ouer redyly* in MS.—" grace were
wane " (24,*b*), " *cran* (?) written after ' wane '
in another hand " (F)—" While I over-delve
it " (24,*c*), *ouer dylew yt* in MS.—" into thi[*s*]
yard " (25,*b*), supplied by M—" pow[*d*]er of Paris "
(25,*d*), supplied by M—" Ye shall [*see*] *a* good
sport " (25,*d*), supplied by M : Brandl, however,
suggests that *a*=have, which provides, I think
on reflection, a better reading without altering
the text—" Be as *be* may . . . Mercy be wroth "
(26,*a* and *b*), " these lines are added at the bottom
of the page " (F), *be* is *it* in original—" I shall *sleep* "
(26,*b*), ?MS. *skepe* (F)—" rideth over the gallows "
(26,*d*), *galouf* in MS. for *galous*—" And thy own wife
brethel " (27,*a*), see Brethel, *ante* (382,*d*): F in a
footnote (p. 22) says, " Qy. *bethell*, M," but M (p. 338)
has " Qy. *brethell* " !—" Adieu, fair *master* " (27,*b*),
F suggests *master*[*s*]—" such a *likely* man " (27,*d*),
lyghly which F reads *lygh*[*t*]*ly*=likely—" ye have
sco[u]red a pair of fetters " (28,*d*), *scoryde* in MS. :
see *Scoured*, *post*, 461,*a*)—" *that* sweet mouth " (28,*d*),
þo in MS.—" do *it* [*in*] forma " (29,*c*), " fo " is
struck out after *it* in MS. : *in* is supplied by M—
" his side-gown may be *sold* " (29,*d*), *solde* in F
and M, but F has a note " solde MS., tolde M "
which I do not understand : M at all events is
intelligible in noting the *solde* of his text as " MS.
tolde " ; but which is correct ?—" spare that ye
may " (30,*a*), so in MS and F, which I have followed :
M reads *mow* (to rhyme with *yow*, p. 30, line 1),
and notes his departure from the original—" beshrew
your ears, *a* fair hand " (30,*b*), *&* in MS. and F :
M reads *a*—" Curia *tenta generalis* " (30,*c*), *Carici*
in MS.: see Curia, *ante* (391*a*)—" makest much
[*tarrying*] " (30,*d*), supplied by M and adopted
by F—" I can[*not*] express this inconvenience "
(32,*d*), [*not*] supplied by M and adopted by F—
" *Christus* et *omnia jura* " (33,*c*), *sit* in MS. :
emended by Kittredge in M—" Equity to be
laid over part[l]y " (33,*d*), *party* in MS : this line
was a puzzler to M and B in consequence of the

wretchedly inaccurate copy of the text supplied to them, and on which they had to work. The variations are characteristic : F is direct from MS. and collated (?); M and B are copies of a copy made by the same person at different times : these differ alike one with the other, and with the F copy. (F) " Equyte to be leyde ou*er* p*a*rty, & mercy to prevayll." (M) O quyte to be leyde ou*er*, p*e*rty & mercy to prevayll ! (B) O, quyte to be leyde, ou*er* p*a*rty *and* mercy to prevayll ! The readings adopted or suggested are—(F) As given above. (M) Equyte to be leyde ou*er*, pety & mercy to prevayll ! (B) O, quyte to be lewyde, ou*er* pety *and* mercy to prevayll ! From this it will be seen that all differ with one another and from myself in interpreting this line : I offer mine as a suggestion —" with these cursed caitiffs " (34,*a*), *cayftys* in MS.—" nigh dead in the crick " (34,*c*), *my* in MS. : corrected by M and B, and adopted by F, to *ny*— " Hic, hic, hic " (34,*c*), M says a line is wanted here rhyming with the third line lower down to complete the stanza—" a *cepe* coppus " (34,*d*), so in original which says M may be intentional : he reads *cape corpus*—" give the rope just to *thy* neck " (35,*d*), *pye* in MS. : restored by M and B— " *He is* so timorous " (36,*a*), *He ys ys* in MS.— " To see your *solicitious* face " (36,*b*), *solaycyose* in MS. : M reads *solacyose* ; B *solicitose* — " What ! ask mercy yet once again ? " (36,*c*), F says that from this point to " good perseverance " (40,*b*) the MS. is in another hand—" my *worst* transgression " (36,*c*), *wernt* or *werunt* in MS. : F has *werst* : M has *wekit*—" dolorous *fears* " (36,*d*), *seris* in MS. : F has *feris* : M has *feres* ; and B suggests *sores* — " this sinful sinner to *redeem* " (36,*d*), so in MS. : M and B suggest *reduce* for the rhyme's sake—" *Nam hec . . . non sunt* " (36,*d*), F " notes " this passage : " Ps. lxxvi (lxxvii, Engl.), II, ' *hæc mutatio dexteræ Excelsi* ' ; ' *Verte impios, et non erunt*'—*Prov.* xii. 7 "—" as Himself doth *precise* " (37,*b*), M says " *precyse* does not rhyme : qy. *preche*, or, as Kittredge suggests, *precysely teche* "—" *Nolo mortem, &c.* " (37,*b*), " *Nolo mortem impii, sed ut convertatur impius a vita sua, et vivat,* Ezech. xxviii. II " (F)—" he will [*be*] reducible "

(37,*b*), M—" Inciine your capacity," etc. (37,*d*),
in MS. this line reads, " My doctrine is convenient,
Incline your capacity " : the change is due to M—
" as *I* said before " (38,*a*), *he* in MS. (M)—" cause
of great grievan*ce* " (38,*b*), " *ge* in MS. altered to
ce or *se* " (F)—" Not to the *lowli'st* joy " (38,*d*),
F reads *holest*, and " notes " M's query of MS.
being miswritten for *loliest* or *lest* : B also suggests
lo[*w*]*l*[*i*]*est*—" Scripture doth *prove* " (38,*d*), *prewe*
in MS. and followed by F : M has *prove*—" my
suavious solace " (38,*d*), to B : F has *suatius* ;
M has *solatius*—" my *inexcusable* reproof " (39,*a*),
so in MS. : M suggests *inexorable* may be better—
" fantastical visions, *sedulously* sought " (39,*b*),
sedociusly in MS. : the emendment is to M : B
reads *seducively*—" *Libere velle*," etc. (40,*a*), *Libere
welle liebere welle* (Kittredge in M)—" Dominus
custodi[a]t te " (40,*b*), *custodit se* in MS. (M)—
" my *several* patrociny " (40,*c*), " ? MS. suuerall
(several, individual). Kittredge suggests *special* "
(F)—" *Search* your conditions " (40,*c*), in original
Serge—" O Liber," etc. (40,*d*), see *Macro Plays*.

MAN OF ARMS (M28,*c*), a sarcasm : Mischief is loaded
with fetters.

MANITORY, " my doctrine *manitory* " (M39,*b*), warning.

MARKET, " about our *market* depart " (R207,*d*), here
generic for business, affairs.

MARY MASS (R202,*b*), a mass in honour of the Virgin
Mary : specifically festivals held on Candlemas
Day (2 February), the assumption (15 August), and
the latter Marymass, the nativity of the Virgin
(8 September). The asseveration was common in
the sixteenth century ; moreover, a covert allusion to
the trouble of Queen Mary as regards the celebration
of the mass in her late brother's time may be intended.

MAS (*passim*), master : in Respublica *mace*.

MASS, see Prime.

MASSHIP, " I trow we shall his *masship* trim " (R230,*d*),
mastership.

MAST, " *mast* Wealth " (WH289,*d*), master.

MATINS, see Prime.

MEASURE, "*Measure is treasure*" (M12,*b*), proverbial. "Men wryte of oold how *mesour is tresour.*"— Lydgate, *Min. Poems* (Percy Soc.), 208 (*c.* 1430).

MEDWALL (HENRY). Mr. T. Seccombe, writing in the *Dictionary of National Biography*, says he "flourished in 1486"; but beyond the fact that he was chaplain to John Morton (who became Archbishop of Canterbury in 1486, and died in 1500), little is known of this early writer of interludes. The only work of his extant is *Nature* (see pp. 43–133). Bale mentions another interlude not now extant, but ascribed to Medwall, "Of the Finding of Truth, carried away by Ignorance and Hypocrisy." This was diversified by the introduction of a fool, an innovation which commended it to Henry VIII. when it was produced before him at Richmond, Christmas 1516. Apart from this feature the piece was misliked, and the King "departyd before the end to hys chambre."

MEEK, "Except that man himself do *meek*" (WH 279,*b*), abase, humble.

MELL, "not suffer to *mell*" (R213,*a*)—"with such high matters to *mell*" (R235,*b*),—"will not *mell*" (R250,*b*), meddle.

MEMBER, "I scannot *member* his name" (R212,*d*), —"to *member* in my heart" (R234,*d*), remember: in original *membre*.

MEMENTO, "*Memento, homo*," etc. (M15,*b*): see *Job* xxxiv. 15.

MENGE, "I shall *menge* his corn" (M24,*a*), mix, or ? scatter.
> "The busy bee, her honey now she *mings*."
> —Surrey, *Songs and Sonnets* (1557), Description of Spring.

MERCHANT, "prattling *merchant*" (*passim*), fellow, chap: frequently in depreciation.

MERE, "be used *mere*" (WS174,*a*), simply, solely, "single-eyed," unquestionably, downright.
> "This is *mere* falsehood."
> —Shakespeare, *Winter's Tale* (1604), iii. 2.

MET, " I hope to have his foot *met* " (M23,*d*), caught.

MICH, " cost him even as *mich* " (N67,*c*), much.
"Alle the *myche* tresour that traytour had wonnene
To commons of the contré, clergye and other."
—*Morte Arthure, MS. Lincoln,* f. 66.

MISCHIEVE, " herself to *mischieve* " (IP313,*d*), harm, injure.
" Grant, I may ever love, and rather woo
Those that would *mischief* me, than those that do."
—Shakespeare, *Timon of Athens* (1609), iv. 3.

MISERICORDIA, " put out the *i* of Misericordia, and without an *i* play e'en plain trussing corda " (R243,*d*); the pun survives to this day.

MISERY, " harlotry, *misery*, treachery " (R263,*d*), miserliness, parsimony, coveteousness. " But Brutus, scorning his (Octavius Cæsar's) *misery* and niggardliness, gave unto every band a number of wethers to sacrifice."—North, *Plutarch* (1578), p. 215.

MISH, MASH, see Driff, draff.

MISWOMEN (IP320,*c*), a generic reproach : here = strumpets, wantons.
" Fly the *miswoman*, least she thee deceiue."
—Chaucer, *Remedy of Love.*

MO (*passim*), more.

MOME (*passim*), clown, buffoon, blockhead, fool.

MOON, " made you believe the *moon* was a green cheese " (R265,*c*), bamboozled or deceived you ; the proverbialism is, in truth, of respectable antiquity : also *cream cheese.*

MORROW, " on Sundays, *on the morrow* " (M31,*c*), in the morning.

MOSELLING, " I fell down *moselling* " (JE363,*d*), original *moselynge* ; ? drunk (cf., muzzling, muzzy) : the E.E.T.S. editors gloss *meselynge* = diseaseful, from *measle*, but the context would bear my own " shot." " In *meselynge* glotonye, with goode metis and drynkys trye, I norche my syster Lecherye " (*Castell of Persev.* [E.E.T.S.], 144, 2258).

MOT, MOUGHT (*passim*), might.

MOUNSIRE, " *Mounsire* authority " (R197,*c*)—(also R224,*b*), an early corrupted form of " Monsieur " : cf. modern *Mounseer*.

MUMCHANCE (WH286,*a*), a game of hazard with cards or dice : see Nares.

NAM, " *Nam hæc est mutatio, dexteræ Excelsi : vertit impios, et non sunt* " (M36,*d*), see *Psalm* lxxvii. 11, and *Prov.* xii. 7.

NAMNOT, NAMMOT (R267,*d*), am not : the double negative, *ne am not*.

NARSE (WS153,*b*), arse : the transference of the *n* of the indefinite article, and a similar process in respect to the *n* of " mine," " thine," etc. is not infrequent in M.E. ; cf. " naunt," " nuncle," " nam," " newt," " nickname," etc.

NATURE. The text will be found on pages 41–133, together with a reduced facsimile of the title-page of the unique copy now in the British Museum (C34,*e*54). Bound up with it, at the end of the volume, are two duplicate leaves. In several places (see 105,*c* ; 106,*d* ; 112,*d* ; 114,*a*) the lower margins have suffered by cutting ; otherwise it is a good copy, but without date, place, or printer's name. It is well printed, probably by John Rastell, between 1510–20, and is in excellent preservation. When printing my own text, I was not aware that a fragment comprising two complete and well-preserved pages had been discovered in an album consisting entirely of " Specimens of the English Printers from Caxton to Robert Barker," which Sir John Fenn had collected for the completion of Ames-Herbert's *Typographical Antiquities*, and which was offered for sale by Mr. Bernard Quaritch in his Catalogue, No. 237 (pp. 97–99), the price affixed being £280. For the foregoing particulars I am indebted to *Materialen zur Kunde des alteren Englischen Dramas*, so ably edited by Prof. Bang of Louvain University and other well-known English, American, and Continental scholars. I have, so far, been unable to trace the subsequent history of this volume ; but I am not without hopes, later on, of being in a position to supply full and detailed particulars.

What more nearly concerns the present purpose is the
fact that in vol. xii. of *Materialen* are given facsimiles
of parts of each of these two pages, by means of which
two out of the four lines cut away, each on different
pages, have been restored, viz. at 112,*d* and 114,*a*—
a fortunate and happy circumstance (see *Corrigenda, etc., infra*). Another fragment was known to
exist at the Bodley. This is mentioned by Mr. Greg
in his *Handlist of English Plays* ; but no particulars
are furnished, and on enquiry at the Bodley no trace
of the fragment could at first be found. I, thereupon, made search, and at last unearthed it, finding
it buried in a mass of uncatalogued early printed
scraps. This was after delving through a dozen
volumes of similar miscellaneous material, so let it
now be ear-marked for future reference. The Bodley
shelf-mark is Rawl. 4° 598 (12). It came into the
Bodleian with the Rawlinson collection of MSS. and
printed books in 1755. The fragment (Aiiii) is small,
and is apparently of the same edition as the British
Museum copy, and the extra leaves. As the Quaritch
fragment is also undoubtedly of similar parentage, it
is unlikely that the play was printed more than
once. The Bodley fragment comprises (*a*) " But,
if Reason tickle . . ." (last line p. 49) down to
" . . . that from above is sent " (p. 50, 11th line of
text from bottom) ; and (*b*) " No well-advised body
. . . "(page 51, 11 lines from top) down to " It
shall not skill as for this intent " (p. 52, 2 lines from
top). By this it will be seen that this recovery does
not serve to restore either of the two missing lines,
not restored by the other fragments. *Nature* was
produced before Archbishop Morton in Henry vii.'s
reign (see 51,*c* ; 88,*b*) ; and Bale states that it was
translated into Latin. A period of nearly three days
seems to have elapsed between the representation
of Parts I. and II. (see 90,*d*). Other allusions I have
dealt with in this Note-Book as they occur. Of
the author little is known save what is revealed by
the play, and Bale's mention (see *Medwall*). From
the former it is evident, however, as Prof. Gayley
first pointed out, that he must have possessed a
remarkably vivid imagination, or have enjoyed a
closer acquaintance than might be expected of one
of his cloth with the seamy side of London life ; for

there are few racier or more realistic bits of description in our early literature than the account given by Sensuality of Fleyng Kat and Margery, of the perversion of the hero by the latter, and of her retirement when deserted to that house of " Strayt Religyon at the Grene Freres hereby," where " all is open as a gose eye." Dr. Gayley remarks that though " the plot is not remarkable, nor the mechanism of it, for almost the only device availed of is that of feigned names, still the author's insight into the conditions of low life, his common sense, his proverbial philosophy, his humorous exhibition of the morals of the day, and his stray and sudden shafts at the foibles of his own religious class, would alone suffice to attract attention to this work. And even more remarkable than this in the history of comedy is Medwall's literary style; his versification excellent and varied, his conversations witty, idiomatic, and facile. Indeed, he is so far beyond the ordinary convention that he writes the first bit of prose to be found in our drama." *Nature* has only once before been reprinted in modern times, in Prof. Brandl's admirable *Quellen* series. The present text is taken direct from the British Museum copy, and has been re-collated with the original in proof: mere misprints I have, as a rule, not noted. It is proper to point out that the " Humility " of the " Names of the Players " (p. 42) appears in the text, except in one instance, as " Meekness " ; likewise that " Good Occupation " is the " Good Business " of the text ; " Pride " also is occasionally given as " Pry. Co." *Corrigenda, Amended Readings, etc.:* The *Names of the Players* (42,*b* and *c*), these are from the end of play—" things here *below* " (44,*b*) *by low* in original—" To *the* which end " (50,*b*), original *ye* —" nor *yet* so furious " (51,*b*), original *yt* —"*point* oversight" (51,*c*), original has *point of* ; my mistake —" use thee as a *servant* " (52,*b*), original *servand* — " As *far* as " (57,*d*), original *for* — " And let thy *word* be *cousin* to thy deed " (59,*a*), original *world . . . consyn*—" *See* that ye commit " (59,*b*), original *So*—" to every man's *guise* " (60,*b*), original *ges*—" my chief *counsellor* " (60,*c*), original *conselour*—" *Sens*. Lord ! ye say well " (61,*b*), between this and the previous line Dr. Brandl points

out that a line has been dropped, but there is no
break in the original copy—" To put him*self* "
(61,*c*), in original *selse*—" [*He goeth out . . .*] " (64,*d*),
considerable confusion exists in the original from
this point to the end of the next page. The lines
beginning " Worldly Affection," " Come hither ! "
are assigned to *The World*, whereas it is clear that
The World goes out, and *Mankind*, calling to *Worldly
Affection* (who comes in), continues his speech,
addressing the new comer. From this point the
speeches now given, rightly I think, to *Worldly
Affection* are in original to *The World*, except the
last on page 65, which appears as a continuation of
Mankind's speech. I may remark that Dr. Brandl
differs—" [*Pride*]. Who dwelleth here " (66,*c*),
in original *Pry. Co.*—" worn gilt *spurs . . .* cutted
whores " (66,*d*), original *sperys . . . horys*—" How
say ye, *sirs* " (67,*a*), original *syrst* : Brandl suggests
reading *fyrst*—" *Allez . . . vous avant !* " (69,*c*),
original *Ale seygniour ale vouse auant* "—" judge in
common *pleas* " (71,*c*), original, *place* —" Sir ! bid
him welcome," etc. (72,*b*), in original the catch-cue
to " *Sens*." is repeated here ; the present inter-
polated " direction " makes the action clear—
" *Man.* Me ? " (73,*a*), in original *Man.* is misprinted
as part of text, *Man me ?*—" The *world* told me "
(73,*c*), read *World*—"Where they *shall*" (93,*b*), original
misprinted *shalbe*—" Sirs, God speed *ye* ! " (112,*d*),
original *you*—" [*A line has been shaved away at the
foot of the page*]" (112,*d*), this is now restored from the
Quaritch fragment, " *Had I set a done* (=adown)
my gear." A line similarly shaved off at 114,*a* is
also restored by " I *wene he wyll be dede* "—" great
scorn and disdain " (120,*c*), original *storn*—" mind
and good *will* " (121,*b*), Dr. Brandl suggests reading
lust—" to the uttermost " (122,*d*), Dr. Brandl suggests
uttermest—" He *speaketh* sometime " (126,*a*), so in
original, Dr. Brandl prints *seeketh*—" [*Help*] to reform " (128,*d*), this word is cut away at the foot of
the page : the same mishap has occurred at " in this
case " (130,*a*).

NE, " *ne* would " (N124,*a*), not, neither.

NEAT, " a horse and a *neat* " (M26,*c*), an ox, bullock,
cow, heifer : now rare.

NEC, " *nec* in hasta," etc. (M18,*c*), see 1 Reg. xvii. 47—
" Non in gladio, *nec* in hasta. . . ."

NECK-VERSE, " he could his *neck-verse* " (M27,*d*), a
verse on which one's neck depends, in allusion to
hanging : originally " a Latin verse printed in black
letter (usually the beginning of the 51st Psalm),
formally set before one claiming benefit of clergy,
. . . by reading which he might save his neck "
(*O.E.D.*). See other volumes of this series.

NEEDINGS (M34,*d*), "relieving nature," doing that is
necessary.

NEGLIGENCE, (*a*) "if it please your *negligence* " (M21,*a*),
i.e. if an " interval " will be acceptable : this usage
=a pleasing relaxation of attention, or absence of
restraint, was common enough.
    (*b*) " Committed to my *negligence* " (N83,*a*), in
sarcasm.

NEMBLE, " now am I *nemble* " (IP337,*d*), nimble : cf.
trimble=tremble.

NEMESIS (R., *passim*), the embodiment of retributive
justice ; this passage serves the *O.E.D.*, being nearly
half a century earlier than the first given by Dr.
Murray.

NESH, " tender and *nesh* " (IP337,*b*), succulent, juicy.

NEST, see Feather.

NEW GUISE, see Guise.

NEW JET, see Jet.

NEW YEAR, " in *the worship of the new year* " (IP334,*c*),
i.e. at the next jollification.

NIL, see Suffer.

NINE STOCKS, " sit in *nine stocks* " (R220,*d*). Mr. Magnus
thinks the meaning of this somewhat obscure sentence to be that the culprit shall be sentenced to
the stocks nine times running ; note the exigency
of a rhyme to *mine locks*.

NINNAT (R., *passim*), ne will not.

NOLD, " The skitb[r]ains *nold not* " (R267,*b*)—" for
she *nolde* suffer " (N45*a*), would not be—n[e w]o[u]ld:
cf. Namnot, etc.

NOLI ME TANGERE, " He is a *noli-me-tangere* " (M23*b*), generic for anybody or anything repellant, an awkward tempered person. " He was wont to say of them that they were of the tribe of Dan, and were *noli me tangere's*."—R. Naunton, *Frag. Reg.* (*c.* 1630), 18 (1870).

NOLO, " *Nolo mortem peccatoris, inquit* " (M37,*b*): see *Ezekiel* xxviii. 11—" *Nolo mortem impii, sed ut convertatus impius a vita sua, et vivat.*"

NOMINATION, " that is my *nomination* " (R199,*d*), name, designation. " Because of these two effectes . . . hath it the *nomination* of kayes."—Frith (*d.* 1533), *Workes*, p. 58.

NON, see Inventus.

NONAGE, " the *nonage* of this gentleman " (N53,*d*), legal minority. " My parents deceased in mine *nonage*."—*Godly Queen Hester*, Anon. Pl., 2 Ser. (E.E.D.S.), 257,*c*.

NONNY, see Hey.

NOURICE, " thy tender *nourice* " (N46,*d*), nurse. " Flatterers ben the devil's *nourices* that nourish his children with milke of losengrie."—Chaucer, *Cant. Tales* (1383), Persones Tale.

NYMPHS, " at her *nymphs* " (R251,*b*), *i.e.* handmaidens, waiting women.

OAR, see Boat.

OBEDIENT, " subdued to reason as his *obedient* " (N55,*d*), one subject to authority, a subordinate : an earlier instance of the substantive use of *obedient* than that recorded in the *O.E.D.* by a century and a quarter.

OBSTINANT, " if he be *obstinant* " (IP346,*b*), obstinate : the *O.E.D.* records the word as a substantive, earmarking it " rare," and giving a single quotation only, but the adjectival form is absent.

OCCUPY, " a merchant's place to *occupy* " (IP339,*b*), formerly *occupy* was almost as hard-worked a verb as the modern American *fix*. Amongst other senses it meant, take possession, seize, enter upon, hold, have in possession, enjoy, reside in, tenant, stay, abide, employ, busy about, engage, make use of, etc.

ODIBLE, " as carene is *odible* " (M32,*d*)—"dispectuous and *odible* " (M33,*b*), hateful, odious. "His face was so hatefull and so *odyble*."—Lydgate, *Chron. Troy* (1412–20), III. xxiv.

OLD BOY, " play ever . . . *the old boy* " (N75,*b*), as one who has become skilled, clever, knowing through practice and experience ; foreshadowing the slang usage : cf. " olde souldier, *veteranus* " (Huloet., 1552).

OM (*passim*), them—'em.

ONT (*passim*), on it—on[i]t.

OPRAY, OPRY, " *opray* counsel " (N71,*c*)—" such *opry* " (N71,*c*), not in *O.E.D.*: ?=*operary*, practical.

ORGANS, " Piers Pickpurse playeth at *organs* " (R240,*a*), *i.e.* as if fingering an organ : formerly organs (pl.) denoted a single instrument.

OSCULARE, " *osculare fundamentum* " (M8,*c*), the modern vulgar jeer wrapped up in Latin.

OTHER (*passim*), either.

OVERBLISS, " he may *overbliss* it " (M17,*c*), overbless : Nought sarcastically says that Mankind may treat his land too well by using it as a jakes.

OWETH, " he *oweth* to be magnified " (M3,*b*), ought. " Forgotten was no thing That *owe* be done."——*Chaucer's Dreme* (*c.* 1500), 1405.

OWL-FLIGHT, " in the *owl-flight* " (M25,*d*), when owls go abroad, dusk ; here under cover of night. "He ran away by nyght In the *owle flyght* Lyke a cowarde Knyght."—Skelton, *Dk. Albany* (*c.* 1529), 312.

OYEZ (*passim*). "Hear ye" : a call (usually three times given) to command silence and attention.

PAINFUL, " *painful* ministers " (R234,*b*), " Young, *painful*, tractable " (WS137,*d*), careful, diligent, painstaking : cf. *careful*=full of care ; *hateful*=full of hate, etc. " Vertuous sermons and *painefull* preaching."—Stapleton, tr. *Bede's Hist. Ch. Eng.* (1565), 79.

PALE, " four kine to my *pale* " (R229,*a*), an enclosed space, limit : here=holding.

PARDON, " forty days of *pardon* " (M8,*c*), an indulgence, a papal warrant of forgiveness of "faults" : see other volumes of this series.

PARIS GATES (N67,*a*), ? the entrance to Paris Garden ;
see Halliwell and Nares.

PARLEMENT, " A *parlement*, a *parlement*," (M35,*a*),
conference, consultation, talk.
" He sent to his barrons a *parlement* to hold."
—*Robert de Brunne*, p. 244.

PARTICIPABLE, " be *participable of* " (M3,*d*), partakers
of.

PARTY, see Mankind, *Amended Readings*.

PASH, PASSHE (*passim*), (*a*) the Passover, Easter-tide,
properly Pasch.
(*b*) " *Pash* head ! *pash* brain " (WS143,*b*), smash,
dash to pieces.
" And *pash* the jaws of serpents venomous."
—Marlowe, 1 *Tamburlaine* (1590), i. 1.

PASS, " I do not *pass* " (WS147,*c*), care, reck, mind :
see other volumes of this series.

PASSEIVE, " we *passeive* " (R212,*a*), perceive.

PASSIBLE, " obedient and *passible* " (M33,*a*), able to
feel or suffer. " Therein he assumed human nature,
mortal, and *passible*."—Chr. Sutton, *Godly Medita-
tions* (1622), p. 24 (ed. 1849).

PATROCINY, " my several *patrociny* " (M40,*c*), patron-
age, protection, defence, support. " To take hym
and his pore causis into your *patrocynye* and protection."—Wolsey, *Lett. to Gardener* (1529) in Strype,
Eccl. Mem., 1. App. xxxiii. 92.

PATUS, " I beshrew your *patus* " (M21,*c*), head : mock
Latin.

PAUL'S STEEPLE, etc. (*passim*), Paul's (Poules, Paules,
Powlys, Pawles, etc.), *i.e.* St. Paul's Cathedral in
London, a favourite lounge and business resort in
the sixteenth and seventeenth centuries, — hence
frequent allusions in old writers.

PEAK, " bold to *peak* in " (R255,*d*), peep. " That
other pries and *peekes* in euery place."—Gascoigne,
Steele Glas. (1576), 68 (Arber).

PEASON, (*a*) " *peason* knaves " (R213,*c*), peasant
knaves : a generic reproach=low fellow, rascal,
" villain." Possibly also with an eye on the chief

food staple of the lower classes in Tudor times, pease (or peason) and beans.

(*b*) see Peson.

PEERS, " with all their old *peers* " (IP346,*c*), associates, companions: *perers* in original. " Children sittynge in Cheepynge . . . cryinge to her *peeris*."—Wyclif, *Matt.* xi. 16 (1382).

PERMOUNTED, " how ye beeth *permounted* " (R256,*c*), ? a portmanteau word *promoted* + *mounted*.

PERSECUTED " how shall this redress be well persecuted " (R269,*c*), pursued (Magnus).

PERSWAGED, " cham *perswaged* " (*passim*), persuaded.

PERVERSIOUS, " this *perversious* ingratitude " (M33,*b*), perverse.

PERVERTIONATE, " that ever be *pervertionate* " (M10,*c*), perverse.

PERZENT, whom itch do *perzent* " (R211,*a*), represent.

PESON, " piss my *peson* " (M12,*c*), what *peson* means is somewhat obscure. The recorded meanings are (1)=pl. of pease; (2) a staff-like instrument used for weighing purposes before scales were employed, and so, maybe, a staff. The context, however, would seem to suggest *peason* as a shortened or popular name of the *peasecod doublet*, a long-breasted garment carried down to a long peak in front, having the lower part stiffly quilted and projecting.

PESTEL, " a *pestel* on him " (R199,*a*), *i.e.* a *pestilence*.

PETTICOAT, " *have at thy petticoat* " (R270,*d*); cf. " I'll pay him o' th' *petticoat*."—*Misogonus*, Anon. Pl., 2 Ser. (E.E.D.S.), 157,*b*. " I dare jeopard a groat, If he may reach them, will have on the *petticoat*."— *Jacob and Esau*, 2 Anon. Pl., 2 Ser. (E.E.D.S.), 77,*c*.

PEW, " God give him an ill *pew* " (JE363,*c*), in original pue: a rare transferred usage of the common word = " station, situation, allotted place " (O.E.D.). " Ye lat me peyne here in a peynfull *pewe*, That is a place of grete doloures."—*Pety Job* (*c.* 1400) 555, in 26 *Pol. Poems*, 139.

PIE, " hands be in the *pie* " (R191,*d*), the modern " finger in the pie " is more modest; the present example is the earliest given in the *O.E.D.*

PIKE, " *pike* thee home " (WS157,*a*)—" they bad me
pike me home " (R256,*a*), walk, be off, get home.
Mr. Magnus glosses the Respublica example, " pick."
" He bad them then go *pyke* them home." — *Ane
Ballat of Matrymonie (c.* 1570) in Laing, *Pop. Poet.
Scotland,* ii. 77.

PIP, " God send them both the *pip* " (R215,*c*), properly a disease peculiar to poultry and the like, but
frequently used jocosely by old writers for various
diseases in human beings, specifically, however,
of the pox. " I have a master : I wolld he had ye
pyppe."—*Play Sacram (c.* 1460), 525.

PISS, see Rods.

PLAIN, " did not ich *plain* me to you ? " (R229,*d*),
complain, lament, bewail.
  " Erles & barons at ther first samnyng,
  For many maner resons *pleyned* of the king."
                    —*Robert de Brunne,* p. 312.

PLAYERS (THE NAMES OF THE). The following refer-
ences to Players' Names in this volume and the
Play in which they occur may be of service.
  Abstinence (N); Abundance (IP); Actio (JE);
Adulation (R); Avarice (R).
  Bodily Lust (N).
  Charity (N); Chastity (N); Colhazard (IP);
Comfort (WS); Confidence (WS); Conscience (IP).
  Diligence (WS).
  Envy (N and IP); Eugenio (JE); Evil Counsel
(JE); Experience (WS).
  Fame (WS); Favour (WS).
  Garcon (N); Gluttony (N); Good Occupation (N).
  Hance (WH); Health (WH); Honest Recreation
(WS); Humility (N).
  Idleness (WS); Idleness (JE); Ill Will (WH);
Impatient Poverty (IP); Ingnorancy (WS); Inno-
cency (N); Insolence (R); Instruction (WS);
Irisdision (JE).
  Justicia (R).
  Liberality (N); Liberty (WH).
  Man (N); Mankind (M); Mercy (M); Mischief
(M); Misericordia (R); Misrule (IP); Mundus (N).
  Nature (N); Nemesis (R); New Guise (M);
Nought (M); Now-a-days (M).

Oppression (R).

Patience (N) ; Pax (R) ; Peace (IP) ; People (R) ;
Poverty (IP); Pride (N); Prologue (R); Prosperity (IP).
Quickness (WS).

Reason (N and WS) ; Remedy (WH) ; Respublica
(R) ; Riches (WS).

St. John the Evangelist (JE); Science (WS) ;
Sensuality (N) ; Shame (WS) ; Shamefacedness (N) ;
Shrewd Wit (WH); Sloth (N); Strength (WS) ;
Study (WS) ; Sumner (IP).

Tediousness (WS) ; Titivillus (M).

Veritas (R).

Wealth (WH) ; Wit (WS) ; Worldly Affection (N) ;
Worship (WS) ; Wrath (N).

PLETTE, " whom should I *plette* " (IP341,*d*), plead.
 " About eftsoones for to *plete*,
 And bring on you advocacies new ? "
 —Chaucer, *Troilus and Creseide*, ii.

PLEYSERIS, " ye may be *pleyseris* with the angels
above " (M40,*d*), so in original : Manly suggests
partakers.

POLICATE, "such a *policate* wit " (R213,*b*), polished :
? a compound of *polished* + *delicate*, or a corruption
of *politic* = sharp, clever, well-devised.

POLL, " I see you would *poll* me " (R220,*c*), plunder,
pillage, rob.

POPULORUM, " by his precious *populorum* " (R259,*b*)
A coinage of no special worth save a bare record.

PORT, "Wealth hath great *port* " (WH279,*d*), carriage,
mien, bearing, state. " With another *port*."—*Jacob
and Esau*, Anon. Pl., 2 Ser. (E.E.D.S.), 72,*c*. " Keep
house, and *port*, and servants as I should."—Shakespeare, *Taming of the Shrew* (1593), i. 1.

POTESTATE, " a worthy *potestate* " (N71,*b*), potentate,
chief authority. " And whanne thei leeden you
unto synagogis and to magistratis and *potestatis* ;
nyle ye be bisy how or what ye schulen answere, or
what ye schulen seye."—Wycliffe, *Luke* xii.

POTICARY (N125,*a*), apothecary : see Heywood, *The
Four P.P.*

PRECISE, " as Himself doth *precise* " (M37,*b*), to deter-
mine with precision : cf. Fr. *preciser*.

PRECLAIR, "*preclair* pre-eminence" (IP347,*d*), illustrious, eminent. "That puissant prince *preclair*." Lyndesay, *Monarche.*

PREYS, "the gubbins of booties and *preys*" (R183,*d*), spoil, plunder.

PRYKE, "*pryke* not your felicities" (M4,*b*), fix.

PRIME, "mass and matins, hours and *prime*" (M31,*c*) —"by *prime*" (JE360,*c*), the first of the canonical hours, succeeding to lauds.

PRIVITY, see Jewels.

PROMIDENCE, "climbing up aloft for promidence" (R212,*d*), ? prominence, predominance.

PROUT, "zo thick *prout* whorecop" (R256,*b*)—"maketh us *prout*" (R256,*c*), proud : in original *prowte* and *prout* respectively ; A.S. prut.

PUDDINGS, see Dogs.

PURVEY, PURVEYED, "*purvey* such a lad" (N68,*b* ; also 65,*c*)—"hath *purveyed* me" (N43,*c*), provide, plan, contrive : specifically to supply provisions.

PUTTOCK (JE363,*b*), properly the common kite, but also applied to other birds of prey.

QUALIFIED, "would not be *qualified*" (R224,*c*), appeased, mollified, calmed. "Whan the quene was thus *qualyfyed*"—tr. *Pol. Verg. Eng. Hist.* (*c.* 1540), 210 (Camden, No. 29).

QUORUM, see Justices of Quorum.

RAIL, "if thou *rail* too far" (N52,*b*), wander, roam. "I *rayle*, I *straye* abrode, *je trace, je tracasse*. He doth naught els but *rayle* here and there."—Palsgrave, *Lang. Franc.* (1530), 678, 1.

RAISE, "is that the great love ye *raise* her" (WS147,*a*), bear : cf. the now (except as regards cattle) rare sense of *raise*=beget.

RAT, "we have smelled a *rat*" (R187,*a*), one of the earliest instances of this proverbial saying.

RATHER, "later or *rather*" (R188,*c*), earlier. "Aftir me is comun a man, which was maad bifor me ; for he was *rather* than Y."—Wyclif (1388), *John* i. 30.

RAUGHT, "*raught* to Cumberland" (R254,*a*), reached.

REBATED, "openly *rebated*" (R197,*a*) : see Respublica, *Var. readings*, etc.

RECH, "For other wealth I not *rech* (WH278,*c*), strive or reach out for.

RECREATORY, "my singular *recreatory*" (M38,*d*), source of comfort, "joy" : the only quotation in the *O.E.D.*

RECUMBENTIBUS, "a shrewd *recumbentibus*" (M20,*b*) —"speak to Mankind for the *recumbentibus* of my jewels" (M22,*c*), "a knock-down blow" (*O.E.D.*), but the second example does not quite fit this sense which seems to refer to the position of the object attacked, rather than the act of attacking.

RED CAP, "him that wears the *red cap*" (WH303,*c*). Remedy seems to have worn a red cap : ? as the symbol of spiritual authority. The term is of rare occurrence ; only two examples of so early a date are quoted in the *O.E.D.*, both from State papers— (*a*) "Captaine *Redde Cappe*, one of the rebelles of the last yere" (1549); (*b*)=*red-hat*=cardinal (1539).

REDE, "by my *rede*" (N121,*d*), counsel. Also as verb.

REDFORD (JOHN), musician, poet, and writer of interludes, was, according to Hawkins, organist and almoner of St. Pauls. Tusser, in his autobiographical poem, mentions him as master of the children of St. Paul's about 1535. As a musician, his instrumental works are well known, consisting mainly of florid counterpoint upon a plain song. As master of the children at St. Paul's, it was part of his duty to provide dramatic entertainments. A quaint specimen of his skill in this respect is afforded by his "Wit and Science." This is preserved among the additional MSS. at the British Museum (No. 15,233), the memorandum book in which it is written, and of which the original binding is still in excellent condition, containing some musical sketches (possibly memoranda only), and fragments of two other moralities, one of them in Redford's name. The date of his death is unknown, but as Sebastian Westcott was master of

the children of St. Paul's in 1559, probably Redford
had died before that date.

The fragments of other interludes, probably both
by Redford, included in add. MSS 15,233, are as
follows :—

[*Fragment No.* 1.]

*   *   *   *   *   *

D. Marye, Tom, such poyntes God send him mani !
T. Well, go to, mok on ! your mokes bere can I,
    Tyll we shall once be evin, I truste.
G. Nay, Tom, all Malles lay in the dust,
    And syns we have droonke all of one cup,
    Shake handes lyke freends ! all quarelles give up !
D. Ye, by my sowle, and syns the payne is past,
    Let us be merye, and care awey cast.
I. What els, Tom, syns we have leve to play ?
    Let us be merye all thys long daye !
          Fynis, quod Master Jhon Redford.
              Here the syng Hey nony nonye,
                 and so go forth syngyng.

In the MS. this fragment is cancelled with a pen.

[*Fragment No.* 2.]

The other fragment of an interlude (cancelled in
the MS.) is as follows :—

CORAGE.

    Shall we three joyne in unitee
    To cheere these gestes ?

KYNDNES.

      By my trothe, ye.
CLENNES *cumth in and* CON. *steylyth away.*
Not so, my friends, here me speake.   Mum !

CORAGE.

Where is Concupiscence becum ?

CLENNES.

My presens hath put her to flyght !
Where Clennes doth in place apeere,
Ther is Concupiscence gone quighte.

This is not signed by Redford ; it is only conjectur-ally his.

The other works of Redford's in the MS. book (additional MSS. 15,233) appear to be separate poems, with titles (some apparently inserted in his reprint by Halliwell Phillips). The numbers to the right refer to the pages in Halliwell Phillips's reprint.

1. Lamentation of boys learning the prick song.
(14 stanzas of 4 lines each)   62
2. " Nolo Mortem peccatoris : hœc sunt verba Salvatoris."   (23 stanzas of six lines each) 68
3. Long have I been a singing man."
(8 stanzas of six lines each)   80
4. " Will and Power."   (3 stanzas of seven lines each)   86
5. " The Pleasure of Godliness."
Besides some irregular opening lines.
(22 stanzas of six lines each)   92
6. " The goodness of all God's gifts."
(11 stanzas of seven lines each)   97
7. " The sinfulness of man."
(8 stanzas of eight lines each)   100

REDUCIBLE, " he will be *reducible* " (M37,*b*), reclaim-able.

REFRAIT, " harp both on *refrait* " (N59,*d*), refrain, burden.   " Of ther song the *refreit* was of pees."— Lydgate in *Pol. Poems* (1443), II., 211 (Rolls).

REMORD, " thou ought to *remord* " (IP316,*b*), feel remorse.   " *Remord* and rew, and pondir weill my parte."—A. Scott, *Poems* (*c.* 1560), xiii. 38 (S.T.S.).

REMOTION, " to you . . . have recourse and *remotion* " (M3,*d*), inclination to.

REN (*passim*), run.

REPORTURE, " to make *reporture* " (N100,*c*), mention, report.   " To hyr I wyll goo and make *reportur.*" —*Digby Myst.* (*c.* 1485), III., 2084 (1882).

RESIDED, " one *resided* me with a bowl of water" (JE358,*a*).   I have been unable to arrive at any satisfactory explanation of this passage.

RESPUBLICA. The text is given on pp. 177–272. The original forms one of the Macro plays in manuscript, now the property of Mr. J. H. Gurney of Keswick Hall, near Norwich : see Macro Plays and Manuscripts, *ante*. *Respublica* has been three times previously printed in modern times—(*a*) by Mr. John Payne Collier in *Illustrations of Old English Literature*, I. (1866), B. M. press-mark, 2326, *c* ; (*b*) by Prof. Brandl in *Quellen*, etc. (1904) ; and (*c*) by the Early English Text Society (Extra Series xciv.), edited by Mr. Leonard A. Magnus, LL.B., " from Mr. Gurney's unique Macro MS. 115 " (1905), B. M. press-mark, Ac. 9926/60. I do not know how Mr. Collier got his copy ; Dr. Brandl states his copy was made for him by Dr. Emeke, " and we both have collated it." Whether the copy was made direct from the original manuscript, or whether it was (as in the case of *Mankind* (*q.v.*) a copy of a copy, or further, whether the collation of the proof-sheets was with the original or with the copy is not stated : still even the last is *something* towards assurance, for the ways of the modern " comp." and the oversight of the average " reader " are, at times, passing strange. Yet Mr. Magnus by his remark, " Prof. Brandl had to make his edition from a copy of the manuscript," seems to infer that the German editor was unable to get into close contact with the original. This uncertainty is unfortunate, for were we sure of the contrary, there would have been immediate and well-founded confidence in the fidelity of Prof. Brandl's text. But worse remains. Mr. Magnus, beyond saying that " the manuscript has been kindly lent by the owner," nowhere, so far as I can read, mentions that the copy of the same as prepared for the printers had, when in proof, been compared with the original manuscript. My own experience in collating the three copies of *Mankind* (*q.v.*), made respectively for the E.E.T.S., Prof. Manly, and Prof. Brandl, does not tend to reassure one. Indeed, the sampling of Mr. Manly's printed sheets in another direction has convinced me that though the text may be, and probably is, substantially accurate, yet it would be folly to waste valuable time in furnishing, for this play, even the simplest of textual notes and criticism. Knowing, by experience, the weighty trustworthiness of Prof. Brandl's work in respect to other plays, I commenced by modernising his text, at the same time collating it with that of Collier, only to find, when I came to compare it with the E.E.T. Society's edition, just the same obviously careless miscripts and blunders that I found when collating *Mankind*. This estimate was confirmed when I tested the value of the work done on *Respublica*, apart from the text, in the same fashion that I tested the worth of *Mankind*. Taking pages xviii. (four lines from bottom) to xxii. (two lines from top) of Mr. Magnus' *Introduction* (E.E.T.S., Extra Series xciv.), to prove the accuracy of the quotations and references, what is the result ? In 124 lines there are no fewer than forty errors in quotation, reference figures, and the like, or more than one mistake for every three lines ! ! ! I fear little faith can be placed in the accuracy of the text of the play when such a result is forthcoming in respect to the very structure of the setting. Nor is this an isolated or specially selected weak spot : these particular pages attracted attention as providing an obviously distinctive chance of checking the work done. Turn again to the glossary references, and taking a column haphazard, the second column of page 79, and the same process of verifying the printed page shows five blunders in thirty-four entries from *Cale* to *Creature*. Or, take page 66 of the notes, and one reaps four blunders in twelve lines (Notes, l. 439– l. 581)! I cannot therefore help feeling uncertain about the text of the play itself, and as I have been unable, as yet, to get access to the original, I prefer to save useless labour by sending forth my own text without comment of any kind. As a matter of course the E.E.T.S. version is no doubt nearest the original, and, in doubtful cases I have, equally of course, followed it in preference to the Collier or Brandl versions ; but it must not be taken as worth more than it really is. I can only once again express a sincere hope that some one will in the near future be allowed to reproduce these invaluable Macro Plays in facsimile. *Respublica* is noteworthy in more respects than one. Obviously written by a Catholic, it is the Reformation in its

social and political, and not in its doctrinal, aspect
that forms the pivot of the action of the play.
The calmest judgments of posterity incline to the
view that the mainspring of the revolt against the
Papacy in England rested more on zeal as the
tool of worldliness than, as elsewhere, on worldliness
as the tool of zeal. A king whose character was
despotism itself personified, unprincipled ministers,
a rapacious aristocracy, a servile Parliament, such
were the instruments by which England was delivered from the yoke of Rome. The work which
had been begun by Henry, the murderer of his
wives, was continued by Somerset, the murderer
of his brother, and completed by Elizabeth, the
murderer of her guest. By Reformers and Catholics
alike, religion was made the tool of spoliation,
rapine, and oppression. The Reformation left
the country morally and materially bankrupt, and
Catholic though Mary was, much seems to have been
expected of her by the nation at large. Indeed, the
great mass of the people cared little or nothing for
the factional strife of either camp, except so far as
it affected them from a social point of view. Hence
the *motif* of *Respublica* and its curiously moderate
tone. It would really seem that Queen Mary
was possessed of a softness not usually credited
to her, and that she succumbed to political faction
as her brother before her and her sister after her
succumbed. It is, therefore, this aspect—the social
aspect—of the great upheaval with which the
author of *Respublica* is concerned, and no more
pithy or pungent contemporary narrative or satire
exists. Apart from the regrettable shortcomings
of Mr. Magnus' volume in other respects, he has
done useful yeoman service to English scholarship
by tracing and emphasising, point by point, the
action of the play in its relation to policital events,
practically identifying the play as a stage version of
the events of the reign of Edward vi. I can only
refer my readers to his altogether admirable analysis
—a statement of fact and resumé which happily is
not and cannot be marred by the evil influence of
inaccuracy of reference and quotation. Further,
if Mr. Magnus' essay be read in conjunction with
that portion of Hallam's *Constitutional History of*

England, which concerns this period—Macaulay's famous review of the same will serve admirably— and with Book II. of Burnett's *History of the Reformation*, the key will be found to emphasise the points made by Mr. Magnus, and to illustrate and explain the political and social allusions with which *Respublica* abounds. On the question of authorship, Mr. Magnus also attempts an attribution, suggesting Udall, the author of *Ralph Roister Doister*. His facts and inferences are, to my mind, inconclusive ; as he himself admits. Identity of phraseology, tricks of style, similarity of orthography, and the like, are at best uncertain grounds to form the basis of Tudor attributions. Very shortly the *corpus* of pre-Shakespearean drama now in progress will enable the student to tackle his subject to more purpose than heretofore.

RESTED, " would have *rested* me " (IP316,*c*), a contracted form of *arrest*.

RESTORITY, " it is *restority* " (R222,*c*), restorative note the exigency of the rhyme.

RICEPUDDING-CAKE (R. *passim*), Respublica (*q.v.*).

RINGWORM, " a *running ringworm* " (M28,*a*), *i.e.* the mark of the halter round New Guise's neck.

RODS, " *rods in piss* " (R219,*b*), a reckoning in store.

ROND, " *rond* in your ear " (M14,*c*), whisper.

ROOM, " to have with him a *room* " (N49,*d* ; 50,*a*), post, office, station, position. " To have and enjoy that office and *room*."—Holinshed, *Scotland* (an. 1543).

ROYALS, "give us *red royals*" (M21,*b*), *i.e.* give us gold, not coppers : *red*=gold is frequently found in old writers, though it is now only used in thieves' slang. The *royal* was a gold coin of varying value, from 10s. to 30s. : see other volumes of this series. " Ich shall not mis of *red ones* to haue store."— T. Howell, *Poems* (1568), i. 91 (Grosart).

RUTTER, " A *rutter*, huffa gallant " (N77,*c*.), trooper, horseman : also a swaggering, dashing gallant. That this last mentioned is the sense is clear from the phrase *huffa gallant*, which in old writers is commonly put into the mouths of roisterers and dashing men of fashion : see *Four Elements, Hick-scorner*, etc.

RUTTERKIN, " what *rutterkin* have we here (IP332,*b*), a rutter : see previous entry.

SAD, " *sad* a-sleep " (M26,*c*), sound, firm, not to be easily awakened. " It was founded on a *sad* stoon." —Wyclif, Luke vi.

SAINT AUDREY, " *St. Audrey's* holy bend " (M28,*a*), *bend*=band : see Nares, *s.v.* Tawdry.

SAINT CATHERINE'S (JE361,*c*). This is probably St. Catherine's near Guildford, which was one of the stations on the " Pilgrim's way " from Winchester to Canterbury, the route lying also through Kent. From St. Catherine's, which stands on a knoll just to the south of Guildford, the " way " leads up through " The Chantries " to St. Martha's Chapel, which crowns a considerable hill, thence proceeding eastward into Kent.

SAINT CHAD (IP336,*c*). Of course this saint was picked for the rhyme's sake. St. Chad was better known by his Saxon name of St. Ceadda, a Northumbrian by birth. His early life was spent in a monastery in Ireland. In 664 he succeeded Bishop Cedda, his brother, as abbot of Lastingham. Subsequently he became Bishop of York, but resigned the bishopric on a question arising as to the regularity of his consecration, retiring to his old office at Lastingham. On the death of Jaruman, bishop of Mercia, Ceadda was induced to enter the episcopate once more. He died at Lichfield in 672. He has always been a popular saint in the English Calendar, his festival falling on the 2nd March.

SAINT CHARITY (M11,*b*), see *Anon. Plays* (E.E.D.S.), 3 Ser., 293,*d*.

SAINT GABRIEL'S MOTHER (M35,*b*), perhaps a reference to the Virgin Mary. There are three St. Gabriels, of whom the one recognised in the gnostic systems is the more likely. He was the angel specially associated with the conception of the Virgin Mary, and according to some versions was Jesus Himself taking the form of the angel Gabriel for the purpose of preparing the Virgin, in a physical sense, for the miraculous conception.

SAINT GEORGE, "*Saint George thee borrow*" (R208,*a*), whether merely used as a salutation or referring to some song is not clear : as regards the phrase, see Udal, *Works* (E.E.D.S.), 146,*d*.

SAINT HUGH (IP341,*a*). There are no less than *four* St. Hughs who were bishops, viz. : — Hugh, 9th Bishop of Geneva, early in 7th century ; Hugh, 13th Bishop of Alby, said to have been in possession of the See when the Saracens took the city in 722 ; Hugh, 37th Bishop of Paris, died in 730 ; Hugh, 18th Bishop of Séez, in latter half of 8th century. There is also a legendary St. Hugh, patron of the Abbey of Tewkesbury, who is said to have buried Brihtric, King of Mercia, in the chapel of St. Faith at Tewkesbury, and to have been buried there himself in 812. According to *Dictionary of Christian Biography*, the story is an impudent fabrication.

SAINT QUINTIN (M13,*b*) came into Gaul with St. Lucian of Beavais, and was martyred by the Romans under Rectiovarus.

SAINT TRUNNION, see Heywood, *Works* (E.E.D.S.), I., *272,d*.

SALLET, " for lack of a *sallet* " (R229,*b*), a light helmet, chiefly used by foot-soldiers in the fifteenth century : see God's Good. " Many a time, but for a *sallet*, my brain-pan had been cleft with a brown-bill."— Shakespeare, 2 *Henry VI.*, ix. 10.

SANCTO, " *Cum sancto . . . perverteris* " (M15,*c*), see *Psalm* xvii. 27.

SCAMBLE, SCAMBLING, " I doubt not to *scamble* and rake " (R187,*c*)—" fall thus to *scambling* " (R194,*d*)— " as quick *scambling* as ever I saw " (R221,*c*), *i.e.* pilfer and plunder when and how possible ; see " Catch that catch may " (R187,*b*), and cf. Cotgrave, " *Scamblingly*, catch that catch may."— " Much more being *scambled* up after this manner." —Holinshed, *Chronicle* (Epis. Dedic.).

SCAPE, " the *scape* of extreats " (R183,*d*), trick, cheat : see Respublica. " They readily pardon all faults and *scapes* committed by negligence."—North, *Plutarch*, p. 206.

SCOTTLING, " a pretty *scottling* " (M6,*d*), scuttling.

SCOURED, " *scoured* a pair of fetters " (M28,*d*), a very
common piece of Old Cant=to go, or lie, in, or wear
fetters : usually, " to *scour* the cramp-rings or
derbies." " Then to the quier-ken to *scoure* the
cramp-ring."—Dekker, *Beggar's Curse* (1608). " And
'cause we are poor made to *scour* the cramp-ring."
—Dekker, *Lanthorne and Candlelight.* The original
is *scoryde.*

SECTOURSHIP, see Respublica.

SECULE, " *secule* thyself " (IP342,*d*), ? a misprint for
secure.

SEREFUL, " a *sereful* man " (N81,*c*), I suspect from
the context that this is a misprint for fearful=full
of fear, timid.   Or it may be akin to the use
of *sere* by Ascham, characterised by Nares as
" peculiar " to that writer=individual, particular,
single : whence *sereful* would mean " peculiar,"
" full of idiosyncracies," " difficult."

SHAKED, " They *shaked* me up " (R255,*d*), shook.

SHALCH, " what *shalch* zai to om " (R.,*passim*), shall
I—shal[1 i]ch.

SHALES, " served but with *shales* " (R214,*d*), shells.

SHARINGS (R183,*c*), shearings.

SHENT, " you will be *shent* " (N105,*c*, *et passim*),
blamed.

SHROUD CELL (M17,*c*), ? privy place, such as the
crypt of a church : shrouds are properly places
under ground : the meaning is that Mankind has
met Mercy privately.

SIDE, see ALOFT.

SIDE-GOWN, " his *side-gown* may be sold " (M29,*d*),
long   gown :   cf.   " side-sleeves "=long   sleeves.
There are examples enough in Nares.

SI DIDERO (M20,*d*), *i.e.* " I'll pay you back with profit "
(E.E.T S. ed.).

SIGHING, " weeping, *sighing*, and sobbing " (M32,*d*),
the *sythynge* of the original seems worth recording.

SIKER, "*siker* thyself, man!" (N51,*b*), secure, make all safe, assure

> "Now be we duchesses both I and ye,
> And *sikerde* to the regals of Athenes,
> And both hereafter likely to be queenes."
> —Chaucer, *Legend of Ariadne.*

SIKERNESS, "In one is *sikerness*" (N55,*b*), certainty, security, sureness : see previous entry.

SILVER HOOK (IP345,*d*), a bribe.

SINDONS, "the *sindons* in which were wrapped the chalices" (R221,*d*), a wrapper of cotton or linen. "There were found a book and a letter, both written in fine parchment, and wrapped in *sindons* of linen." —*Bacon.*

SINGULAR, "my sing'lar solace" (M36,*c*)—"my . . . *singular* recreatory (M39,*a*), unique : in original *singler* and *synguler* respectively.

> "Some villain, ay, and *singular* in his art."
> —Shakespeare, *Cymbeline* (1605), iii. 4.

SIR WILL—SIR WILLIAM OF TRENTRAM (JE356,*b* ; 357,*a*) : see Trentham.

SLEET, "I will not *sleet* my love to greet" (WS172,*c*), neglect.

SLEIGHT (*passim*), art, skill, dexterity, expertness : generic in both a good and bad sense.

SLIPED, "*sliped* down to the hard knee" (N77,*c*), sloped : note the rhyme with "striped."

SLIPPER, "A *slipper* sugar-mouthed whorecop" (R212,*c*), "the ground be *slipper* and sliding" (JE363,*d*), slippery. "I know they *bee slipper* that I have to do wyth, and there is no holde of them."— Barnes, *Workes* (1573), p. 283.

SLITHER, "make you to *slither*" (M7,*c*), slide, glide : still dialectical.

SLOUTHY, see Flouthy.

SMATTERING, "a *smattering* face" (M27,*b*),?a wanton face: cf. *smoterlich*=wanton ; also *smorterest place* (N95,*a*), *place* being considered as a misprint for "piece."

> "We wyll have cousynge Besse also,
> And two or thre proper wenchis mo,
> Ryght feyr and *smotter* of face."—
> *Four Elements,* Anon. Pl., 1 Ser. (E.E.D.S.), 22,*b.*

SMORTEREST, " the *smorterest* place " (N95,*a*) : see previous entry.

SMOULT, " gay, *smoult* smirking whorecop " (R214,*b*), smooth.

SOCKET, " his wife's *socket* " (M8,*c*), *vulva*.

SONDE, " God . . . send us of His *sonde* " (M24,*b*), message, dispensation.
  " Fyve yeer and more, as liked Cristes *sonde*,
  Er that hir schip approched unto londe."
      —Chaucer, *Cant. Tales* (1383), 5322.

SORT (*passim*), company, assemblage, knot of people, gang : see other volumes of this series.

SOVEREIGNS, " *sovereigns* I beseech you " (M3,*d* ; also IP347,*a*), *i.e.* the audience, " Masters," " excellencies " : cf. M.E. *soverainly*=above all.

SOWNETH (JE360,*b*), soundeth : see other volumes of this series.

SPADIBUS, " in *spadibus* " (M18,*c*), spades ; cf. Breadibus.

SPARLING, " my own . . . *sparling* " (WS162,*c*), properly the smelt : formerly colloquial for " gull," " simpleton," and (so it would appear) as an endearment. Probably, however, the exigencies of a rhyme with " darling " influenced the author. Later, the cry, " Westward for smelts ! "=on the spree, in search of conies, male or female.

SPECIAL, " my predelict *special* " (M39,*a*), favourite : most frequently used of a paramour, male or female.

SPIRITUALTY, " an officer of the *spiritualty* " (IP 343,*c*), the hierarchy of the Church : here=an officer of the Ecclesiastical Courts.

SQUAT, " *squat* out ons brain " (R256,*d*), squash.

STARVE, see Grass.

STATE, " a great *state* " (N68,*d*)—" haled up with *states* " (R267,*c*)—" to compare with a *state* " (IP339,*c*), a person of rank or importance. " When *states* . . . sit in the cool."—Heywood, *Works* (E.E.D.S.), II., 258,*b*.

STATT, see Stow.

STILE, see Hedge.

STORE, "*store* is no sore" (R184,*c*), in Heywood, *Works* (E.E.D.S.), 12,*c* ; 176,*d*.

STOW, "*stow, statt, stow !*" (M32,*b*), "*Stow, stow,* says Halliwell, was formerly addressed to a hawk by a falconer to make it come to his fist."

STRUSSIONERS, "such *strussioners* as these" (R265,*c*), destructioners + constructioners.

STUD, "Doth you *stud* your brains" (R228,*b*). People's perversion (perhaps intentional) of "study."

SUFFER, "he *will not suffer*" (R213,*a*) ; in original *nil not*, and it should have been so printed in text. *Nil*=will not n[e w]il[l] : cf. namnot, ninnat.

SUPERATE, "now it is *superate*" (M15,*a*), conquered, overcome.

SUPERSEDEAS (R261,*d*), a writ having in general the effect of a command, to stay or forbear, on good cause shown, any ordinary proceedings which might otherwise be proceeded with : hence a stay, a stop. "To give a *supersedeas* to industry."—Hammond, *fl.* 1605–60), *Works*, i. 480.

TAGETIVE, "Am I a *tagetive*" (WH277,*c*). I can find no trace of this word. Can Wealth be regarded as offended at being spoken to as if he were one of the " tag " or rabble ?

TANE (WH294,*b* ; 305,*a*), taken.

TENDERANCE, "cometh of great *tenderance*" (N52,*d*), watchfulness.

THE, "God let you never *the*" (M., *et passim*), prosper, thrive.

THIRLETH, "a short prayer *thirleth* heaven" (M25,*a*), ascends to, pierces, penetrates. "If ony *thirle* or make an hole in a feble walle."—*Gesta Romanorum*.

TIDE, "tarry here this *tide*" (M23,*d*), time, season.

TINKERS, "though *tinkers* should lack work" (R213,*d*), cf. " Like Banbury tinkers, that in mending one hole make three."

TO, "thou must needs *to*" (N50,*d*), elliptic ; *i.e.* " go to."

TO-BEATEN, "all *to-beaten*" (M19,*c*), *to*=A.S. prefix implying deterioration, destruction, or completeness ; *i.e.* beaten unmercifully.

To-GLORIED, " all *to-gloried* " (M34,*c*) : see previous
   entry. *To-gloried*=finically fine or grandiloquent
   (*i.e.* your phraseology is destructive of " measure ").

TORITY, " ye give me *tority* " (R266,*c*), authority.

TRENTHAM (SIR WILLIAM OF TRENTHAM).   As already
   stated (see *John Evangelist*) the entrances and
   exits, and the connection between different parts
   of this play of *John the Evangelist*, are by no means
   obvious.   At 356,*b*, Eugenio, referring to Irisdision,
   says he may well be called " witless Sir Will ";
   and when Eugenio speaks of the coming of Sir
   William of Trentham (357,*a*), in comes John the Evangelist.   The most feasible explanation is that the
   part of John the Evangelist was played by a parish
   priest whose name was Sir William of Trentham.
   The clerical use of *Sir = dominus* is common,
   but the only reference I can find to Trentham
   (near Stoke-on-Trent) is in the 5th volume
   of *Magna Britannia*," pp. 92 and 154.   In both
   places there is mention of a monastery of " Canons
   Regular of St. Augustine, built in the reign of
   William Rufus.   According to Dugdale and Speed
   it was valued, at the time of the dissolution, at
   £106, 3s. 10d. per annum.   As the rule of the
   Augustines enjoins poverty, chastity, and humility,
   my suggestion receives confirmation of a sort at
   359,*b* and *c*, where " wilful poverty " is enjoined.
   As regards Irisdision, who is obviously the same
   as John the Evangelist and Sir William of Trentham,
   this is a puzzle.   Eugenio is Greek, but an attempt
   at making Greek of Irisdision is not quite satisfactory, and may seem somewhat far-fetched.
   Iris in Greek mythology was a messenger of the
   gods, who are sometimes noted collectively by
   Dis — is Irisdision intended to mean " a divine
   messenger " ?

TREPITT, " take you here a *trepitt* " (M7,*d*), blow.

TRISE, " *trise* him out at your gates " (M21,*d*), haul,
   pull.

TRUST, (*a*) " *in trust is treason* " (M33,*b*), in Heywood
   (*Works*, E.E.D.S., II., 67,*c*).
      (*b*) " best be *trust* " (R196,*a*), *i.e.* Avarice has
   called his minions back to coach them, and bids

them be ready (*to truss*=to tuck up the gown and
generally to prepare oneself). On the other hand,
Mr. Magnus (E.E.T.S.) says, "Mr. Daniel has ex-
plained this phrase as a nickname for a dishonest
fellow, with a by-play on *trussed* (*i.e.* hanged)."

UNCURTESS, "so *uncurtess*, so inconsiderate" (M33,*b*;
34,*a*), unthoughtful, careless, uncivil.

UNDERFONG, "war or battle to *underfong*" (N90,*a*),
undertake, manage, wage.

UNRIGHTFUL, "In *unrightful* to say pride of him
than " (JE366,*c*), the passage is obscure or corrupt ;
unrightful occurs in Bale (*Works*, E.E.D.S.), 59,*c*—
"justices *unrightful*."

UNTHRIFTS RENT (JE364,*c*)—"let us go to *Unthrift's*
a while " (JE361,*c*), a *rent*=tenements or houses
let out to others ; often named after the proprietor :
Fulwood's *Rents*, Holborn, is (1907) a case in point.

UNTIL (*passim*), to, unto.

VALESLIE, "you liest *valeslie*" (R210,*c*), valorously.

VOWELS : "worship of the five vowels " (M22,*c*), the
passage as it stands is obscure. Furnivall and Pollard
read *v. vowellys*,Manly,*v voli ellys*,andBrandl, *volvellys*.
I have perforce followed the first-named as the most
likely to be according to the original, but in view
of the uncertainty as to the accuracy of either transcript, little can be said (see *Mankind*). Manly (whom
the E.E. Text editors follow) suggests *vij* (*or xx*)
devellys ; Brandl *dewellys ?* The phrasing is suggestive, "worship" (cf. "worship of the new year":
see *New Year*), and " v vowels," which of course
is distinctive, but I am quite at a loss to suggest
an explanation. If the allusion is to gaming,
vowels may be a miscript for *volvelles*, quite a different
word. Whitney says of it—" A small and generally
circular movable plate affixed to an engraving
containing a dial or lottery, and made to carry
the index hand or pointer." There is a paragraph
in *Notes and Queries* (Sixth Series, vol. xi. p. 217)
referring to " volvelles," and it seems pretty evident
from this that they were well known as instruments
of chance ; there is an allusion in Withers' *Emblems*,
where he makes use of the " Index " or " volvelle "

in a moral sense. One could understand the " worship of *volvelles*," if this were a gambling game, as one can understand the " worship of dice."

WALSINGHAM WHISTLE (M20,*c*), probably an allusion to the " Wishing Wells " at Walsingham (Norfolk). Persons drinking of them were said to obtain the fulfilment of any wish made while drinking. *Nought*, appealed to, said he could " pipe on a Walsingham whistle," *i.e.* wish for what he wanted, and perhaps get it. Apparently he does, for he wished for the entry of *Titivullus*, who appears.

WALTER, " I love ill to *walter* " (JE364,*a*), tumble, roll about. " To turne or *walter* in mire " (Baret, 1580).

WART, " che *wa'r't*, a false harlot you art " (R210,*c*), war[ran]t.

WAT, " some great *wat* " (N69,*b*)—" Brother *wat* " (WH297,*a*), a wight, a man.

WAY, " *do way, do way* " (M6,*c*), away, away !

WEALTH AND HEALTH is one of the recently-recovered " lost " plays (see Preface), and is of unknown authorship. The text is given on pp. 273–309, from a photograph copy of the original now in the British Museum, together with a reduced facsimile of the title-page. The B.M. entry is—

> WEALTH. An enterlude of Welth and Helth, very mery and full of pastyme, newly att his [*i.e. att this*] tyme imprinted. B. L. [London, 1565 ?] 4°. [C.34,i.25.

The collation is sixteen leaves, Ai (title with back blank) to Div. in 4s. The play is wretchedly printed on very thin paper, and simply bristles with printer's errors. I have taken no heed of most of these in the present text which I have collated twice with the old copy. I think I have succeeded in producing a substantially correct version of the original, any specially doubtful point being noted *infra*. This, however, must be taken with one reservation—so far as the state of the typography would allow I have given the Dutch and Spanish jargon exactly as it appears in the old text. It was simply impossible to make sense out of it. Many of the words have no resemblance to anything

in Dutch. It was submitted to Dutch and German
scholars to no effect. The sense occasionally
can be gleaned—for example, that Hance was a
drunken Hollander who wanted to get an engage-
ment as gunner by the English. But the whole
is evidently a caricature of Dutch, with which
the author obviously had no acquaintance beyond
a few scattered words, and the "patter" was put
in simply to tickle the ears of the groundlings. As
regards date, the British Museum Catalogue suggests
"? 1565" for this recovered copy ; but Hazlitt
states that the play was licensed in 1557-8, and
printed by John Waley in 1558. There is little
internal evidence to help to a decision. Hance
(300,*c*) says he has been in England "this darteen
(thirteen) year," and if we deduct this from 1557-8
we get 1544-5, which is close enough to the times
of Anne of Cleves (1540), the "Flander's mare"
of Henry VIII., to suggest that the play may have
been written and played a year or two earlier than
the date of its entry at Stationers' Hall. There
are two references to the Sovereign (301,*b* and 308,*d*),
Queen Elizabeth, who succeeded 17th Nov. 1558,
but these allusions do not, of course, reveal anything.
Corrigenda, Amended Readings, etc.: Title-page
(274), a reduced facsimile being given (273), direct
comparison may be made : though very indistinct,
there are traces of the lines of a written inscription
on the lower half of the page—*Names of Players*
(275 *et seq.*), these are given in margin ; in places
dropped a little out of line, but nowhere so that
the commencement of the speech is not easily
identified—" praise yourself *too* much ye may "
(276,*a*), original *so*—" *Yet* no displeasure " (276,*b*),
original *Yeth*—" to you no *dispraise* " (276,*b*), in
original *dyspayre*—" am I a *tagetive* " (277,*c*), original
tagetyve, but the first " stamp " may be anything :
see *Tagetive*—" I, Wealth, *have* all treasure "
(278,*a*), original *hatg* : the close alphabetical juxtaposition of *v* and *t* on the one hand and *e* and *g*
of the misprint (for so I take it) is curious : see
supra—" *their* pain is such " (280,*c*), original *there*—
" *Ill-W*. Why, I came," etc. (284,*a*), throughout
the original Ill Will, who is given his full name
in the stage direction marking his entrance, is

" tagged " in the margin *Will*—" *H*[*eal*]*th.* Whose,"
etc. (284,*a*), the letters in square brackets are
rubbed away, but the speech seems to be to Health
rather than Wealth. See Health's speech, 283,*b*.—
" and *kindred* too " (284,*d*), original *kinred*—
" lest that I *mar*" (285,*d*), so I think in original :
the letters are blurred, but the portions visible
indicate the rubbed-out strokes : if so, note the
three rhymes, *were, near, mar* : Dr. Murray gives
mer(*e* as a form current from the 13th to the 16th
centuries—" I *came* my way " (286,*c*), original
can—" *Ill-W.* I would come in " (286,*c*), in original
this speech is given to Wit, but clearly that is a
mistake—" *Hance* Beerpot, a scon router " (287,*a*),
so in original, which there seemed no need to modern-
ise to Hans : see *ante*—" his name is War " (287,*c*),
in view of recent discussion in *N. and Q.* note the
rhyme with *mar*—" with your *gound ? stand near* "
(287,*c*), this may possibly read " with your gound-
stand near ? "—" I am very glad " (289,*d*), the next
line is very indistinct, and even the paper at this
place is opaquer than elsewhere, so debarring
restoration in that wise : it *looks* like " Some
crafty wile for him [I would] ye had," but *I would*
is very doubtful, unless we reckon on a glaring
misprint—" they shall not *flit* " (290,*c*), original
flye—" [*Health*]. Sirs ! now go your way " (291,*c*),
the name is not in original, but the lines are apparently as now attributed—" *w'out* blane " (294,*b*),
wout in original—" If a man be never so . . . ."
(295,*a*), the line appears to have got loose, and
in printing this has caused extra blurring : *so*
may not be correct ; what follows looks like " so
. . good and b . . . . be but thrifty " :
but it is uncertain to a degree—" Speak ! be not
afraid " (295,*d*), in original *afryde*—" What *sayest*
thou in his face " (296,*a*), obviously misprinted
in the original : the word meant may be *seest*—
" for *these* years twenty " (296,*b*), *this* in original—
" as good *know* " (296,*d*), in original *no*—" And
your subtilty known " (297,*a*), in original *Aud our
ſubtillitte knowen*—" *Ill-W.* Peace ! no mo words "
(297,*b*), in original this is given to *Wit*—" with
kindness my *heart* do kill " (299,*b*), *herye* in original
—" *magt not* do thereto " (300,*a*), *aot* in original—

" I understand thee well " (300,*d*), *Ic* in original :
the author has forgotten himself in this instance—
" *Wit. I will go to fetch them* " (304,*d*), in original
I Iyf Зo to fetch tham—" should *lean* to man's life "
(305,*a*), in original *leaue*—

WHERE, " *where* he go " (JE354,*d*), whether.

WHISTER, " *whister* him in the ear " (N77,*d*), whisper.

WHITE WINE (JE361,*a*), an allusion, I suppose, to the
rotten eggs shied at a victim in the pillory.

WIDGE, " chad a *widge* " (R229,*a*), horse. In a recent
number of *Notes and Queries* appeared the following,
which seems worth quoting, as exemplifying the
survival in Tudor-English dialect of an A.S. word
that itself had only a limited vogue. " In South-
Western dialect, *widge*, a horse (mare) . . . from
M.E. *wig*, A.S. *wicg*. The . . . word is only
found in poetry, and with moderate frequency ;
while in other Teutonic languages *wigg*, horse, occurs
solely, to my knowledge, in O. Sax., *The Heliand*,
and there but once. Stratmann's *Mid. Eng.
Dictionary* (ed. H. Bradley) gives a solitary example
of *wig*, horse, in *Early English Homilies* (ed. R.
Morris), rendering the more notable its survival
to the above date. The word is not in Halliwell's
Dictionary." (H. P. L.)

WIT AND SCIENCE, BY JOHN REDFORD. The text,
collated anew in proof with the original manuscript in
the British Museum (Add. MSS. 15,233), will be found
on pages 135–175, together with a reduced facsimile
of the penultimate page of the manuscript (p. 136),
and the concluding lines of the same with Redford's
signature (p. 175). This last facsimile has been
included because nowhere in the Museum Catalogue
does Redford's name occur ; the play has never
been catalogued as his though his name appears
both in the MS. and in the Shak. Soc. reprint (Ac.
9485.33). A good deal of confusion and uncertainty
has existed concerning the identity of this and two
other Wit plays, a question which I discuss in
Anon. Plays (E.E.D.S.), *Series IV.*, now in the
press. I refer the reader to this volume, which will
reach subscribers in due course. Besides the
Shakespeare Society's reprint, Prof. Manly has

included *Wit and Science* in his *Specimens of the Pre-Shakespearean Drama*. The MS. is in the shape of a memorandum book, the lines running across the short width of the page. There has been no cutting of the margins. It was purchased at the sale of the Bright MSS. in 1844, and the binding is without doubt contemporary with the MS., though it has apparently been patched here and there. *Corrigenda, Amended Readings, etc.*: " The better hold out *he* may" (138,*b*), *ye* in manuscript, which Halliwell follows : Prof. Manly has *he*—" *Study*. Yea, hold your peace . . . that way" (139,*c*), Halliwell in his reprint (1848) reads thus :—

Yea, hold your peace, best ! we here now stay,
For, Instruction, I like not that way.

" *Good, sir* " (141,*b*), original *God, sir*—" *Striketh him* " (144,*d*), this stage direction, which is not in manuscript, should, of course, have been put within brackets—" Give ear to *that* we sing and say " (145,*c*), so in MS. ; *what* in transcript of song in Shakespeare Soc. Papers, II. 78 : it may also be noted that in the same transcript the commencement of the fifth stanza inserts *an* not in the MS. which reads " After eye given "—" *Here cometh in* HONEST RECREATION," etc. (145,*a* to 146,*b*), this stage direction in MS. is continuous, and the song is given at the end of the play. I have inserted it here as more convenient —" while we *him* bear " (146,*b*), *here* in MS., which is followed by Halliwell ; I have accepted Prof. Manly's amendment—" *Rea.* I wot well that " (146,*d*), in MS. these words are followed in the same line by the first five words of the next line, " The more to blame ye " ; the scribe finding out his mistake crossed them through, and then re-wrote them in the next line as in text—" *Here* COMFORT, QUICKNESS, STRENGTH *go out* " (147,*a*), in the margin, very small, between the speakers' names as if by an afterthought, is written, " Al go out save Honest "— " Sure call a blow or twain" (162,*d*), Halliwell says " the scribe here began to write the preceding speech of Science but erased it." Reference to the manuscript shows that the previous line originally ran, " By the mass, *madam, ye can no good*," and that the words in italics were then crossed through and the line re-written as in the present text. The next line, commencing " And thou shalt sure," etc., has apparently been written in after the mistake was discovered ; it occurs at the end of a page. At the top of the next page of the MS. the word " Art " is written, and then crossed through, as if the writer had begun to write the lines ascribed to Science (162,*d*) commencing " Art a - swearing, too ? "—" Welcome, mine own " (171,*c*), in the MS. this song appears in another part of the book quite distinct from the play, but as it is obviously intended to be sung here it is restored to its place. Therefore the stage directions *supra* and *infra* (171,*c*, 172,*d*) are continuous in the MS.—" life's end [end] it " (174,*d*), in the MS. the line reads with *life's end end it*, but the second *end* is crossed through, erroneously it would seem.

WOLPIT, OUR LADY OF (IP315,*d*). *Woolpit* is about eight miles east of Bury-St.-Edmunds. Taylor in his *Index Monasticus* (p. 117) includes it in a list of shrines, images, etc., in Suffolk to which pilgrimages were made. The manor was given to the monks of Bury-St.-Edmunds prior to the Conquest. They were possessed of it in the time of Edward I., and probably continued in possession till the dissolution of the monasteries.

WONNING (JE363,*d*), dwelling.

WORNE, " the wild worm is come into his head " (N98,*d*) ; cf. " maggot in brain."

WOTE, " half a *wote* " (N67,*c*), *i.e.* " half I wot."

WRIT OF PRIVILEGE (IP316,*d*), a writ to deliver a privileged person from custody when arrested in a civil suit.

YEAR-DAY, " my father's *year-day* " (M32,*b*), either birthday or the anniversary of death.

ZEE, see A ZEE.

ZEMBITY (R230,*a*), semblity ; Magnus suggests " dissemble."

ZORYLESS (R212,*d*), sorryless (for sorriness).